MAIMONIDES:
A COLLECTION OF CRITICAL ESSAYS

MAIMONIDES

A COLLECTION OF CRITICAL ESSAYS

Edited, with an introduction and bibliography, by
JOSEPH A. BUIJS

University of Notre Dame Press
Notre Dame, Indiana

© 1998 by
University of Notre Dame Press
Notre Dame, Indiana 46556
http://www.undpress.nd.edu

Reprinted in 2001

Library of Congress Cataloging-in-Publication Data

Maimonides : a collection of critical essays.
  Bibliography: p.
  1. Maimonides, Moses, 1135–1204.   2. Philosophy,
Jewish.   3. Philosophy, Medieval. I. Buijs, Joseph A.
B759.M34M32   1998   181'.06   87-40617
ISBN 0-268-01368-3 (pbk)

Contents

III. ISSUES IN ETHICS, LAW, AND POLITICS

IV. THE INFLUENCE OF MAIMONIDES

Acknowledgments

The articles collected here deal with philosophical issues in the thought of Maimonides. Not only were these issues problematic in his day; they continue to be of significance to various discussions carried out in our day in such areas as epistemology, metaphysics, ethics, politics, philosophy of law, and philosophy of religion. The articles were selected to represent a wide spectrum of philosophical concerns and recent Maimonidean scholarship. The thought of Maimonides has been the focus of study by specialists in Jewish thought and in the history of philosophy. His philosophical contributions, alongside those of other notable philosophers, merit discussion by a wider contemporary philosophical audience, both student and professional.

Acknowledgments for permission to reprint are given with each of the articles. I am grateful to both the authors and publishers for their cooperation. I am also particularly thankful to Professors Harold J. Johnson, Arthur Hyman, and Ruth Link-Salinger for their advice at various stages; to Professors Francis Landy, Brian Inglis, and David Louch for checking the translation of several foreign quotations; to Marie Beck for her continual patience and expertise in retyping much of the manuscript; and to the editorial staff at University of Notre Dame Press for their professional assistance in the production of this book.

Several colleagues and reviewers made helpful suggestions on the contents of this volume. While some of their suggestions were incorporated and thus, no doubt, improved the collection, various constraints inevitably limit the final choice of articles. For this I assume full responsibility.

J. A. B.

Introduction

JOSEPH A. BUIJS

1

Moses ben Maimon (1135–1204), the celebrated medieval Rabbi and philosopher now commonly known by the name Maimonides, was a man of his time and tradition. His time was the cultural, intellectual climate of twelfth-century Moorish Spain; his tradition, the Judaism into which he was born and to which he remained committed. Both provide the context from which, and within which, he developed his philosophical thinking.

Judaism is very much a religion of law and tradition. It is founded on the Mosaic Law, the Torah, which the prophet Moses communicated to the people of Israel. The Torah contains both religious and moral directives. Their study, interpretation, and application gave rise to an oral tradition of beliefs and practices that received formal expression in the Talmud. Its juridical focus on religious, moral, and social prescriptions formed the study of *halakah* (traditional law); summaries of Jewish belief and practice, brief commentaries thereon, and related non-legal issues formed the study of *aggadah* (legend). Subsequent talmudic studies sought to apply the Mosaic Law and to extend Jewish tradition to the everyday and constantly new situations of Jewish life. Knowledgeable in this rabbinic tradition, Maimonides himself contributed to it through several major works, his letters, and his responsa to Jewish communities throughout the Middle East and southern Europe.

Twelfth-century Spain had become the center of Greek and Arabic learning under Abbasid rule. Arabic scholars not only disseminated Greek culture but made original contributions in such areas as mathematics, medicine, astronomy, science, and philosophy. The predominant philosophical framework was Aristotelian, alongside the political and ethical views of Plato. The understanding of Aristotle, however, was very much imbued with Neoplatonic elements, derived from Plotinus and Proclus and mistakenly attributed to Aristotle; it was also nuanced by Aristotle's Greek

1

and Arabic commentators. This Greek and Arabic learning influenced Jewish scholars in Spain as elsewhere. Maimonides was steeped in this wide and varied intellectual culture.

Among Jewish medieval thinkers, Maimonides enjoys the same status as Averroes (1126–1198) among Arabs and Thomas Aquinas (1225–1274) among Christians. Yet unlike both, he wrote neither philosophical treatises as such nor commentaries on the works of Aristotle—except for a brief summary on Aristotelian logic written in his youth. Indeed, the work that is considered his philosophical *opus magnum, The Guide of the Perplexed,* is explicitly addressed to educated Jews who may have become puzzled about aspects of their religion. Moreover, Maimonides purportedly disavows that the *Guide* is a philosophical work and intentionally excludes from it those issues that he suggests are adequately treated by other philosophers. Yet he does presuppose from his reader a knowledge of Greek science and philosophy, insists on demonstrative knowledge, and in one way or another touches on a number of philosophical issues also handled by other medieval thinkers, before and after him.

Maimonides, to be sure, uses philosophy within a Jewish context. He raises philosophical issues as a result of religious concerns. But that is not to say that Maimonides is merely a Jewish philosopher in some narrow sense or that he is only a religious philosopher in a broader sense. Rather, it is to acknowledge the initial context for an understanding of his thought. A philosophical understanding, however, is not restricted to a historical setting. It includes a justification of views, and this is not settled merely by explaining the context in which those views arose. Thus, a Jewish religious context, as in the case of Maimonides, may legitimately give rise to philosophical problems. It does not follow that this context also determines Maimonides' philosophical response. Nor does it follow that his response is philosophically adequate. As with other thinkers in the history of thought, Maimonidean issues can be seen as philosophical in their own right, once they are extracted from the historical context in which they arose. His views, though admittedly enigmatic and intriguing to a twentieth-century reader, are thus of more than historical interest.

Some of the issues in Maimonidean thought are specifically Jewish. The nature of Mosaic prophecy or the uniqueness of the Mosaic Law are some examples. Others are more broadly religious. Among these are proofs for the existence of God, the nature of theological language, and the status of divine attributes. Both types of issues, however, raise more fundamental philosophical concerns dealing with the status of religious truth, knowledge and justification, the purpose of laws in general, the perfection and proper end of human beings, universals. Such concerns parallel a number of preoccupations of twentieth-century philosophers in diverse areas.

Therein lies the contemporary interest in Maimonides' philosophical views. His insights, I believe, are as equally revealing and challenging to the contemporary reader as they were to medieval thinkers.

Whether his views are, in the end, philosophically acceptable remains an open question that calls for reflection and critical scrutiny. The articles collected in this volume contribute to that end. With few exceptions, they have been chosen to reflect philosophical issues that have preoccupied Maimonidean scholars over the past twenty years. They have also been chosen with the twentieth-century philosophical reader in mind. The articles have been divided into four sections. The first deals with a general problem of interpretation that Leo Strauss raised anew in this century and that pervades the approach to virtually any other issue. The next two sections correspond to the Aristotelian distinction between theoretical and practical philosophy that Maimonides acknowledges in several works. Thus, the one section discusses both metaphysical and epistemological issues, which in medieval philosophy tend to go hand in glove; among these are issues that we would classify within the philosophy of religion. The other section raises issues in ethical, political, and legal theory. The final section illustrates the influence of Maimonides on later medieval philosophy through his theory of divine attributes and negative theology.

2

Maimonides was born on March 30, 1135, in Cordoba, Spain. He received his early instruction from his scholarly father, Rabbi Moses ben Joseph. When the Almohads, an Islamic sect, conquered Cordoba in 1148, the young Maimonides wandered with his family through Spain until they settled some twelve years later in Fez, Morocco. There they were hardly safe from the Almohad persecution of Jews. Thus in 1165, the family left Fez and, after a brief sojourn in Palestine, settled in Fostat, south of Cairo, Egypt. The following year Maimonides suffered the loss of his father and, some years later, of his younger brother David, who had been providing for the family as a jewel merchant. Having to assume that task himself, Maimonides undertook the practice of medicine and eventually became the personal physician to the vizier of Saladin. About the same time he became the recognized head of the Jewish community in Egypt. He died on December 13, 1204, and was buried in Tiberias in Galilee.

Maimonides is often affectionately named the RaMBaM, an acronym from Rabbi Moses ben Maimon. In the Latin West, he was frequently mentioned simply as Rabbi Moyses or Rabbi Moyses Aegyptius.

His first work is *A Treatise on Logic (Makālah Fi-Ṣinā'at al-Manṭiḳ* in Arabic; *Millot ha-Higgayon* in Hebrew), written at the age of sixteen in Arabic. It is a brief exposition of logical terms and related concepts used in Aristotelian philosophy.

His *Book of Illumination* (*Kitāb al-Sirāj* in Arabic; *Sefer ha-Ma'or* in Hebrew) is usually titled *Commentary on the Mishnah*. It was started in 1158 when Maimonides was twenty-two years of age and was completed ten years later. It is a rabbinic commentary on parts of the Talmud, originally written in Arabic and later translated into Hebrew. Two separate treatises are of particular interest. One is an introduction to his commentary on "Sayings of the Fathers" (*Pirke Avot*), under the more usual title of "Eight Chapters" (*Shemonah Perakim*), which deals with psychology and ethics; the other is an introduction to the tenth chapter of the Tractate Sanhedrin (*Perek Ḥelek*), which contains Maimonides' thirteen principles of faith and a discussion of eschatological themes. Two other works focus on Jewish law. The *Book of Commandments* (*Sefer ha-Mitzvot*) lays out a general scheme for classifying the many Jewish commandments and prohibitions. The *Mishneh Torah* (Repetition of the Law), his only major work originally written in Hebrew, is a fourteen-book codification of Jewish law. The first part, *Book of Knowledge* (*Sefer ha-Madda*), contains a number of general and theoretical topics, preliminary to the later juridical development.

The *Guide of the Perplexed* (*Dalālat al-Ḥā'irīn* in Arabic; *Moreh Nevukhim* in Hebrew), already mentioned as Maimonides' philosophical *opus magnum*, was written some time before 1190. Its three books deal with a number of issues that might trouble a person educated in science and philosophy yet committed to Judaism. In addressing those concerns, Maimonides deals with such philosophical issues as religious knowledge, the existence of God, divine attributes, creation, prophecy, divine providence, divine foreknowledge, the rationality of Jewish prescriptions and prohibitions, and the end or ultimate happiness of human beings. Although originally written in Arabic (with Hebrew characters), the *Guide* was soon translated into Hebrew by Samuel ibn Tibbon (c. 1160–c. 1230), still within the life of Maimonides and with his approval, and later again by Judah al-Ḥarizi (1170–1235). Both Hebrew versions, in turn, received Latin translations: ibn Tibbon's version later circulated under the title of *Dux perplexorum* and *Doctor perplexorum;* al-Ḥarizi's, variously under the title of *Dux neutrorum, Dux dubiorum,* or *Dux dubitantium.* Christian medieval thinkers seemed to have read the Latin translation from al-Ḥarizi's version. Spinoza (1632–1677) is known to have studied the ibn Tibbon version in Hebrew, whereas Leibniz (1646–1716) carefully read and annotated its Latin translation. Numerous commentaries have been written on the *Guide,* most of them still unpublished.

In addition, Maimonides wrote responsa, letters, and several treatises. Of note are the *Treatise on Resurrection* (*Ma'amar Teḥiyyat ha-Metim*); the *Letter on Apostasy* or *Treatise on Martyrdom* (*Iggeret ha-Shemad*), addressed to the Jews in Morocco suffering persecution; the *Epistle to Yemen* (*Iggeret Teman*), rebutting the claims of a pseudo-Messiah; and the *Letter on Astrology to the Rabbis of Marseilles,* discussing sources of truth and the inadequacy of astrology as a science.

3

A fundamental problem of interpretation underlies an understanding of Maimonidean thought. The problem arises in different ways.

In one way, a question of interpretation emerges because of the apparently disparate concerns of Maimonides the Rabbi and Maimonides the philosopher. This difference is evident in his two monumental works. On the one hand, there is the juridical focus of the *Code,* the *Mishneh Torah,* and on the other, the more theoretical focus of the *Guide.* Hence some ask the question: Is there an overall and consistent interpretative approach? Are we to interpret Maimonides as a Rabbi, a philosopher, or both? An answer carries implications for a more general issue in the thought of Maimonides, namely, the relationship between religion and philosophy.

In another way, the *Guide* itself poses a question of interpretation because of its stated audience, purpose, and style. On the surface, its audience are educated Jews committed to their religion; its purpose, to handle scriptural and related religious concerns that might trouble them; and its style, intentionally elusive so as to conceal the author's true views from an educated reader who might easily misunderstand and yet to reveal them to the educated reader who could understand. Consequently, the *Guide* contains levels of meaning: an explicit, exoteric one for the general reader and an implicit, esoteric one for the more select reader. Hence some ask the question: Are Maimonides' real views expressed by his explicit teachings or by an implicit one? More importantly, by what criteria do we determine what his real views are? For some, already early in the history of Maimonidean studies, the problem came to be cast as a question of Jewish orthodoxy, expressed exoterically, versus some form of Aristotelianism, argued esoterically. Which, then, correctly characterizes Maimonides' position in the *Guide*?

The problem pervades Maimonidean studies. Section One deals with some of its representative views, arguments, and applications.

In the article "Interpreting Maimonides," Arthur Hyman first sketches a general framework for any understanding of the *Guide* and then identifies what he calls a "naturalistic" and a "harmonistic" approach among modern commentators. He explains how each differs in their understanding of the purpose of the *Guide,* the extent of its esoteric teachings, and its predominant philosophical issues. In particular, the "naturalistic" approach tends to emphasize a political scope alongside a hidden, esoteric teaching, whereas the "harmonistic" approach tends to stress an epistemo-logical-metaphysical scope and, on some issues at least, is willing to take Maimonides' stated exoteric view as the intended one.

The next selection exemplifies the "naturalistic" approach. Leo Strauss considers the *Guide* to be thoroughly esoteric in its real teachings and, despite its extensive use of philosophy, basically a non-philosophic work. These contentions he argues in "The Literary Character of the *Guide for the Perplexed."* His textual analyses of the *Guide's* subject matter and purpose show that these are akin to the *kalam,* a tradition of theological argumentation in both Islam and Judaism. *Mutakallimun,* proponents of the *kalam,* connote theologians in contrast to philosophers. They sought to defend religion, often against the perceived threat of Greek philosophy. Their methods of justification had much in common with the rational demonstrations of the philosophers, although they clearly differed in their starting principles. Maimonides agrees with the goals of the *mutakallimun,* namely, to justify fundamental religious beliefs; he objects to their arguments, which he claims were based on false premises. On Strauss' analysis, then, the *Guide* pertains to *aggadah,* rather than *halakah.* It seeks to explain the foundations or roots of Judaism, not its conventional practices. It seeks to justify fundamental Jewish beliefs. But unlike the traditional *kalam,* it does so in terms of true beliefs and rational demonstrations.

The elusive style, Strauss goes on to explain, is dictated by the *Guide's* subject matter and purpose. Except within specified limits, there were talmudic prohibitions against explaining certain scriptural "secrets," the foundations of the Law, lest these "secrets" mislead believers. Yet Maimonides felt compelled to explain these foundations to certain believers by a public means of communication. Thus he faced a moral dilemma, which he solved by using various literary devices to conceal his intended teachings from the general public and yet to reveal them to a select reader. As Strauss concludes, "The *Guide* is then devoted to an esoteric explanation of an esoteric doctrine." But Strauss' conclusion raises some troublesome questions. Does interpreting the *Guide* raise a similar moral problem, whether and to whom to communicate its esoteric explanations? Are the *Guide's* teachings then totally inaccessible to the modern philosopher?

In "The Philosophical Character of Maimonides' *Guide—* A Critique of Strauss' Interpretation," I reformulate Strauss' view and assess its arguments. I challenge the underlying premise that, for Maimonides, there is a dichotomy between being a Jew and being a philosopher, by discussing the relationship between religious belief and philosophical reason. I contend that, for Maimonides, these are mutually dependent, one on the other. If so, then philosophy is not just incidental, but integral, to the program of the *Guide*.

Virtually any issue in the *Guide* raises the specter of a hidden, esoteric teaching implied by Maimonides' explicit language. But two discussions are particularly troublesome, that on the nature of prophecy and that on the origin of the world. Maimonides lists three opinions on each issue and adds that his position on the one is like his position on the other. His treatment here is troublesome because some of the opinions allude to conventional Jewish beliefs and others to contrary philosophical positions. Maimonides' ambiguity, intentional or otherwise, has led commentators to ask, Which view does he espouse on the origin of the world? Which on the nature of prophecy? How does the list of views on cosmogony relate to the list of views on prophecy? While recent commentators tend to agree that on one or all of these issues there is an implicit esoteric view different from Maimonides' stated exoteric view, they disagree on what that view is. And while they also tend to agree that Maimonides' exoteric view on cosmogony is a traditional Jewish belief in creation, they differ over his esoteric view and its intended correlate on prophecy.

In "A Third Approach to Maimonides' Cosmogony-Prophetology Puzzle," Warren Zev Harvey addresses these questions anew against the background of this recent discussion.

An underlying issue is whether Maimonides upholds the Mosaic Law, as he seems to do publicly and exoterically, or whether he sides with Aristotelian philosophy, albeit veiled and esoterically. Harvey contends that Maimonides did not choose one over the other. Rather, his commitment to both the Mosaic Law and Aristotelian philosophy is unfaltering. His real intention, according to Harvey, is to present a more nuanced understanding of both. Upholding what he considers an "obvious correspondence," based on the order in which Maimonides lists the views on cosmogony and later those on prophecy, Harvey goes on to argue that on cosmogony Maimonides espouses an Aristotelian position, along with the contention that this is not incompatible with the Mosaic Law. On prophecy, instead, Maimonides modifies its traditional understanding as a supernatural event, by claiming that prophecy is a natural event, whose occurrence may nevertheless be prevented by miraculous intervention. A miracle, however, is itself a natural event but one that involves the will of God. Consequently, on this interpretation, the foundation of Maimonides' worldview includes both the Aristotelian laws of change and the divine will.

Similar issues are discussed, again, in the selection by Alfred L. Ivry on Maimonides' understanding of divine omniscience and providence. The question of interpretation forms the explicit framework for his discussion in Section Two. The question of Maimonides' commitment to Judaism alongside Aristotelian philosophy also emerges in the treatment of his ethical views by Marvin Fox in Section Three. And Isaac Franck, in connection with Maimonides' theory of divine attributes in Section Four, alludes to Strauss' insistence on a secret teaching.

4

Many of the epistemological and metaphysical issues of Maimonides parallel those of his Islamic and Christian counterparts. Among these are the relation between faith and reason, between religion and philosophy; the existence and nature of God; the status of divine attributes; the meaning of theological language; problems dealing with specific attributes such as omniscience, omnipotence, and providence; the process of change in natural events, the role of human free will, and the nature of miracles; the creation versus the eternity of the world; the nature of the soul or intellect as well as its natural perfection and immortality.

What motivates Maimonides to address these issues is often the belief in God. This belief is central to Judaism, as it is to any religion, but Maimonides hardly accepts it uncritically, because either in its scriptural or its philosophical context the belief is problematic, as are other religious beliefs in relation to it. Indeed, in the *Guide* he seeks to replace traditional religious beliefs, which he considers often misleading and at times mistaken, with true beliefs about the reality of God and related matters. The one point generates a fundamental metaphysical question about the existence and nature of God; the other, a fundamental epistemological question about the nature and scope of true beliefs or knowledge.

In the *Guide* Maimonides alludes to three kinds of knowledge: of the educated, of prophets, and of God. All three raise similar questions. What is distinctive of that knowledge? How is it attained? What, as a result, is known? In general Maimonides suggests an Aristotelian epistemology, in which knowledge is a function of intellectual apprehension and rational demonstration. But the theory is sorely tested in the case of both prophetic knowledge and divine knowledge. The knowledge of prophets, unlike that of the educated, proves to be troublesome because of its purportedly special status and content. The knowledge of God, unlike human knowledge in general, proves to be troublesome because of Maimonides' theory of divine attributes and negative theology.

In the first selection of Section Two, "The Limitations of Human

Knowledge according to Al-Farabi, ibn Bajja, and Maimonides," Shlomo Pines touches on a number of epistemological issues. But his focus is on two apparently contradictory contentions: that knowledge or contemplation is the ideal of human perfection and that the scope of knowledge is severely restricted. On Maimonides' epistemology, according to Pines, the intellect can only cognize objects abstracted from the percepts of sensation or the imagination. From this it follows that there is no knowledge beyond the sublunar realm of material entities. This conclusion is consistent with Maimonides' negative theology, which denies that we can know *what* God is. But what, then, can Maimonides mean by urging his reader toward knowledge of God as the ideal of human perfection? Since Maimonides allows knowledge of God's actions in the world, Pines interprets the ideal to refer, not to theoretical contemplation, but to a practical and political end. He traces these views to the influence of Alfarabi (c. 870–950) by way of Ibn Bajjah (c. 1070–1138; Avempace to the Latins). Along the way, he comments on Maimonides' views on immortality, prophetic knowledge, and the division and ranking of the sciences. By way of conclusion, Pines compares Maimonides to Kant in his critique of traditional metaphysics and in his according primacy to the practical life.

Whether the ideal of human perfection is a practical or a theoretical end in the thought of Maimonides, it still presupposes the fact that God exists. Like other medieval philosophers, he took this to be a matter of demonstration.

In "Maimonides' Proofs for the Existence of God," William Lane Craig systematically analyzes Maimonides' four arguments. There are two from motion, one from contingency and necessity, and one from potentiality and actuality. The Maimonidean proofs are reminiscent of Avicenna (980–1037) before him and of Aquinas after him. Maimonides prefaces these proofs with twenty-six premises derived from Aristotelian philosophy. Craig's reformulations show how the Aristotelian premises figure in Maimonides' proofs. They establish not only the fact of God's existence but also His incorporeality, simplicity, and incomparability, which, in turn, are the premises to Maimonides' theory of divine attributes and negative theology.

The next selection deals with one consequence of these proofs for Maimonides' theory of existence. Existence can *not* be an attribute or an accident in the case of God; it *is* in the case of everything else. Commentators have criticized this view. Alexander Altmann argues that the criticism is based on a misunderstanding. In "Essence and Existence in Maimonides," Altmann draws on the parallel thesis in Avicenna, who considered existence an accident, not in the logical sense of a predicate but in the ontological sense of the effect of an agent's efficient cause. Thus,

Maimonides' thesis serves, on the one hand, to incorporate the will of God into the causal process and, on the other, to demarcate a radical distinction between God as totally uncaused and all other creatures as in some way fundamentally caused.

In "Maimonides on Modes and Universals," Harry A. Wolfson takes up one aspect of the problem of divine attributes. Among Islamic and Jewish thinkers, this problem received similar responses as the general problem of universals. Analogous to the realist position on universals, some held divine attributes to be real entities, distinct within God's essence. Others, akin to the nominalist position, took divine attributes to designate mere names that refer to God's absolutely simple essence. A third view, somewhat like the conceptualist position on universals, called divine names "modes." Neither real entities nor mere names, modes were meant to imply a conceptual difference in thought but not an ontological difference in God's essence. Various formulae were often used ambiguously to express quite different views on divine attributes. By analyzing the formulae alluded to in the *Guide*, Wolfson explains Maimonides' position on divine attributes and his rejection of the theory of modes. Because of the special case of God, however, a theory of divine attributes is logically distinct from a theory of universals. Maimonides is clearly a nominalist on divine attributes; he is an Aristotelian realist on universals in general.

His nominalism on divine attributes entails a negative theology, the thesis that meaningful language about God can only say what He is *not* and hence that we cannot know *what* God is but only what He is *not*. Terms referring to knowledge, power, life, and the like can be predicated of God and other creatures only equivocally. When such terms are predicated of God, the proposition amounts to a tautology, asserting that God is God; otherwise the proposition contradicts absolute divine simplicity. Negative propositions, denying attributes to God, are neither tautologous nor contradictory to the divine essence. Rather, they have the effect of removing God from the range of human conceptualizations.

Maimonides' negative theology, however, needs to be qualified in two respects. First, it is not just imperfections that are to be denied to God, anything that suggests corporeality, for instance; it is, more specifically, the privation of corresponding perfections that are to be denied to God. We can intelligibly and truthfully say, for example, "God is not ignorant" and "God is not weak." But Maimonides would also contend that these propositions do not logically entail "God is knowledgeable" and "God is powerful," because there is a logical difference between a privation and a negation. Second, despite his insistence on negative language, he allows the predication of actions, which describe the effects of God's agency, on the grounds that such predication does not countenance divine simplicity.

To say what God did, for Maimonides, does not entail anything descriptive about God's essence. Nuanced though his views may be on theological language, they are nevertheless extremely troublesome, both logically and ontologically. The two later selections in Section Four, by Seymour Feldman and Isaac Franck, deal with aspects of Maimonides' negative theology.

Several issues dealt with in the *Guide* imply divine agency; among these are prophecy, miracles, and divine providence. The last selection in this section explains Maimonides' approach to one of these issues, namely, divine providence.

In "Providence, Divine Omniscience, and Possibility: the Case of Maimonides," Alfred L. Ivry also brings forward an esoteric teaching. Providence and omniscience are related in that without knowledge there can be neither just rewards nor just punishments; nor indeed any kind of care. In the case of God's knowledge, however, there is the question whether God knows only species in their intelligible form, i.e., their universal essence, or also particular members in their individual material substratum. The latter seems precluded on Maimonides' epistemology, if God does not acquire knowledge by way of sensation and abstraction, as human beings do. Yet Maimonides admits that providence extends to individual human beings, although it does not to individual members of other species. On Ivry's analysis, Maimonides' theory of emanation is the link between God's knowledge and providence. While matter is created, forms emanate from God. Providence, too, is the result of emanation and thus extends to individual human beings in virtue of their intellects and their cognition of forms. In addition, Ivry briefly touches on the problem of evil, the question of divine will and freedom, and the question of possibility in relation to omnipotence. In conclusion, he notes the significant influence of Neoplatonic elements in Maimonides' epistemology and metaphysics.

5

The Aristotelian domain of practical sciences covers ethical and political issues. So does *halakah*. But here, too, Maimonides brings a distinctively philosophical outlook to the Jewish tradition of jurisprudence. And the extent of his commitment to Judaism alongside a commitment to Aristotelian philosophy emerges anew for practical issues, as it did for theoretical ones. His political views, however, owe more to Plato than to Aristotle.

In the *Guide* and elsewhere, Maimonides addresses himself to a number of philosophical, ethical, and political problems: the nature of virtue and its criteria; the nature of human perfection and the ethical end of human beings; the role of prophets; the rational justification of laws, especially in connection with the range of Jewish prescriptions and prohibitions implicit in the Mosaic Law; the nature of the state and, in particular, of the Jewish nation. The selections in Section Three highlight central issues and views in Maimonides' political theory, legal theory, and ethical theory, respectively.

In "Maimonides, the Disciple of Alfarabi," Lawrence V. Berman sketches a theory of development of religion that Maimonides adopted from Alfarabi and applied to Judaism. On this theory in Alfarabi, religion comes after philosophy, but there is an ascending progression in the latter and a descending one in the former. On the one hand, there is a progression in philosophy from spurious beliefs based on sophistical arguments, to probable beliefs based on dialectics, and finally to true beliefs based on demonstration. On the other hand, religion leads to jurisprudence, which works out the implications of religion in its beliefs and practices, and to theology, which defends religion. The philosopher-statesman provides the link between philosophy and religion. As Plato had argued, only the philosopher-statesman on the basis of his knowledge can properly legislate for others so as to assure social order. Maimonides alludes to a similar ascending and descending progression, but he incorporates philosophy into the development of Judaism. Thus, on the ascending rung, religion culminates in Mosaic prophecy, in which legislative authority combines with the highest level of human knowledge. On the descending rung, Judaism, that is, the Mosaic Law, leads to jurisprudence, exemplified by Maimonides' *Code,* and to theology, exemplified by his *Guide.* To Berman, Maimonides is a theologian in Alfarabi's sense and the *Guide* "his major theologico-political opus." In this conclusion, Berman shows an affinity to the interpretation of Leo Strauss.

In "The Purpose of the Law according to Maimonides," Miriam Galston deals with Maimonides' general treatment of laws. Maimonides distinguishes conventional laws of civil states from the revealed law of Moses. The latter, moreover, excels the former. Maimonides also claims that laws can be given a rational justification, if they are proper laws. He justifies laws in general and defends the superiority of the Mosaic Law in particular in terms of both spiritual and political well-being. Galston analyzes this multilayered concept. She clarifies several important distinctions in Maimonides: between the concepts of revealed, divine, and conventional laws; between kinds of societies according to the laws that govern them; between health and perfection of both the body and the soul; and between correct opinions and necessary beliefs. The Mosaic Law is a legal system *par excellence,* according to Maimonides, for several reasons. First, it not only aims at health of the body and of the soul, but it also promotes their corresponding perfections. Health of the body includes a social well-being; perfection of the soul has intellectual connotations. Second, the Mosaic Law reinforces behavior by beliefs necessary for the stability of the political order. Third, it allows for individual perfection in terms of correct opinions held for their own sake, rather than for their political utility. Other legal systems, Maimonides claims, fall short of these aims in one way or another.

Human perfection also enters into the discussion of Marvin Fox, "The Doctrine of the Mean in Aristotle and Maimonides: A Comparative Study." But human perfection, for Maimonides, consists in a religious ideal, the contemplation and imitation of God. Fox questions how this ideal squares with Maimonides' acceptance of the Aristotelian theory of the mean. The religious ideal taken from *halakah*, it seems, is not a mean between the extremes of excess and caution, nor is it determined by prudential wisdom. In light of his examination of both Aristotle and Maimonides, Fox suggests that Maimonides' ethical theory operates at two levels. The Aristotelian-philosophical level proposes a theory of the mean that suffices to insure general social order. The religious-Jewish level proposes an ethical ideal for individual human perfection. The one is, at best, a precondition for the other. The theory of the mean allows for changing standards; the theory of individual perfection derives from the fixed norms of the Torah. In the ethical sphere, then, Fox also draws a difference between Maimonides' commitment to Judaism and his commitment to Aristotelian philosophy, limiting the latter because of the former.

6

Maimonides' influence was extensive in his lifetime; it has continued unabated since. It can be seen directly or indirectly in medieval as well as modern thought, among both Jewish and non-Jewish thinkers.

Within medieval Jewish thought Maimonides generated a number of controversies regarding his Jewish orthodoxy or his interpretation of Aristotle. Gersonides (1288–1344), for instance, who also developed his views within an Aristotelian framework, nevertheless differed from Maimonides on language about God, on Mosaic prophecy, on providence and omniscience. The difference, to be sure, is in part explained by the fact that Gersonides tended to follow an Averroistic interpretation of Aristotle, whereas Maimonides relied on Alfarabi and Avicenna. Whatever the reason, later Jewish medieval thinkers reacted favorably or unfavorably to Maimonides, but never with indifference.

Within Christian medieval thought Maimonides came to be highly regarded for his general approach to religious problems and for his views on specific issues. The respect is particularly noticeable in Thomas Aquinas, who showed a similar deference to Aristotelian philosophy as did Maimonides. The Rabbi's influence on Aquinas' proofs for the existence of God has already been mentioned. Another point of common interest is the problem of theological language, which the two selections in Section Four both take up.

In "A Scholastic Misinterpretation of Maimonides' Doctrine of Divine Attributes," Seymour Feldman first gives a general exposition of Maimonides' theory of divine attributes. The theory hinges on a logical distinction between essential, accidental, and relational attributes on the one side, and attributes of action on the other. Only attributes of action are positively predicable of God, according to Maimonides, because in describing what God did—rather than what He is—these do not entail multiplicity in God's essence. Thus to say "God is merciful," for example, is to describe certain effects of God's agency, not a disposition or quality in God. Predecessors of Maimonides, however, understood this proposition to mean either that God is the cause of mercy or that divine acts of mercy are like human acts of mercy. Thus they tended to classify attributes of action with relational attributes. Maimonides clearly did not. As Feldman maintains, later Christian scholastics, among them Thomas Aquinas (1225–1274) and John Duns Scotus (1265–1308) misunderstood Maimonides on this point. They interpreted Maimonides' attributes of action relationally or causally. The issue is significant when assessing the Maimonidean theory of theological language in relation to the well-known theory of analogy in Aquinas.

In the final selection, "Maimonides and Aquinas on Man's Knowledge of God: A Twentieth Century Perspective," Isaac Franck sets a twofold task: to show the close parallel between Maimonides and Aquinas on negative theology and to defend this theology against a number of recent criticisms. These criticisms, Franck argues, either misunderstand the central thrust of negative theology or else beg the question against it. The negative theology of both Maimonides and Aquinas claims that while we can know *that* God exists, we can not know *what* He is. Hence, we can only know what He is *not*. Although a radical thesis, Franck suggests on behalf of Maimonides and Aquinas that it is intelligible and defensible.

Among modern and later thinkers, Maimonidean strands are discernible as well. The tenor of his philosophical thought, however, is as often criticized as it is absorbed. Spinoza, for instance, shows an affinity with Maimonidean views in some aspects of his philosophy, although he is critical of the medieval Rabbi's attempt to synthesize philosophy with religion.

Leibniz, on the other hand, developed or refined a number of his well-known themes as a result of his reading the *Guide*. Likewise, among modern Jewish thinkers, Moses Mendelssohn (1729–1786), to mention an early post-enlightenment philosopher, seems to reflect some of Maimonides' rationalism, whereas Ahad Ha'am (1856–1927) later severely criticized it.

Noting a fundamental difference between the medieval and modern mind, one recent commentator nevertheless has asked whether there are any twentieth-century Maimonidean thinkers (Warren Zev Harvey, "The Return of Maimonideanism," *Jewish Social Studies* 42 [1980]: 249–268). His response is that there are and he lists Leo Strauss among them. Even if this contention is disputed, Maimonides' approach to philosophical and religious issues remains significant by way of the problems he raised as well as the methods he used, if not also the solutions he offered.

SECTION I

Issues of Interpretation

Interpreting Maimonides

ARTHUR HYMAN

Maimonides' *Guide of the Perplexed* is a difficult and enigmatic work which many times perplexed the very reader it was supposed to guide. Its technical subject matter, the elitist audience for which it was composed, its allusory and contradictory style, and its apparently eclectic philosophical foundations have challenged a long line of interpreters who attempted to clarify the details of Maimonides' views and to determine his over-all philosophic orientation. This line of interpreters, which extends from Maimonides' days until our very own, may, in fact, be said to have been started by Maimonides himself. For, when in his *Ma'amar Tehiyyat ha-Metim*, Maimonides reaffirmed his belief in the literal meaning of the resurrection of the dead against charges that he denied this principle, he became the first interpreter of his own views.

In this brief paper I shall undertake a three-fold task. I shall begin by analyzing some of the features of the *Guide* of which any interpreter must take account. Then I shall describe some aspects of the interpretation of Maimonides by modern scholars, showing that modern interpreters may be divided into two basic groups. And finally, I shall make two suggestions concerning further research that may help to clarify Maimonides' views.

I

By his own admission, Maimonides did not compose a purely philosophic work, thereby setting himself off from the philosophic tradition of his day. Unlike his Islamic predecessors — Alfarabi, Avicenna, Ibn Bajjah

Gesher 5 (1976): 46–59. Reprinted by permission of the author and *Gesher*. Translations added to the text in brackets are those of the editor with the help of David Louch.

— and his contemporary Averroes, who composed commentaries on Aristotle's works, *summae* of his views, and philosophic treatises of their own, Maimonides had no intention to add to the philosophic literature of his day or to become an innovator in the realm of philosophic speculation. This was already clear from his early program in the *Commentary on the Mishnah,* according to which he had in mind to write a "Book of Prophecy" and a "Book of Correspondence," devoted respectively to an account of prophecy and an exposition of difficult Midrashim (cf. *Guide* I, Introduction). More explicitly, he writes in *Guide* II, 2: "Know, that my purpose in this Treatise of mine [the *Guide*] was not to compose something in the natural science [physics], or to make an epitome of notions pertaining to the divine science [metaphysics] . . . For the books composed concerning these matters are adequate." "If however," he adds, "they should turn out not to be adequate with regard to some subject, that which I shall say concerning that subject will not be superior to anything else that has been said about it." (English citations are taken from S. Pines' translation of the *Guide*).

If then the *Guide* is not a work of purely philosophic speculation, what then are the subjects with which it deals? Maimonides foregoes characterizing the contents of the *Guide* by means of a single word or phrase, describing them instead in three-fold fashion. In the Introduction to the *Guide* he first states that it is the purpose of his work to explain the equivocal, derivative, and amphibolous terms appearing in the scriptural texts and to clarify scriptural parables which are obscure. Then again, he describes the subject matter of the *Guide* by the rabbinic terms *Ma'aseh Merkabah* and *Ma'aseh Bereshit* which in all of his works he identifies with physics and metaphysics. Finally, he states that the *Guide* is devoted to "the science of the Law in its true sense" (*hokhmat ha-Torah 'al ha-emet*), "the secrets [of the Law]" (*ha-sodot*), and "the mysteries of the Law" (*sitrei Torah*). That the secrets of the Law discussed in the *Guide* are not co-extensive with the totality of physical and metaphysical knowledge, may be gathered from an incidental enumeration that Maimonides himself provides. In a chapter advocating the moderate intellectual enlightenment of the masses (*Guide* I, 35), he states emphatically that the secrets and mysteries of the Law must be concealed from them, listing as such secrets: divine attributes, creation, God's governance of the world and His providence for it; divine will, apprehension, knowledge, and names; and prophecy and its various degrees. Comparing this list with the topics forming the subject matter of the *Guide*, one discovers that it contains all the topics of the work with the exception of the section, at the end of the book, devoted to the reasons for the commandments (*ta'amei ha-mitzvot*). From these observations one may conclude that, whatever else the *Guide* may be, it is a book of scriptural exegesis devoted to the secrets of the Law. The purpose of Maimonides' exegesis remains, however, still to be determined.

Just as the *Guide* is restricted to a limited subject matter, so is it restricted to a limited audience. Maimonides wrote for Jews and for Jews of a special kind at that. That the work was not written for pure philosophers is clear from what has been seen so far as well as from the fact that most of the subjects discussed in the *Guide* are of little interest to those concerned with pure philosophic speculation. Nor is the work addressed to the masses, to those who are beginners in speculation, or to those scholars who are only engaged in the legal study of the Law—though all of these may derive some benefit from the work. Who then are those to whom the *Guide* is addressed? Maimonides, in his Introduction, describes the addressee of the *Guide* as someone who is "perfect in his religion and character," that is someone who is a devoted Jew and who, at the same time, has "studied the sciences of the philosophers and come to know what they signify." The reader so described has been perplexed by the conflict between the literal meaning of scriptural terms and parables and what he has learned in the philosophical disciplines. He is concerned that were he to follow the teachings of philosophy he would have to renounce the foundations of the Law, and were he to accept literally the scriptural terms and parables, he would have to sacrifice the discoveries of his mind. Once again it must be left open how Maimonides resolves the perplexity of his reader.

The literary character of the *Guide* imposes further difficulties of interpretation—difficulties occasioned by halakic considerations as well as principles of philosophic prudence. The *Mishnah* in *Hagigah* II, 1 enjoins the public teaching of *Ma'aseh Bereshit* and *Ma'aseh Merkabah,* holding that *Ma'aseh Bereshit* may be taught to only one person and *Ma'aseh Merkabah* only to one who is wise and able to reason for himself. Maimonides in *Mishneh Torah, Hilkhot Yesodei ha-Torah* II, 12 and IV, 11 codifies this mishnaic principle as binding law and this presents him with a problem in writing the *Guide.* For if *Ma'aseh Bereshit* and *Ma'aseh Merkabah* are identical with physics and metaphysics, how can he write a book devoted to these topics, especially since presenting one's views in writing is public teaching par excellence. Aware of this dilemma, Maimonides justifies his writing the *Guide* in three-fold fashion. First of all he invokes the biblical verse: "It is time to do something for the Lord, for they have infringed Thy Law" (Ps. 119:126). This is the same verse that had been used to justify the writing down of the *Mishnah,* another work the writing down of which had been legally enjoined. To the biblical verse he adds as additional justification the rabbinic saying "Let all thy acts be for the sake of Heaven" (Ab. II, 17).

Then again, Maimonides takes cognizance of the halakic injunction in the literary form of his work. He begins the *Guide* with an Introductory Letter, addressed to a former student, Joseph ben Judah Ibn Sham'un, whom he had previously tested to make sure that he was wise and able to reason for himself. Since then the work has the form of a personal communication addressed to someone who has fulfilled the qualifications of the halakah, the writing of the *Guide* cannot, strictly speaking, be said to be public teaching.

Maimonides, however, was well aware that his work would become available to people at large (in fact he aided Samuel Ibn Tibbon in translating the *Guide* into Hebrew) and so he had to look in still another direction to observe the teachings of the halakah. This he did by using methods of contradiction. Enumerating in the Introduction to the *Guide* seven types of contradictions that appear in books and compilations, Maimonides states explicitly that he will use two of these in the work. One of these is the use of contradictions for pedagogic reasons, the other to conceal his true opinions. Concerning the latter he writes: "In speaking about very obscure matters it is necessary to conceal some parts and to disclose others. Sometimes in the case of certain dicta this necessity requires that the discussion proceed on the basis of a certain premise, whereas in another place necessity requires that the discussion proceed on the basis of another premise contradicting the first one." There has been no greater challenge to interpreters than to locate these contradictions and to discover how they may be resolved.

We have so far spoken about problems occasioned by the subject matter of the *Guide*, the audience to which it is addressed, the method of contradiction which Maimonides uses, but there is one further aspect of the work which invites the interpreter's attention. It is the overall orientation of Maimonides' philosophic views. It is a commonplace among the students of Maimonides that he was an Aristotelian in his philosophic orientation, but hardly anyone has clarified what kind of Aristotelianism he embraced. This question becomes acute once it is realized that two types of Aristotelianism were current in Maimonides' days—that of Avicenna and that of Averroes. Avicenna's Aristotelianism manifested a strong Neoplatonic coloration and it had a certain theological bend. By contrast, Averroes' Aristotelianism was of a more naturalistic kind. Averroes undertook to restore the true Aristotelian teachings by cleansing them of Neoplatonic accretions and he accused Avicenna of having capitulated to theological considerations on certain points. Hence, one may contrast the theologically colored Aristotelianism of Avicenna with the more naturalistic one of Averroes. What kind of evidence does Maimonides provide for assessing his position on this philosophic controversy?

Maimonides mentions both philosophers in his writings. He mentions Averroes in a well-known letter to Samuel Ibn Tibbon, the first Hebrew translator of the *Guide*, and also in a letter to Joseph ben Judah, the addressee of the *Guide*. Scholars are agreed that Maimonides became acquainted with the views of Averroes too late to consider them in his *Guide*. (See S. Pines, "Translator's Introduction," *Guide of the Perplexed* [Chicago, 1963], pp. lix–lxi, cviii, and H. A. Wolfson, *Crescas' Critique of Aristotle* [Cambridge, Mass., 1929], p. 323). However this does not preclude that Maimonides' Aristotelianism may have been of an Averroean kind, since Maimonides associated himself with Andalusian Aristotelianism — an Aristotelianism which was naturalistic in its orientation.

Maimonides also mentions Avicenna in the letter to Samuel Ibn Tibbon, but while he recommends Averroes without any reservation, he attaches some strictures to the study of Avicenna. Comparing Avicenna and Alfarabi he writes: "Though the works of Avicenna manifest great accuracy and subtle study, they are not as good as the works of Abu Nasr al-Farabi." (A. Marx, "Texts by and about Maimonides," *Jewish Quarterly Review*, n. s., 25 [1934–35]: 380). This somewhat negative opinion must be balanced by the observation that in the continuation of this passage Maimonides advocates the study of Avicenna's works and that on a number of crucial philosophic issues on which Avicenna and Averroes held conflicting opinions he follows Avicenna's views. Thus, for example, he follows Avicenna (against Averroes) in holding that essential attributes applied to God must be understood as negations and in recognizing the validity of the proof of the existence of God known as the proof from necessity and contingency.

With these backgrounds in mind, we can now proceed to a discussion of some aspects of modern Maimonides interpretations.

II

The modern study and interpretation of Maimonides may be divided into two periods. The first of these extends from the 1840s until the early 1930s; the second from the early 1930s until today. Of the studies which appeared during the first of these two periods one may single out Scheyer's *Das psychologische System des Maimonides* (1845) and Rosin's *Die Ethik Maimonides* (1876), but scholars would probably agree that the Arabic edition and annotated French translation contained in S. Munk's *Le Guide des Egarées* (1856–66) mark the high-point of the scholarly accomplishments of this period. Research during this period was hampered by the lack of adequate editions of the parallel Arabic texts and by the absence of monographic studies devoted to the Islamic philosophers on whom Maimonides drew. Thus, for example, Scheyer in his just mentioned study of Maimonides' psychological teachings had to rely on citations in the Hebrew commentaries on the *Guide* for his knowledge of Maimonides' Islamic philosophic antecedents.

The turning point came in the early 1930s with the appearance of Julius Guttmann's *Die Philosophie des Judentums* (1933), Leo Strauss' seminal *Philosophie und Gesetz* (1935), and H. A. Wolfson's magisterial studies. The Arabic texts of Maimonides' Islamic predecessors now started to appear and so did monographs on their thought.

While Maimonides scholarship during the second period was devoted primarily to articles and monographs on specific problems within Maimonides' thought, certain trends in the overall interpretation of his position started to emerge. There were those scholars, primarily Strauss, Pines, and, more recently, Berman who proposed what may be called the naturalistic interpretation of Maimonides; and there were those, primarily Julius Guttmann, H. A. Wolfson, and the present writer who tended toward a more harmonistic interpretation.

The pioneering study of the naturalistic interpretation was Leo Strauss' *Philosophie und Gesetz* — a work, judging by the footnotes, partially influenced by Leon Gauthier's *La théorie d'Ibn Rochd (Averroès) sur les rapports de la religion et de la philosophie* (1909) which Strauss himself describes as a "meisterhafte Analyse" [masterful analysis] of Averroes' *Fasl al-Maqal* (p. 70, n.1). Gauthier's work, together with his own researches on the political writings of Alfarabi, brought Strauss to emphasize the political dimensions of Maimonides' thought and the esoteric nature of his exposition. Strauss pointed out that Maimonides (as the Muslim Aristotelians) followed Aristotle in his physical and metaphysical views, but his political teachings were Platonic. Through the intermediacy of Alfarabi, Maimonides accepted the Platonic notion that the ideal state consists of three classes of men, each one of which performs the function for which it is fit. (It should be noted that Maimonides reduces these classes to two — the elite, literally "the perfect ones," and the masses.) The ideal state can only come to be when there exists a philosopher-king in whom there are combined the virtues of the philosopher and the statesman. Pagan societies never produced a philosopher-king, so that the ideal state never came to be among them. By contrast, the advent of the scriptural prophets, particularly Moses, created the possibility of the ideal state and the ideal law. Manifesting an interest in the political function of the prophet more than in the psychological processes productive of prophecy, Strauss and those who follow his approach, point out that Moses, for Maimonides, becomes the embodiment par excellence of Plato's philosopher-king and that the state which Moses founded and the Law he brought are the embodiment of the Platonic ideal.

Strauss continued his studies of Maimonides in "The Literary Character of the *Guide for the Perplexed*" (in S. W. Baron, ed., *Essays on Maimonides: An Octocentennial Volume* (New York, 1941]; appeared also in Strauss' *Persecution and the Art of Writing* [Glencoe, Ill. 1952]; and is reprinted in this volume,) and his "How to Begin to Study the *Guide of the Perplexed*" (in S. Pines' English translation of the *Guide* [Chicago, 1963]). Strauss' insistence on the esoteric character of the *Guide*, his detailed analysis of its literary structure, and his painstaking investigation of its dominant themes imply a certain theory concerning Maimonides' overall views. The position of Strauss and those who follow his interpretation may be gathered from their account of two characteristic Maimonidean topics — prophecy and prophetic knowledge, and creation. From Maimonides' account of these two topics it appears, at first glance, that the prophet possesses knowledge beyond the natural knowledge attained by philosophers and that the world was created. But it may be asked: Are these Maimonides' real views? Might it not be the case that Maimonides' overt statements are simply an exoteric exposition, while in his esoteric views he maintains that there is no special prophetic knowledge and that he agrees with the Aristotelians that the world is eternal?

Strauss' answer to the question appears to have undergone a change as his researches progressed. In his early *Philosophie und Gesetz* he seems to have accepted that Maimonides is the proponent of special prophetic knowledge and of creation (pp. 76–79), but one gains the impression that in his later "The Literary Character of the *Guide for the Perplexed*" and "How to Begin the Study of the *Guide of the Perplexed*" he moved toward the naturalistic interpretation of Maimonides' views. While Strauss' allusive style makes it somewhat difficult to locate his views with precision, S. Pines defends the naturalistic orientation of the *Guide* in more overt fashion. Pines, in fact, speaks of the "naturalistic aspect" of Maimonides' thought and he ascribes to him "a certain naturalistic hard-headedness" ("Translator's Introduction," pp. xcvii and cix).

Pines' stance receives clarification from his interpretation of a passage appearing in the Introduction to the *Guide*. In this passage Maimonides states that the knowledge of the "Secrets of the Law" comes to select individuals, the prophets, like bolts of lightning and that Moses received this kind of knowledge in preeminent, singular fashion. At first glance one gains the impression — and this is the opinion of most of the commentators — that Maimonides describes here a kind of intuitive illumination that only prophets can attain. Pines, however, interprets the passage in another fashion. Citing a passage from Ibn Bajjah's *Risalat al-Ittisal,* Pines explains that while it is true that Moses alone was the recipient of the highest kind of intuitive knowledge, this knowledge was within the natural powers of the human mind. Thus, Pines concludes his interpretation by stating: "When Maimonides borrowed part of his imagery from Ibn Bajja, he must have been aware that all his readers, who were more or less familiar with the main philosophic texts of his time, would tend to identify the man receiving the lightning flashes with the highest type of philosopher and not, as the passage might suggest, with the prophets" (ibid., p. cvi).

If it is then correct that Strauss and his followers see in Maimonides primarily a philosopher committed to a naturalistic interpretation of Aristotle's views, what then is the purpose of Maimonides' scriptural exegesis in the *Guide* and how does he resolve the perplexities of his reader? The answer to this question is that the *Guide* is a transitional book. The reader for whom the work was written is a believing and practicing Jew who, having studied the philosophical sciences, has become perplexed by the literal meaning of scriptural terms and parables. To this reader Maimonides wants to show that the judicious, esoteric interpretation of Scripture reveals that the secrets of the Law are identical with the pure philosophic teachings. This was a position which Averroes had also made his own. But in spite of this philosophic orientation, Maimonides, unlike Spinoza later on, requires that the philosopher must observe the commandments of Jewish Law. For while the practices contained in the Law have only a secondary function in producing the contemplative state, which for Maimonides is the goal of human life, they are necessary for the stability of the state, of which even the philosopher has need.

Let us now turn briefly to the second exegetical trend—that which has been described as the harmonistic interpretation. Whereas Strauss and his followers emphasize the political dimensions of Maimonides' thought, these merit less attention in the researches of scholars following the harmonistic trend. Guttmann in his *Philosophie des Judentums* barely mentions Maimonides' political views, and his account of prophecy concentrates on the psychological processes of the prophet rather than on his political function. That this is not simply due to the fact that this work appeared before Strauss' *Philosophie und Gesetz* is evident from the Hebrew version of Guttmann's work which appeared in 1950. Not only did Guttmann see no need to revise his earlier views; in fact he argues against Strauss' thesis in a footnote (*Ha-Philosophiah shel ha-Yahadut*, p. 394, n.476b; *Philosophies of Judaism*, p. 434, n.125). While Guttmann's reaction to Strauss has so far been largely a matter of conjecture, a recently published posthumous work by him has helped to explicate his views. In his *Philosophie der Religion oder Philosophie des Gesetzes?* (*Proceedings, The Israel Academy of Sciences and Humanities*, vol. 6 [Jerusalem, 1974])

Guttmann shows his appreciation of Strauss' study of the political and legal dimensions of Maimonides' thought, but reiterates at the same time his conviction that theoretical philosophic concerns lie at the center of Maimonides' thought. "Auch wenn man Strauss den schlechthinnigen Primat des Gesetzes zugeben wolle," writes Guttmann in a salient passage, "ware es doch nur das Recht des Philosophierens, das im Gesetz begründet ist. Ihre sachliche Grundlegung vollzieht die Philosophie selbst, und ihr innerer Aufbau wird durch den sachlichen Zusammenhang ihrer Probleme bestimmt" [Even if one were to concede to Strauss the absolute primacy of the Law, it would still be only the right to philosophize that is grounded in the Law. Philosophy establishes its own essential foundation and its internal structure is determined by the essential coherence of its problems] (p. 168).

It is similarly interesting to note that H. A. Wolfson, who has written on many aspects of Maimonides' thought, did not devote a study to his political views. Instead, proponents of the harmonistic trend turned their attention to Maimonides' physical, psychological, and metaphysical views out of the apparent conviction that these topics provide the most important issues of the *Guide*.

While proponents of the harmonistic interpretation are aware of Maimonides' use of contradictions, they do not place this principle at the center of their interpretation of the *Guide*. Hence, they take Maimonides at his word when he affirms his belief in creation, when he makes prophecy in some way dependent on the will of God, and when he holds that prophets can acquire knowledge which is not available to the philosopher. H. A. Wolfson expresses this point of view when he writes: "They both [Hallevi and Maimonides] agree that God acts with free will and that in His action there is therefore an element of grace and election, opposing thereby the view which they both attribute to Aristotle and to the philosophers in general that God acts by the necessity of His nature" ("Hallevi and Maimonides on Prophecy," *Jewish Quarterly Review,* n. s., 32 [1942]: 345). Guttmann speaks in a similar vein when he writes: "Even with regard to speculation the prophet transcends the pure philosopher, for cognition rises in him to speculative heights that surpass the boundaries of that which can discursively be grasped" (*Philosophie des Judentums,* p. 195, my own translation).

What, then, according to the harmonistic interpretation is the complexion of Maimonides' thought and what is the purpose of the *Guide*? H. A. Wolfson, in his very first published study, answered this question by felicitously describing Maimonides as an Aristotelian, though with limitations. By that he meant that "[it was Maimonides' aim] to show that Scriptures and Talmud, correctly interpreted, strictly harmonize with the philosophical writings of Aristotle" ("Maimonides and Halevi: A Study in Typical Attitudes towards Greek Philosophy in the Middle Ages," *Jewish Quarterly Review,* n. s., 2 [1912]: 307). However this harmonization was limited in the sense that the human mind had only a limited capacity for truth. Beyond that—in areas such as creation, prophetic knowledge, and so forth—Scripture provided a truth not available to the unaided human intellect. In writing the *Guide* it was Maimonides' task to show that Scripture, properly interpreted, contains the truths of Aristotelian physics and metaphysics but that, in addition, it provides knowledge which man cannot attain by his own natural powers. In somewhat different language, Guttmann makes the same point when he writes, "Maimonides' theistic Aristotelianism made room for the creator-God of the Bible within his philosophic outlook, thereby effecting metaphysically a real synthesis between biblical religion and Aristotelianism" (*Philosophie des Judentums,* p. 205, my own translation).

III

Confronted by these two divergent interpretations, what is the contemporary interpreter to do and can he ever hope for a resolution of this dilemma? Isadore Twersky has given expression to the interpreter's problem when he writes in his *Maimònides Reader*: "This dialectic and these difficulties [of the *Guide*] continue to befuddle and divide students of the *Guide* concerning Maimonides' true intention and actual religious stance. There is little agreement among scholars in this area" (p. 21, note).

Having studied Maimonides consistently for some twenty-five years, I have no clear-cut answer to our question. My own preference is for the harmonistic interpretation, though I can not close my eyes to the merits of the naturalistic school (See my "Some Aspects of Maimonides' Philosophy of Nature," *La filosofia della natura nel Medioevo* [Milan, 1966], pp. 209–218 and "Maimonides' Thirteen Principles," *Jewish Medieval and Renaissance Studies,* ed. A. Altmann [Cambridge, Mass., 1967], pp. 119–144). I want to conclude, however, with two suggestions for future Maimonidean studies which, to my mind, will help to clarify our problem. My first suggestion is to investigate anew Maimonides' psychological doctrines. Admittedly this is not easy, since his discussion of psychological topics is rather scant. But we now have good editions of psychological writings of Alfarabi, Avicenna, Ibn Bajjah, and Averroes and their judicious use will undoubtedly be of help. Specifically, one should investigate once again the nature of the illuminative experience described in the Introduction of the *Guide.* My second suggestion is to probe further the relation of Maimonides' teachings to those of the Ash'arite Ghazali. While it is evident that Maimonides' stance is quite different from that of Ghazali, still scholars have suggested that what has been called Ghazali's occasionalism may have had some influence on Maimonides' thought. While, then, an answer to the question: "What is the correct interpretation of Maimonides' thought?" may lie at the end of a long road, studies such as those suggested might help to move us along the way.

The Literary Character of the *Guide for the Perplexed*

LEO STRAUSS

ἡ γὰρ ὕστερον εὐπορία λύσις τῶν
πρότερον ἀπορουμένων ἐστί, λύειν
δ' οὐκ ἔστιν ἀγνοοῦντας τὸν δεσμόν.
— Aristotle

[for what follows is, of course,
the solution of those very difficulties,
and no one can untangle a knot which
he does not see.
Metaphysics III, 1, 995a29]

Among the many historians who have interpreted Maimonides' teaching, or who are making efforts to interpret it, there is scarcely one who would not agree to the principle that that teaching, being essentially medieval, cannot be understood by starting from modern presuppositions. The differences of view between students of Maimonides have thus to be traced back, not necessarily to a disagreement concerning the principle itself, but rather to its different interpretation, or to a difference of attitude in its application. The present essay is based on the assumption that only through its most thoroughgoing application can we arrive at our goal, the true and exact understanding of Maimonides' teaching.[1]

From *Essays on Maimonides, An Octocentennial Volume,* edited by Salo Wittmayer Baron (New York: Columbia University Press, 1941), pp. 37–91; also in Leo Strauss, *Persecution and the Art of Writing* (Glencoe, Ill.: Free Press, 1952), pp. 38–94.

Abridged for this volume and reprinted by permission of Columbia University Press.

The English translation of the above Greek quote is that of Richard Hope (Columbia University Press, 1952). All other translations and transliterations added to the text in brackets are those of the editor with the help of Frances Landy.

I. THE SUBJECT MATTER

The interpreter of the *Guide for the Perplexed* ought to raise, to begin with, the following question: To which science or sciences does the subject matter of the work belong? Maimonides answers it almost at the very beginning of his work by saying that it is devoted to the true science of the law.

The true science of the law is distinguished from the science of the law in the usual sense, i.e., the *fiqh*.[2] While the term *fiqh* naturally occurs in the *Guide* on more than one occasion, the explanation of its meaning has been reserved for almost the very end of the work. *Fiqh* is the exact determination, by way of "deduction" from the authoritative statements of the law, of those actions by means of which man's life becomes noble, and especially of the actions of worship.[3] Its most scientific treatment would consist in a coherent and lucid codification of the law, such as achieved by Maimonides in his *Mishneh Torah,* which he calls "our great work on the *fiqh.*" In contradistinction to the legalistic study of the law, which is concerned with what man ought to do, the true science of the law is concerned with what man ought to think and to believe.[4] One may say that the science of the law in general is divided into two parts: a practical part which is treated in the *Mishneh Torah,* and a theoretical part which is treated in the *Guide.* This view is confirmed by the fact that the former work deals with beliefs and opinions only insofar as they are implied in prohibitions and commands, whereas the *Guide* deals with commands and prohibitions only in order to explain their reasons.

The relation between the two parts, or kinds, of the science of the law may be described in a somewhat different way by saying that, whereas science of the law in the usual sense is the study of the halakah, the true science of the law corresponds to the aggadah. As a matter of fact, the *Guide* is a substitute for two books, planned by Maimonides, on the non-legal sections of the Bible and the Talmud. But, above all, its most important feature, which distinguishes it from all philosophic as well as halakic books, is also characteristic of a part of the aggadic literature.[5]

Since Maimonides, however, uses an Islamic term to designate the ordinary science of the law, it may be worth while to consider what Islamic term would supply the most proper designation for that science of the law which is the subject of the *Guide.* Students of the *fiqh* deal with the actions prescribed by the law, but do not deal with the "roots of religion," i.e., they do not attempt to prove the opinions or beliefs taught by the law. There seems to be little doubt that the science dealing with those roots is identical with the true science of the law.[6] Since the students of the roots are identified by Maimonides with the *Mutakallimûn,* the students of the *kalâm*, we shall say that the true science of the law is the *kalâm*.[7] It is true that Maimonides vigorously attacks the *kalâm*; yet in spite of his ruthless opposition to the assumptions and methods of the *Mutakallimûn*, he professes to be in perfect harmony with their intention.[8] The intention of the science of *kalâm* is to defend the law, especially against the opinions of philosophers.[9] And the central section of the *Guide* is admittedly devoted to the defense of the principal root of the law, the belief in creation, against the contention of the philosophers that the visible world is eternal.[10] What distinguishes Maimonides' *kalâm* from the *kalâm* proper is his insistence on the fundamental difference between intelligence and imagination, whereas, as he asserts, the *Mutakallimûn* mistake imagination for intelligence. In other words, Maimonides insists on the necessity of starting from evident presuppositions, which are in accordance with the nature of things, whereas the *kalâm* proper starts from arbitrary presuppositions, which are chosen not because they are true but because they make it easy to prove the beliefs taught by the law. Maimonides' true science of the law and the *kalâm* thus belong to the same genus,[11] the specific difference between them being that the *kalâm* proper is imaginative, whereas that of Maimonides is an intelligent or enlightened *kalâm*.

The tentative descriptions of the true science of the law which have been set forth thus far are useful, and even indispensable, for the purpose of counteracting certain views more commonly held of the character of the *Guide*. In order to arrive at a more definitive description of the subject matter of that work, we have to make a fresh start by reminding ourselves again of the authoritative statements with which it opens.

Maimonides states that the intention of his work is to explain the meaning of biblical words of various kinds, as well as of biblical parables. Such an explanation is necessary, because the external meaning of both lends itself to grave misunderstanding. Since the internal meaning, being hidden, is a secret, the explanation of each word or parable is the revelation of a secret. The *Guide* as a whole is thus devoted to the revelation of the secrets of the Bible.[12] *Secret*, however, has manifold meanings. It may refer to the secret hidden by a parable or word, but it also may mean the parable or word itself which hides a secret. With reference to the second meaning, the *Guide* may more conveniently be said to be devoted to the explanation of the secrets of the Bible. Thus the true science of the law is nothing other than the explanation of the secrets of the Bible, and in particular of the Torah.

There are as many secrets of the Torah as there are passages in it requiring explanation.[13] Nevertheless, it is possible to enumerate at least the most momentous secret topics. According to one enumeration, these topics are: divine attributes, creation, providence, divine will and knowledge, prophecy, names of God. Another enumeration, which seems to be more lucid, presents the following order: *ma'aseh bereshit* (the account of creation), *ma'aseh merkabah* (the account of the chariot, Ezekiel 1 and 10), prophecy, and the knowledge of God.[14] However those two enumerations may be related to each other, it is certain that *ma'aseh bereshit* and *ma'aseh merkabah* occupy the highest rank among the secrets of the Bible. Therefore, Maimonides can say that the first intention, or the chief intention, of the *Guide* is the explanation of *ma'aseh bereshit* and *ma'aseh merkabah*. The true science of the law is concerned with the explanation of the secrets of the Bible, and especially with the explanation of *ma'aseh bereshit* and of *ma'aseh merkabah*.[15]

II. A PHILOSOPHIC WORK?

The finding that the *Guide* is devoted to the explanation of the secret teaching of the Bible seems to be a truism. Yet it is pregnant with the consequence that the *Guide* is not a philosophic book.

The fact that we are inclined to call it a philosophic book is derived from the circumstance that we use the word "philosophy" in a rather broad sense. We commonly do not hesitate, for example, to count the Greek Sophists among the philosophers and we even speak of philosophies underlying mass movements. The present usage may be traced back to the separation of philosophy from science — a separation which has taken place during the modern centuries. For Maimonides, who knew nothing of "systems of philosophy" and consequently nothing of the emancipation of sober science from those lofty systems, philosophy has a much narrower or a much more exact meaning than it has at the present time. It is not an exaggeration to say that for him philosophy is practically identical with the teaching as well as the methods of Aristotle, "the prince of the philosophers," and of the Aristotelians.[16] And he is an adversary of philosophy thus understood. It is against the opinions of "*the* philosophers"[17] that he defends the Jewish creed. And what he opposes to the wrong opinions of *the* philosophers is not a true philosophy, and in particular not a religious philosophy or a philosophy of religion, but "our opinion, i.e., the opinion of our law," or the opinion of "us, the community of the adherents of the law," or the opinion of the "followers of the law of our teacher Moses."[18] He obviously assumes that the philosophers form a group[19] distinguished from the group of adherents of the law and that both groups are mutually exclusive. Since he himself is an adherent of the law, he cannot possibly be a philosopher, and consequently a book of his in which he explains his views concerning all important topics cannot possibly be a philosophic book. This is not to deny that he acknowledges, and even stresses, the accordance which exists between the philosophers and the adherents of the law in every respect except as regards the question (which, however, is the decisive question) of the creation of the world. For certainly such an accordance between two groups proves their nonidentity.

There is, perhaps, no greater service that the historian can render to the philosopher of our time than to supply the latter with the materials necessary for the reconstruction of an adequate terminology. Consequently, the historian is likely to deprive himself of the greatest benefit which he can grant both to others and to himself, if he is ashamed to be a micrologist. We shall, then, not hesitate to refrain from calling the *Guide* a philosophic book. To justify fully our procedure we only have to consider Maimonides' division of philosophy. According to him, philosophy consists of two parts, theoretical philosophy and practical philosophy; theoretical philosophy in its turn is subdivided into mathematics, physics, and metaphysics; and practical philosophy consists of ethics, economics, "government of the city," and "government of the great nation or of the nations."[20] It is obvious that the *Guide* is not a work on mathematics or economics; and there is practically complete agreement among the students of Maimonides that it is not devoted to political science of either kind. Nor is it an ethical treatise, since Maimonides expressly excludes ethical topics from the *Guide*.[21] The only sciences, then, to which that work could possibly be devoted are physics and metaphysics, which occupy the highest rank among the sciences.[22] This view seems to be confirmed by Maimonides' professions (1) that the chief intention of the *Guide* is to explain *ma'aseh bereshit* and *ma'aseh merkabah,* and (2) that *ma'aseh bereshit* is identical with physics, and *ma'aseh merkabah* with metaphysics.[23] For these two statements seem to lead to the inference that the chief intention of the *Guide* is to treat of physics and metaphysics. This inference is contradicted, however, by another express statement of Maimonides, according to which all physics and an unlimited number of metaphysical topics are excluded from the *Guide*. He mentions in this connection particularly the doctrine of separate intelligences.[24] Thus the only philosophic subject treated, as such, in the *Guide* seems to be the doctrine of God.[25] But Maimonides excludes further all subjects proved, or otherwise satisfactorily treated by the philosophers and leaves no doubt that the philosophers succeeded in proving the existence of God as well as his unity and incorporeity.[26] In accordance with this, Maimonides clearly states that these three doctrines do not belong to the secrets of the Torah,[27] and hence neither to *ma'aseh bereshit* nor to *ma'aseh merkabah,* the principal subjects of the *Guide*. Thus we are led to the conclusion that no philosophic topic of any kind is, as such, the subject matter of the *Guide*.

We are then confronted with the perplexing contradiction that Maimonides, on the one hand, identifies the main subjects of the *Guide* with physics and metaphysics, the most exalted topics of philosophy, while on the other hand, he excludes from the field of his investigation every subject satisfactorily treated by the philosophers. To solve that contradiction one might suggest that the *Guide* is devoted to the discussion of such "physical" and "metaphysical" topics as are not satisfactorily treated by the philosophers. This would amount to saying that the subjects of the *Guide* are "physics" and "metaphysics," insofar as these transcend philosophy, and consequently that the *Guide* is not a philosophic book.

Yet the objection may be raised that this suggestion disregards Maimonides' explicit and unqualified identification of *ma'aseh bereshit* with physics and of *ma'aseh merkabah* with metaphysics. If we assume for the time being that this objection is sound, we seem to have no choice but to admit that the question of the subject matter of the *Guide* does not allow of any answer whatsoever. But, as a matter of fact, the very obviousness of the only possible answer[28] is the reason why that answer could escape our notice. The apparently contradictory facts that (1) the subject matter of the *Guide* are *ma'aseh bereshit* and *ma'aseh merkabah*, and that (2) Maimonides, in spite of his identifying *ma'aseh bereshit* with physics and *ma'aseh merkabah* with metaphysics, excludes physics and metaphysics from the *Guide*, may be reconciled by the formula that the intention of the *Guide* is to prove the identity, which to begin with was asserted only, of *ma'aseh bereshit* with physics and of *ma'aseh merkabah* with metaphysics. Physics and metaphysics are indeed philosophic disciplines, and a book devoted to them is indeed a philosophic book. But Maimonides does not intend to treat physics and metaphysics; his intention is to show that the teaching of these philosophic disciplines, which is presupposed, is identical with the secret teaching of the Bible.[29] The demonstration of such identity is no longer the duty of the philosopher, but is incumbent upon the student of the true science of the law. The *Guide* is then under no circumstances a philosophic book.[30]

As a corollary we have to add that the *Guide* cannot be called a theological work, for Maimonides does not know of theology as a discipline distinct from metaphysics. Nor is it a book of religion, for he expressly excludes religious, together with ethical topics from the subject matter of his work.[31] Until we shall have rediscovered a body of terms which are flexible enough to fit Maimonides' thought, the safest course will be to limit the description of the *Guide* to the statement that it is a book devoted to the explanation of the secret teaching of the Bible.

III. THE CONFLICT BETWEEN LAW AND NECESSITY

When Maimonides embarked upon the explanation of the secrets of
the Torah, he was confronted with the apparently overwhelming difficulty
created by the "legal prohibition"[32] against explaining those secrets. The
very same law, the secrets of which Maimonides attempted to explain, forbids their explanation. According to the ordinance of the talmudic sages,
ma'aseh merkabah ought not to be taught even to one man, except if he
be wise and able to understand by himself, and even to such a one only
the "chapter headings" may be transmitted. As regards the other secrets
of the Bible, their revelation to many people met with scarcely less definite
disapproval in the Talmud.[33] Explaining secrets in a book is tantamount
to transmitting those secrets to thousands of men. Consequently, the talmudic prohibition mentioned implies the prohibition against writing a
book devoted to their explanation.[34]

This prohibition was accepted by Maimonides not only as legally binding, but also as evidently wise; it was in full accordance with his own considered judgment that oral teaching in general is superior to teaching by
writing. This view may be traced back to an old philosophic tradition.[35]
The works of Aristotle, which were known to Maimonides, are "acroa-
matic" and not "exoteric," and his method of expounding things betrays
more often than not its provenance from Platonic or Socratic dialectics.
Even *the* classical statement about the danger inherent in all writing may
have been known to Maimonides, for the famous doctrine of Plato's *Phae-
drus* had been summarized by Fārābī in his treatise on Plato's philosophy.[36] Be this as it may, not the ambiguous advice of the philosophers but
the unequivocal command of the law was of primary importance to Maimonides.[37]

If a book devoted to the explanation of the secrets of the Bible is
prohibited by law, how then can the *Guide*, being the work of an obser-
vant Jew, be a book? It is noteworthy that Maimonides himself in the *Guide*
never calls it a book, but consistently refers to it as a *maqâla (ma'amar)*.[38]
Maqâla (just as *ma'amar*) has several meanings. It may mean a treatise;
it is used in that sense when Maimonides speaks, for instance, of the *Treatise on Government* by Alexander of Aphrodisias. But it may also mean—
and this is its original connotation—a speech. Maimonides, by refraining
from calling the *Guide* a book and by calling it a *maqâla,* hints at the essentially oral character of its teaching. Since, in a book such as the *Guide*,
hints are more important than explicit statements, Maimonides' contentions concerning the superiority of oral teaching very probably have to
be taken quite literally.

If the *Guide* is, in a sense, not a book at all, if it is merely a substitute for conversations or speeches, then it cannot be read in the way we may read, for instance, Ibn Sina's *Al-Shifâ,* or Thomas Aquinas's *Summa theologica.* To begin with, we may assume rather that the proper way of studying it is somehow similar to the way in which traditional Judaism studies the law.[39] This would mean that if we wish to know what Maimonides thinks, say, about the prophecy of Moses, it would not be sufficient to look up that chapter of his work which is explicitly devoted to that subject, and in which we might find perfectly clear and apparently final statements about it; nor would it be sufficient to contrast the latter with divergent statements unexpectedly occurring in other chapters. We would also have to take into account analogous "decisions" given by Maimonides with regard to entirely different "cases," and to make ourselves familiar with the general rules of analogy which obtain in oral discussions of that kind. Producing a clear statement of the author, in the case of a book like the *Guide,* is tantamount to raising a question; his answer can be ascertained only by a lengthy discussion, the result of which may again be open, and intended to be open, to new "difficulties." If it is true that the *Mishneh Torah* is but the greatest post-talmudic contribution to the oral discussions of the halakah, then it may be asserted with equal right that Maimonides, while writing the *Guide,* continued the aggadic discussions of the Talmud. And just as the *Mishneh Torah,* far from terminating the halakic discussions, actually served as a new starting point for them, in the same way the *Guide,* far from offering a final interpretation of the secret teaching of the Bible,[40] may actually have been an attempt to revive the oral discussion thereof by raising difficulties which intentionally were left unsolved.

But although the method employed by Maimonides in the *Guide* may come as near as is humanly possible to the method of oral teaching, the *Guide* does not for that reason cease to be a book. Consequently the very existence of the *Guide* implies a conscious transgression of an unambiguous prohibition. It seems that Maimonides for a while intended to steer a middle course between oral and confidential teaching, which is permitted, and teaching in writing, which is forbidden. That kind of writing which comes nearest to confidential conversation is private correspondence with a close friend. As a matter of fact, the *Guide* is written in the form of letters addressed to a friend and favorite pupil, Joseph.[41] By addressing his book to one man, Maimonides made sure that he did not transgress the prohibition against explaining *ma'aseh merkabah* to more than one man. Moreover, in the *Epistula dedicatoria* addressed to Joseph, he mentions, as it were in passing and quite unintentionally, that Joseph possessed all the qualities required of a student of the secret lore and explains the necessity of written communication by his pupil's departure.[42] This justification would have held good if Maimonides had refrained from making public these private "letters to a friend." In spite of this inconsistency and in spite of his evident determination to write the *Guide* even if he had never met Joseph, or if Joseph had never left him,[43] it would be a mistake to assume that the dedicatory epistle is wholly ironical. For we need only ask ourselves: what was the ultimate reason for Joseph's premature departure, and we are going over from the sphere of private and playful things to the sphere of public and serious matters. Joseph's departure, we may say, was the consequence of his being a Jew in the Diaspora. Not a private need but only an urgent necessity of nation-wide bearing can have driven Maimonides to transgressing an explicit prohibition. Only the necessity of saving the law can have caused him to break the law. . . .[44]

The law requires that only the "chapter headings" be transmitted. Maimonides decided to abide by that precept. But the law goes further: it requires that even those "chapter headings" be not transmitted even to one, except he be wise and able to understand by himself. As long as the secret teaching was transmitted by oral instruction, that requirement was easily complied with: if the teacher had not known the pupil for a long time beforehand, as probably was almost always the case, he could test the pupil's intellectual capacities by having a talk with him on indifferent subjects before he started to explain to him some of the secrets of the Bible. But how can the author of a book examine his readers, by far the greater part of whom may not yet be born when the book is published? Or does there exist some sort of examination by proxy which would allow the author to prevent incompetent readers not only from understanding his book —this does not require any human effort —but even from finding out the very formulation of the "chapter headings"? To see that such a device does exist, we have only to remind ourselves of how a superior man proceeds if he wishes to impart a truth, which he thinks not to be fit for everybody's use, to another man who may or may not be able to become reconciled to it. He will give him a hint by casting some doubt on a remote and apparently insignificant consequence or premise of the accepted opinion. If the listener understands the hint, the teacher may explain his doubts more fully and thus gradually lead him to a view which is of necessity nearer the truth (since it presupposes a certain reflection) than is the current opinion. But how does he proceed, if the pupil fails to understand the hint? He will simply stop. This does not mean that he will stop talking. On the contrary, since by suddenly becoming silent he would only perplex the pupil without being of any help to him, he will continue talking by giving the first, rather revealing sentence a more conventional meaning and thus gradually lead him back to the safe region of accepted views. Now this method of stopping can be practiced in writing as well as in speech, the only difference being that the writer must stop in any case, since certainly the majority of readers must be prevented from finding out the "chapter headings." That is to say, the writer has to interrupt his short hints by long stretches of silence, i.e., of insignificant talk. But a good author will never submit to the ordeal of indulging in insignificant talk. Consequently, after having given a hint which refers to a certain chapter of the secret teaching, he will write some sentences which at first glance seem to be conventional, but which on closer examination prove to contain a new hint, referring to another chapter of the secret teaching. By thus proceeding, he will prevent the secret teaching being prematurely perceived and therefore inadequately understood; even those readers who not only noticed but even understood the first hint and might understand further hints directly connected with it, would experience considerable difficulty even in suspecting the second hint, which refers to a different section of the argument. It is hardly necessary to add that there are as many groups of hints as there are chapters, or subdivisions of chapters, of the secret teaching, and that in consequence an ingenious author has at his disposal almost infinite possibilities of alternatively using hints of different groups.

We are now in a position to appreciate the bearing of the following statement of Maimonides: "You will not demand from me here [in the *Guide*] anything except chapter headings; and even those headings are, in this treatise, not arranged according to their intrinsic order or according to any sequence whatsoever, but they are scattered and intermingled with other subjects, the explanation of which is intended."[45] It is true Maimonides makes this statement with regard to his explanation of *ma'aseh merkabah* only. But there can be no doubt that he has followed the same method in his explanation of *ma'aseh bereshit* and, indeed, of all the secrets of the Torah.[46] It is for this reason that the whole work has to be read with particular care, with a care, that is, which would not be required for the understanding of a scientific book.[47] Since the whole teaching characteristic of the *Guide* is of a secret nature, we are not surprised to observe Maimonides entreating the reader in the most emphatic manner not to explain any part of it to others, unless the particular doctrine had already been clearly elucidated by famous teachers of the law,[48] i.e., unless it is a popular topic, a topic only occasionally mentioned in the *Guide*.

The *Guide* is devoted to the explanation of an esoteric doctrine. But this explanation is itself of an esoteric character. The *Guide* is, then, devoted to the esoteric explanation of an esoteric doctrine. Consequently it is a book with seven seals. How can we unseal it?

IV. A MORAL DILEMMA

No historian who has a sense of decency and therefore a sense of respect for a superior man such as Maimonides will disregard light-heartedly the latter's emphatic entreaty not to explain the secret teaching of the *Guide*. It may fairly be said that an interpreter who does not feel pangs of conscience when attempting to explain that secret teaching and perhaps when perceiving for the first time its existence and bearing lacks that closeness to the subject which is indispensable for the true understanding of any book. Thus the question of adequate interpretation of the *Guide* is primarily a moral question.

We are, however, entitled to object to raising that moral question because the historical situation in which we find ourselves is fundamentally different from that of the twelfth century, and therefore we ought to be justified in not taking too personally, so to speak, Maimonides' will. It is true, at first glance, that objection seems to beg the question: it is based on the assumption that it is possible to have a sufficient knowledge of the historical situation of the twelfth century without having a true and adequate knowledge of the secret teaching of Maimonides. Yet, if one looks more closely, one sees that by the historical situation no historian understands the secret thoughts of an individual, but rather the obvious facts or opinions which, being common to a period, give that period its specific coloring. We happen to be excellently informed by competent historians about the opinions prevalent in the twelfth century, and each of us can see that they are fundamentally different from those prevalent in our time. Public opinion was then ruled by the belief in the revealed character of the Torah or the existence of an eternal and unchangeable law, whereas public opinion today is ruled by historic consciousness. Maimonides himself justified his transgression of the talmudic injunction against writing on the esoteric teaching of the Bible by the necessity of saving the law. In the same way we may justify our disregard of Maimonides' entreaty not to explain the esoteric teaching of the *Guide* by appealing to the requirements of historic research. For both the history of Judaism and the history of medieval philosophy remain deplorably incomplete, as long as the secret teaching of Maimonides has not been brought to light. The force of this argument will become even stronger if we take into consideration that basic condition of historic research, namely, freedom of thought. Freedom of thought, too, seems to be incomplete as long as we recognize the validity of any prohibition to explain any teaching whatsoever. Freedom of thought being menaced in our time more than for several centuries, we have not only the right but even the duty to explain the teaching of Maimonides, in order to contribute to a better understanding of what freedom of thought means, i.e., what attitude it presupposes and what sacrifices it requires.

The position of Maimonides' interpreter is, then, to some extent, identical with that of Maimonides himself. Both are confronted with a prohibition against explaining a secret teaching and with the necessity of explaining it. Consequently, one might think it advisable for the interpreter to imitate Maimonides also with regard to the solution of the dilemma, i.e., to steer a middle course between impossible obedience and flagrant transgression by attempting an esoteric interpretation of the esoteric teaching of the *Guide*. Since the *Guide* contains an esoteric interpretation of an esoteric teaching, an adequate interpretation of the *Guide* would thus have to take the form of an esoteric interpretation of an esoteric interpretation of an esoteric teaching.

This suggestion may sound paradoxical and even ridiculous. Yet it would not have appeared absurd to such a competent reader of the *Guide* as Joseph ibn Kaspi, who did write an esoteric commentary on it. Above all, an esoteric interpretation of the *Guide* seems to be not only advisable, but even necessary.

When Maimonides, through his work, exposed the secret teaching of the Bible to a larger number of men, some of whom might not be as obedient to the talmudic ordinance nor as wise as he was, he did not rely entirely on those readers' compliance with the law or with his own emphatic entreaty. For the explanation of secrets is, as he asserts, not only forbidden by law, but also impossible by nature:[49] the very nature of the secrets prevents their being divulged. We are then confronted with a third meaning of the word "secret": secret may mean not only the biblical word or parable which has an inner meaning, and the hidden meaning itself, but also, and perhaps primarily, the thing to which that hidden meaning refers.[50] The things spoken of by the prophets are secret, since they are not constantly accessible, as are the things described by the ordinary sciences,[51] but only during more or less short and rare intervals of spiritual daylight which interrupt an almost continuous spiritual darkness; indeed they are accessible not to natural reason, but only to prophetic vision. Consequently, ordinary language is utterly insufficient for their description; the only possible way of describing them is by parabolic and enigmatic speech.[52] Even the interpretation of prophetic teaching cannot but be parabolic and enigmatic, which is equally true of the interpretation of such an interpretation, since both the secondary and the primary interpretation deal with the same secret subject matter. Hence the interpretation of the *Guide* cannot be given in ordinary language, but only in parabolic and enigmatic speech. That is why, according to Maimonides, the student of those secrets is required not only to be of mature age, to have a sagacious and subtle mind, to possess perfect command of the art of political government and the speculative sciences, and to be able to understand the allusive speech of others, but also to be capable of presenting things allusively himself.[53]

If each student actually had to meet all these conditions, we should have to admit at once, i.e., before any serious attempt has been made to elucidate the esoteric teaching of the *Guide*, that the interpretation of that work is wholly impossible for the modern historian. The very intention of interpreting the *Guide* would imply an unbearable degree of presumption on the part of the would-be interpreter; for he would implicitly claim to be endowed with all the qualities of a Platonic philosopher-king. Yet, while a modest man, confronted with the requirements which we have indicated, will be inclined to give up the attempt to understand the whole *Guide*, he may hope to make some contribution to its understanding by becoming a subservient part of the community of scholars who devote themselves to the interpretation of the *Guide*. If that book cannot be understood by the exertions of one man, it may be understood by the collaboration of many, in particular of Arabists, Judaists, and students of the history of philosophy. It is true that when speaking of the conditions to be fulfilled by students of the secret teaching, Maimonides does not mention disciplines such as those just alluded to; as a matter of fact, he thought very slightly of history in general.[54] But in all justice it may be said that he did not know, and could not know history in the modern sense of the word, a discipline which, in a sense, provides the synthesis, indispensable for the adequate understanding of the secret doctrine, of philosophy and politics. Yet, however greatly we may think of the qualities of the modern historian, he certainly is neither per se able to understand esoteric texts nor is he an esoteric writer. Indeed the rise of modern historic consciousness came simultaneously with the interruption of the tradition of esotericism. Hence all present-day students of Maimonides necessarily lack the specific training required for understanding, to say nothing of writing, an esoteric book or commentary. Is, then, an interpretation of the *Guide* altogether impossible under the present circumstances?

Let us examine somewhat more closely the basic assumption underlying the conclusion at which we have just arrived, or rather upon which we have just come to grief. Maimonides, it is true, states in unambiguous terms that direct and plain communication of the secrets of the things, or of the secrets of the Torah, is impossible by nature. But he also asserts in no less unambiguous terms that such a communication is forbidden by law. Now a rational law does not forbid things which are impossible in themselves and which therefore are not subject to human deliberation or action; and the Torah is the rational law par excellence.[55] Consequently the two statements appear to be contradictory. Since we are not yet in a position to decide which of them is to be discarded as merely exoteric, it will be wise to leave the question open for the time being and not to go beyond briefly discussing the possibilities of an answer. There are three possible solutions: (1) Maimonides may actually have believed in the unavoidable necessity of speaking enigmatically of secrets; (2) he may have conceded the possibility of plainly discussing them; (3) he may have approved some unknown intermediary position. There is, then, certainly a prima facie probability in the ratio of two to three that the first solution, which is wholly incompatible with our desire to understand the *Guide*, has to be ruled out. But even if the first solution had to be ultimately accepted, we need not be altogether despondent, since we may very well reject that view as erroneous. Esotericism, one might say, is based on the assumption that there is a rigid division of mankind into an inspired or intelligent minority and an uninspired or foolish majority. But are there no transitions of various kinds between the two groups? Has not each man been given freedom of will, so that he may become wise or foolish according to his exertions?[56] However important may be the natural faculty of understanding, is not the use of this faculty or, in other words, method, equally important? And method, almost by its very definition, bridges the gulf which separates the two unequal groups. Indeed, the methods of modern historical research, which have proved to be sufficient for the deciphering of hieroglyphs and cuneiforms, ought certainly to be sufficient also for the deciphering of a book such as the *Guide*, to which access could be had in an excellent translation into a modern language. Our problem reduces itself, therefore, to detecting the specific method which will enable us to decipher the *Guide*. What are, then, the general rules and the most important special rules according to which this book is to be read?

V. SECRETS AND CONTRADICTIONS

The clue to the true understanding of the *Guide* is provided by the very feature of that book which, at first glance, seems to make it for all modern generations a book sealed with seven seals. I am referring to the fact that it is devoted to the esoteric explanation of an esoteric text. For it is merely a popular fallacy to assume that such an explanation is an esoteric work of the second power, or at least twice as esoteric, and consequently twice as difficult to understand as is the esoteric text itself. Actually, any explanation, however esoteric, of a text is intended to be helpful for its understanding; and, provided the author is not a man of exceptional inability, the explanation is bound to be helpful. Now, if by the help of Maimonides, we understand the esoteric teaching of the Bible, we understand at the same time the esoteric teaching of the *Guide*, since Maimonides must have accepted the esoteric teaching of the law as the true teaching. Or, to put it somewhat differently, we may say that, thanks to Maimonides, the secret teaching is accessible to us in two different versions: in the original biblical version, and in the derivative version of the *Guide*. Each version by itself might be wholly incomprehensible; but we may become able to decipher both by using the light which one sheds on the other. Our position resembles then that of an archeologist confronted with an inscription in an unknown language, who subsequently discovers another inscription reproducing the translation of that text into another unknown language. It matters little whether or not we accept Maimonides' two assumptions, rejected by modern criticism, that the Bible is an esoteric text, and that its esoteric teaching is closely akin to that of Aristotle. As far as Maimonides is concerned, the Bible *is* an esoteric book, and even the most perfect esoteric book ever written. Consequently, when setting out to write an esoteric book himself, he had no choice but to take the Bible as his model. That is to say, he wrote the *Guide* according to the rules which he was wont to follow in reading the Bible. Therefore, if we wish to understand the *Guide*, we must read it according to the rules which Maimonides applies in that work to the explanation of the Bible.

How did Maimonides read the Bible, or rather the Torah? He read it as the work of a single author, that author being not so much Moses as God himself. Consequently, the Torah was for him the most perfect book ever written as regards both content and form. In particular, he did not believe (as we are told to believe by modern biblical criticism) that its formal deficiencies — for instance, the abrupt changes of subject matter, or repetitions with greater or slighter variations — were due to its having been compiled by unknown redactors from divergent sources. These deficiencies were for him purposeful irregularities, intended to hide and betray a deeper order, a deep, nay, divine meaning. It was precisely this intentional disorder which he took as his model when writing the *Guide*. Or, if we accept the thesis of modern biblical criticism, we have to say that he took as his model a book which unintentionally lacks order and that by so doing he wrote a book which intentionally lacks order. At any rate the *Guide* certainly and admittedly is a book which intentionally lacks order. The "chapter headings" of the secret teaching which it transmits "are not arranged according to their intrinsic order or according to any sequence whatsoever, but they are scattered and intermingled with other subjects."[57] Instances of apparently bad composition are so numerous in the *Guide* and so familiar to its students that we need not mention here more than one example. Maimonides interrupts his explanation of biblical expressions attributing to God place, local movement, and so on (I, 8–26) by an exposition of the meaning of *man* (I, 14) and by a discussion of the necessity of teaching *ma'aseh bereshit* esoterically (I, 17), just as the Bible itself interrupts the story of Joseph by inserting into it the story of Judah and Tamar. Consequently, whenever we are confronted in the *Guide* with an abrupt change of subject matter, we have to follow the same rule of interpretation which Maimonides was wont to follow whenever he had to face a similar apparent deficiency of the Bible: we have to find out, by guessing, the hidden reason of the apparent deficiency. For it is precisely that hidden reason, accessible only to guesswork, which furnishes a link between the scattered "chapter headings," if not a "chapter heading" itself. Certainly the chains of reasoning connecting the scattered "chapter headings," and possibly even some "chapter headings" themselves, are not stated within the chapters, but are written with invisible ink in the empty spaces between the chapters, between the sentences, or between the parts of the *Guide.* . . .

Both the Bible, as Maimonides was wont to understand it, and the *Guide* are esoteric books. To cite but one other assertion of the author, his intention in writing the *Guide* was that the truths should flash up and then disappear again.[58] The purpose of the *Guide* is, then, not only to reveal the truth, but also to hide it. Or, to express the same thing in terms of quantity, a considerable number of statements are made in order to hide the truth rather than to teach it.

But what is the difference between the esoteric method of the Bible and that of the *Guide*? The authors of the Bible chose, in order to reveal the truth by not revealing it, and not to reveal it by revealing it, the use of words of certain kinds and of parables and enigmas.[59] Parables seem to be the more important vehicle, for Maimonides speaks of them much more fully than he does of the kinds of words in question.[60] Thus the suspicion arises that the species of esoteric books to which the Bible belongs is parabolic literature. That suspicion leads us to raise the question whether parables and enigmas are indispensable for esoteric teaching. As a matter of fact, that question is raised by Maimonides himself. After asserting that nobody is capable of completely explaining the secrets and that therefore every teacher speaks of them by using parables and enigmas, he goes on to say that, if someone wishes to teach the secrets without using parables and enigmas, he cannot help substituting for them obscurity and briefness of speech.[61] This remark may refer to an extreme case which is not likely to occur, but it also may suggest a possible innovation. Whether or not that case is likely and whether Maimonides is willing to make the innovation,[62] the substitution indicated by him is certainly possible. Thus his remark implies the admission that there exists a species of unparabolic esoteric literature and, consequently, that the species of esoteric books to which the Bible belongs may rightly be described as parabolic literature.

The question of how to avoid parables and enigmas when speaking of the secrets is taken up again by Maimonides a little further on in the general introduction to his work, in his discussion of the explanation of parables. He discusses that question by telling us a story. He narrates that once upon a time he had intended to write two books in order to explain the parables of the Bible and those of the Midrashim, but that when attempting to write these books he was faced by a dilemma. Either he could give the explanation in the form of parables, which procedure would merely exchange one individual for another of the same species, or he could explain the parables in unparabolic speech, in which case the explanation would not be suitable for the vulgar. Since the explanations given in the *Guide* are not addressed to the vulgar, but to scholars,[63] we may expect from the outset that they would be of an unparabolic character. Moreover, we know from Maimonides' earlier statement that parabolic and enigmatic representation of the secret teaching can be avoided: it can be replaced by obscurity and briefness of speech, i.e., by ways of expression which are suitable exclusively to scholars who, besides, are able to understand of themselves. Above all, in the case of an explanation of parabolic texts, it is not only possible, but even necessary to avoid parabolic speech: a parabolic explanation would be open to the objection, so aptly made by Maimonides himself, that it merely replaces one individual by another individual of the same species, or, in other words, that it is no explanation at all. What is then, the species of speech, different from that of parabolic speech, the use of which Maimonides had to learn after he had decided to write the *Guide* instead of the two popular books? What is the species, of which all expositions of the truth, given in the *Guide*, are individuals? To answer this question, we must first raise the more general question as to what is the genus which includes the species, hitherto unknown, of the expositions of the truth characteristic of the *Guide*, as well as of the species of parabolic expositions? The answer to this question, which no careful student of the *Guide* can help raising, is given by Maimonides in the last section of the general introduction to his work, where he quite abruptly and unexpectedly introduces a new subject: the various reasons for contradictions occurring in various kinds of books. We already know the hidden motive underlying this sudden change of subject matter; that hidden motive is the somewhat disguised question of the method characteristic of the *Guide* or, to speak more generally and vaguely, the question of the genus including the esoteric methods of both the Bible and the *Guide*. To the latter question, Maimonides gives here the rather undisguised answer that the genus looked for is contradictory speech. To the former question, he answers with equal clarity that the contradictions met with in the *Guide* are to be traced back to two reasons: to the requirements of teaching obscure matters, i.e., of making them understood, and to the requirements of speaking, or writing, of such matters. The contradictions caused by the former are bound to be known to the teacher (provided he did not make them deliberately), and they escape the pupil until he has reached an advanced stage of training; that is to say, they certainly escape the vulgar. But as regards the contradictions caused by the latter requirements, they always are deliberately made, and the author must take the utmost care to hide them completely from the vulgar.[64] Those disclosures of Maimonides enable us to describe the form of the esoteric teaching of the *Guide*: Maimonides teaches the truth not by inventing parables (or by using contradictions between parabolic statements) but by using conscious and intentional contradictions, hidden from the vulgar, between unparabolic and unenigmatic statements.[65]

From this result the inference must be drawn that no interpreter of the *Guide* is entitled to attempt a "personal" explanation of its contradictions. For example, he must not try to trace them back to the fact, or assumption, that the two traditions which Maimonides intended to reconcile, i.e., the biblical tradition and the philosophic tradition, are actually irreconcilable; or, more philosophically but scarcely more adequately, to explain them by assuming that Maimonides was on the track of philosophic problems transcending the horizon of the philosophic tradition, but was unable to free himself sufficiently from its shackles. Such attempts would serve a useful purpose if meant to explain highly complicated and artificial reconciliations of contradictions. They are both erroneous and superfluous if they are destined to explain contradictions which, if unintentional, would betray not the failure of a superior intellect in the face of problems either insoluble or very difficult to solve, but rather scandalous incompetence.[66] All these attempts would tacitly or expressly presuppose that the contradictions had escaped Maimonides' notice, an assumption which is refuted by his unequivocal statements. Therefore, until the contrary has been proved, it must be maintained that he was fully aware of every contradiction in the *Guide*, at the very time of writing the contradictory sentences. And if the objection is made that we ought to allow for the possibility that unconscious and unintentional contradictions have crept into the *Guide*, since philosophers hardly inferior to Maimonides have been found guilty of such contradictions, we answer by referring to Maimonides' emphatic declaration concerning the extreme care with which he had written every single word of his book and by asking the objectors to produce similar declarations from those books of other philosophers which they may have in mind. Therefore the duty of the interpreter is not to explain the contradictions, but to find out in each case which of the two statements was considered by Maimonides to be true and which he merely used as a means of hiding the truth.

Maimonides has raised the question whether contradictions caused by the requirements of speaking, or writing, of obscure matters are also to be found in the Bible: he demands that this question be very carefully studied.[67] In fact, it reveals itself as being the decisive question, once one has looked beneath the surface of the teaching of the *Guide*. Since he does not answer it explicitly, it must here be left open. Neither can we discuss here the related questions as to whether the Maimonidean method of teaching the truth was influenced by a philosophic tradition; whether it is characteristic of a particular kind of philosophic literature; and whether, in accordance with the terminology of the philosophic tradition, the *Guide* ought not to be described rather as an exoteric work. If this description should ultimately prove correct, the meaning of the term "addition" would have to undergo a profound change: it would not mean the decisively important secret teaching which is added to the conventional view, but rather the imaginative representation which is added to the undisguised truth. . . .[68]

Returning to Maimonides' use of contradictions, one may assume that all important contradictions in the *Guide* may be reduced to the single fundamental contradiction between the true teaching, based on reason, and the untrue teaching, emanating from imagination. But whether this be the case or not, we are certainly in need of a general answer to the general question: Which of the two contradictory statements is in each instance considered by Maimonides as the true statement? That answer would be *the* guide for the understanding of Maimonides' work. It is provided by his identification of the true teaching with some secret teaching. Consequently, of two contradictory statements made by him, that statement which is most secret must have been considered by him to be true. Secrecy is to a certain extent identical with rarity; what all people say all the time is the opposite of a secret. We may therefore establish the rule that of two contradictory statements in the *Guide* or in any other work of Maimonides that statement which occurs least frequently, or even which occurs only once, was considered by him to be true. He himself alludes to this rule in his *Treatise on Resurrection,* the most authentic commentary on the *Guide*, when he stresses the fact that resurrection, though a basic principle of the law, is contradicted by many scriptural passages, and asserted only in two verses of the Book of Daniel. He almost pronounces that rule by declaring, in the treatise mentioned, that the truth of a statement is not increased by repetition nor is it diminished by the author's failure to repeat it: "you know that the mention of the basic principle of unity, i.e., His word 'The Lord is one', is not repeated in the Torah."

To sum up: Maimonides teaches the truth not plainly, but secretly; i.e., he reveals the truth to those learned men who are able to understand by themselves and at the same time he hides it from the vulgar. There probably is no better way of hiding the truth than to contradict it. Consequently, Maimonides makes contradictory statements about all important subjects; he reveals the truth by stating it, and hides it by contradicting it. Now the truth must be stated in a more hidden way than it is contradicted, or else it would become accessible to the vulgar; and those who are able to understand by themselves are in a position to find out the concealed statement of the truth. That is why Maimonides repeats as frequently as possible the conventional views which are suitable to, or accepted by the vulgar, but pronounces as rarely as possible contradictory unconventional views. Now a statement contradictory to another statement is, in a sense, its repetition, agreeing with it in almost every respect and differing only by some addition or omission. Therefore we are able to recognize the contradiction only by a very close scrutiny of every single word, however small, in the two statements.

Contradictions are the axis of the *Guide*. They show in the most convincing manner that the actual teaching of that book is sealed and at the same time reveal the way of unsealing it. While the other devices used by Maimonides compel the reader to guess the true teaching, the contradictions offer him the true teaching quite openly in either of the two contradictory statements. Moreover, while the other devices do not by themselves force readers to look beneath the surface — for instance, an inappropriate expression or a clumsy transition, if noticed at all, may be considered to be merely an inappropriate expression or a clumsy transition, and not a stumbling block — the contradictions, once they are discovered, compel them to take pains to find out the actual teaching. To discover the contradictions or to find out which contradictory statement is considered by Maimonides to be true, we sometimes need the help of hints. Recognizing the meaning of hints requires a higher degree of understanding by oneself than does the recognition of an obvious contradiction. Hints are supplied by the application of the other Maimonidean devices.

To make our enumeration of those devices somewhat more complete, and not to mention intentional sophisms and ironical remarks, we shall first briefly clarify our foregoing remark on Maimonides' extensive use of words of certain kinds. We may call those words secret words. His secret terminology requires a special study, based upon a complete index of words which have, or may have, secret meaning. These words are partly ambiguous, as in the instances mentioned above, and partly unambiguous, such as *âdamiyyûn, fiqh, dunyâ*. In the second place we may mention various kinds of apostrophes to the reader and mottoes prefixed to the whole work or to individual parts. Another device consists in silence, i.e., the omission of something which only the learned, or the learned who are able to understand of themselves, would miss. Let us take the following example. Maimonides quotes in the *Guide* four times, if I am not mistaken, expressly as an utterance of Aristotle, and with express or tacit approval, the statement that the sense of touch is a disgrace to us.[69] Such fourfold repetition of an express quotation in a book so carefully worded as the *Guide* proves that the quotation is something like a *leitmotif*. Now, that quotation is incomplete. Maimonides omits two words which profoundly alter its meaning. Aristotle says: δόξειεν ἂν δικαίως (ἡ ἀφὴ) ἐπονείδιστος εἶναι [and it is rightly a matter of opinion that the sense of touch is a disgrace].[70] Maimonides omits, then, those two words which characterize the utterance as an ἔνδοξον [a matter of opinion]. Readers of the *Guide*, cognizant of the teachings of the "prince of philosophers," naturally noticed the omission and realized that the passages into which the quotation is inserted are of a merely popular, or exoteric character. If one examines the four quotations more closely, one notices that while in the second and third citation Maimonides mentions the name of Aristotle, but not the work from which it is taken, he expressly cites the *Ethics* in the first passage, thus intimating that its source is a book based mainly on ἔνδοξα [matters of opinion]. In the last quotation Maimonides adds the remark that the quotation is literal, but two or three lines further on, while speaking of the same subject, he refers to the *Ethics* and the *Rhetoric*, i.e., to books devoted to the analysis of ἔνδοξα [matters of opinion]. There can be no doubt that Maimonides was fully aware of the fact that his citation from Aristotle actually reflected popular rather than philosophic opinion. It is still less doubtful that Maimonides, while agreeing with the complete statement of Aristotle, viz., that the sense of touch is popularly considered disgraceful, by no means believed in the soundness of this popular judgment. As a matter of fact, he contradicted it quite openly by denying any difference in dignity between the senses and by ascribing to the imagination of the vulgar the distinction between senses which are supposed to be perfections and those believed to be imperfections.[71] The reader of the *Guide*, familiar with the main controversial topics of the Middle Ages, will at once realize the bearing of Maimonides' misquotation: the statement of Aristotle, as cited by Maimonides, would afford an excellent justification of ascetic morality — for what Maimonides would call "exaggeration"—and in particular for an ascetic attitude toward sexuality.[72] And the reader who looks up the passages in question in the *Guide* will notice that one of these misquotations is inserted into what Munk calls the "définition générale de la prophétie." Another characteristic omission is Maimonides' failure to mention the immortality of the soul or the resurrection of the body, when he attempts explicitly to answer the question of Divine Providence.[73] He begins his discussion (III, 16–24) by reproducing the philosophic argument against individual providence, mainly based on the observation that the virtuous are stricken with misery, while the wicked enjoy apparent happiness. It is therefore all the more perplexing that he pays no attention to what Leibniz has called[74] "le remède [qui] est tout prêt dans l'autre vie." Neither does he mention that remedy in his express recapitulation of the view of Providence characteristic of the literal sense of the Torah.[75] On the other hand, he elsewhere explains in the same context the "good at thy latter end" alluded to in Deuteronomy 8:16 as the fortitude acquired by the privations from which Israel had suffered while wandering through the desert.[76]

The fourth and last kind of hints to be indicated here are the *rashei perakim.* This expression, which we have hitherto rendered as "chapter headings," may also mean "beginnings of chapters." In some cases, indeed, Maimonides gives us important hints by the initial word or words of a chapter. The opening word of the section devoted to the rational explanation of biblical commandments (III, 25–49) is the noun, *al-af'âl* ("the actions"). The *af'âl,* synonymously used with *a'mâl,* constitute the second half of the law, the first half consisting of *ârâ'*[77] ("opinions"). Thus this opening gives us a hint that all the preceding chapters of the *Guide* (I–III, 24) are devoted to the "opinions," as distinguished from "actions," which are taught or prescribed by the law. The initial words in the first chapter (III, 8) devoted to theodicy, or the question of providence, is the expression "All bodies which come into existence and perish." These words indicate that this whole group of chapters (III, 8–24) deals exclusively with bodies which come into existence and perish, and not with bodies or souls which do not come into existence or perish. That this guess is correct is shown by other remarks of Maimonides.[78] From this opening, moreover, we must draw the inference that all preceding chapters (I, 1–III, 7) are devoted to things which do not come into existence and perish, and in particular to souls or intelligences which do not come into existence and perish, i.e., to *ma'aseh merkabah.* This inference is confirmed by Maimonides' statement, made at the end of Book III, Chapter 7, that all the preceding chapters are indispensable for the right understanding of *ma'aseh merkabah,* whereas in the following chapters not a word will be said, either explicitly or allusively, about that most exalted topic. Equally important are the beginnings of Book III, Chapter 24, which opens with the ambiguous word *'amr,* which may mean "thing" as well as "command,"[79] and the beginning of the very first chapter of the whole work.

Necessity has led us to make such incoherent and fragmentary remarks about Maimonides' methods of presenting the truth that it will not be amiss if we conclude this chapter with a simile which may drive home its main content to those readers who are more interested in the literary than in the philosophic question. There are books the sentences of which resemble highways, or even motor roads. But there are also books the sentences of which resemble rather winding paths which lead along precipices concealed by thickets and sometimes even along well-hidden and spacious caves. These depths and caves are not noticed by the busy workmen hurrying to their fields, but they gradually become known and familiar to the leisured and attentive wayfarer. For is not every sentence rich in potential recesses? May not every noun be explained by a relative clause which may profoundly affect the meaning of the principal sentence and which, even if omitted by a careful writer, will be read by the careful reader?[80] Cannot miracles be wrought by such little words as "almost," "perhaps," "seemingly"? May not a statement assume a different shade of meaning by being cast in the form of a conditional sentence? And is it not possible to hide the conditional nature of such a sentence by turning it into a very long sentence and, in particular, by inserting into it a parenthesis of some length? It is to a conditional sentence of this kind that Maimonides confides his general definition of prophecy.[82]

VI. THE *GUIDE* AND THE CODE

As we have seen, the *Guide* is devoted to the true science of the law, as distinguished from the science of the law in the usual sense, the *fiqh*. It remains to be considered whether, according to Maimonides, the two kinds, or parts, of the science of the law are of equal dignity or whether one of them is superior to the other. . . .

To sum up, according to Maimonides the *Mishneh Torah* is devoted to *fiqh*, the essence of which is to deal with actions; while the *Guide* deals with the secrets of the Torah, i.e., primarily opinions or beliefs, which it treats demonstratively, or at least as demonstratively as possible. Demonstrated opinions or beliefs are, according to Maimonides, absolutely superior in dignity to good actions or to their exact determination. In other words, the chief subject of the *Guide* is *ma'aseh merkabah*, which is "a great thing," while the chief subject of the *Mishneh Torah* is the precepts, which are "a small thing." Consequently, the subject of the *Guide* is, according to Maimonides, absolutely superior in dignity to the subject of the *Mishneh Torah*. Since the dignity of a book, *caeteris paribus*, corresponds to the dignity of its subject, and since, as is shown by a comparison of Maimonides' own introductory remarks to the two books, he wrote the *Guide* with no less skill and care than his code, we must conclude that he considered the *Guide* as absolutely superior in dignity.

This conclusion, based on the general principle underlying his entire work and nowhere contradicted by him, that knowledge of the truth is absolutely superior in dignity to any action, is reinforced by some further statements or hints. We have started from the distinction made by him at the very beginning of the *Guide* between the true science of the law and the *fiqh*: the former deals chiefly with the secrets of the Bible or, more generally, with opinions and beliefs both secret and public;[83] in other words, it demonstrates the beliefs taught by the law. Maimonides repeats this distinction in the last chapter, in a somewhat modified manner; he there distinguishes three sciences: the science of the Torah, wisdom, and *fiqh*.[84] The science of the law, or the science of the Torah, does not demonstrate the basic principles taught by the law, since the law itself does not demonstrate them.[85] The *fiqh*, which at the beginning of the *Guide* had been identified with the science of the law, is now clearly distinguished from it or from the science of the Torah, as well as from wisdom.[86] Wisdom is the demonstration of the opinions taught by the law. Now the *Guide* is devoted to such demonstration; hence the true science of the law, mentioned at the beginning as the subject of the work, is identical with wisdom, as distinguished from both the science of the law and from the *fiqh*. Maimonides repeats, then, the distinction between the true science of the law and the science of the law; yet he no longer calls the former a science of the law, but wisdom, and no longer identifies the (ordinary) science of the law (or of the Torah) with the *fiqh*. The relation of wisdom to the *fiqh* is explained by a simile: the students of the *fiqh*, arriving at the divine palace, merely walk around it, whereas only speculation on the "roots," i.e., demonstration of the basic truths taught by the law, leads one unto the presence of God.[87]

Though Maimonides discloses his view at the end of his work only, he does not fail to give hints of it on previous suitable occasions. When he tells the story of his abandoned plan to write two books on the parables of the prophets and the Midrashim, he states that he had intended those books for the vulgar, but later realized that such an explanation would neither be suitable for, nor fill a need felt by the vulgar. That is why he has limited himself to that brief and allusive discussion of the basic truths of the law, which is to be found in his code. In the *Guide*, however, he goes on to say, he addresses himself to a man who has studied philosophy and who, while believing in the teachings of the law, is perplexed in regard to them.[88] Those sentences, enigmatic and elusive as they are, show clearly that the *Guide* was not addressed to the vulgar, nor the *Mishneh Torah* to the perplexed. Are we, then, to believe that the latter was written for students of philosophy who had not become perplexed as regards the teachings of the law? Hardly, since Maimonides does not tire of repeating that the code is devoted to the *fiqh* and consequently is addressed to students of *fiqh*, who may or may not be familiar with philosophy. This is also shown by his failure to discuss in the *Mishneh Torah* the basic truths of the law, according to his primary and main intention and only, as it were, incidentally or haphazardly.[89] Evidently the *Mishneh Torah* was written also for people who had not studied philosophy at all and therefore were not perplexed; in other words, it was addressed to "all men."[90] This is quite clearly the meaning of the following passage in the *Guide:* "I have already explained to all men the four differences by which the prophecy of our teacher Moses is distinguished from the prophecy of the other prophets, and I have proved it and made it manifest in the Commentary on the Mishna and in the *Mishneh Torah.*" The meaning of "all men" (*al-nâs kâffa*) is incidentally explained in connection with a synonymous phrase (*ğamî' al-nâs*): "all men, i.e., the vulgar."[91] This allusion to the exoteric character of the code and the commentary naturally has to be taken into account, not only in the interpretation of these two works but also for the adequate understanding of all quotations from them in the *Guide*.

We conclude: The *Mishneh Torah* is primarily addressed to the general run of men, while the *Guide* is addressed to the small number of people who are able to understand by themselves.

NOTES

1. In the notes Roman and Arabic figures before the parentheses indicate the part and chapter of the *Guide*, respectively. The figures in the parentheses before the semicolon indicate the page in Munk's edition, and the figures following the semicolon indicate pages and lines in Joel's edition. For the first book of the *Mishneh Torah*, I have used M. Hyamson's edition (New York, 1937).

2. I, Intro. (3a; 2, 14f., 26f.).

3. III, 54 (132b; 467, 20-25); cf. III, 27 (59b; 371, 29); 51 (123b; 455, 21-22).

4. II, 10 (22b; 190, 14); I, Intro. (11a-b; 13, 3-5). Cf. the passages quoted in note 3.

5. I, Intro. (5b and 11b; 5, 18ff and 13, 12-15). Cf. I, 70 (92b; 120, 4-8); 71 (94a; 121, 25-28).

6. III, 51 (123b-124a; 455, 21-23). Cf. III, 54 (132a-b; 467, 7-9) with I, Intro. (3a; 2, 12-14).

7. I, 71 (96b-97a; 125, 12). Cf. I, 73 (105b; 136, 2) Maimonides was called a שרשי [shareshī: an exponent of roots or foundations] by Messer Leon; see M. Steinschneider, *Jewish Literature* (London, 1857), p. 310.

8. II, 19 (40a; 211, 24-25); I, 71 (97b; 126, 4-5). Cf. also I, 73 (111b; 143, 6).

9. Farabi, *'Ihsâ al-'ulûm,* ch. 5. (See the Hebrew translation of Falakera's *Reshit Hokmah,* ed. David, p. 59ff.). Farabi's discussion of the *kalâm,* and the framework of that discussion, are of decisive importance for the understanding

of the *Guide.* Cf. also Plato's *Laws,* X, 887b, 8 and 890d, 4–6. I, 71 (94b, 95a; 122, 19–22; 123, 2–3).

10. I, 71 (96a; 124, 18–19); II, 17 (37a; 207, 27–28).

11. Cf. Aristotle, *Eth. Nich.,* 1098a, 8–10.

12. I, Intro. (2a–3b, 6a, 6b–7a; 2, 6–29; 6, 12–19; 7, 10–8, 3). Cf. ibid. (2a, 8a; 1, 14; 9, 6).

13. See in particular III, 50 *in princ.*

14. I, 35 (42a; 54, 20–26); II, 2 (11a–b; 176, 18–23).

15. II, 29 (65b; 243, 17–19); III, Intro. (2a; 297, 5–7). Cf. the distinction between *fiqh* and secrets of the Torah in I, 71 (93b; 121, 20–22) with the distinction between *fiqh* and the true science of the law at the beginning of the work. For an interpretation, see A. Altmann, "Das Verhältnis Maimunis zur jüdischen Mystik," *Monatsschrift für Geschichte und Wissenschaft des Judentums* 80 (1936), 305–330.

16. I, 5 *in princ.*; II, 23 (51a; 225, 4). I. Heinemann goes too far, however, in stating (*Die Lehre von der Zweckbestimmung des Menschen im griechisch-römischen Altertum und im jüdischen Mittelalter* [Breslau, 1926], p. 99, n.1) that "*Failasûf* heisst nicht Philosoph, sondern steht für Aristoteles oder Aristoteliker" [*Failasûf* does not mean philosopher, but stands for Aristotle or Aristotelian]. Cf. I, 17, 71 (94b; 122, 26–28); II, 21 (47b; 220, 20); III, 16 (31a; 334, 22–24), where *falsafa* or *falâsifa* other than Aristotelian are mentioned.

17. Cf., for instance, III, 16 *in princ.*

18. Cf., for instance, II, 21 (47a; 220, 17f); II, 26 (56a; 230, 30); III, 17 (34b; 338, 21), 21 (44b; 351, 17–18).

19. That kind of group, one individual case of which is the group of the philosophers, is called by Maimonides פרקה or פריק [*firqah* or *firīq:* sect or school] (Ibn Tibbon: כת [*kath*]. The Greek equivalent is αἵρεσις [*airesis:* school of philosophy]; cf. G. Bergsträsser, *Hunain ibn Ishâq über die syrischen und arabischen Galen-Uebersetzungen* [Leipzig, 1925], p. 3 of the Arabic text); cf. II, 5 (33a; 203, 17f.); III, 20 (42a; 348, 16).

20. *Millot ha-higgayon,* ch. 14. Cf. H. A. Wolfson, "The Classification of the Sciences in Medieval Jewish Philosophy," *Hebrew Union College Jubilee Volume* (1925), 263–315.

21. III, 8 *in fine.* Cf. I, Intro. (11a–b; 13, 3–5).

22. III, 51 (124a; 456, 1–4).

23. I, Intro. (3b; 3, 8–9). Cf. n. 15.

24. II, 2 (11a–12a; 176, 3–27). Cf. also I, 71 (97b; 126, 13–15). As regards the philosophic doctrine of the sublunary world, cf. II, 22 (49b–50a; 223, 15–17); for that of the soul, cf. I, 68 *in princ.*

25. Notice the identification of *ma'aseh merkabah,* or metaphysics, with the doctrine of God in I, 34 (40b; 52, 24–25).

26. I, 71 (96b; 124, 29–125, 6); II, 2 (11a–12a; 176, 3–27). Cf. II, 33 (75a; 256, 21–25).

27. I, 35.

28. That is to say, the only answer which could be given if the suggestion made in the foregoing paragraph is ruled out. Cf., however, pp. 41ff., below.

29. As regards the identification of the teaching of revelation with the teaching of reason in medieval Jewish philosophy, cf. Julius Guttmann, *Die Philosophie des Judentums* (Munich, 1933), p. 71f.

30. Cf. also above n. 5 and below n. 47 and n. 51.

31. III, 8 *in fine*.

32. III, Intro. (2a and b; 297, 16 and 25).

33. I, Intro. (3b–4a; 3, 9–19); 33 (36a; 48, 19–21); 34 (40b; 52, 24–53, 3); III, Intro.

34. I, Intro. (4a; 3, 19–20); III, Intro. (2a; 297, 15–16).

35. I, 71 (93b; 121, 14–24); III, Intro. (2b; 297, 25–26). Cf. I, 17 and Intro. (4a; 3, 19–20).

36. Cf. Falakera's Hebrew translation of Fārābī's treatise in *Reshit ḥokmah,* ed. David, p. 75 bottom.

37. The inferiority of writing is also indicated by the designation of those biblical works which had not been composed by prophets proper as "writings." Cf. II, 45 (94a, 95b; 283, 1–5; 284, 21–285, 3).

38. This fact is pointed out by Abravanel in his *Ma'amar ḳaṣer bebi'ur sod ha-moreh.* Ibn Tibbon, in his preface to his translation of the *Guide,* calls it הספר הנכבד הזה מאמר מורה נבוכים [*ha-sefer ha-nikebad ha-zeh ma'amar moreh nebukim*: this excellent book, the treatise of *The Guide of the Perplexed.*]

39. Cf. H. A. Wolfson, *Crescas' Critique of Aristotle* (Cambridge, 1929), p. 22ff. Maimonides indicates the similarity between the prohibition against writing down the oral law and that against writing down the secret teaching of the law; see I, 71 *in princ.*

40. Cf., for instance, III, Intro. (2b; 298, 1–2); I, 21 (26b; 34, 10–12).

41. Cf. in particular II, 24.

42. These observations on the *Ep. ded.* cannot furnish a sufficient interpretation of that remarkable piece of literature, but deal merely with its more superficial meaning. Maimonides mentions Joseph's poems in order to show that the latter possessed the indispensable ability of expressing himself beautifully; cf. I, 34 (41a; 53, 14) with I, Intro. (7a–b; 8, 7–8). As regards the other qualities of Joseph, see Shem Tob's commentary on the *Ep. ded.*

43. It is controversial whether Maimonides finished the *Guide* before he made the acquaintance of Joseph or thereafter. According to Z. Diesendruck, "On the Date of the Completion of the Moreh Nebukim," *Hebrew Union College Annual* 12–13 (1937–1938): 496, the *Guide* was finished in 1185, i.e., at about the time when Joseph's sojourn with Maimonides began. Even if the *Guide* was not finished before the year 1190, which is the latest possible date (see ibid., pp. 461, 470), it certainly had been conceived and partly elaborated before Joseph's arrival.

44. I, Intro. (9b; 10, 28–29) in the interpretation of Fürstenthal and Munk.

45. I, Intro. (3b; 3, 11–14).

46. II, 29 (46a; 244, 10f.). Cf. I, Intro. (3b–4b; 3, 17–4, 22); 17, 35 (42a; 54, 20–28). See also III, 41 (88b; 409, 16).

47. I, Intro. (8b; 9, 26–10, 2); ibid. (3b; 3, 11–14); ibid. (4b; 4, 12–15).

48. I, Intro. (9a; 10, 4–8).

49. I, Intro. (3b; 3, 15). Cf. I, 31 *in princ.*

50. "Secrets of the being and secrets of the Torah," II, 26 (56b; 232, 5). For the distinction between various meanings of "secret," cf. Bacon, *Advancement of Learning,* ed. G. W. Kitchin, p. 205.

51. I, Intro. (4b; 4, 15). This passage implies a fundamental distinction between esoteric and exoteric sciences. As regards such distinctions, cf. I. Goldziher, *Kitâb maʿânî al-nafs* (Berlin, 1907), pp. 28-31. According to a usual distinction, "the exterior science" (*al-ʿilm al-barrânî*) is identical with Aristotelian philosophy and also with the *Kalâm*; "the interior philosophy" (*al-falsafa al-dâḫila* or *al-falsafa al-ḫâṣṣa*), treated by the *muhakkikûn,* deals with "the secrets of nature." The teaching of esoteric science is the knowledge *al-maḍnûn bihi.* Cf. I, 17 *in princ.,* 35 (41b; 54, 4), 71 (93b; 121, 20).

52. I, Intro. (4a; 4, 4-7). See the commentaries of Ephodi and Shem Tob on the passage. I, Intro. (4a-b; 3, 23-4, 20).

53. I, 34 (41a; 53, 12-19), 33 (37b; 48, 22-25).

54. Cf. Baron, *Outlook,* 3-4.

55. III, 26. Cf. III, 17 (33a-b; 337, 8-15).

56. M. T. Teshubah 5, 2.

57. I, Intro. (3b; 3, 11-14).

58. I, Intro. (3b; 3, 14).

59. I, Intro. (5a; 5, 11 and 16).

60. Cf. the index to Munk's Guide, *s.vv.* "allégories" and "noms."

61. I, Intro. (4b-5a; 4, 11-13, 17-19, 26-28).

62. I, Intro. (9b; 10, 24-28).

63. Cf. I, Intro. (5b; 5, 18-25) with ibid. (3a and 4b; 2, 11ff. and 4, 8-12).

64. I, Intro. (10a, 10b, 11b; 11, 19-26 and 12, 7-12 and 13, 13-15).

65. Cf. I, Intro. (10a; 11, 13-16). Cf. the somewhat different interpretation followed by Altmann, op. cit., 310f.

66. Cf. I, Intro. (10b; 12, 4-7).

67. I, Intro. (11b; 13, 6-8).

68. For the two meanings of *addition,* cf. I, Intro. (7a-b; 8, 6, 15), on the one hand, and ibid. (8a; 9, 8), on the other. Cf. also in the *Treatise on Resurrection* the beginning of the treatise proper. The importance of the term "addition," for instance, for the doctrine of attributes may be indicated here in passing.

69. II, 36 (79a; 262, 11-12); 40 (86b; 272, 4-5); III, 8 (12b; 311, 9-10); 49 (117a; 447, 1-2). Cf. also III, 8 (14a; 313, 18-19).

70. *Eth. Nic.* 1118b2. I am naturally following that interpretation of the passage cited, on which is based the Arabic translation as quoted by Maimonides. Cf. Averroes *ad loc.*: "et justum est nos opinari a nobis [sic] quod sensus iste opprobriosus est nobis" [and we are rightly of the opinion that this sense is a disgrace to us]. Cf. *De anima,* 421a 19-26.

71. I, 47, 46 (51b-52a; 68, 16-21); 2 (14a; 16, 22-17, 3).

72. Cf., in this connection, III, 8 (14a-b; 313, 22-314, 14).

73. This is not to deny that Maimonides mentions here the "other world," in connection with such views of Providence as he rejects or the truth of which

he neither discusses nor asserts. The phrase in II, 22 (46a; 354, 3–4), "the thing which remains of man after death," is naturally noncommittal with respect to the immortality of the individual soul. Cf. I, 74 (121b; 155, 9–10).

74. *Théodicée*, §17.

75. III, 17 (34b–37b; 338, 21–343, 5).

76. III, 24 (52b–53a; 362, 10–363, 4). Cf. M. T. Teshubah 8, 1–2.

77. Cf. in particular III, 52 (130b; 464, 26–465, 5) with Farabi, *'Iḥṣâ al-'ulûm*, chap. 5 (or the Hebrew translation by Falakera, in *Reshit ḥokmah*, ed. by David, p. 59). For the two Arabic words for "actions," cf., for instance, III 25 (57a; 368, 8 and 10).

78. III, 23 (50b–51a; 360, 1–14); 54 (135a 470, 21–26).

79. Cf. III, 24 (54a; 364, 16 and 20f.).

80. Cf. in this connection I, 21 (26a; 33, 11–17), 27 *vers. fin.*

81. Cf. III, 19 (39a; 345, 6).

82. II, 36 (78b–79b; 262, 2–263, 1). Cf. Munk, *Guide* II, 284, n. 1. Other examples of the same method occur in III, 51 (127b; 460, 27–461, 1) [cf. Munk, *Guide* III, 445, n. 2] and III, 18 (39a; 344, 22).

83. Cf., for example, I, 1 (12a; 14, 14), 18 (24a; 30, 7) with I, 35.

84. III, 54 (132b; 467, 18–20).

85. III, 54 (132a–b; 467, 2–9, 13–14).

86. III, 54 (132a–b; 467, 18–23 and 7 and 13–14). Cf. III, 41 (88b; 409, 15–16); M. T. Talmud Torah, 1, 11–12.

87. III, 51 (123b–124a; 455, 21–28). In his commentary on this chapter, Shem Tob relates that "many talmudic scholars have asserted that Maimonides had not written this chapter, and that, if he did write it, it ought to be suppressed, or rather, it would deserve to be burned."

88. I, Intro. (5b–6a; 5, 18–6, 11).

89. I, Intro. (3a; 2, 13–16); 71 (97a; 125, 23–24).

90. Cf. M. T. Yesodei ha-torah, 4, 13.

91. II, 35 *in princ.*; III, 22 (45b; 353, 10). Cf. also M. T., Intro., 4b, 4–19 (Hyamson), and *Ḳobeṣ*, II, 15b.

The Philosophical Character of Maimonides' *Guide*—A Critique of Strauss' Interpretation*

JOSEPH A. BUIJS

Is Maimonides' *The Guide of the Perplexed* a philosophical book or not? Modern scholars have generally conceded that it is.[1] But Leo Strauss has recently cast doubt on that view, arguing instead that the *Guide* can be properly understood only when the contemporary reader recognizes it to be a Jewish book.[2] Strauss does not, of course, deny the obvious use of a philosophical method nor the interspersed discussions of acknowledged philosophical topics, throughout the *Guide*. What he does deny is that the *Guide's* general content, its scope and purpose, can be appropriately viewed as being philosophical. If he is right, then comprehension of the *Guide* is limited to a restricted, Jewish audience. For, unless the contemporary reader were to adopt the point of view that Strauss' Jewish interpretation implies, he would run the risk of misrepresenting the *Guide's* content, interpreting it in a way that is both contrary to its underlying presuppositions and alien to Maimonides' intentions. This risk would apply in particular to specific issues, especially when these are extracted from the broader context of the *Guide*.[3]

I believe that Strauss is too restrictive in his interpretation. Admittedly, the *Guide* is not a simple book. But it is not as intransigent and inaccessible to a contemporary reader — particularly a philosopher, be he Jewish or not — as Strauss suggests. Although the *Guide* is, historically, a Jewish book in that it was written by a Jew and explicitly for Jews, that fact need not, nor does it, preclude its being also a philosophical one in its fundamental scope and purpose.

Strauss' interpretation hinges basically on two arguments. One is that

Judaism 27 (1978): 448–457. Reprinted by permission of *Judaism*.

59

Maimonides cannot be viewed as a philosopher nor the *Guide* as a philosophical book, because, for Maimonides, there is an incompatibility between being a Jew and being a philosopher and, on fundamental issues, he chooses the former as against the latter. The other is that the *Guide*'s proper subject matter is an explanation of prophetic and scriptural secrets and, therefore, does not, nor does it intend to, deal with any philosophical topic as such.

In his article, "The Literary Character of the *Guide for the Perplexed,*" Strauss focuses on the science with which the *Guide* purportedly deals. Maimonides himself states that this is "the science of Law in its true sense" (I, Intro.). Plausibly enough, Strauss compares this science to Islamic *kalām*, since Maimonides identifies the *mutakallimūn* as students of the foundations or roots of religion (1, 71), which is also the subject matter of a true science of the Law in Maimonides' sense (I, Gen. Intro., 71; II, 2; III, 51, 54). Maimonides, however, persistently disagrees with the basic premises and methods of the *mutakallimūn* (I, 71). Nevertheless, he seems to be in agreement with them on at least one point—their intention to defend religious beliefs, especially against the rational criticisms of the *falāsifah*. The prime example of this, Strauss notes, is Maimonides' "defense of the principal root of the law, the belief in creation, against the contention of the philosophers that the visible world is eternal."[4] Thus, although Maimonides starts from evident propositions that are true in accordance with the way things are, rather than, as do the *mutakallimūn,* from arbitrarily chosen ones that facilitate demonstrations of religious beliefs, Maimonides' enlightened *kalām,* according to Strauss, shares with the Islamic *kalām* proper the intention of opposing the opinions of philosophers when these conflict with religious doctrine. Since Maimonides views philosophy as virtually identical with the teachings of Aristotle and of the Aristotelians, he is, therefore, opposed to philosophy and philosophers in this restricted sense. From this Strauss concludes:

> And what [Maimonides] opposes to the wrong opinions of *the* philosophers is not a true philosophy, and in particular not a religious philosophy, or a philosophy of religion, but "our opinion, i.e., the opinion of our law," or the opinion of "us, the community of the adherents of the law," or the opinions of the "followers of the law of our teacher Moses." He obviously assumes that the philosophers form a group distinguished from the group of adherents of the law and that *both groups are mutually exclusive.* Since he himself is an adherent of the law, he cannot possibly be a philosopher, and consequently a book of his in which he explains his views concerning all important topics cannot possibly be a philosophic book (II, 15, 21, 26; III, 17, 20, 21).[5]

The claim that Maimonides does not advance a religious philosophy or a philosophy of religion I discuss below. What is evidently central to Strauss' argument here is a presumed mutually exclusive distinction between being a Jew and being a philosopher, at least in the limited sense of being a follower of Aristotle.

In his other article, "How to Begin to Study *The Guide of the Perplexed*," Strauss once more attributes this incompatibility to Maimonides, but without its Aristotelian restriction. He claims, moreover, that this incompatibility constitutes a fundamental premise to an understanding of the *Guide*. His reason is that

> Philosophers are men who try to give an account of the whole by starting from what is always accessible to man as man; Maimonides starts from the acceptance of the Torah. A Jew may make use of philosophy and Maimonides makes the most ample use of it; but as a Jew he gives his assent where as a philosopher he would suspend his assent (cf. II, 16).[6]

There is no objection to Strauss' characterization of a philosopher. But does Maimonides espouse the mutually exclusive distinction that Strauss requires for his Jewish interpretation?

In the first place, if, for Maimonides, being a Jew and being a philosopher are incompatible, one needs to explain his repeated emphasis on philosophy throughout the *Guide*. To be sure, Maimonides intends to uphold the religious beliefs of Judaism, as he does in the case of the belief in a purposeful creation of the world (II, 16). He explicitly addresses the *Guide* to Jews confirmed in their religious beliefs. Yet he also addresses it specifically to those Jews acquainted with the philosophical sciences, purportedly in order to remove the perplexity which they encounter from a conflict between religious tenets based on prophetic authority, on the one hand, and philosophical teaching based on rational demonstrations, on the other (I, Intro.). Furthermore, he emphasizes the importance of the philosophical sciences, as he knew them, not only for intellectual development in general, but, also, for the knowledge of God in particular (I, Intro., 33, 34, 55; III, 51, 54). But if, in the end, the issues central to Judaism are already decided, so to speak, in favour of religious assent, why does Maimonides nevertheless insist on prerequisites that prominently include the philosophical sciences? The response that this is merely propaedeutic will not do, since it fails to consider specifically *how* and *to what extent* Maimonides uses philosophy in relation to religion and his acceptance of the Torah. That use, as I argue below, is not merely propaedeutic but integral to the *Guide*'s scope and purpose.

Secondly, in order to maintain the distinction in question as an exclusive one, Strauss must admit that Maimonides gives his assent to scriptural teachings *in spite of* philosophical considerations. But this cannot be maintained.

On the issue of creation in time versus the eternity of the world — which Strauss claims to be the decisive one — Maimonides does, indeed, adopt a belief in the former because it is taught in Scriptures. But he opts for the scriptural teaching only after he has critically considered the arguments for both alternatives and has found them demonstratively inconclusive. He argues that creation in time is at least a logical possibility, since its opposite, the eternity of the world, has not been demonstrated (I, 71; II, 16).[7] In fact, he lessens the impression of disagreement with Aristotle on this issue by claiming that the latter did not intend to demonstrate the eternity of the world (II, Intro., 15). By "demonstration" here he means an incontrovertible proof, based on self-evident premises that entail indubitable conclusions (I, 71; II, 3, 15).[8] Since both opinions lack a demonstration in this sense, there is at least no reason to reject the literal teachings of Scriptures on the origin of the world. Had it been otherwise, Maimonides says, he would have reinterpreted figuratively the scriptural texts about creation, just as he reinterprets figuratively the scriptural texts about God's corporeality, because the denial of God's corporeality has been demonstrated (II, 25). But he gives some rational support, nevertheless, to the belief in creation in time by arguing that it is less doubtful than the belief in the world's eternity because of the former's coherence with a number of other beliefs about the nature of God, man, and the world (II, 19, 22, 23, 25).

What is actually at issue in this dispute is which view is compatible with a belief in divine purpose and will. The belief in creation in time clearly implies a creator and, hence, is compatible with a divine will and purpose, while the belief in the world's eternity is held to imply, on its Aristotelian conception, that the process of generation and corruption proceeds by a continuous causal necessity. As this could misleadingly be understood to exclude a divine purpose and the possibility of divine intervention in the world — both of which are central to Judaism — Maimonides adopts the belief in creation in time. Here Strauss might reassert that Maimonides sides with the adherents of the Law against the philosophers. But, even on this issue, Maimonides notes that the world's eternity need not logically preclude a divine purpose and will, so that even if this belief were undeniably true, it need not be incompatible with a basic Jewish belief (II, 19, 22). Since the belief in the world's eternity is not undeniably true and since it raises numerous problematic questions, it is more reasonable, Maimonides suggests, to accept the belief in creation in time with its obvious implication of a belief in a divine purpose and will.

On the question of divine purpose, as on the question of creation in time, Maimonides allows his faith to be guided by reason. In other words, reason may not be *sufficient,* but it is at least *necessary,* to establish the fundamental beliefs of Judaism. Rather than giving his assent *in spite of* philosophical considerations, as Strauss would have us believe, Maimonides gives his assent only *in accordance with* them. But this surely is not an indication of a mutually exclusive distinction between being a Jew and being a philosopher, between assenting to faith and following reason.

Strauss' first argument rests on a questionable premise. His second argument is equally problematic.

As already stated, Maimonides concerns himself in the *Guide* with a true science of the Law. The contents of this science are expressed in scriptural and rabbinic teachings but are couched in figurative and parabolic terms because they are secrets whose meaning cannot be made accessible to all (I, Intro., 33; III, Intro.). However, since such secret teachings concern the very foundations or roots of Judaism, they are important to a Jew who is seriously intent, not only on practicing, but on understanding his religion. Furthermore, Maimonides recognizes the perplexity that would be encountered by a religious Jew, educated in the secular sciences, in attempting to unravel the "internal" or figurative meaning of these secret teachings from their "external" or literal one (I, Intro.). Thus, he undertakes to remove this perplexity by at least providing the means of understanding scriptural and rabbinic secrets within the intellectual capabilities of a select audience (Epistle Ded.; I, Intro.). The two most important secrets, he notes, are *ma'aseh bereshit,* the Account of the Beginning, and *ma'aseh merkabah,* the Account of the Chariot (I, Intro.; II, 2, 29; III, Intro.).

Since a true science of the Law amounts to an explanation of prophetic secrets and since this is admittedly the principal subject matter of the *Guide,* Strauss wonders whether it includes any philosophical topics as such. He appeals to Maimonides' classification of philosophy into theoretical and practical parts. Following Aristotle, the former is subdivided into mathematics, physics, and metaphysics; the latter into ethics, economics, government of the city, and government of the great nation (or nations).[9] Now, the only philosophical topics that might be included in the subject matter of the *Guide* are those relating to physics and metaphysics, since the *Guide* obviously does not deal with mathematics, economics, or political science of either kind nor, by Maimonides' own admission, with ethical matters (III, 8). Maimonides asserts, however, that "the *Account of the Beginning* is identical with natural science [physics], and the *Account of the Chariot* with divine science [metaphysics]" (I, Intro.). Yet he also explicitly dismisses from the scope of the *Guide* those physical and metaphysical topics adequately treated by the philosophers (II, 2). Consequently, only the doctrine of God, which is extensively discussed, remains as a possible philosophical topic. But Maimonides admits that the existence, unity, and incorporeality of God, to which he devotes most of his discussion on God, were adequately demonstrated by the philosophers. These three tenets, therefore, do not belong to the prophetic secrets that Maimonides wants to explain. Consequently, Strauss concludes that "no philosophic topic of any kind is, as such, the subject matter of the *Guide*."[10]

Here the difficulty arises of how one is to interpret Maimonides' explicit identification of the two most important scriptural secrets with the two principal domains of (Aristotelian) philosophy. On this point, Strauss most noticeably diverges from the traditional interpretation of the *Guide*'s general scope and purpose.[11] Taken quite literally, Maimonides' identification substantiates the generally accepted view that Maimonides seeks to reconcile Judaism with philosophy and that, therefore, the *Guide* is eminently philosophical. Strauss correctly contends that Maimonides' intention is not to treat of physics and metaphysics as such, entirely for their own sake. Rather, he claims, it is

> to prove the identity, which to begin with was asserted only of *ma'aseh bereshit* with physics and of *ma'aseh merkabah* with metaphysics; . . . to show that the teaching of these philosophical disciplines, which is presupposed, is identical with the secret teaching of the Bible.[11] [And Strauss continues] The demonstration of such identity is no longer the duty of the philosophers, but is incumbent upon the student of the true science of the law.[12]

Why is this demonstration not the duty of a philosopher? Why is a student of the true science of the Law not also a philosopher? If the role of the philosopher and that of the student of the Law were clearly disparate, as Strauss assumes, then he might be right. But, as I argued above, this assumption cannot be attributed to Maimonides. And, as I will clarify below, the roles of the philosopher and of the student of the Law *qua* seekers of truth coincide. For, although both may arrive at truth by means of different sources, they cannot, in principle, be in disagreement. Any differences between a philosopher and a student of the Law must be due to other, perhaps practical, considerations. Moreover, both are governed by the same logical principles of demonstration. Maimonides' objection to the *mutakallimūn* is precisely that their methods are not demonstrative in the sense of being rationally convincing and grounded on true premises (I, 71). Therefore, even if Maimonides' intention is to demonstrate the identity in question and Strauss means by "demonstration" what Maimonides would understand by this term, then Maimonides is, indeed, engaged in philosophy. Not only is the method, but also the subject matter, of the

Guide one which falls within the realm of philosophy. Demonstrations require valid inferences and indubitably true premises. These requisites, according to Maimonides, invariably involve one in various philosophical disciplines. This may not amount to a discussion of philosophical topics as such, as Strauss would want, but it is, nevertheless, philosophical and integral to the scope and purpose of the *Guide*.

In his later article, "How to Begin to Study *The Guide of the Perplexed*," Strauss offers a slightly different interpretation of the same issue. Here he distinguishes a public and speculative teaching from a secret and exegetical teaching in the *Guide*. Because of Jewish legal proscriptions that restrict the revelation of prophetic secrets—of which Maimonides was well aware (I, Intro., 33, 71; III, Intro.)—Maimonides intentionally uses literary devices, such as contradictory and contrary claims, to conceal his explanations from the general public and common Jewish believer. What unites the secret exegetical parts with the public speculative parts of the *Guide*? If it is thought that speculation demonstrates the foundations of the Law, then, Strauss contends, speculation should precede exegesis, which is obviously not the order in the *Guide*. If it is maintained that exegesis deals with the same subject matter as that public teaching which is demonstrated by speculation, then, Strauss claims, there is no reason to consider the exegesis a secret teaching. Why, then, does Maimonides explicitly identify one with the other? To this question Strauss now responds:

> What [Maimonides] means by identifying the core of philosophy (natural science and divine science) with the highest secrets of the Law (the Account of the Beginning and the Account of the Chariot) and therewith by somehow identifying the subject matter of speculation with the subject matter of exegesis may be said to be *the secret par excellence of the Guide*.[13]

To speak of "the secrets of the *Guide*" is consistent with Strauss' view that the *Guide* is modelled on the Scriptures.[14] Since the Scriptures, by their metaphorical language and parabolic narratives, conceal certain teachings, so that they are accessible only in part and to a few, they contain esoteric doctrines. Since the *Guide* is devoted to an explanation of these secret teachings and abides by the legal proscriptions surrounding their explanations, it, too, Strauss concludes, is esoteric in its teachings. But this view poses a serious problem for any one seeking to understand the *Guide*, especially in those instances in which Maimonides apparently contradicts himself intentionally to conceal his real meaning from the common believer. Yet one cannot but take Maimonides seriously when he says that "The diction of this Treatise has not been chosen at haphazard, but with great exactness and exceeding precision, and with care to avoid failing to explain any obscure point" (I, Instruction). Now, with respect to the asserted identity of the Account of the Beginning with physics and the Account of the Chariot with metaphysics, Maimonides would have left an obscure point unexplained, if one were to adopt Strauss' view that what this identity means to assert is a secret of the *Guide*.

While conceding that Maimonides does not intend to treat of physics and metaphysics as such, there seems to be no reason to refuse to take him literally here, as scholars have usually done. Moreover, Maimonides explicitly admits that he has mentioned this identity in the *Mishneh Torah*, his legal Code (I, Intro.). But that work, on Maimonides' admission, was written for the general Jewish public and, therefore, presumably contains a public teaching (I, Intro.).[15] Is one to conclude, rather implausibly, that what was expressed in his Code as a public teaching is now, as explicitly stated in the *Guide*, a secret teaching? Even so, Maimonides cautions against a precipitous introduction to philosophical speculation without suitable abilities and prerequisites, for that may lead to confusion about, and ultimately rejection of, one's religion (I, 33, 34, 36, 60). This implies, however, that the philosophical sciences, claimed to be identical in content and truth with the prophetic secrets, should not, like these secrets, be divulged randomly and openly to the general public.

Strauss might object to my critique of his arguments by claiming that they rely on the explicit statements of Maimonides, which cannot be an accurate gauge of the latter's real intentions because Maimonides is revealing prophetic secrets while at the same time concealing them from the general public. Strauss might even suggest, in particular, that Maimonides' claim to an exact choice of words is itself problematic and its interpretation perhaps a secret of the *Guide*. But that would virtually close the book to any understanding, in its general scope as well as in particular details. If Strauss does mean this, then how could Maimonides even seriously propose to guide his readers through their perplexity? To claim, for example, that (i) the *Guide* is entirely written with precision but that (ii) the real meaning of its specific claims is also concealed would embroil Maimonides in an untenable situation. Yet this is what an interpreter of the *Guide* would encounter if he were to follow the implications of Strauss' interpretation.

What, more precisely, is the general character of the *Guide*? It can plausibly be viewed as an attempt to present a systematic philosophy of Judaism or of religion. Strauss denies this, presumably because philosophy of religion does not fall within Maimonides' classification of philosophy and, hence, was unknown to him.[16] But, while the term "philosophy of religion" was not current in medieval times and while it is not incorporated into the Aristotelian classification of philosophy that Maimonides accepted, by and large, there is ample textual evidence in the *Guide* to substantiate the interpretation that Maimonides does, indeed, intend to present a philosophy of religion or, specifically, a philosophy of Judaism.

First, Maimonides signals a theoretical intent, on the one hand, by addressing a select type of reader who is cognizant of the philosophical sciences (Epistle Ded.; I, Intro.) and, on the other, by his contrasting a true science of the Law with a legalistic study and excluding the latter from the scope of the *Guide*. A legalistic study of the Law, dealing with religious, moral, and social prescriptions incumbent upon Jewish adherents (III, 54), must be comprehensible to all, since all Jews are obligated to adhere to them in their daily lives. But a true science of the Law, dealing with its foundations and, consequently, a justification of its practical implications, is not comprehensible to all Jewish believers alike, since it requires a suitable preparation and intellectual development which they could not all be expected to have (I, Intro., 33–35).

Secondly, he indicates his religious intent, not only by the individual topics that are discussed, but by a unity of concerns expressed in the first and last chapters of the *Guide*. While the first introduces the two main themes of any theistic religion, namely, God and man, and initiates an explication of the proper concept of God, the last focuses on the natural end of man and his religious comportment as a result of his relationship to, and knowledge of, God.[17]

What unites these two aspects into a common objective is Maimonides' persistent quest for truth. This is evidenced by his repeated insistence on "intellectual beliefs," "intellectual apprehensions," apprehensions of "the true reality" of things, and of "the true essences of things," especially in connection with a knowledge of God as the basis of worship (I, Intro., 43, 57, 59; III, 51, 52, 54). These contrast with the false, "imaginary beliefs" on which, according to Maimonides, the *mutakallimūn* base their religious doctrines (I, 71). Intellectual beliefs result in knowledge; if they are indubitably true on the grounds of being self-evidently or demonstratively so (I, 50, 51). Implicit here is a unitary conception of beliefs and truth. Whether they originate from the Scriptures or from the philosophical sciences, beliefs are true in so far as apprehensions correspond to reality (I, 50). But, while the common believer accepts the truth of scriptural claims on the basis of tradition by way of prophetic authority, Maimonides accords a priority to the acceptance of truth on the basis of reason or demonstration (III, 51, 54). And this superior acceptance, as previously noted, relies on logic, physics, and metaphysics in their Aristotelian conception, for the first involves the principles of demonstration and the latter two, speculative truths about reality.

By admitting a superiority of philosophical knowledge based on demonstration over traditional knowledge based on prophecy, Maimonides does not minimize the importance of revelation and faith. The Scriptures, the textual source of revelation and faith, derive from prophecy and this, like reason in philosophy, is, according to him, a source of knowledge and truth (I, Intro., 35; III, 24).[18] But insofar as either kind of knowledge entails truth, the claims of prophecy and those of philosophy cannot in principle contradict each other, because, if different sources of truth were, in fact, to establish conflicting truths, the notion of truth itself would become incoherent. Rather than either subjugating faith to reason or reason to faith, Maimonides puts them on an equal footing.[19] Apparent conflict between them arises only as a result of difficulties of interpretation; in respect of truth, they converge. Prophets couch what has been revealed to them in figurative terms, because their claims, having a practical as well as a theoretical objective, must be accessible to all. They appeal, therefore, to the imagination, rather than the intellect, of the common believer (I, 26, 33; II, 43, 47). But it is men of speculation, or philosophers, in Maimonides' sense of the term, who are capable of interpreting and, hence, of understanding, the true meaning of these claims (I, 33; III, Intro., 54).

In summary, the *Guide* is essentially devoted to religion, to Judaism. In this sense it is a Jewish book. But it is also undeniable that Maimonides' approach is fundamentally theoretical, and this is the basis for calling the *Guide* a philosophical book. His prime concern lies with the foundations or roots of his religion. While these are initially given in prophecy, Maimonides seeks to aid his select readership in their comprehension and justification of these foundations. And this task invariably involves one in philosophy—not only as a pedagogical tool but, also, as an element integral to the task itself. Consequently, Maimonides can be said to provide a philosophy of religion or a philosophy of Judaism. Contrary to Strauss' implications, the *Guide*, in its general scope and purpose, is accessible to a contemporary philosopher, Jewish or not, for one can surely understand the claims of a religion and assess their purported justifications without espousing that religion's practice and underlying presuppositions.

NOTES

*I indicate within parentheses references to *The Guide of the Perplexed*: the book in Roman numerals and the chapter in Arabic numerals. Direct quotations are taken from the translation by Shlomo Pines (Chicago: Chicago University Press, 1963).

1. Typical of this view is the laudatory comment of Alexander Marx: "*The Guide of the Perplexed* is the greatest philosophic book produced in Judaism"

("Moses Maimonides," *Maimonides Octocentennial Series II* [N.Y.: Maimonides Octocentennial Committee, 1935], p. 24). Julius Guttmann similarly remarks about the *Guide*'s achievement that it made "Maimonides the leading philosophical figure of the late Jewish Middle Ages" (*Philosophies of Judaism,* trans. David W. Silverman [N.Y.: Rinehart and Winston, 1964], p. 152).

2. Cf. his "The Literary Character of the *Guide for the Perplexed,*" in *Essays on Maimonides, An Octocentennial Volume,* ed. Salo Wittmayer Baron (N.Y.: Columbia University Press, 1941), pp. 37–91; reprinted in this volume. Cf. also his "How to Begin to Study *The Guide of the Perplexed,*" Introductory Essay to the *Guide,* pp. xi–lxi. In another study, Strauss contends that Maimonides' *Mishneh Torah,* at least in its first book, is more philosophical than the *Guide* because it begins with philosophy and turns to the Torah. By implication, he suggests that the *Guide* neither begins nor ends with philosophy. Cf. Strauss, "Notes on Maimonides' Book of Knowledge," in *Studies in Mysticism and Religion,* ed. Ephraim E. Urback et al. (Jerusalem: Magnes Press, 1967), pp. 269–283.

3. A recent discussion illustrates this point; cf. Norbert Samuelson, "On Knowing God: Maimonides, Gersonides, and the Philosophy of Religion," *Judaism* 18 (1969): 64–77 and Shubert Spero, "Is the God of Maimonides Truly Unknowable?" *Judaism* 22 (1973): 66–78. Samuelson argues that Maimonides mistakenly seeks to identify the God of the philosophers with the God of Abraham, Isaac, and Jacob, whereas Spero defends this identity. But, if Maimonides intends to concern himself with the religious conception of God to the exclusion of the philosophical conception, then both interpretations are misguided.

4. Strauss, "Literary Character," p. 39; this volume, p. 32.

5. Ibid., pp. 41–42 (my emphasis); this volume, pp. 33–34.

6. Strauss, "How to Study," p. xiv.

7. Actually, Maimonides lists three opinions: (1) the Jewish belief in the world's creation in time from nothing; (2) the belief in the co-eternity of matter with God, which he attributes to Plato; and (3) the Aristotelian belief in the eternity of time and motion (II, 13). Since (3) entails that the process of generation and corruption is itself eternal, while (1) and (2) do not, (3) is contradictory to both (1) and (2).

8. He contrasts demonstrations (*burhān*) with proofs (*dalīl*) and uses the latter in connection with both creation in time and the eternity of the world (I, 71, 75, 76; II, 3, 15). For a clarification of this distinction and the requisites of a demonstration, see his *Treatise on Logic,* trans. Israel Efros (New York: American Academy for Jewish Research, 1938), ch. 7, pp. 41–47.

9. Cf. ibid., ch. 14, pp. 61–65.

10. Strauss, "Literary Character," p. 43; this volume, pp. 34–35.

11. Ibid., p. 44; this volume, p. 35.

12. Ibid.

13. Strauss, "How to Study," pp. xvi–xvii (my emphasis).

14. Cf. Strauss, "Literary Character," pp. 45–53; this volume, pp. 36–43.

15. Cf. Maimonides, *Mishneh Torah,* in *A Maimonides Reader,* ed. Isadore Twersky (New York: Behrman House, 1972), Intro., pp. 39–40, and Bk. I: Knowledge, p. 47.

16. Cf. the quotation cited above, p. 61.

17. Cf. Samuel Atlas, "The Contemporary Relevance of the Philosophy of Maimonides," *Central Conference of American Rabbis Yearbook* 64 (1954): 201-202.

18. Cf., especially, his *Treatise on Logic,* ch. 8, p. 47; and his "Letter on Astrology," in *A Maimonides Reader,* p. 465.

19. For a development of this relationship cf. Isaac Franck, "Maimonides' Philosophy Today," *Judaism* 4 (1955): 104-109.

A Third Approach to Maimonides' Cosmogony-Prophetology Puzzle

WARREN ZEV HARVEY

I

Maimonides' *Guide of the Perplexed*[1] is a book of puzzles. Worried lest his radically intellectualist teachings harm the unschooled reader incapable of replacing naive faith with reasoned conviction, Maimonides took extraordinary precautions to conceal them from him. He cut up his arguments as with a jig saw, placed the pieces in careful disarray, and tossed in a goodly number of extra pieces which seemingly fit but do not. His presupposition, of course, was that any reader keen enough to piece together his puzzles would be intellectually prepared to cope with his teachings. No one will gainsay that Maimonides did a superb job of concealment. After almost eight centuries, students of the *Guide* are still trying to figure out how to solve its puzzles.[2]

One puzzle in the *Guide* concerns the relationship between cosmogony and prophetology. In *Guide* II, 13, Maimonides describes three opinions on the creation of the world; then in II, 32, he describes three opinions on the phenomenon of prophecy, and remarks: "The opinions of people concerning prophecy are like their opinions concerning the eternity or creation of the world. I mean by this that just as the people to whose mind the existence of the deity is firmly established have, as we have set forth [in II, 13], three opinions concerning the eternity or creation of the world, so are there also three opinions concerning prophecy."[3] Maimonides does not say anything more about the relationship between the two sets of opinions, but it seems reasonable to infer that there is a correspondence between the three opinions on creation and the three opinions of prophecy.[4]

Harvard Theological Review 74 (1981): 287–301. Copyright 1981 by the President and Fellows of Harvard College. Reprinted by permission.

What this correspondence might be, however, is certainly not evident. The puzzle before us, therefore, is: Just *how* do the three opinions on creation correspond to the three opinions on prophecy? Our puzzle is particularly confusing because Maimonides' teachings on both creation and prophecy are themselves puzzles, and scholars remain until this day in wide disagreement as to what Maimonides really believed about these two subjects. To solve the puzzle of the cosmogony-prophetology correspondence, therefore, involves solving — at least in part — the two puzzles of creation and prophecy.

The cosmogony-prophetology puzzle has recently received detailed attention in two independently written essays: Lawrence Kaplan's "Maimonides on the Miraculous Element in Prophecy"[5] and Herbert Davidson's "Maimonides' Secret Position on Creation."[6] According to the solution endorsed by Kaplan, the first opinion on creation corresponds to the third opinion on prophecy, the second opinion on creation to the first on prophecy, and the third opinion on creation to the second on prophecy; i.e., 1:3, 2:1, 3:2. According to Davidson, the correspondence is 1:1, 2:3, 3:2.[7] The current discussion of this puzzle would, I think, be lacking if some words were not said in favor of the most obvious correspondence, namely, 1:1, 2:2, 3:3, and this is what I intend to do in what follows. In fact, it seems to me that this most obvious of correspondences is indeed the one intended in Maimonides' esoteric teaching.[8]

II

Before I adduce my arguments in favor of 1:1, 2:2, 3:3, it will be helpful here to set down briefly Maimonides' comments on each of the two sets of three opinions. In his presentation of both sets, Maimonides describes not only the opinions themselves but also those who hold them. The three opinions on creation in II, 13, are briefly: (1) creation of heaven and earth after absolute nonexistence[9] by God's will, (2) creation in time of heaven and earth out of eternal matter, (3) eternity *a parte ante* of heaven and earth. These three opinions are said to be held respectively by: (1) "all who believe in the Law of Moses," (2) "all of the [modern?] philosophers of whom we have heard reports and whose discourses we have seen" and also Plato, (3) Aristotle and the Aristotelians. The three opinions on prophecy in II, 32, are briefly: (1) God turns whomsoever he wishes into a prophet, (2) prophecy is a natural human perfection, (3) prophecy is a natural human perfection but can be miraculously prevented by God. These three opinions are said to be held respectively by: (1) the vulgar both among the pagans and among those who profess our Law, (2) the philosophers,

(3) us, i.e., this opinion is "the opinion of our Law and the foundation of our doctrine."

Let us now proceed to the arguments in favor of 1:1, 2:2, 3:3.

III

The argument for the correspondence of 1:1 is obvious, and has been stated succinctly by Davidson: "The parallelism is perfect: both the existence of the world and the appearance of a prophet are construed as sheer miracles, the coming into being of something from nothing."[10] To be sure, 1:1 almost certainly implies that Maimonides' attribution of the first opinion on creation to "all those who believe in the Law of Moses" is not to be taken at face value, but should be revised to read: "*the vulgar* among those who believe in the Law of Moses"; for if the first opinion on creation corresponds to the vulgar opinion on prophecy, then it seems that it too is a vulgar opinion. Such a revision of Maimonides' attribution of the first opinion on creation indicates, of course, that while in his exoteric teaching Maimonides advocated this opinion, in his esoteric teaching he rejected it. This, in fact, is Davidson's view,[11] and I believe that it is correct.[12]

Kaplan, as indicated above, prefers 1:3 to 1:1, and this is of course in accordance with Maimonides' explicit claims that the first opinion on creation is held by "all who believe in the Law of Moses" and that the third opinion on prophecy is "the opinion of our Law." According to 1:3, 2:1, 3:2, the correspondence favored by Kaplan, it would seem that all believers in the Law of Moses, including Maimonides himself, hold 1:3. Kaplan, however, does not commit himself to this proposition, since he leaves open the possibility that Maimonides esoterically held 3:2. Kaplan's analysis is based on the premise (which I consider correct) that prophecy according to Maimonides is a natural human perfection. Kaplan argues accordingly that *if* Maimonides did indeed hold the belief that the world was miraculously created after absolute nonexistence by the will of God, then it would follow that he should hold that God is able to perform miracles in nature, and that God is thus able to prevent miraculously the occurrence of the natural phenomenon of prophecy (i.e., Maimonides would hold 1:3). However, Kaplan concomitantly argues, *if* Maimonides held the Aristotelian theory of eternity, then he would not be able to speak of miracles, and would simply hold that prophecy is a natural phenomenon, period (i.e., Maimonides would hold 3:2). Kaplan is forced to leave open the possibility that Maimonides held 3:2 instead of 1:3, because he does not wish to deny the possibility that Maimonides held the Aristotelian theory of eternity.[13] To my mind, however, it is inconceivable that *if* Maimonides held 1:3, 2:1, 3:2, he would endorse 3:2, for this would suggest that he was dissociating himself from the unequivocal position of the Law of Moses (viz., 1:3), i.e., that he was *rejecting* the Law of Moses in favor of Aristotelian philosophy.[14] What seems correct to me (for reasons which will be given below) is that Maimonides did hold the Aristotelian theory of eternity, but that he did not consider it to be in conflict with the true doctrine of the Law (i.e., he held 3:3). As for the argument that if Maimonides held the Aristotelian opinion on cosmogony (3) he could not speak of miracles, and thus could not hold the opinion of "the Law" on prophecy (3), it is sufficient to remark that although the Aristotelian theory of eternity, as Maimonides understands it, does indeed seem to rule out supernatural phenomena, Maimonides' mention of miracle in his presentation of the opinion of "the Law" on prophecy need not be taken as referring to a *supernatural* miracle.[15]

IV

The argument for 2:2 is based on the clear correspondence of attributions: each of the corresponding opinions is attributed to "the philosophers." Now, with regard to the second opinion on cosmogony, it is evident that "the philosophers" must be understood as "the *non-Aristotelian* philosophers," since according to Maimonides the Aristotelian philosophers did not hold the second opinion, but rather the third. If, then, Maimonides as a good Aristotelian held the third opinion on cosmogony (which I think he did, as I shall explain below), he would in effect here be setting his own opinion (3) in contradistinction to that of "the philosophers" (2). Similarly with regard to prophetology, Maimonides sets his own opinion (3) in contradistinction to that of "the philosophers" (2).

With regard to the attributions, therefore, the relationship between 2 and 3 in cosmogony seems to be analogous to that between 2 and 3 in prophetology. Moreover, there is a similar analogy with regard to the subject matter. In both the cosmogony and the prophetology discussions, 3 is presented as being like 2, with one exception. In the cosmogony discussion, it is reported that those who hold 3, like those who hold 2, assert that "something endowed with matter can by no means be brought into existence out of that which has no matter," *but* that unlike those who hold 2, they assert that "the heaven is in no way subject to generation and passing away."[16] In the prophetology discussion, similarly, it is reported that 3 is identical with 2 "except in one thing," viz., that according to 3 "it may happen that one who is fit for prophecy . . . should not become a prophet."[17]

If we are justified in arguing that the relationship between 2 and 3 in the cosmogony discussion is analogous to that between 2 and 3 in the prophetology discussion, we would certainly be justified in going one step further, and in arguing that the relationships between 1, 2, and 3 in the two discussions are analogous. Thus, 1 in both discussions is the vulgar opinion; 2 in both discussions is the "philosophic" opinion; and 3 in both discussions is the "philosophic" opinion with one exception.

Davidson, as indicated above, argues for 2:3, and thus attributes to Maimonides the Platonic view on creation (although he allows that Maimonides might after all have held 1:3).[18] That Maimonides could have held the Platonic view on creation is emphatically rejected by Kaplan, who argues (I think decisively) that in Maimonides' judgment "a doctrine that affirms that the heavens are subject to generation and passing-away in effect denies the possibility that there exists a rational, natural order," and such a doctrine would have had to have been rejected by Maimonides, who, like Aristotle, believed in "a fixed natural order."[19] Kaplan's pairing 2:1 is based on his conclusion that for Maimonides the Platonic view on creation is unscientific, and thus it should correspond to the unscientific opinion of the vulgar concerning prophecy.[20] Kaplan's argument for 2:1 is compelling, except that it is not at all clear that the second opinion on cosmogony is more unscientific than the first.

V

In my judgment, Maimonides held 3:3. In other words, he held the Aristotelian position on cosmogony (3), in spite of his exoteric support of the position that the world was created after absolute nonexistence (1); and he held the position on prophecy which he said he does (3).

The question of whether Maimonides, despite his many disclaimers, did hold the Aristotelian theory of eternity was debated by medievals and continues to be debated by moderns. As we have seen, for example, Kaplan leaves the question open (maintaining that Maimonides held *either* 1:3 or 3:2) and Davidson answers negatively (maintaining that Maimonides held 2:3 or alternatively 1:3).[21] It seems to me, however, that there is ample evidence in the *Guide* to indicate that Maimonides did advocate the Aristotelian theory, and some of this evidence will be summarized presently. Before this summary, however, two comments are in order.

First, to avoid a common misunderstanding, it should be emphasized that to conclude that Maimonides held Aristotle's theory of eternity is *not* to say that he denied creation, and it is *not* to say that he denied religion; rather, it is to say that he denied what he considered to be the vulgar notion of creation and the vulgar notion of religion. Thus already in the thirteenth century, the philosophically astute kabbalist Abraham Abulafia argued in his esoteric commentary on the *Guide* that it is an error to consider the creation and eternity of the world as exclusive disjuncts, for the world may be *both* created (*ḥadaš*) and eternal *a parte ante* (*qadmon*).[22] According to Abulafia, the notion of continuous or eternal creation is found, for example, in the words of the morning prayer, "He creates [*mĕḥaddeš*] each day continuously [*tamid*] the work of creation."[23] The compatibility of creation and eternity was not infrequently affirmed in the medieval Maimonidean literature. In his well-known commentary on the *Guide*, for example, the fourteenth-century Maimonidean philosopher, Moses of Narbonne, speaks of the crucial theological importance in Maimonides' system of the proposition of "the eternity of the world, which is to say, the eternal creation [*ha-bĕri'a ha-niṣḥit*]."[24]

Second, it should be remarked that to conclude that Maimonides held Aristotle's theory of eternity is *not* to say that he thought that the theory had been proved. His explicit statements to the effect that the theory has not been proved are, it seems clear to me, to be accepted as straightforward expressions of his true opinion.[25] However, if Maimonides thought that the theory had not been proved, he *also* thought that Aristotle himself did not think it proved.[26] Maimonides, as far as I understand him, embraced the theory of eternity for the same reason that he thought Aristotle had embraced it: namely, it conforms to the nature of what exists, i.e., it conforms to our empirical observation of the continuous motion of the heavens.[27]

We turn now to our summary of the evidence on behalf of Maimonides' advocacy of the Aristotelian theory of eternity.

To begin with, Maimonides states in *Guide* I, 71, that in his proofs for the existence, unity, and incorporeality of God (in II, 1–2), and in his discussion of these subjects in his works on rabbinic law (e.g., *Mišne Tora*, Yĕsode ha-Tora, i), he always presupposes the *eternity of the World* in order "not to cause the true opinion . . . to be supported by a foundation [viz., the doctrine of creation after nonexistence] that everyone can shake and wish to destroy, while other men think that it has never been constructed,"[28] Maimonides, it is true, claims that his presupposition of the eternity of the world is merely methodological, and does not imply his commitment to it.[29] Nevertheless, an examination of Maimonides' proofs in *Guide* II, 1–2, testifies that *our knowledge of God* is based on the Aristotelian premise of eternity.[30] More significantly, in my opinion, an examination of Maimonides' statements in his great Code, the *Mišne Tora*, reveals that the Aristotelian premise of eternity is indeed *required* for the fulfillment of the divine *commandments* to know God and to know that he is one,[31] and that Abraham our father had in fact come to know God on the basis of the Aristotelian premise of eternity.[32]

Again, an examination of Maimonides' comments in the *Guide* on the biblical narrative of creation shows that for him the Hebrew word *bara'* ("created") in the first verse of Genesis does not designate coming into being *after* nonexistence (Arabic: *ba'd al-'adam*), but rather coming into being *from* nonexistence (Arabic: *min al-'adam*), which seems to mean that it designates the continuous ontic dependence of creation on Creator, or if you will, the continuous information of matter by the Form of the world.[33] Similarly, according to Maimonides, the first word in Genesis, *bĕ-rešit* ("In the beginning"), does not refer to a *temporal* beginning, but rather to a "principle" (Arabic: *mabda'*) in the philosophic sense of the Greek *archē*.[34] Moreover, the Arabic word *al-bāri'* ("Creator") occurs in the *Guide* more than twenty times in contexts which are at least compatible with the Aristotelian theory of eternity, but *not even once* in a context suggesting the doctrine of creation after nonexistence.[35]

Again, Maimonides reports in *Guide* II, 28, that "many adherents of our Law" attributed to King Solomon the belief in the eternity of the world. Although Maimonides makes a point of protesting that Solomon could not have harbored such a belief, his explication of the scriptural verses in question gives the distinct impression that Solomon did indeed hold the Aristotelian position.[36]

Again, Maimonides hints that three distinguished rabbis held the theory of eternity. On the basis of a dictum in the *Chapters of Rabbi Eliezer,* Maimonides suggests in *Guide* II, 26, that the tanna Rabbi Eliezer ben Hyrcanus held that the "throne of glory" is the heavens (i.e., the celestial spheres or, perhaps more precisely, the diurnal sphere), and that it is eternal *a parte ante.*[37] On the basis of dicta of the amoraim Rabbi Abbahu and Rabbi Judah ben Simon, Maimonides suggests in *Guide* II, 30, that they held the eternity *a parte ante* of time.[38]

Finally, what on the face of it appears to be fundamentally objectionable to Maimonides in the Aristotelian theory of eternity is that it denies God's will and affirms necessity.[39] Inspection of the relevant texts, however, shows that Maimonides does speak of God's "volition" (Arabic: *irāda*) in his presentation of Aristotle's theory of eternity.[40] Besides, Maimonides' teaching that God's will, wisdom, and essence are one and inscrutable effectively strips the concept of God's will of any cognitive meaning.[41] Similarly, Maimonides claims that as opposed to Aristotle who had held that all things exist by divine necessity, he holds that they exist by divine *purpose.*[42] However, he completely neutralizes this claim when he subsequently pronounces that the word "purpose" is used equivocally when applied to the purposes of men and of God.[43] Moreover, in several critical texts Maimonides openly advances the doctrine of divine necessity.[44] It is noteworthy in this connection that in explaining Aristotle's notion of the necessary derivation of the world from God, Maimonides writes in *Guide* II, 20, that "this necessity is somewhat like the necessity of the derivation of an intellectum from an intellect,"[45] words which recall his own position put forth in I, 68, concerning the unity of intellect and intellectum in God.[46] In fine, if both Aristotle and Maimonides maintain the doctrine of divine necessity, and if both also speak about divine will, then on the allegedly crucial question of divine necessity and divine will there is no evident difference between Aristotle and Maimonides. What had been thought to be Maimonides' fundamental objection to Aristotle's theory of eternity now appears to be no objection at all.

Much more could be said in support of the proposition that Maimonides held the Aristotelian theory of the eternity of the world, but this is not the place to elaborate on the problem, and in any case the preceding summary of the evidence suffices for our purposes.[47] Having indicated the grounds for assigning to Maimonides the third opinion on creation, let us now examine the grounds for assigning to him the third opinion on prophecy.

At the outset, we may state that Maimonides' position on prophecy is not nearly as problematic as his position on creation. Surely he did not hold the opinion of "the vulgar" (1). It is imaginable, however, that despite his explicit affirmation of the opinion of "the Law" (3), he really held the opinion of "the philosophers" (2). The view that Maimonides esoterically held the opinion of "the philosophers" has been entertained by some medieval and modern commentators, and — as we have seen — it is left open as a possibility by Kaplan.[48] However, there does not seem to me to be any good reason to reject Maimonides' explicit affirmation of the opinion of "the Law." For as Kaplan's highly sensitive reading of Maimonides' statements on prophecy in *Guide* II, 32, shows conclusively,[49] there is no essential distinction between the theory of prophecy of "the philosophers" (2) and that of "the Law" (3). Now if there is no essential distinction between 2 and 3, then there would seem to be no good reason to insist that Maimonides held 2 instead of 3. The proviso mentioned in Maimonides' presentation of 3 which is not found in his presentation of 2, viz., that God can miraculously prevent prophecy, has — as Kaplan explains — nothing whatsoever to do with the theory of prophecy proper. The point of the proviso is simply that according to the Law miracles *can* happen (even though they may be interpreted as purely natural phenomena), and thus just as God (to use Maimonides' own examples) miraculously prevented King Jeroboam from moving his hand (I Kgs. 13:4), and just as he miraculously prevented the soldiers of the King of Aram's army from seeing

(2 Kgs. 6:18), so too he can miraculously prevent a person naturally fit to prophesy from prophesying.[50] The question of just what Maimonides had in mind by his curious reference to the miracle of preventing prophecy need not detain us here.[51] What is important is only that according to Maimonides the Law has a notion of miracle and the philosophers do not, and that Maimonides — for reasons which have nothing to do with his epistemology of prophecy — accepts the notion of miracle (even if he interprets all miracles as natural phenomena).[52]

In affirming that there is no essential distinction between the theory of prophecy of "the philosophers" (2) and that of "the Law" (3), we are in effect pointing to a significant parallel between 2 and 3 in cosmogony and 2 and 3 in prophetology. For with regard to the opinions on cosmogony, Maimonides tells us explicitly that in essence there is "no difference" between the opinion of "the philosophers" (2) and that of Aristotle (3), since both entail the belief in eternity *a parte ante,*[53] or — to put it another way — both preclude the doctrine of temporal creation after nonexistence, and both cohere with that of eternal creation, i.e., with the doctrine that "creation" refers to the ontic or causal dependence of the world upon God.[54] We have already observed (see above, section IV) that in both the cosmogony and prophetology discussions, 3 is presented as being just like 2 but with one exception. It now appears that we may add that in both cases this one exception is not essential to the issue at hand. Just as with regard to cosmogony the essential choice is between the unscientific opinion of "creation after nonexistence" (1) and the scientific opinion of eternal creation (2, 3), so with regard to prophetology the essential choice is between the unscientific opinion of prophecy as a supernatural phenomenon (1) and the scientific opinion of prophecy as a natural phenomenon (2, 3). Moreover, it seems that both with regard to cosmogony and prophetology Maimonides chose 3 over 2 for reasons which have to do with his naturalistic theory of miracles,[55] or more generally with his belief (which is neither part of his doctrine of creation proper nor part of his doctrine of prophecy proper, but which of course influences both these doctrines) that *all* phenomena are to be understood in accordance with "the nature of what exists."[56]

VI

In what has preceded, I have tried to present the basic arguments for the correspondence 1:1, 2:2, 3:3, as the solution to the cosmogony-prophetology puzzle of *Guide* II, 13 and 32. Admittedly, solutions to the puzzles of the *Guide* are never apodictic. It can always be argued that wrong pieces have been crassly forced into critical places in the puzzle, and that the pretty picture intended by Maimonides has been distorted out of recognition. However, I believe that a comparison of the three suggested solutions will show that 1:1, 2:2, 3:3 is not less likely than 1:3, 2:1, 3:2, or 1:1, 2:3, 3:2; and even if it is concluded that all three are equally likely, then I believe the nod should be given to 1:1, 2:2, 3:3, simply because it is, after all, the obvious correspondence, and unless there are reasons to think otherwise it may be supposed that this is the correspondence that Maimonides had in mind.

In any case, my purpose in writing down the foregoing comments on the cosmogony-prophetology puzzle was simply to contribute to the current discussion of the puzzle by presenting a third approach for the consideration of students of the *Guide*. I do not delude myself that I have solved the puzzle to everyone's satisfaction, and I know that even those readers who will agree with me about the solution may disagree with me about the reasons I have put forth in its defense, and perhaps they will find even better reasons.

NOTES

1. Page references to the *Guide* will be to Shlomo Pines's English translation (*The Guide of the Perplexed* [Chicago: University of Chicago, 1963]), although in quotations this translation may sometimes be modified.

2. In his Introduction to the *Guide* (pp. 5-20), Maimonides advises his philosophic reader (cf. p. 10, 1.21, and n. 24) on how to uncover the esoteric meaning of the book. E.g., he writes: "If you wish to grasp the totality of what this treatise contains . . . then you must connect its chapters one with another; and when reading a given chapter, your intention must be not only to understand the totality of the subject of that chapter, but also to grasp each word that occurs in it . . . even if that word does not belong to the intention of the chapter. For the diction of this treatise has not been chosen at haphazard . . . and nothing has been mentioned out of its place, save with a view of explaining some matter in its proper place" (p. 15). A valuable key to Maimonides' esoteric teaching is his discourse on the "seven causes" of contradictory and contrary statements (pp. 17-20), and perhaps in particular his comments on the *seventh* cause: "In speaking about very obscure matters, it is necessary to conceal. . . . Sometimes . . . this necessity requires that the discussion proceed [in one place] on the basis of a certain premise, whereas in another place [it] proceeds on the basis of another premise contradicting the first one. In such cases, the vulgar must in no way be aware of the contradiction; the author accordingly uses some device to conceal it by all means" (p. 18). On the esotericism of the *Guide*, see Leo Strauss, *Persecution and the Art of Writing* (Glencoe, Ill.: Free Press, 1952), pp. 38-94; reprinted in this volume;

see also his "How to Begin to Study *The Guide of the Perplexed,*" in Pines's translation of the *Guide,* pp. xi–lvi.

3. *Guide,* p. 360.

4. As Isaac Abrabanel observes in his Commentary on *Guide* II, 32, if only the similarity between the two sets of opinions were the number 3, then Maimonides might as well have said that the opinions on prophecy are like the Patriarchs, or like any other trio. See *More Něbukim* with Commentaries of Ephodi, Shem Tob ben Joseph ibn Shem Tob, Asher Crescas, and Isaac Abrabanel (Warsaw: Goldman, 1872), 66a. Abrabanel's observation is translated in Alvin Reines, *Maimonides and Abrabanel on Prophecy* (Cincinnati, Ohio: Hebrew Union College, 1970), pp. 4–5.

5. *Harvard Theological Review* 70 (1977): 233–256.

6. In Isadore Twersky, ed., *Studies in Medieval Jewish History and Literature* (Cambridge, Mass.: Harvard University, 1979) pp. 16–40.

7. The solution endorsed by Kaplan was, it seems, first explicitly suggested by the sixteenth-century rabbinic scholar Mordecai Jaffe, and has been held in the present century by S. Atlas and J. Kafih (see Kaplan, "Maimonides and the Miraculous Element," pp. 249–250). The solution endorsed by Davidson is what Kaplan calls "the standard explanation of the correspondence"; it was explained in detail by Abrabanel and has been accepted by modern scholars like S. Munk, M. Friedländer, Z. Diesendruck, and Reines (see Kaplan, "Maimonides and the Miraculous Element," pp. 251–252, n. 42).

8. I have not seen this solution suggested in either the medieval or modern literature. However, it is perhaps implicit in the esoteric comments of some of the medievals.

9. This opinion, according to which the world was created "*after* absolute pure nonexistence (Arabic: *ba'd al-'adam al-mahḍ al-muṭlaq*)" (p. 281, ll. 8–9) is *not* identical with the opinion that the world was created *ex nihilo* (Arabic: *min al-'adam*). It implies that *before* creation there had been nonexistence, whereas the opinion of creation *ex nihilo* may be interpreted to signify the continuous creation of existence out of nonexistence, or the eternal information of matter (=*nihil*). In other words, it is incompatible with the theory of the eternity of time, whereas the opinion of creation *ex nihilo* is compatible with it. See Sara Klein-Braslavy, *Peruš ha-Rambam lě-Sippur Běri'at ha-'Olam* (Jerusalem: Israel Society for Biblical Research, 1978), pp. 81–90. The distinction between creation after nonexistence and creation *ex nihilo* is ignored by both Kaplan and Davidson, as well as by most scholars who have written on Maimonides' cosmogony. On concepts of creation in medieval Arabic literature, see Harry A. Wolfson, *The Philosophy of the Kalam* (Cambridge, Mass.: Harvard University, 1976), pp. 355–372.

10. "Maimonides' Secret Position," 23. "Nothing" must be understood here as "no matter" (see previous note).

11. Ibid., 24–26. On p. 36, however, Davidson expresses reservations about this view (and, indeed, about his entire analysis of Maimonides' position on creation), both on the grounds that the evidence he has assembled is "not unambiguous," and on the grounds that Maimonides may have been "less immune to error

and carelessness than he and his readers through the centuries have imagined."
While on the cosmogony Davidson thus expresses uncertainty as to whether Maimonides held 1 or 2, he voices no doubt that on prophetology Maimonides held
3. In his view, therefore, Maimonides' own position on the cosmogony-prophetology
correspondence is if not 2:3, then 1:3. That 1:3 is (according to his own analysis)
composed of *non*-corresponding opinions would presumably be taken by Davidson simply as evidence that Maimonides did not, as the "thoroughgoing esoteri-
cists" suppose, write the *Guide* with "exceeding precision" (see p. 25).

    12. With regard to the possible objection that Maimonides had to have held
the first opinion on creation since it is necessary for his conception of prophecy,
see Maimonides' instructions to his reader in *Guide* I, 71: "You should not ask
how prophecy can be true if the world is eternal, before you have heard our discourse concerning prophecy" (p. 181). This comment as Pines observes, "tends to
produce the impression that prophecy can be true (or valid) even if the world is
eternal" (Introduction to his translation of the *Guide,* p. cxxviii n. 115). However,
whatever "impression" this comment produces, its plain meaning is that until the
reader has studied Maimonides' discourse on prophecy, he has no right to conclude that the doctrine of creation after nonexistence is necessary for Maimonides' conception of prophecy. Now, Maimonides' discourse on prophecy begins at
Guide II, 32, and ends at II, 48. Since Maimonides' presentation of the three opinions on prophecy appears in II, 32, right at the beginning of that discourse, it is
obvious that in examining that presentation the reader has no right to presume
that only the first opinion on creation is compatible with Maimonides' conception
of prophecy. See also Maimonides' affirmation of the compatibility of prophecy
and eternity in *Guide* II, 16, p. 294.

    13. "Maimonides on the Miraculous Element," 256.

    14. That Maimonides considered Judaism and philosophy to be mutually
exclusive has admittedly been maintained by Leo Strauss in several works; e.g.,
Persecution, pp. 42–43; see this volume, pp. 33–34; and "How to Begin to Study
the *Guide,* p. xiv. Strauss thereby raises the question of whether Maimonides in
his esoteric doctrine did indeed ultimately reject the Law of Moses for Aristotelian
philosophy. Cf. also Pines's remark; "that Maimonides realized the true issue between philosophy and religion, or religious Law, does not necessarily mean that
. . . he . . . chose religion" (Introduction to his translation of the *Guide*, p. cxxviii).
Nonetheless, I think that there is no justified doubt about Maimonides' uncompromising commitment to the Law of Moses, even if it is *also* true (as I think it
is) that his commitment to philosophy was likewise uncompromising. On the in-
tegration of Judaism and philosophy in Maimonides, see Twersky, "Some Non-
Halakic Aspects of the Mishneh Torah," in A. Altmann, ed., *Jewish Medieval and
Renaissance Studies* (Cambridge, Mass.: Harvard University, 1967), pp. 95–118;
idem, *Introduction to the Code of Maimonides* (New Haven, Conn.: Yale University, 1980); Arthur Hyman, "Maimonides' Thirteen Principles," in Altmann, *Studies,*
pp. 119–144; idem, "Interpreting Maimonides," *Gesher* 5 (1976): 46–59; reprinted
in this volume; and David Hartman, *Maimonides: Torah and Philosophic Quest*
(Philadelphia: Jewish Publication Society, 1976); and see my review of Hartman's
book in the *Journal of the History of Philosophy* 17 (1979): 86–88, and my "Po-

litical Philosophy and Halakhah in Maimonides" (in Hebrew), *Iyyun* 29 (1980): 198–212.

15. In *Guide* II, 25, p. 328, Maimonides comments that Aristotle's theory of eternity would not contradict the Law if miracles are "interpreted"; and in II, 29, pp. 345–346, he suggests that miracles are "in nature." See also Maimonides' *Eight Chapters,* 8 (ET in J. I. Gorfinkle, ed., *The Eight Chapters of Maimonides on Ethics* [New York: Columbia University, 1912], pp. 90–91; and in R. L. Weiss and C. Butterworth, eds., *Ethical Writings of Maimonides* [New York: New York University, 1975], pp. 87–88).

16. *Guide* II, 13, p. 284.

17. Ibid., II, 32, p. 361.

18. See above, n. 11.

19. "Maimonides on the Miraculous Element," 250, 253.

20. Ibid., 249–251.

21. Kaplan's view that on cosmogony Maimonides held 1 or 3 but surely not 2 is corroborated with extensive evidence by Klein-Braslavy, *Peruš ha-Rambam* (summary of findings, pp. 256–266). Davidson's view that on cosmogony Maimonides held 1 or 2 but surely not 3 has been held recently by some other scholars, e.g., S. Feldman in his article on "Creation and Cosmogony," *Encyclopaedia Judaica* 5, col. 1067–69; however, the evidence for this view is not convincing, being based on unargued rhetorical statements of Maimonides, e.g., at *Guide* II, 25, p. 330. Cf. below, n. 55.

22. *Sitre Tora,* MS. Paris, hébr. 768 (Hebrew University Microfilm, no. 12327), 137b–140b; MS. Paris, hébr. 774 (Hebrew University Microfilm, no. 12332), 147b–149b.

23. Ibid., MS. 768, p. 140a; MS. 774, p. 149a. A similar use of this phrase (from the *yoṣer 'or* blessing preceding the morning reading of the *Šěma'*) is found, e.g., in Isaac Albalag, *Tiqqun ha-De'ot,* ed., G. Vajda (Jerusalem: Israel Academy of Sciences and Humanities, 1973), 31, l. 1; in Hasdai Crescas, *Or Adonay,* IIIA, 1,5 (Ferrara: Abraham Usque, 1555), 24viii, l. 16; in Joseph Solomon Delmedigo, *Noblot Ḥokma* (Basel: Samuel Askenazi, 1631), 97b, l. 20; and in modern times in Franz Rosenzweig, *Star of Redemption,* Introduction (New York: Holt, Rinehart and Winston, 1971), 2.111. Another liturgical text cited by Abulafia (loc. cit.) as indicating the notion of eternal creation is "today is the birth of the world" (Additional Service, New Year, after sounding of ram's horn).

24. Commentary on the *Guide,* Introduction, ed. J. Goldenthal (Vienna: K. K. Hof- und Staatsdrukerei, 1852), 1b, l. 18. Cf. "Epistle on *Shi'ur Qomā*" ed. A. Altmann, in *Studies* (cited above, n. 14), p. 259, l. 128 (trans. pp. 276–277), where Narboni—like Abulafia (see preceding note)—cites the prayer, "today is the birth of the world." On the compatibility of creation and eternity in the medieval Hebrew philosophic literature, cf. also, e.g., the references to Albalag, Crescas, and Delmedigo in the preceding note. A recent study of the theory of eternal creation in late Antiquity and in the Middle Ages is S. Feldman, "The Theory of Eternal Creation in Hasdai Crescas and Some of His Predecessors," *Viator* 11 (1980): 289–320. Feldman, however, does not consider the possibility that Maimonides held the theory (cf. above, n. 21).

25. E.g., *Guide*, I, 71, p. 180; II Introduction, p. 241; II, 15–16; II, 17, p. 298; II, 19, pp. 307–308; II, 22, p. 320; II, 23, p. 322; II, 25, pp. 328 and 330. On Maimonides' general skepticism, see Pines, "The Limitations of Human Knowledge according to Al-Farabi, ibn Bajja, and Maimonides," in Twersky, ed., *Studies* (cited above, no. 6), pp. 82–109; reprinted in this volume.

26. *Guide* II, Introduction, p. 240; II, 15, pp. 289–292; II, 19, pp. 307–308.

27. "For [Aristotle's] opinion [concerning eternity] is nearer to correctness than the opinions of those who disagree with him insofar as inferences are made from the nature of what exists [Arabic: *min tabī'at al-wujūd*]" (*Guide* II, 15, p. 292; cf. III, 17, p. 468). "That which exists [*al-wujūd*] does not conform to the various opinions, but rather the correct opinions conform to that which exists" (ibid., I, 71. p. 179). Similarly, Maimonides remarks that his proofs for the existence, unity, and incorporeality of God—which presuppose the eternity of the world (see following note)—are "derived from the nature of existence [*min tabī'at al-wujūd*] that can be perceived and that is not denied except with a view to safeguarding certain opinions" (ibid., p. 182). Cf. Maimonides' summation of the arguments for creation after nonexistence put forward by the Kalam: "they have abolished the nature of what exists (*tabī'at al-wujūd*] and have altered the original disposition of the heavens and the earth by thinking that by means of these premises it would be demonstrated that the world was created in time . . . [and thus they] have destroyed for us the demonstrations of the existence and oneness of the Deity and of the negation of His corporeality, for [these] demonstrations . . . can only be taken from the permanent nature of what exists [*min tabī'at al-wujūd*], a nature which can be seen and apprehended by the senses and the intellect" (ibid., I, 76, pp. 230–231; cf. I, 71, pp. 179–181). In sum, science has no choice but to base itself on "that which exists," even when dealing with questions which apparently cannot be absolutely decided on that basis.

28. *Guide* I, 71, p. 182.

29. Ibid. Cf. also I, 76, p. 231; II, Introduction, p. 235 and 239.

30. I.e., on premise 26 ("time and motion are eternal, perpetual, and existing *in actu*"), *Guide* II, Introduction, pp. 239–240. Not only does this premise figure critically in Maimonides' proofs, but apparently there can be no such proofs without them, "for [these] demonstrations . . . can only be taken from the permanent nature of what exists" (see above, n. 27).

31. See *Book of Knowledge* (ET, M. Hyamson [Jerusalem: Boys Town, 1962]), Yĕsode ha-Tora 1:1–7, where God's existence (1:5) and unity and incorporeality (1:7) are inferred from the empirical observation that "the [diurnal] sphere spins continuously"; that this phrase is understood by Maimonides as denoting the Aristotelian theory of eternity is clear from Maimonides' remarks in *Guide* II, 2, p. 252. Cf. my "The Question of the Incorporeality of God in Maimonides, Rabad, Crescas, and Spinoza" (in Hebrew), in S. Heller Wilensky, et al., ed., *Tĕpisat ha-Elohut bĕ-Maḥăšaba ha-Yĕhudit* (Haifa: University of Haifa, 1981). Cf. also Strauss, "Notes on Maimonides' Book of Knowledge," in *Studies in Mysticism and Religion presented to Gershom G. Scholem* (Jerusalem: Magnes, 1967), pp. 269–272; and Twersky, *Introduction* (cited above, no. 14), p. 448, n. 224.

32. *Book of Knowledge,* 'Akum 1:3, where Abraham (in the spirit of Yĕsode ha-Tora 1:7; cf. preceding note) is portrayed as having inferred the existence of God from the continuous spinning of the diurnal sphere.

33. *Guide* II, 30, p. 358; III, 10, p. 438. Cf. above, n. 9. And see Klein-Braslavy, *Peruš ha-Rambam,* pp. 81–82, and 86–87.

34. *Guide* II, 30, pp. 348–349. Cf. Klein-Braslavy, *Peruš ha-Rambam,* pp. 114–131. And cf. Hasdai Crescas's interpretation in Wolfson, *Crescas's Critique of Aristotle* (Cambridge, Mass.: Harvard University, 1929), pp. 290–291, p. 664 nn. 34–35.

35. See Abraham Nuriel, "The Question of a Primordial or Created World in the Philosophy of Maimonides" (in Hebrew), *Tarbiz* 33 (1964): 372–387; cf. I. Ravitsky's response, *Tarbiz* 35 (1966): 333–348. The word *al-bāri'* occurs in *Guide* I, 10, p. 36; I, 15, p. 41; I, 22, p. 52; I, 51, p. 113; I, 53 (twice), pp. 119, 122; I, 56, p. 130; I, 68, p. 165 (overlooked by Nuriel); I, 69 (four times), pp. 169–70; II, 11, p. 274; II, 12, p. 279; II, 14, p. 288 (in explicit reference to the Aristotelian theory of eternity); II, 19, p. 302 (in explicit reference to the Aristotelian theory of eternity); II, 20, p. 313 (in explicit reference to the Aristotelian theory of eternity); III, 12, p. 446 (cf. p. 443, l. 3, where the underlying Arabic is *bāri'hu*); III, 13 (twice), pp. 448, 451. Maimonides, it may be remarked further, shows similar care with regard to the use of the Hebrew *bore'* ("Creator") in the *Book of Knowledge.* Strauss has called attention to Maimonides' avoidance of the Hebrew root *br'* in Yĕsode ha-Tora I ("Notes" [cited above, n. 31] 272). The first text in which a derivative of this root is predicated of God is Yĕsode ha-Tora II:3, where the verb *bara'* is used in a context identical to that of *al-bāri'* in *Guide* II, 11.

36. Thus, Maimonides states (p. 334) that "people thought" that Solomon's words, "And the earth abideth forever [*lĕ 'olam*]" (Eccl. 1:4), indicate the eternity *a parte ante* of the world. However, he goes on to explain that "the word '*olam* does not signify [only] eternity *a parte post* unless it is conjoined with the word '*ad*"; but in the verse in question '*olam* is *not* conjoined with '*ad* (p. 335). It seems to be implied, therefore, that these words of Solomon's—as well as similar texts where '*olam* appears without '*ad* (e.g., Eccl. 3:4, cited on pp. 335–336; but perhaps Gen 21:33, cf. references on p. 645)—do indeed indicate the eternity *a parte ante* of the world.

Maimonides' exegeses in *Guide* II, 28, are followed closely by Spinoza in *A Theologico-Political Treatise,* 6 (trans. R. H. M. Elwes [New York: Dover, 1951]), p. 96 (on Ps. 148:6, Jer. 31:35, and esp. on Eccl. 1:1–9 and 3:14). On Eccl. 1:9, cf. also Maimonides' *Eight Chapters,* 8 (Gorfinkle, 90; Weiss-Butterworth, 87; cited above, n. 15).

37. See also *Guide* I, 9 and 70. Note the different interpretations of Lam. 5:19 in I, 9 (p. 35; cf. I, 10, p. 37) and in II, 26 (p. 331); in this verse '*olam* appears without '*ad* (see preceding note), and so its meaning is not restricted to eternity *a parte post.* In III, 2 (p. 422; on Ezek. 1:26), the throne of glory has been understood by some medieval and modern commentators as symbolizing the convexity of the diurnal sphere. On the throne of glory in the *Guide* see Klein-Braslavy, *Peruš ha-Rambam,* p. 89 and 132; Aviezer Ravitzky, *The Thought of R. Zerahia b. Isaac*

b. Sheltiel Hen & the Maimonidean-Tibbonian Philosophy in the 13th Century (in Hebrew) (Doctoral diss., The Hebrew University of Jerusalem, 1977), pp. 258-263, cf. p. 236 n. 1; Wolfson, "Halevi and Maimonides on Prophecy," *Jewish Quarterly Review* 33 (1942/1943): 78-79 (reprinted in his *Studies in the History of Philosophy and Religion,* ed. I. Twersky and G. H. Williams [Cambridge, Mass.: Harvard University, 1972], volume 2, pp. 115-116); idem *Repercussions of the Kalam in Jewish Philosophy* (Cambridge, Mass.: Harvard University, 1979), pp. 113-120. Cf. G. Vajda, *Recherches sur la philosophie et la kabbale dans la pensée juive du Moyen Age* (Paris: Mouton, 1962), p. 412, s.v. "Trône (de Gloire)"; M. Idel, "A Fragment of Asher ben Meshulam of Lunel's Philosophical Writings" (in Hebrew), *Kiryat Sefer* 50 (1975): 150, 152-153.

38. Cf. Klein-Braslavy, *Peruš ha-Rambam,* pp. 128-245.

39. See *Guide* II, 19-21.

40. Ibid., II, 13, p. 284, lines 30-31 ("all that exists has been brought into existence . . . by God through his volition").

41. Cf. ibid., I, 53, p. 122; I, 69, p. 170; II, 18, p. 302; III, 13, p. 456.

42. Ibid., II, 19, p. 303; II, 21, pp. 316-17.

43. Ibid., III, 20, p. 483; cf. II, 18, p. 301; II, 21, p. 315.

44. E.g., "the works of the Deity . . . are of necessity established as they are, for there is no possibility of something calling for a change in them" (ibid., II, 28, p. 335; note the exegesis of Deut. 32:4 on p. 336, and cf. I, 16, p. 42, and III, 25, p. 506). Cf. below, n. 46.

45. Pp. 313-314.

46. Cf. "His knowledge of things is not derived from them. . . . On the contrary, the things . . . follow upon His knowledge, which preceded and established them as they are . . . . He also knows the totality of what necessarily derives from all His acts" (III, 21, p. 485).

47. As Klein-Braslavy remarks, the very existence of ambiguities in Maimonides' position on creation is itself evidence that he held the theory of eternity: "If Maimonides had been of the opinion that the world was created [after nonexistence], he would have said it . . . explicitly and unequivocally, for the opinion of creation [after nonexistence] is the view acceptable to the vulgar man" (*Peruš ha-Rambam,* p. 256). If Maimonides' ambiguities were intended to conceal something from the vulgar, it surely was not the doctrine of the creation of the world after absolute nonexistence!

48. See above, n. 13. Regarding the medievals, see Kaplan, "Maimonides and the Miraculous Element," 240.

49. Ibid., 247-248.

50. "[W]ould anyone argue," asks Kaplan rhetorically, "that it is a fundamental principle of [the Law's] theory of vision that God can miraculously blind a person or that it is a fundamental principle of [the Law's] physiology that God can paralyze a person's arm?" (ibid., 248).

51. See ibid., 238-248, 252-253. However, *pace* Kaplan (237-238 n. 18), I suspect that Yĕsode ha-Tora *does* underlie Maimonides' reference to the miraculous prevention of prophecy (cf. Yĕsode ha-Tora 7:5 with the problematic phrase in *Guide* II, 32, discussed by Kaplan on 246-247 n. 38). See following note.

52. It may be argued that since according to Maimonides *all* miracles (including of course those recorded in 1 Kings 13:4 and 2 Kings 6:18) are natural phenomena (see above, n. 15), the provision about the miracle in the opinion of "the Law" (3) on prophecy is wholly meaningless, and that consequently there is *absolutely* (i.e., not only essentially) no distinction between the opinion of "the philosophers" (2) and that of "the Law" on prophecy. However, it seems to me that it is a mistake to equate the naturalistic interpretation of miracles with the denial of all meaning to the notion of miracle, just as it is a mistake to conclude that a thoroughgoing physical determinist can have no use for terms such as "will," "accident," or "luck." In point of fact, Maimonides himself seems to have been a thoroughgoing physical determinist (see Pines, "Notes on Maimonides' Views concerning Human Will," *Scripta Hierosolymitana* 6 [1960]: 195–198; and Altmann, "The Religion of the Thinkers," in S. D. Goitein, ed., *Religion in a Religious Age* [Cambridge, Mass.: Association for Jewish Studies, 1974] pp. 35–45), and there are analogies and connections between his treatment of will, accident, and luck, and his treatment of miracle (cf., e.g., *Guide* II, 48). Altmann ("The Religion of the Thinkers," p. 41) has called attention to the "striking parallel" between Maimonides' comments in *Guide* II, 32, concerning the miraculous prevention of prophecy and his comments in *Eight Chapters,* 8 (Gorfinkle, pp. 95–96; Weiss-Butterworth, pp. 90–91; cited above, nn. 15, 36) concerning the miraculous prevention of human choice. While in *Guide* II, 32, Maimonides likens the prevention of prophecy to the prevention of motion from Jeroboam's hand and the prevention of sight from the King of Aram's soldiers, in the *Eight Chapters* he had likened the prevention of prophecy to the prevention of motion from Jeroboam's hand and the prevention of sight from the Sodomites (Gen. 19:11). It is most likely that in the case of both the miraculous prevention of human choice and the miraculous prevention of prophecy (which itself may be seen as an instance of the miraculous prevention of human choice), Maimonides had in mind a certain phenomenon (probably psychological, but possibly physical or political) which prevents human beings from acting in accordance with their natural abilities. Regarding the prevention of human choice, see also *Book of Knowledge,* Tesuba 6:3. On the relationship between Maimonides' theory of human choice and his statement that God may miraculously prevent prophecy, cf. also Eliezar Goldman, "Maimonides' View of Prophecy" (in Hebrew), in *Samuel K. Mirsky Memorial Volume* (New York: Yeshiva University, 1970), pp. 203–210. According to Goldman's analysis of Maimonides, "the divine will which is spoken of in connection with prophecy is none other than the choice of the prophet" (210), and similarly the divine will which can prevent prophecy is none other than "human choice, whose source is the pre-eternal divine will" (208–209).

53. *Guide* II, 13, p. 285.

54. Maimonides' statement (ibid., p. 283) that according to the opinion of "the philosophers" (2), "there exists a certain matter that is eternal . . . and that [God] does not exist without it, nor it . . . without Him [cf. I, 9, p. 35, on Lam. 5:19; cf. above, n. 37] . . . [but that this matter does not have] the same rank in what exists as He . . . but He is the cause of its existence," holds good also according to the Aristotelian opinion (3).

55. Regarding cosmogony, the only "argument" mentioned by Maimonides in favor of 2 as opposed to 3 is that according to 2 "all the [biblical] miracles [taken literally] become possible" (*Guide* II, 25, pp. 329–330); but given Maimonides' views on the "fixed natural order" (cf. Kaplan's remarks cited above, n. 19), it seems that this is really an argument *against* 2: Davidson, to be sure, thinks otherwise (see "Maimonides' Secret Position," 20–22); cf. above, n. 21. Similarly with regard to prophetology, it is the theory of miracles (however it is to be understood) which separates the otherwise identical 2 and 3.

56. See above, n. 27.

SECTION II

Issues in Epistemology
and Metaphysics

The Limitations of Human Knowledge according to Al-Farabi, ibn Bajja, and Maimonides

SHLOMO PINES

One of the most perplexing problems posed by the *Guide of the Perplexed* — and to my mind a fundamental one — relates to two apparently irreconcilable positions held by, or attributed to, Maimonides. On the one hand, he sets very narrow limits to human knowledge; on the other, he affirms that man's ultimate goal and man's felicity consist in intellectual perfection, that is, in knowledge and contemplation (*theoria*).[1] It is hard to admit that a knowledge that includes neither metaphysics — the cognition of God and immaterial beings, that is, separate intellects — nor celestial physics is man's final end. I will attempt to show that an unpublished text of Ibn Bajja[2] throws light on the antecedents of this problem and thus clarifies the issue.

The text in question is one of the treatises of Ibn Bajja collected in MS Pococke 206 of the Bodleian Library. It deals with a lost but much quoted work of al-Farabi, his *Commentary on the Nicomachean Ethics,* concerning which it provides important new information. I have tried to show that, given the evidence — Ibn Bajja's quotations and those of other authors — we are justified in asserting that al-Farabi's *Commentary* was a seminal work[3]: the necessity to disprove one of its theses may have shaped Averroes' thinking on the hylic intellect, and its Latin translation may have provided Marsilius of Padua with one of his most incisive formulae. It may have also given Ibn Bajja's reflections a new turn.

In this chapter I shall *inter alia* consider the possibility that the di-

From *Studies in Medieval Jewish History and Literature,* edited by Isadore Twersky (Cambridge, Mass.: Harvard University Press, 1979), pp. 82–109. Reprinted by permission of the author and of the Center for Jewish Studies, Harvard University.

rect or indirect influence of this work of al-Farabi may account for some distinctive traits of Maimonides' thought. A translation of a small section of Ibn Bajja's text follows. (In the MS on which it is based some words are missing.)

> [The following belongs also] to his [Ibn Bajja's] Discourse: As to what is believed about Abū Nasr [al-Farabi] regarding that which he says in his *Commentary* on the Book of *Ethics,* namely that after death and demise[4] there is no afterlife,[5] that there is no happiness except political happiness,[6] that there is no existence except that which is perceived by the senses and that that through which it is said another existence than the one which [has just been mentioned comes about] is nothing but an old wives' tale. [I am of the opinion that] all this [that which is believed about al-Farabi] is false, [that those are lies] used to attack Abū Nasr [al-Farabi]. For Abū Nasr [al-Farabi] has made these remarks at his first reading [of the *Ethics*[7]]. But what he says on this subject does not resemble these statements of his that are entailed by a demonstration.

It is worth noting that in this rather involved passage Ibn Bajja does not deny al-Farabi's having made the remarks which were used to denigrate him. The point he wishes to make is that these pronouncements do not carry much weight and need not be taken seriously; unlike other statements by al-Farabi, they are not backed by a demonstration. This objection does not seem to be wholly correct. Al-Farabi based his negations on a logical argument (which Ibn Bajja apparently found unconvincing).[8]

In the passage quoted above one bit of information is new and startling: al-Farabi is reported to have affirmed that there is no happiness except political happiness.[9] This phrase, which is identical with a formula found in the *Defensor Pacis* of Marsilius of Padua, denies that happiness (*eudaimonia*) is achieved by contemplation (Greek *theoria*). In the framework of the Aristotelian system this means that intellectual perfection is not the final end of man. This view seems to be due to the fact that, according to al-Farabi, metaphysics, regarded as cognition of the immaterial entities, is a science that transcends human capacity. The other statements attributed in the passage to al-Farabi can by and large be matched by quotations from the *Commentary* on the *Ethics* found in a variety of sources. But reference to political happiness provides a clue for this interpretation. They negate traditional philosophy at least as much as they negate naive religion, which perhaps was not foremost in al-Farabi's mind when he made the observations under discussion.

The consequences of al-Farabi's position are spelled out by Ibn Bajja in a passage that occurs some lines after the one translated:

A statement (*qawl*) made by al-Farabi [in the work in question], which does not resemble other statements of his [is concerned with the opinion] attributed by him to some[10] of the Ancients; [according to al-Farabi] they [opposed] a violent negation [to the teaching concerning the separation[11] of the soul from the body]. Now this is not the doctrine (*qawl*) of one of the ancients, but that of the miscreant (*dāllīn*) *Ikhwān al-Safā*.' It is an evident [consequence] of this doctrine that happiness [consists] in a [human] individual being a part of the city in such a way that he serves[12] [it] in a manner appropriate to his degree so that he and the people [of the city] obtain many good things[13] perceived by the senses, [things] that pertain to civic[14] [life] and that procure pleasure in ways consonant with the interests of the community.[15] [In] serving [the latter] in a manner appropriate to his station he [helps] to bring about both for himself and for the people [of the city] the most excellent political circumstances, those that are most favorable for the permanent existence (*baqā'*) in security of the [human] species throughout the length of durable existence (*Tūl al-baqā'*).

This is a model for a state, the activities of whose inhabitants are wholly directed toward material security and welfare, a totalitarian state which is clearly an end unto itself. In imputing this conception to the Ikhwān al-Safā', Ibn Bajja has probably had in mind their Ismā'ili leanings.[16] On the other hand, it seems evident that only his immense respect for al-Farabi prevents him from taxing the author of the *Commentary* on the *Ethics* with this conception.[17]

In our text Ibn Bajja's view of the objectives that should be pursued in civic governance (*al-tadbīr al-madanī*) seems to be more or less identical with the doctrine expounded by al-Farabi in such treatises as *Ārā' Ahl al-Madīna al-Fādila*. Ibn Bajja makes it plain that civic government, especially in the case of a virtuous city (*al-madīna al-fādila*), may be of great help in the furtherance of intellectual development, that is, in bringing about in man the existence of an intellect cognizing many intellecta.[18] Some of these intellecta are mentioned: God, His angels, His scriptures, His messengers, all His creatures. The "degree" of these cognitions, that is, their greater or lesser adequation to true intellection varies, since it depends on the degree of the cause of the cognition.[19]

This enumeration of intellecta resembles in part a similar enumeration occurring in *Ārā' Ahl al-Madīna al-Fādila*[20]: Al-Farabi lists in that passage the things and matters that the people of the Virtuous City know (*ma'rifa*). He does not have in mind intellection in the strict sense of the word. Thus there may exist some excuse for the conjecture[21] that in the passage cited Ibn Bajja's reference to intellecta in connection with the knowledge of God and the angels lacks semantic rigor. Or he may have been guilty of inconsistency.

In the text under discussion there is no indication that Ibn Bajja at the time of writing had renounced the philosophical politics advocated by al-Farabi,[22] that is, the obligatory participation of the philosopher qua philosopher in public affairs. Such a renunciation is a main theme of this *Tadbīr al-Mutawahhid*. This attitude could be fully explained by the political climate of his time, in which the revolutionary, partly philosophical, propaganda of the Ismā'īlīs had spent its force.[23] It would be mere speculation to imagine that his revulsion from the reduction of all human goals to the pursuit of political happiness propounded by al-Farabi in the *Commentary* on the *Ethics* may have been one of the factors which had brought about this renunciation.

In his *Commentary,* al-Farabi maintained the mortality of the soul[24] and of human intellection. In the first place I shall try to place in a historical perspective his assertion concerning the soul. One of the interesting points about this assertion is that the *Commentary* on the *Ethics* may have been the earliest work written by an Arab philosopher in which this conception was spelled out. Al-Kindi professed belief in the separate existence of the soul. Al-Farabi himself refers in other works, as is pointed out by Ibn Tufayl,[25] to the afterlife of the soul. The aggressive tone which he apparently used, in the *Commentary* on the *Ethics,* in denying this afterlife, may be due to the circumstance that no Arab philosopher had previously formulated this denial (which may be regarded as a necessary consequence of some formulae of Aristotle's *De Anima*).

After al-Farabi, the belief that the individual souls have an afterlife is criticized by Ibn Butlan, a Christian philosopher from Baghdad.[26] This critique may be derived directly or indirectly from al-Farabi's *Commentary,* whose doctrine on the point in question may have been adopted by the philosophers of Baghdad. Avicenna, on the other hand, taught that the individual souls continued to exist after death. I have suggested elsewhere[27] that this may be one of the main questions in which the two doctrines and philosophical traditions posited by Avicenna — the occidental tradition, which to a large extent is represented by the philosophers of Baghdad, and the oriental tradition, which may be assimilated to the personal opinions of Avicenna — are supposed to be in total disagreement.

As regards the Intellect, Averroes quotes in the *Long Commentary* on the *De Anima*[28] from al-Farabi's *Commentary* on the *Ethics* an argument by which the Cordovan philosopher seems to have been so impressed that, in order to be able to answer it with a show of reason, he conceived his well-known theory concerning the hylic intellect. "If it had been possible for a substance subject to generation and corruption to intellect abstract forms (*formas abstractas*), that is, forms that are totally separate from matter, it would have been likewise possible (*possibile esset*) for the nature of the contingent (*natura possibilis*) to become necessary." In other words human cognition transcends temporality. This argument clearly entails the denial, as far as men are concerned, of the highest kind of knowledge which is free of any recourse to sense data: it is the knowledge in which the knower, the known, and the act of knowing are identical. The abstract forms to which al-Farabi refers are, among other things, God and the separate intellects: man can have no knowledge either of the former or of the latter.

The Arab and Jewish philosophers who had accepted al-Farabi's conception of the mortality of the individual soul, that is, by and large all the philosophers with whom Avicenna's influence was paramount,[29] tried to construct theories that might legitimate the rejection of the view of the human intellect propounded in al-Farabi's *Commentary* on the *Ethics*. An account of these theories would make up a considerable part of the history of Arab and Jewish philosophy.

I have made a brief study of Averroes' position;[30] in this chapter Ibn Bajja will be the only Arab philosopher (except for al-Farabi) with whom I shall deal in this connection. It would seem that he had no less than two[31] theories on the point at issue. One of them is set forth in the text in which he quotes and criticizes al-Farabi's *Commentary* on the *Ethics*. According to this theory, man has an intellect that grasps intellectual objects (*ma'qūlāt*) by means of insight (*basīra*), the latter being a divine faculty[32] that emanates from the active intellect but is not identical with it. This faculty relates to the percepts of the imagination in a way analogous to the relation between the senses and their percepts. It grasps, by means of something analogous to light that subsists in it, quiddities[33] of the percepts of the imagination. To speak metaphorically, it chisels these percepts into shape. For example, we grasp in this way the quiddities of the celestial motions and thus the noblest objects of cognition are actualized in us.

It is man's own essence that grasps the quiddities actualized in it, and for this it has no need of a body. Man's intellect (which exercises this activity) is perdurable, it is immortal. It belongs to the category of intellect, although it is the lowest among them.

This conception of Ibn Bajja calls for the following observations: the percepts of the imagination undergo a transmutation when they are transferred to the sphere of the intellect, are actualized in man's essence, become objects of intellection. It is true that after this transmutation they have no relation to matter and to sensual objects. There is, however, in what may be called the epistemological section of the text,[34] no reference to objects of intellection that were not prior to their transmutation percepts of the imagination (and before that percepts of the senses). The fact that the quiddities of the celestial movements are regarded as the noblest objects of intellection is in keeping with the foregoing observation.

This doctrine is similar in many respects to views expounded by al-Farabi in *R. al-'Aql wa'l-Ma'qūl*, mentioned by Ibn Bajja in the text under discussion. The main difference seems to be that the cognition of forms that have no connection with matter, and never have had, is regarded as possible in this treatise by al-Farabi and is not mentioned at all in Ibn Bajja's text. It is tempting to suppose that this omission is due to the influence of al-Farabi's *Commentary* on the *Ethics,* but there is no proof.

What appears to be a different theory is set forth in other treatises by Ibn Bajja. I have profited by A. Altmann's masterly analysis of this theory,[35] but for my purposes here I shall put a somewhat different emphasis on various points. The treatise I shall refer to in this connection is Ibn Bajja's *Risālat al-Ittisāl,*[36] the *Epistle on Conjunction.* In the first lines of the treatise Ibn Bajja speaks of the "knowledge"[37] for which he had found demonstration and of the "greatness" and "remarkable characters" (*gharāba*) of the matter (p. 103). The indications he gives show that the conception expounded in the *Epistle* was influenced by nonperipatetic sources, one of which he did not recognize as such: on page 112 he quotes Alexander of Aphrodisius' *K. fi-l-Suwar al-Rūhāniyya.* In point of fact this treatise is an extract from Proclus' *Elements of Theology.* However, he also refers explicitly (pp. 114–115) to Plato's theory of ideas,[38] which he criticizes. I shall not go into the details of Ibn Bajja's doctrine, referred to both in the Kuzari and in Maimonides, concerning the unity of the human intellect, that is, the identity of the intellect which subsists in different human individuals.

The doctrine of the unity of the intellect is not mentioned in the treatise of Ibn Bajja which gives his views on the *Commentary* on the *Ethics.* A second point of disagreement between this text and the *R. al-Ittisāl* may be found in the fact that according to the former the objects of intellection that are divorced from matter and are actualized in the intellect are transmuted percepts of imagination that have been grasped by the divine faculty called insight. In the *R. al-Ittisāl* the higher objects of intellection have as their substrata not percepts of the imagination but other objects of intellection.

The following passage from this treatise goes even further (and is perhaps not quite consistent with the statement, based on other passages,[39] that has just been made concerning the doctrine of the treatise):

> From what I have said it has become clear that there are three degrees: the first is the degree of the multitude (*al-jumhuriyya*); it is the natural degree (*al-martaba al-tabi'iyya*). For them the object of intellection is bound up with the material forms. They only know it through and from them, [de-

rived] from them (*'anhā*) and with a view to them (*lahā*). All the practical crafts (*al-sanā'i' al-'amaliyya*) pertain to this (p. 112).

The second is theoretical cognition (*al-ma'rifa al-nazariyya*). It is at the summit of the natural [cognition]. [The difference is that] the multitude look first at the [material] substrata (*al-mawdū'āt*) and [only] in the second place and for the sake of the substrata, at the object of intellection. The theoreticians of the natural sciences[40] [on the other hand] look first at the object of intellection and [only] in the second place, and for the sake of the object of intellection, [to which they] liken them,[41] at the material substrata. For this [reason] the propositions employed in the sciences contain all of them a subject (*mawdū'*) and a predicate[42] which is referred to (*al-mushār ilayhi*). For this [reason] the propositions are universal (*kulliyya*). It is evident that in our statement "every man is an animal," there is a third [term] which the Arabs omit, in expressing the meaning [contained] in this statement, as they omit the particle[43] [which is known as] the copula (*al-rābita*). For our statement "every man is an animal" indicates that which is indicated [by the statement] "everything that is a man is an animal" and "whatever thing is described as being a man is also described as being an animal." [Statements which present] similar [modes of] expression are either tautological or they indicate aspects[44] that are concomitant and equivalent.[45] It is clear that this differs from the meaning of our statement "man is a species" as an object of intellection . . . [A person who has achieved] this degree of theory[46] sees the object of intellection, but only through an intermediary, as the sun is seen[47] in water, for what is visible in water is [the sun's] image, and not [the sun] itself. The multitude sees an image of the image; this is similar to the sun's casting its image into water, and this image being reflected in a mirror and being seen in the mirror, which does not [contain the particular thing[48]] that is reflected. The third degree is that of the happy ones that see the thing [as it is] in itself (p. 113).[49]

In the treatise there are also other accounts of the three (or four) degrees; some of the variation in the terms and the imagery used are of some interest. On page 114, there is an interpretation of the myth of the cave. There are people dwelling in almost total darkness; there are people, they are the great majority, who are aware of the existence of the intellect; they are compared to the cave dwellers who do not see light as separate from colors. Then there are the men of speculation,[50] who may be compared to people who have come out of the cave, and separately see the light and all the colors. Finally there are the happy ones who might be compared to people whose sight has been transmuted to light.

On page 117 the people belonging to the second degree, the men of speculation, are referred to as the *tabī'iyyūn,* the physicists, the men studying natural sciences, who use definitions. They see the intellect, but jointly with other things.

Aristotle and other happy (men) belong to the third degree. In spite of appearances, they are "one in number,"[51] for there is no difference between them except in externals.

On page 116, people belonging to the second degree are likened to "a polished surface (*al-sath al-saqīl*), as [for instance] the surface of a mirror which makes itself seen and in which other things may be seen. He is nearer to deliverance (*takhallus*) than [the people belonging to] the first degree and yet he is in a state that is subject to corruption (*bālin*) People belonging to the third degree are most like . . . the sun itself. However [in point of fact] nothing that is a material body is like unto them . . . They are not subject to corruption and passing away."[52]

A summary of some of the main points of the theories which have been discussed would seem to be in order. But before this I shall make a brief reference to a relevant doctrine of Alexander of Aphrodisias, which may help to bring the other theories into focus.

According to Alexander,[53] a (human) intellect *in actu,* which is identical with the act of intellection, intellecting something subject to corruption is itself subject to corruption. If however the object is not subject to corruption, neither is the intellect; this being a consequence of the identity of the intellect with the object of intellection. We may surmise that in the *Commentary* on the *Ethics* al-Farabi had in mind *inter alia* the doctrine of Alexander. What the *Commentary* appears to mean[54] is that, since man is incapable of intellecting abstract forms, his intellect cannot be transmuted into a perdurable substance; nothing in man escapes death. The abstract forms that cannot be *cognized* by man certainly include the separate intellects; they may also have included forms that, according to other theories, one of the theories of Ibn Bajja for instance, the human intellect is able to abstract from sense percepts or percepts of the imagination.

Given the logic of the doctrinal system deriving from Alexander, it should have been, and apparently was, a moot question whether the cognition of such abstract forms survives the death of the body, that is, is immortal. Gersonides, who discusses this point at some length, answers the question in the affirmative and concludes that this is the only kind of immortality vouchsafed to man,[55] men being unable to cognize and achieve union with the active intellect. This may have also been in substance the conclusion of Ibn Bajja in the theory I have dealt with in the first place. However, according to Ibn Bajja's "second" theory, man can transcend this degree of cognition, intellect incorporeal entities, attain identity with the active intellect.

These preliminary observations may possibly help us find the right perspective in our inquiry concerning Maimonides' views as expressed or hinted at in the *Guide of the Perplexed,* on the limitations of human knowledge and on the final end of man. They will help us in the first place to give a narrower and perhaps clearer definition of the object of our inquiry.

With a view to this, reference will be made to Maimonides' Introduction to the *Guide* (page 7 of my translation): "We are like someone in a very dark night over whom lightning flashes time and time again. Among us there is one for whom the lightning flashes time and time again, so that he is always, as it were, in unceasing light . . . That is the degree of the great one among the prophets, to whom it was said: *But as for thee, stand thou here by Me*[56] . . . Among them there is one to whom the lightning flashes only once in the whole of his night; that is the rank of those of whom it is said: *they prophesied, but they did so no more.*[57] There are others between whose lightning flashes there are greater or shorter intervals. Thereafter comes he who does not attain a degree in which his darkness is illumined by any lightning flash. It is illumined, however, by a polished body or something of that kind, stones or something else that give light in the darkness of the night. And even this small light that shines over us is not always there, but flashes and is hidden again . . . It is in accord with these states that the degrees of the perfect vary. As for those who never even once see a light, but grope about in their night, of them it is said: *They know not, neither do they understand; they go about in darkness.*[58] The truth, in spite of the strength of its manifestation, is entirely hidden from them."

The simile of lightning flashes seems to be derived from Avicenna's *K. al-Ishārāt wa'l-Tanbīhāt*. According to this work[59] experiences of the *'ārifūn* perceiving something of the light of truth may be likened to lightning which flashes momentarily and is then extinguished. These are called moments, *awqāt*, a sufi term. If, however, a person has by dint of (spiritual) exercise attained a certain station, the lightning flash may be transformed into a permanent luminous phenomenon seen in the sky, an experience which has some resemblance with that of Moses in Maimonides' Introduction to the *Guide*. The Avicennian category *'ārifūn*,[60] "those who know," appears to include some of the sufi mystics, those who have attained spiritual degrees and also in all probability the prophets. In Maimonides' Introduction only the prophets appear to see the lightning flashes. If this image refers *inter alia* or exclusively to cognition, as seems likely, it would mean that, according to Avicenna, only the *'ārifūn* or, according to Maimonides, only the prophets are able to cognize intelligibles that are not abstractions of corporeal objects. In the case of Maimonides, the reference in the Introduction to the man whose darkness is illumined "by a polished body" may be adduced in support of this interpretation. The word "polished" (*saqīl*) calls to mind "the polished surface" (*sath saqīl*) to which people belonging to Ibn Bajja's second degree are likened. The simile is somewhat different, but it could have been inspired by *R. al-Ittiṣāl* or by some other treatise by Ibn Bajja. As far as I can see, it means that the people, whose degree in the hierarchy is inferior to that of the prophets, need (like the persons who belong to Ibn Bajja's second degree) for their intellection perception of corporeal objects (the polished bodies).

Maimonides' Introduction thus appears to indicate that only prophets (and not the philosophers belonging to "the third degree" of *R. al-Ittiṣāl*) can cognize incorporeal entities. This seems to mean that the cognition that can be achieved by the prophets is different in kind from that of all other men (including the philosophers) and may be beyond their ken. The possibility that this position of Maimonides may have been determined by theologico-political reasons need not concern us for the moment. What matters is that Maimonides did not consider himself a prophet[61] and certainly did not write with a view to being read by prophets. Everything points to his having envisaged the possibility of his being read by philosophers, and he may have thought that he was one himself. This being so, it is of great significance that, as the common run of people as well as the philosophers (but not the prophets) are concerned, Maimonides may seem to adopt in the Introduction to all intents and purposes the theory that we have designated as Ibn Bajja's "first" doctrine, according to which human intellection depends on the perception or imagination of material objects.

It is not my task in this chapter to find out to what extent various relevant texts of the *Guide* confirm or disprove this interpretation of Maimonides' epistemology. His theologico-political assessment of the superiority of Moses' faculty of intellection over that of other people will concern us only indirectly; it may throw light on the nature and limitations of the intellectual activity of men who are not Moses. Maimonides' views on the other prophets seem to be less significant in the context of this investigation.

In the first place, I shall quote two passages that at first may not seem to accord with or easily to fit into the interpretation referred to above.

This passage occurs in the course of a discussion concerning knowledge of the Name composed of forty-two letters.

"It has been made clear in the books that have been composed concerning the divine science, that it is impossible to forget this science; I mean thereby the apprehension (*idrāk*) of the Active Intellect" (I, 62, my translation p. 152).

"Furthermore the relation of the intellect *in actu* existing in us, which derives from an overflow of the Active Intellect and through which we apprehend the Active Intellect, is similar to that of the intellect of every sphere that exists in the latter," (II, 4, my translation p. 258).

Does the term *idrāk* (apprehension) mean that the human intellect *in actu* cognizes the active intellect in the Aristotelian sense of the verb — in other words does it achieve identity with this intellect, which is separate from matter? An investigation of the way Maimonides employs *adraka, idrāk* shows that this interpretation is not obligatory. This may be inferred from the last chapter of the *Guide* (III, 54, pp. 636 and 638 of the translation), in which we encounter twice the expression: "the apprehension (*idrāk*) of Him, may He be exalted." On page 638 the phrase reads: "It is clear that the perfection of man that may truly be gloried in is the one acquired by him who has achieved, *in a measure corresponding to his capacity,* apprehension of Him, may He be exalted." Given this wording and Maimonides' views on the limits of man's cognition of Deity, it is evident that *idrāk* of God does not mean an intellectual act that brings about the identity of the subject and object of intellection. The meaning of the term is much weaker. It is legitimate to suppose that Maimonides, when referring to man's apprehension of active intellect, likewise gave *idrāk* this weaker meaning. As far as I can see, all the texts of the *Guide* that might seem to postulate man's capacity to cognize immaterial being or to intellect without the help of sense percepts or images are as ambiguous and indecisive as the two that have been quoted.

The reasons for assuming that the opposite thesis was regarded by Maimonides as correct are much stronger and, it seems to me, cannot be gainsaid. Two categories of texts are relevant in this connection: those which describe or characterize in some manner man's cognitive activity and those (more important in this context) which refer to the limitations of the human intellect. Some texts may be held to belong to both categories. The clearest and most detailed description of an act of human intellection found in the *Guide* is this:

> Know that before a man intellectually cognizes a thing, he is potentially the intellectually cognizing subject. Now if he has intellectually cognized a thing (it is as if you said that if a man has intellectually cognized this piece of wood to which one can point, has stripped its form from its matter, and has represented to himself the pure form — this being the action of the intellect), at that time the man would become one who has intellectual cognition *in actu.* Intellect realized *in actu* is the pure abstract form, which is in his mind, of the piece of wood. For intellect is nothing but the thing that is intellectually cognized. (I, 68, pp. 163–164)

This intellectual act is described apparently in order to enable the reader to compare it with the intellection of God, discussed in the second half of the chapter, with which it has both points of similarity and differences. It is doubtless significant that the intellectual cognition of a material object, a piece of wood, is used in this context as an example of human intellection. A question which may spring to mind is whether this choice of an example is intended *inter alia* to produce the impression that all human intellection is of this type.

At this point Maimonides' views on the limitations of human knowledge should be examined. It seems to me that his so-called negative theology admits of two interpretations, which, to some extent at least, are mutually exclusive. Textual evidence may be adduced in support of either of them. To put the matter succinctly, Maimonides may have adopted the doctrine professed by Greek Neoplatonists, Christian theologians, and Muslim mystics and sectarians that the deity is unknowable *per se,* that it cannot be cognized by any conceivable intelligence, that of men or that of the separate intellects if these are assumed to exist; or he may have considered that God, like the separate intellects cannot be grasped by a human intellect,[62] whose activity is dependent on sense data and images. Many of Maimonides' statements seem to be in accord with the first interpretation,[63] but the second appears to account for the following passage (III, 9; translation, pp. 436–437): "Matter is a strong veil preventing the apprehension of that which is separate from matter as it truly is . . . Hence whenever our intellect aspires to apprehend the Deity or one of the intellects, there subsists this great veil interposed between the two." The term "intellects" means in this context the separate intellects. This passage entails at least two conclusions: man cannot cognize God because the human intellect is tied up with the body. For the same reason man cannot cognize the separate intellects.

The second conclusion is of considerable importance, as it appears to mean that man can only know material objects or objects connected with matter. The view, based on III, 9, that according to Maimonides men do not have the capacity to achieve naturally—through an exercise of their cognitive faculty—knowledge of the separate intellects[64] is indirectly confirmed by the *Guide* I, 37, and I, 38. Both chapters refer *inter alia* to God's answer to Moses' request (in Exod. 33) to see His face. In I, 37, Maimonides sets forth his interpretation of Onkelos' translation (Exod. 33:23) of this answer. According to this interpretation Onkelos wished to convey that the text signified that God informed Moses that "there are . . . great created beings whom man cannot apprehend as they really are. These are the separate intellects." The things that can be apprehended in their true reality are those "endowed with matter and form." I, 38, purports to give Maimonides' own explanation of one part of God's answer. According to this explanation Moses was granted the favor of apprehending "all the things created" by God. This clearly implies that as a result of God's response to Moses' request, the latter was given the capacity to know even such transcendent beings as the separate intellects.

Maimonides had no need to give in this context Onkelos' translation or to put on it an interpretation that runs counter to the explanation which is put forward as his own. This way of proceeding may possibly be accounted for by the supposition that he wished to hint that the natural limitations of the knowledge of a corporeal being made it probable that "Onkelos' interpretation" was correct and that Maimonides' own explanation was propounded for theological reasons,[65] a doctrine emphasizing the uniqueness of Moses being needed for the defense of religion.

It is significant that Moses is given a similar role in Maimonides' discussions of astronomy and celestial physics. According to the *Guide*[66] (III, 22 and 24, and elsewhere), no theory intended to explain the nature of the heavenly bodies and to account for their motions can, because of the human limitations, be regarded as certain. Moses is the only human being that may be assumed to have had this knowledge (III, 24, translation p. 327). In this context too the exception made in favor of Moses is in all probability connected with Maimonides' interpretation of Exod. 33:23 and may also be supposed to have been formulated for theological reasons.

It should be noted that as regards astronomy, Maimonides adopts a position that is different from that which is set forth in the text in which Ibn Bajja propounds his "first" theory. As stated above, the essence of the motions of the heavenly bodies is, according to this theory, the most sublime object that can be intellected by man. Maimonides, on the other hand, considers that man can have scientific knowledge (which involves intellection) only of the phenomena of the sublunar world.

At this point the analysis of Maimonides' views on the limitations of the human intellect can be summed up as follows: as in Ibn Bajja's "first theory" the human intellect can only cognize objects perceived by the senses and images deriving from sense data; in contradistinction to that theory, Maimonides is of the opinion that no scientific certainty can be achieved with regard to objects that are outside the sublunar world.

The first of these theses is of considerable importance; it provides, if taken seriously, a criterion which might permit us to distinguish in the philosophy of Maimonides[67] the conceptions that conform to this epistemology and can therefore be regarded as having been reached through the application of a critical method, from those that may be termed "metaphysical" (if the adjective is not given its medieval meaning, but is used, as in many modern writings, in a somewhat pejorative sense). Another possible designation of the conceptions set forth in the *Guide* which, according to Maimonides' epistemology, cannot be verified because they transcend the limits of human knowledge would be to describe them as forming a part of a philosophical theology.

Guide I, 68, is a case in point. The chapter begins (translation, p. 163): "You already know that the following dictum of the philosophers with reference to God . . . is generally admitted (*shuhrat hadhihi al-qawla allatī qālathā al-falāsifa fi'llāh*); the dictum being that He is the intellect as well as the intellectually cognizing subject and the intellectually cognized object (*innahu al-'aql wa'l-āqil wa'l-ma'qūl*) and that those three notions form in Him one single notion in which there is no multiplicity."

It is obvious that, if Maimonides' epistemology is accepted, man cannot possibly[68] have the knowledge of God that is presupposed in the "dictum of the philosophers." In this respect the analogy that is drawn in the chapter between God's and man's intellection does not and probably is not intended to prove anything. It may be significant that Maimonides refers to the *shuhra* (rendered in the translation as "generally admitted") of the "dictum." The Arabic word has the same root as *mashhūrāt,* a term used by Maimonides to denote notions that are generally admitted without either being self-evident indubitable truths or having been proven by rigorous reasoning.

It would thus seem that to Maimonides' mind the so-called Aristotelian philosophical doctrine would be divided into two strata: intellectually cognized notions whose truth is absolute, and which form a coherent system, namely terrestrial physics; a much more comprehensive and ambitious system, namely celestial physics and metaphysics which is concerned with the higher being. However the conceptions and propositions which make up this system cannot be cognized by the human intellect. They are in the best case merely probable. It is, however, possible, but there is no explicit Maimonidean warrant for this hypothesis, that they provide the philosophers with a system of beliefs, somewhat analogous, as far as the truth function is concerned, to the religious beliefs of lesser mortals. It is, however, significant that the thesis concerning the Deity set forth in *Guide* I, 68 is also propounded — as Maimonides quite correctly points out at the beginning of the chapter — in *Mishneh Torah.*[69] In both works, the thesis in question forms a part of a theological system, which may be believed, but cannot be proved to be true. In passages in which this critical (in the Kantian sense) attitude is expounded, Maimonides refers to his sources; he may also have had sources which he does not mention.

The authors whom he explicitly cites in support of his attitude are Aristotle and Alexander of Aphrodisias. Both these authors have occasionally given expression to their awareness of the fact that some of the theories they propound are not certain, but merely plausible, and Maimonides makes much of this. His overemphasis is tantamount to a misrepresentation of the views of these authors.[70] For our purpose it is particularly significant that in *Guide* II, 3, Maimonides makes use of the authority of Alexander in order to buttress his statement "that the opinions held by Aristotle regarding the cause of the motion of the spheres — from which

opinions he deduced the existence of separate intellects — are simple assertions for which no demonstration has been made;" they are however "of
all the opinions put forward on this subject, those that are exposed to the
smallest number of doubts and those that are the most suitable for being
put into a coherent order." This view clearly entails the consequence that
the existence of the separate intellects is merely probable and that no way
has been found to attain certainty with regard to this matter. This being
so, there is no point in setting oneself the aim to intellect or achieve a conjunction with a separate intellect.

When expounding his "critical" attitudes Maimonides does not refer
to Ibn Bajja, but it may be assumed with a certain degree of likelihood
that he was acquainted with what we have called "the first theory" of his
Spanish predecessor.

Finally there is al-Farabi's *Commentary* on the *Ethics*. There is a
quotation in *Guide* III, 18,[71] to this seminal work, whose impact has been
mentioned above. This quotation appears to refer to the moral progress
of human individuals "who have the capacity of making their soul pass
from one moral quality to another." But Maimonides was also exposed
to the influence of other opinions set forth by al-Farabi in this work.

As has been stated, al-Farabi, in this *Commentary,* denies man's ability to intellect incorporeal entities; apparently in connection with this denial, he rejects the conception according to which the human intellect may
survive death. He has nothing but contempt for the belief in the afterlife
(of the soul).

A second point which should be mentioned is that, according to evidence of Ibn Tufayl,[72] al-Farabi propounds in the *Commentary* in question the idea that the imaginative faculty, and it alone, produces prophecy
— the implication being that the intellect has no part in it — and that philosophy is superior to prophecy. It is not a matter of indifference that Maimonides encountered in a work written by al-Farabi, on whom he relied
more than on any other Arab philosopher, a conception which by and large
seems to have corresponded to what was Spinoza's conception of prophecy.
A third point that has already been mentioned, is that Ibn Bajja appears
to indicate that in the *Commentary* al-Farabi made it clear that political
(or civil, *madanī*) happiness was the only happiness that men could
achieve.[73]

What was Maimonides' position with regard to the afterlife and more
especially to the philosophical conception of the survival and permanence
of the intellect?

In the *Sefer ha-Mada'* and the *Treatise on Resurrection*[74] there are
explicit references to the afterlife, which are calculated to leave no room
for doubt as to Maimonides' acceptance of the idea. If, however, one turns

to the *Guide*, one is struck by the meagerness of the evidence found in that work concerning Maimonides' views on the point at issue.

As far as I can see, the only passage in the *Guide* which contains an apparently unambiguous affirmation of the survival of the intellect occurs at the end of III, 51 (translation, p. 628). After having described the death by a kiss of Moses, Aaron, and Miriam, Maimonides goes on:

> The other prophets and excellent men are beneath this degree; but it holds good for all of them that the apprehension of their intellects becomes stronger at the separation . . . After having reached this condition of enduring permanence that intellect remains in one and the same state, the impediment that sometimes screened him off having been removed. And he will remain permanently in that state of intense pleasure, which does not belong to the genus of bodily pleasures, as we have explained in our compilations and as others have explained before us.

In speaking of "our compilations" (*tawālīfunā*) Maimonides refers to *Mishneh Torah,* called by him in the *Guide ta'līfunā al-kabīr,* and no doubt also to other nonphilosophical works of his. The contexts in which these writings are cited in the *Guide* should be examined. It may be a tenable hypothesis that these references are at least sometimes used by Maimonides to indicate that the passages in the *Guide* in which they occur pertain to theology or a theological philosophy which is not wary of putting forward assertions that the limited human intellect is unable to verify. This hypothesis may be *inter alia* valid for the passage quoted above, as its comparison with two other passages tends to show. One of these occurs in I, 74, *Seventh Method* (translation, pp. 220–221). In order to rebut the argument of a believer in the creation of the world in time — who makes the point that if on the one hand the world were eternal and consequently "the number of men who died in the limitless past" were infinite, and, on the other hand, the souls had, as the philosophers say, a permanent existence, there would be an infinite number of souls existing simultaneously, which because of the impossibility of an actual infinite is impossible — Maimonides remarks in the first place "that this is a wondrous method, for it makes clear a hidden matter by something even more hidden . . . It is as if he already possessed a demonstration of the permanence of the souls and as if he knew in what form they last and what thing it is that lasts."

The argument is continued as follows:

> Now you know that regarding the things separate from matter — I mean those that are neither bodies, nor forces in bodies, but intellects — there can be no thought of multiplicity of any mode whatever, except that some of them are the causes of the existence of others . . .
> However, what remains of Zayd is neither the cause nor the effect of

what remains of Umar. Consequently all are one in number, as Abu Bakr Ibn al-Sa'igh (Ibn Bajja) and others who were drawn into speaking of these obscure matters have made clear. To sum up: premises by which other points are to be explained should not be taken over from such hidden matters, which the mind is incapable of representing to itself.

This passage can be interpreted in two different ways. It may be understood as expressing Maimonides' agreement with the theory of Ibn Bajja, which, according to the *Guide*, postulates the permanence and the unity after death of the human intellect; or it may be held to indicate Maimonides' view that the permanent existence of the soul or of the intellect are "hidden matters," which the mind is incapable of representing to itself. On the whole it seems to me[75] that the second interpretation is, more than the first, in line with Maimonides' argument, though as far as "philosophical theology" as defined above is concerned, he may have inclined to Ibn Bajja's opinion. The second passage with which we are concerned occurs in *Guide* I, 72, and is related to the issue of afterlife, in a circuitous way. Maimonides makes the suggestion that the relation of God to the world may be compared to that obtaining between man and the acquired intellect (*al-'aql al-mustafād*), which is separate from the organic body. He then goes on (translation, p. 193): "However, the case of the intellects of the heavens, that of the existence of separate intellects, and that of the representation of the acquired intellect, which is also separate, are matters open to speculation and research. The proofs with regard to them are well-hidden, though correct;[76] many doubts arise with regard to them; the critic may well find in them objects for his criticism and the caviller objects for his cavilling."

There is no need to discuss in connection with this passage the various theories concerning the acquired intellect. Maimonides makes it abundantly clear that the latter has a relation to, but is separate from, the corporeal human individual. It should be added that the philosophical doctrine concerning the afterlife is predicated on the existence of this and/or of the other separate intellects.

Again, as in the passage quoted before this one,[77] Maimonides inclines to accept the argumentation of the philosophers, but points out that these matters are hidden. It is, as it seems to me, on the face of it unlikely[78] that the immortality of the intellect, which in the judgment of the Maimonides of the *Guide* is an obscure and problematic matter, should be considered by him as the goal of the human individual. With regard to another moot question, the eternity of the world or its creation in time, Maimonides endeavors to prove in the *Guide* at great length, that the human reason is incapable of discovering the truth of the matter. It very clearly serves his purpose to drive this fact home. It seems to me probable that he takes a similar agnostic position with regard to the thesis of the permanence of the intellect, but prefers not to expatiate on this matter.

The discussion whether, as Aristotle affirms, the theoretical life is superior to the practical, is in the context of medieval philosophy closely connected with the question of the goal of man. It may seem at first that in this point Maimonides adopts in the *Guide* an attitude conforming to orthodox Aristotelianism; however, a closer scrutiny seems to show that his position is at least ambiguous, and this ambiguity calls for an interpretation.

In this matter, an observation on one of the roles assigned within the frame of reference of the *Guide* to al-'ilm al-ilāhī "the divine science" (the term can often be correctly rendered by "metaphysics") may serve as a starting point.

Al-'ilm al-ilāhī which appears to be a rendering of the *epistēmē theologilee* (used by Aristotle to designate the science of metaphysics) is variously defined by the Arab philosophers.[79] There is no general agreement as to the scope and objects of this discipline. Thus, for instance, some texts (*inter alia* one by al-Farabi) consider the science of being and the investigation of the principles of the particular (*juz'ī*) sciences as forming an integral part of *al-'ilm al-ilāhī*. There is a general consensus on one point: the knowledge of God and the incorporeal entities is regarded as one of the main subject matters of this divine science. According to Avicenna's *Mantiq al-Mash-riqiyyīn* it is its only subject matter, the other areas dealt with in Aristotle's *Metaphysics* being regarded as belonging to another discipline, the general science, *al-'ilm al-kulli*. This terminology partly corresponds to the one used by al-Farabi in *al-Maqāla fī Aghrād al-Hakīm fī Kull Maqāla min al-Kitāb al-Mawsūm bi'l-Hurūf*, but al-Farabi states in his treatise that *al-'ilm al-ilāhlī* forms a part of *al'ilm al-kullī*; the unity of metaphysics is thus preserved.

Given these texts and others that could be adduced, there can be no doubt that God and the immaterial beings are either the unique or one of the main objects of *al-'ilm al-ilāhī*. On the other hand, we know that, according to Maimonides, men other than Moses (whose status is determined by theological rather than philosophical considerations) cannot cognize the immaterial beings or perhaps even know for certain that they exist. And no man without exception can have positive knowledge of God. He can have negative knowledge of Him, and he can know His attributes of action, that is, he can grasp the natural phenomena and their causes. Negative knowledge, which is highly prized by Maimonides, is knowledge of what is not God. It is difficult, or rather impossible, to equate it with the traditional *'ilm ilāhī*. This is also the case with regard to the knowledge of the attributes of action. This knowledge appears to correspond at least in part to natural science.

These preliminary remarks may facilitate the understanding of the difficulty presented by a passage in *Guide* III, 51. In a parable in which God is figured as a ruler dwelling in his palace, various classes of men are differentiated according to their ability to approach the palace or to enter it.

The highest degree, that of Moses, and the second, that of the other prophets, need not concern us for the moment. The other higher degrees are those of the men who engage in science and philosophical speculation. Maimonides enumerates them in an ascending order (translation, p. 619):

> Those who have plunged into speculation concerning the fundamental principles of religion, have entered the antechambers. People there indubitably have different ranks. He, however, who has achieved demonstration, to the extent that that is possible, of everything that may be demonstrated and who has ascertained in divine matters, to the extent that that is possible, everything that may be ascertained, and who has come close to certainty in those matters in which one can only come close to it has come to be with the ruler in the inner part of the habitation.
>
> Know, my son, that as long as you are engaged in studying the mathematical sciences and the art of logic, you are one of those who walk around the house searching for its gate . . . If, however, you have understood the natural things, you have entered the habitation and are walking in the antechambers. If, however, you have achieved perfection in the natural things and have understood divine science (*al-iāhiyyāt*), you have entered in the ruler's place into the *inner court* and are with him in one habitation. This is the rank of the men of science; they, however, are of different grades of perfection.

This hierarchy of the sciences is the traditional philosophical one. It may be added that in the traditional philosophy the place of a particular science in the hierarchy corresponded, as it does in the passage of the *Guide* that has been quoted, to the degree of perfection that the cognition of the subject matter of the science in question conferred upon man. This is justified as far as Alexander of Aphrodisias' doctrine and others similar to it are concerned; for they postulate man's capacity to cognize and thereby to achieve union with immaterial entities.

In Maimonides' epistemology (which may have been formed under the influence of al-Farabi's *Commentary* on the *Ethics* and of Ibn Bajja's "first theory"[80]) this kind of intellection of the immaterial entities and of the union with them consequent upon this are impossible for man. This means that *al-'ilm al-ilāhī*, the divine science, with regard to whose object matter no certainty is possible for man, compares unfavorably (if one accepts Ibn Bajja's "first theory," as Maimonides may have done by and large) with terrestrial physics, for the subject matter of the latter enables man to intellect concepts that endure. This seems to lead to the conclusion that there is a discrepancy between the hierarchy of sciences expounded in III, 51, and Maimonides' epistemology. As has already been pointed out, there exists a conflict between the latter and the traditional philosophical commonplaces.

The final good and the ways of life man should pursue are set forth in the conclusion of the *Guide for the Perplexed* (III, 54, translation p. 638): "It is clear that the perfection of man that may be gloried in is the one acquired by him who has achieved, in a measure corresponding to his capacity, apprehension of Him . . . , and who knows His providence extending over His creatures as manifested in the act of bringing them into being and in their governance . . . the way of life of such an individual, after he has achieved this apprehension, will always have in view loving kindness, righteousness and judgment, through assimilation to His actions . . . as we have explained several times in this Treatise."

Apprehension of God may, in view of the limitations of the human mind, be equated with the knowledge of God's governance. This knowledge characterizes the men who belong to the highest class, mentioned in the parable of the palace in III, 51, the people who have the rank of prophets (translation, p. 620). The last words of the passage quoted from III, 54 refer first and foremost to I, 54.[81] The latter chapter deals with God's favorable answer (Exod. 33:19) to Moses' first request; Moses is shown God's goodness. According to the interpretation of Maimonides this means that Moses learned to know the divine attributes of action, that is, the way the world is governed. The examples of this governance given by Maimonides refer to natural phenomena, some of them assuring the preservation and the permanence of the living beings, such as the production of embryos, the development of their faculties, and the care bestowed by the progenitors upon their offspring. Because of these phenomena God is called merciful, though He is not affected by compassion. In a similar way, because of destructive phenomena such as earthquakes, violent storms, and wars bringing about the extermination of a people, He may be called jealous and vengeful without His being affected by the passions which these epithets appear to refer to.

The three qualities, loving kindness (*hesed*), judgment (*mishpat*), and righteousness (*zedakah*), that according to the conclusion of the *Guide* should be initiated by certain men, are also attributes of action. They do not imply that God in His essence is righteous, just, and full of loving kindness. This applies also to men who become similar to God (I, 54, translation, p. 126): "It behooves the governor of a city, if he is a prophet, to acquire similarity to these attributes, so that these actions may proceed from him according to a determined measure, and according to the deserts of the people who are affected by them and not merely because of his following a passion." To become similar to God in respect of the attributes of action constitutes the highest perfection of man (I, 54, p. 128): "For the utmost virtue of man is to become like unto Him, may He be exalted, as far as he is able; which means that we should make our actions like unto His."

The only positive knowledge of God of which man is capable is knowledge of the attributes of action, and this leads and ought to lead to a sort of political activity which is the highest perfection of man. The practical way of life, the *bios praktikos,* is superior to the theoretical.

It would be easy to challenge this view of the position of Maimonides; there are passages in the *Guide* which appear to disprove it. In part the internal contradiction may be laid at the door of Plato, whose political philosophy had — mainly indirectly, through the intermediary of al-Farabi — deeply influenced Maimonides. This philosophy is profoundly ambiguous (and that of al-Farabi perhaps even more so[82]). The recommendation that the philosopher, considered as the highest type of man, should return to the cave or should engage in political action, must if carried out, lead to a renouncement of the life of thought, that is, to his ceasing to be a philosopher.[83]

This chapter may *inter alia* tend to show that this contradiction need not remain unresolved. If, to use the Platonic image, man, because of the nature of his cognitive faculty is unable, or able only to a limited extent, to leave the cave, as Maimonides, probably under the influence of al-Farabi and the "first theory" of Ibn Bajja, appears to hold, the superiority of the theoretical life may appear as less than evident. Both Kant and Maimonides, the first outspokenly and the second partly by implication, have tried to show that because of the limitations of his mind man is incapable of intellecting some of the main objects of the traditional metaphysics. There may be a correlation between this fact and the tendency of both philosophers and also of al-Farabi to accord primacy to the life of action.[84]

APPENDIX

The Fourth Source of Disagreement and Error
according to the Guide *I, 31*

The following passage occurs in the *Guide* I, 31 (translation pp. 66–67):

> Alexander of Aphrodisias says that there are three causes of disagreement about things. One of them is love of domination and love of strife,

both of which turn man aside from the apprehension of the truth as it is. The second cause is the subtlety and the obscurity of the object of apprehension in itself and the difficulty of apprehending it. And the third cause is the ignorance of him who apprehends and his inability to grasp things that it is possible to apprehend. That is what Alexander mentioned. However, in our times there is a fourth cause that he did not mention because it did not exist among them. It is habit (ilf) and upbringing. For man has in his nature a love of, and an inclination for, that to which he is habituated. Thus you can see that the people of the desert — notwithstanding the disorderliness of their life, the lack of pleasures, and the scarcity of food — dislike the towns, do not hanker after their pleasures, and prefer the bad circumstances to which they are accustomed to good ones to which they are not accustomed. Their souls accordingly would find no repose in living in palaces, in wearing silk clothes, and in the enjoyment of baths, ointments, and perfumes. In a similar way, man has love for, and the wish to defend, opinions to which he is habituated, and in which he has been brought up and has a feeling of repulsion for opinions other than those. For this reason also man is blind to the apprehension of the true realities and inclines towards the things which he is habituated. This happened to the multitude with regard to the belief in His corporeality and many other metaphysical[85] subjects as we shall make clear. All this is due to people being habituated (ilf) to, and brought up on, texts that it is an established usage to think highly of and to regard as true and whose external meaning is indicative of the corporeality of God and of other imaginings with no truth in them, for these [texts] have been set forth as parables and riddles (al-muthul wa 'l-alghāz).

The definitions of causes one, two, and three are taken over by Maimonides from Alexander of Aphrodisias' treatise on *The Principles of the All*.[86] The fourth cause has apparently been added by Maimonides,[87] and it poses a problem. For it seems to indicate that Maimonides considered that "our times," that is, the times when people are brought up on, and taught to venerate, the revealed Scriptures and other religious texts, are less propitious, as far as the acquisition of true knowledge and the avoidance of errors are concerned, than the pagan times in which Alexander of Aphrodisias lived. This is difficult to reconcile with Maimonides' well-known position according to which the hints given in the Scriptures, which are full of parables and riddles help those who have the capacity to become philosophers to achieve true knowledge.

In fact the reference to the fourth cause is derived from a text of Aristotle. A comparison of this text, of Averroes' *Commentary* on the text and of another passage of Averroes with this reference may throw some light on Maimonides' method of composition and perhaps also on his intention.

The text of Aristotle (*Metaphysics,* II, 3, 995a, 2–6) may be rendered as follows: "The habitual is intelligible. The strength of habit is shown by the nomoi in which that which is mythical and childish prevails by force of habit over our knowledge of what it is."[88]

The Arabic translation of the passage quoted by Averroes in his long *Commentary* on the *Metaphysics* (ed. M. Bouyges, Beirut, 1938, I, 42–43) is on the whole accurate: "The thing which is arranged (*jarat bihi*) [in accordance] with habit, with what is familiar (*al-'āda wa'l-alfa*), and in obedience to what has been heard is more intelligible. We come to know the extent to which habits order (*jarat bihi*) things through an examination of the *nomoi* (*nawāmīs*). For you will find that the riddles (*al-alghāz*) and the things resembling idle tales (*al-khurāfāt*) that are in them have such a high [status] in the souls of the people that their true reality cannot be recognized."

It seems to me certain that the passage of the *Guide* quoted above derives directly or indirectly from this text of Aristotle. It may be noted that in the Arabic translation of the *Metaphysics* the word *alfa* occurs, while Maimonides in *Guide* I, 31 uses in a similar sense the cognate word *ilf* (habit). In both passages the word *al-alghāz*, "riddles," is employed in similar contexts. As for the meaning, the two passages treat of the strength of habit and give as an example the uncritical acceptance by men of the riddles that occur in the *nomoi* (according to Aristotle) or in religious texts (according to Maimonides).

The text of the *Metaphysics* cannot, however, be adduced in support of Maimonides'contention that in pagan times (more accurately, the Greek pagan times) people were less apt than in the monotheistic, revealed religions to adopt, because of habit and their upbringing, false notions considered by them part of their religion.

Averroes in his *Commentary* on this text of Aristotle (pp. 43–44) does not explicitly affirm this superiority of paganism over the monotheistic religions, and it is not quite certain whether he gives a hint to this effect in the following passage.

His [Aristotle's] purpose in this passage is to call attention to the things that hinder [man] from attaining the truth in the human sciences . . . The strongest of these [hindrances] is the fact of being brought up since childhood in some opinion. It is the dominant factor[89] in causing [men of] inborn intelligence[90] to turn away from the knowledge of the true realities of things, especially of those that are dealt with in this science [metaphysics]. This is because most of the opinions dealt with in this science [pertain to the religious] nomos (*namusīyya*) and have been invented for the sake of the people (*al-nās*) in order that they should seek [to acquire] virtue (*fadila*) and not in order to make truth known to them. Truth is referred to them in riddle (*alghāzan*). The reason for all this is that the existence of men (*al-nās*) can only become perfect in society (*ijtimā*); and society is only possible through virtue. The acquisition of virtues is therefore a necessary matter for all of them. This, however, is not the case with regard to the acquisition of knowledge concerning the true realities of things. [For] not everyone has the capacity for this. This [lack of capacity] is not found in respect of the opinions pertaining to the religious law (*al-ārā' al-shar'iyya*), nor in respect of the sciences which, preceding [the others] are the first to be studied by man. We may see this happen to many young men, who studied first of all, before [the other sciences] the one which is called among us the science of kalam.

The use of the adjective *shar'iyya* shows clearly that Averroes had in view the Islamic society, but he does not state in so many words that he considered that religious education was less harmful in Greek times. Indeed his words may be construed to mean that the religious upbringing whose effects he deplores is a necessary evil, as society cannot exist without it.

In another work, the *Prœmium* to the *Long Commentary* on Aristotle's *Physics*,[91] Averroes, referring to statements made by Alexander of Aphrodisias in his *Commentary* on the *Physics* with regard to the beneficial effect of the knowledge of the theoretical sciences on the moral character and conduct, remarks (pp. 451f.) that the scholars of his own (Averroes') time do not show the good qualities mentioned by Alexander. This is due to something "unnatural" (*hus min ha-teva'*) that happened to them. The text of the Hebrew translation which treats of this "unnatural" thing is partly unintelligible. The Latin translation (see p. 470, n. 8), which does not concord with the Hebrew is somewhat clearer. The general sense seems to be in part as follows.

The philosophers hold in small esteem the ideal of perfection in which they were educated, not because of the religious law, but because of the people who corrupt the law. On the other hand, they are considered by people in general to be unworthy of playing a part in the life of the city. The consequence is that in Averroes' times most of the philosophers are swayed by worldly desires and do not in fact deserve to be regarded as part of the city. S. Harvey (p. 470) considers that the remark concerning worldly desires may contain a reflection on Ibn Bajja's conduct. It may be added that the statement concerning the philosophers not participating in the life of the city seems to refer to a theory propounded by Ibn Bajja in *Tadbīr al-Mutawahhid*. According to this theory the philosophers should consider themselves strangers in the city. In contradistinction, Averroes and Maimonides endeavored to integrate philosophy into the life of the community.

This text of Averroes appears to refer to the harm caused by the prejudices of Islamic society to the moral character of the philosophers, but it does not mention the hindrance that an upbringing in a society professing a monotheistic, revealed religion constitutes to intellectual development. In the passage in *Guide* I, 31, in which Maimonides added to three causes of disagreement enumerated by Alexander a fourth one (derived from *Metaphysics* 995a, 2–4) for which habit and upbringing are responsible, this hindrance is described at some length. Maimonides may have encountered this idea in some text that is not known to us.[92] But the available evidence does not negate the possibility that in his statement concerning the fourth cause Maimonides may not have been wholly dependent on Aristotle and some commentaries (from whom the greater part of the statement may be assumed to be derived) but may have introduced some traits of his own into the passage, in which he indicates very clearly that it was easier to attain truth in Greek pagan society than it is in Jewish society, whose members are brought up in the veneration of the Scriptures.

NOTES

1. In this context it should be noted that in the *Guide of the Perplexed* Maimonides affirms that the patriarch and Moses combined unremitting intellection and contemplation with practical activity.

2. I intend to edit the text in question.

3. In a paper read in Paris in 1976 at a colloquium on Averroes, "La Philosophie dans l'Économie du Genre Humain selon Averroès: Une Réponse à al-Fārābī." It will be published in the Acts of the Colloquium.

4. Literally, "separation," The manuscript has *al-mawt al-mufārqa* I read *al-mawt wa'l-mafarāqua*. The reading *al mufāriq* is likewise possible.

5. *Baqā'* (the reading is not quite certain), "permanence, permanent existence."

6. Or "civic happiness," *al-sa'āda al-madaniyya.*

7. Another possible translation might be "on his first studying philosophical texts." The phrase might also be rendered "Abu Nasr has in effect made these remarks according to what one understands at the first reading."

8. On Ibn Bajja's views see below.

9. It is difficult to reconcile this report with a statement made by Averroes. According to the Latin translation of the *Grand Commentary* on the *De Anima* (ed. F. Stuart Crawford, Cambridge, Mass., 1953, p. 433), al-Farabi affirmed in his *Commentary* on the *Ethics* that man's final end was speculative perfection, *perfectio speculativa* (*kamāl naẓarī*). This may mean that in the *Commentary* al-Farabi adopted on this point two contradictory positions. The text of Ibn Bajja also points to a certain lack of consistency on al-Farabi's part in the *Commentary*. On the other hand, the purport of Averroes' statement may be that man cannot achieve cognition which transcends speculative knowledge; the latter, which is based

on sense data, is not the highest kind of knowledge. Ibn Bajja uses the term *nazarī* to denote the kind of knowledge possessed by the physicists.

10. Or "one."

11. *Al-mufāraqa.* The word may simply mean death.

12. Or "is served."

13. *Al-khayrāt: bona.*

14. *Al-Madaniyya.*

15. *Al-jamī*, "all, the generality."

16. In point of fact the *Ikhwān al-Safā'* refer time and again to the soul as being an entity that is separate from the body and to the destiny of souls after death. But their critics may not have taken such statements at face value.

17. Al-Farabi does not seem to have adopted throughout the *Commentary* an attitude which Ibn Bajja found inadmissible. The latter refers with approval to a statement made near the end of that text. He also states in a different context that al-Farabi's position regarding the notion of intellect in the *Risālat al-Aql* is quite different from that propounded in the *Commentary.*

18. In some extant political works of al-Farabi, notably the *Tahsīl al-Saāda,* the function of practical reason is occasionally made to appear as almost as important as that of theoretical reason. The total elimination of the latter in the system propounded in the *Commentary* on the *Ethics* could be regarded as an exaggeration, or an outspoken avowal, of this tendency.

19. Perhaps the degree of the intellectum is meant.

20. Ed. Dieterici, p. 69. In the same work, but in a different context, al-Farabi refers to the superior man in whom the active intellect resides (*halla*). This reference is made in the course of an exposition of the theory of prophetic revelation.

21. It is no more than this.

22. In the *Tahsīl al-Sa'āda* and other works.

23. Another explanation appears to be suggested by Averroes, see the appendix.

24. Ibn Tufayl, at any rate, interpreted a statement in the *Commentary* on the *Ethics* as an affirmation of the mortality of the soul. *Hayy ben Yaqdhān,* ed. L. Gauthier (Beirut, 1930), Arabic text, pp. 13–14.

25. Ibid. Ibn Tufayl mentions in this connection *al-Milla al-Fādila* and *al-Siyāsāt al-Madaniyya.* An afterlife of the soul is also part of the doctrine of *Ārā' Ahl al-Madīna al-Fādila.*

26. See S. Pines, "La *'Philosophie Orientale'* d'Avicenne et sa Polémique contre les *Bagdadiens,"* *Archives d'Histoire Doctrinale et Littéraire du Moyen Age,* 27 (1953): 18ff.

27. Ibid., esp. pp. 26–27.

28. See the Latin translation, ed. F. Stuart Crawford, p. 487.

29. And, of course, the Ishrāqī thinkers of Iran.

30. See note 3.

31. In all probability at least three. The doctrine of his *R. al-Wadā'* seems to be somewhat different from that of *R. al-Ittisāl.*

32. Or "force," *quwwa.*

33. Māhiyyāt.

34. This in contradistinction to the theologico-political section treating of the virtuous city.

35. See A. Altmann, "Ibn Bajja on Man's Ultimate Felicity," in *Studies in Religious Philosophy and Mysticism* (London, 1969), pp. 73–106.

36. One of four treatises published in the supplement to A. F. Ahwani's edition of Averroes' *Talkhīs Kitāb al Nafs* (Cairo 1950), pp. 103–118. A subtitle amplifies the title; the topic of the treatise is described as being *ittisāl al-'aql bi' l-insān,* the conjunction of the intellect with man.

37. Or "science," *'ilm.*

38. And to the strictures on the theory found in Aristotle's *Metaphysics.*

39. This inconsistency may possibly be accounted for by the fact that the passages do not appear to treat of the highest "degree" posited by Ibn Bajja, see below.

40. *Al-nuzzār al-tabī'iyyūn,* literally, "the natural theoreticians."

41. The substrata.

42. Literally, "carried, borne" (*mahmūl*).

43. Literally, "the instrument," *adāt.*

44. *Jihāt,* literally, "sides."

45. *Mutalāzima talāzum al-takāfu'.* More or less literally concomitant in a concomitance of equivalence (or equality).

46. Literally, "this theoretical degree."

47. Literally, "appears."

48. *Al-shakhs*; more or less literally, "person," *atomon.*

49. *Al-shay' bi-nafsihi,* the *Ding an sich.*

50. Or theoreticians, *al-nazariyyūn.*

51. Being all of them pure intellect.

52. Ibn Bajja (pp. 114–115) points out that in Plato's theory the forms (*suwar,* the ideas) are called by the name of the things of which they are the form; one and the same definition applies both to the thing and to its form. This is the reason for the absurdities of this theory as set forth in Aristotle's *Metaphysics.* Ibn Bajja eliminates this weakness of Plato's theory by affirming the existence of a third term. He differentiates between the perceived things, forms, and the meanings (ma 'ānī) of the forms. For the third category he also uses the term *ma 'qūl* (intellectum, or object of intellection).

53. See Alexander, *De Anima,* ed. I. Bruns (Berlin, 1887), p. 90.

54. What follows is not spelled out in every particular in the relevant quotation.

55. The relation between the doctrine of Ibn Bajja and that of Gersonides relating to the human intellect will be discussed elsewhere. There is an essential resemblance, but Gersonides elaborated the doctrine in a way that is different from that of Ibn Bajja, if we may go by the evidence of the texts that have been studied.

56. Deut. 5:28. The reference is to Moses.

57. Num. 11:25.

58. Psalms 82:5.

59. Ed. J. Forget (Leiden, 1892), pp. 202–203.

60. '*Ārif* may in the last analysis be a rendering of the term *gnōstikos,* used by early Christian theologians, for instance, Clement of Alexandria, to designate a high spiritual degree. The same Greek term is used to denote the Gnostics, but in their case the connotations are somewhat different.

61. Heschel's hypothesis according to which he might have done so is most unlikely.

62. An interesting discussion of this and related problems in Maimonides' doctrine occurs in W. Harvey, *Hasdai Crescas' Critique of the Theory of the Acquired Intellect,* Columbia University, Ph. D. dissertation, 1973 (University Microfilms, Ann Arbor, Mich., 1974) pp. 40ff., 54ff.

63. In an article entitled "Shī'ite Terms and Notions in the Kuzari" (in *Jerusalem Studies in Arabic and Islam,* II), app. 6, I have attempted to show that some indications point to Maimonides' borrowing one trait of his negative theology from Ismā 'īlī theologians, who professed the doctrine of the unknowability of God *per se* in a very extreme form.

64. The following passage occurs in the *Guide* I, 1: "Man possesses as his proprium something in him that is very strange as it is not found in anything else that exists under the sphere of the moon, namely intellectual apprehension. In the exercise of this, no sense, no part of the body, none of the extremities are used, and therefore this apprehension was likened unto the apprehension of the Deity, which does not require an instrument, although in reality it is not like the latter apprehension, but only appears so to the first stirrings of opinion. It was because of this something, I mean because of the divine intellect (*al-'aql al-ilāhī*) conjoined (*al-muttasil*) with man, that it is said of the latter that he is *in the image of* God and in His likeness." The fact that Maimonides uses in I, 1, the term *al-'aql al-ilāhī* rather than *al-'aql al-fa''āl* tends to show that in this commentary on a biblical verse he is interested in the refutation of speculations concerning the corporeality of God rather than in philosophical epistemology. *Al-'aql al-ilāhī* has no exact philosophical connotation. The meaning of the word *muttasil* in this passage may be clarified by referring to a passage of Avicenna's *De Anima* being the psychological part of *Kitāb al-Shifā',* ed. F. Rahman (Oxford, 1959), p. 247. "While the human soul (a soul that belongs to a) common [man, *al-āmmiya,* apparently a man that is not a prophet] is in a body, it is impossible for it to receive [unto itself] the Active Intellect all at once. . . . If it is said that a certain person knows intelligibles, this means that wherever he wishes, he makes their form present to the perception [*dhihn,* the word in this context is untranslatable] of his soul. The meaning of this is that whenever he wishes he can be conjoined (*yattasil*) with the active intellect in a conjunction in which he (received from the Active Intellect) a representation of the intelligible in question without this intelligible present in his perception (*dhihn*) and represented *in actu* in his intellect all the time . . . This is [different] from what was [the case] prior to his having learnt [to know the intelligible, p. 246]. When he is freed from the body and the accidents of the body, it may be possible for him to be conjoined with the Active Intellect in a complete conjunction." This passage makes it clear that in Avicennian terminology, at least, *muttasil, ittisāl,* with the active intellect need not refer to conjunction in the sense of

total union. The terms may be applied to a man's intellecting one intelligible. As far as the use of the terms is concerned, it does not seem to matter whether the intelligible was or was not intellected in the first place through an act of abstraction applied to a sense datum or an image. In *Guide* I, 1, Maimonides possibly used *muttasil* in the Avicennian sense. If this is so, the passage could conform to the first theory of Ibn Bajja.

65. "Kalāmic" reasons would have been preferable if the term *Kalām* in the sense given it by al-Farabi in *Ihsā' al-'Ulūm* were sufficiently known. The objective of the science of Kalam, as described by al-Farabi, is to protect religion against all forms of attack.

66. Cf. my Introduction to the translation.

67. And of other philosophical authors (Gersonides may be one of them), who by and large accept a similar thesis (even if it is not quite identical).

68. If God is not conceived as a corporeal substance, a hypothesis which would of course be in flagrant contradiction to the doctrine of Maimonides. It may however be noted that some remarks occurring in the *Guide* may engender the suspicion – which is invalidated by other passages of that work – that the God of Maimonides has an intimate connection with the cosmos, that in fact he may be conceived if we use Spinozistic terms, as an idea whose *ideatum* is the world. It is of course difficult or impossible to reconcile a conception of this sort with Maimonides' epistemology, but it could form a part of his philosophical theology as well as of the doctrines of other medieval Jewish and Arabic philosophers.

69. *Sefer ha-Mada*, *Yesode ha-Torah*, II, 9.

70. Maimonides references in the *Guide* to Aristotle and Alexander of Aphrodisias are dealt with at some length in my Introduction to the translation of that work, see pp. lxi–lxxiv.

71. Cf. my Introduction to the translation (pp. lxxix f.).

72. Ed. L. Gauthier, p. 14, of the Arabic text. Speaking of al-Farabi's *Commentary on the Ethic*, Ibn Tufayl refers to "That which he made clear with regard to his reprehensible belief concerning prophecy: it pertains exclusively, as (al-Farabi) thinks, to the imaginative faculty, and he considers that philosophy is superior to it" *mā sarraha bihi min su'i mu 'taqadihi fi 'l nubuwwa wa- 'annaha li'l quwwa al-khayāliyya khāssa bi-za'mihi wa-tafdīlihi al-falsafa 'alayhā*.

73. *In my introduction to the translation of the Guide* (p. lxxx) I state that Ibn Bajja defends al-Farabi against the charge that in his *Commentary* he professes the opinion that there is no afterlife, that there is no happiness except political happiness, and so forth. This is correct as far as Ibn Bajja's wording is concerned. But it can be clearly understood from the text that Ibn Bajja's defense consists in playing down and explaining away the incriminating statements of al-Farabi. He does not deny that the statements in question occurred in the *Commentary*.

In the paper referred to in note 3, I put forward the hypothesis that al-Farabi's view according to which political happiness is the only one which men can achieve might have influenced Marsilius of Padua. A Latin translation of al-Farabi's *Commentary* on the *Ethics* is known to have existed; it was still existant at the time when in the twenties of the fourteenth century Marsilius wrote his magnum opus entitled *Defensor Pacis* (finished in 1324). The passage to which I refer occurs in this treatise in Diccio I, Cap. 1, 7 (ed. W. Kunzmann and H. Kusch, p. 24):

> Possent securius studiosi principantes et subditi tranquille vivere quod est desiderabile propositum in huius operis inicio, necessarium debentibus civili felicitate frui, que in hoc seculo possibilium homini desideratorum optimum videtur et ultimum actuum humanorum.
>
> [That virtuous rulers and subjects may live more securely in tranquility is the desirable outcome I propose at the beginning of this work, an outcome necessary for those who would enjoy civil happiness; moreover, this outcome seems to be the best of the objects of desire possible to man in this world and the ultimate aim of human acts — editor's translation.]

74. Cf. also the 13 principles of religion in Maimonides' *Commentary* on the *Mishnah,* Introduction to *Perek Helek.*

75. I held a different opinion at the time when I prepared the translation. See p. 221, n. 11.

76. Or "The proof with regard to them, even if they are correct, are well hidden."

77. But which precedes it in the *Guide.*

78. The contrary opinion is put forward by W. Harvey in the work quoted above.

79. See S. Pines, "Abstracta Islamica," 6th series, *Revue des Etudes Islamiques* (1938), pp. A51–A53. According to the *Rasā'il Ikhwān al-Safā',* an encyclopedia which did not achieve philosophical respectability, the science of politics also pertains to *al-ʿilm al-ilāhī.*

80. And also rather paradoxically under the influence of Alexander's *Principles of the All.*

81. Possibly Maimonides has deliberately seen to it that both chapters should have the number 54.

82. An exact analysis of al-Farabi's *Tahsīl al-Saʿāda* might show an internal contradiction similar to that which is encountered in the *Guide.* A conception which may point to the influence of the *Tahsīl al-Saʿāda* on the *Guide* is set forth on p. 44 (Hyderabad edition) of this treatise by al-Farabi. This philosopher asserts there that the lawgiver who is the true philosopher has a knowledge that achieves certainty of matters about which the great mass of people have only imaginings and (conceptions due to the influence of) persuasive arguments, *iqnāʾ* (and which thus fall short of certainty). The lawgiver invents these imaginings and conceptions and causes others to entertain them, but they have no place in his own soul. This may be compared with *Guide* II, 36 (translation, p. 373). Maimonides speaking of Moses states there that "the imaginative faculty did not enter into his prophecy."

83. Some observations made by A. Kojève in a debate with Leo Strauss are relevant in this connection. Cf. Leo Strauss, *On Tyranny: A Study of Xenophon's Hiero,* Alexander Kojève's critique of that study (Glencoe, 1963), pp. 159ff. Kojève poses the problem in terms of what he calls the "Epicurean" conception of philosophy. This conception is applicable to some extent at least to Plato's

and Aristotle's philosophy. Kojève's Hegelian answers need not concern us in this context.

84. Employed by Ibn Bajja (see above). It should be stated, however, that the political activity which Maimonides considers as superior to every other way of life has very little or nothing in common with the accomplishment of the moral law which Kant regards as man's principal task. Nor does it consist in — though it may not be incompatible with — the observance of the religious commandments. It should also be noted that the text of the *Guide* gives no prima facie warrant for the view that Maimonides considered — as al-Farabi is supposed to have done — that political happiness is the only one of which man is capable.

The primacy given to the life of action contradicts Aristotle's view, but the epistemology which legitimates this position by demarcating the limits of human knowledge derives probably indirectly in the last analysis, as far as Maimonides is concerned, from certain traits of the Aristotelian doctrine. This may also be partly true in a more complicated way with regard to Kant's epistemology. The relation between the views expressed in al-Farabi's *Commentary* on the *Ethics* and Ibn Bajja's first doctrine, both of which may be supposed to have influenced Maimonides, and the epistemology of Gersonides will be examined elsewhere. The possibility that Judah ha-Levi's and Crescas' critique of the philosophical doctrine concerning the human intellect may owe something to al-Farabi's *Commentary* on the *Ethics* will also be investigated. Ibn Khaldūn's "refutation of philosophy" found in his *al-Muqaddima,* may have also been directly or indirectly influenced by this commentary. See M. Quatremère's, edition of *al-Muqaddima,* III, 215, II. 9–12 (F. Rosenthal's translation, III, 252).

85. Or "divine," *ilāhiyya.*

86. See my translation of the *Guide*, p. 66, note 7, and the translator's introduction, pp. lxvii f.

87. See the translator's introduction.

88. The last part of the passage reads in Greek: *hoi nomoi dēlousin, en hois ta mythōdē kai peidariōdē meizon iskhyei tou ginōskein peri autōn dia to ethos.*

89. Literally, "thing."

90. Literally, "intelligent inborn dispositions."

91. A critical edition of the Hebrew translation of this *Proœmium,* an English rendering, and a reference to the Latin translation of the *Proœmium* are found in Steven Harvey's Ph.D. dissertation "Averroes on the Principles of Nature: The Middle Commentary on Aristotle's Physics, I–II" (Harvard University, 1977), appendix 6, pp. 439–471.

92. Averroes' *Commentary* on the *Metaphysics* was not the only Arabic one. Yaḥyā b. 'Adī's commentary on book 2 of that work is still extant. A reference to it may be found in the contribution made by S. Pines and M. Schwartz to a volume in commemoration of Baneth, which will soon be published in Jerusalem.

Maimonides' Proofs for the Existence of God

WILLIAM LANE CRAIG

By far and away the most significant Jewish philosopher of the Middle Ages is Moses ben Maimon (1135–1204), or Maimonides, affectionately referred to by the Latin scholastics as Rabbi Moses. With Maimonides we reach "the high water mark of medieval Jewish philosophy."[1] He argues the case for God's existence from the standpoint of the philosophers, not the *mutakallimūn,* and he eschews the *kalām* arguments for creation.[2] In the light of Leo Strauss' insistence that the *Guide* is "under no circumstances a philosophic book,"[3] it might be questioned whether our categorizing Maimonides as a representative of the philosophical tradition of theistic argumentation is quite accurate. But while it is true that Maimonides, like the Christian scholastics after him, was really at heart a theologian, his proofs for the existence of God grow exclusively out of the philosophic tradition, not out of *kalām,* and, hence, he may be classed as a philosopher in this sense. Moreover, even Strauss himself points out that

> Maimonides insists on the necessity of starting from evident presuppositions, which are in accordance with the nature of things, whereas the *kalâm* proper starts from arbitrary presuppositions, which are chosen not because they are true but because they make it easy to prove the beliefs taught by the law.[4]

We observed in the preceding chapter that one of the earmarks of philosophy as opposed to *kalām* was that it did not use religious doctrinal positions for its point of departure. In proving God's existence, Maimonides strictly follows this procedure, for he lays down twenty-six proposi-

From William Lane Craig, *The Cosmological Argument from Plato to Leibniz* (London: The Macmillan Press, 1980), pp. 131–157. Reprinted by permission of Macmillan, London and Basingstoke, London, and of Barnes & Noble Books, Totowa, N.J.

tions proven by the philosophers as foundational to his arguments.[5] Thus, in proving the existence of God, Maimonides proceeds as a philosopher.

He opens his proofs for the existence of God by positing twenty-six propositions.[6] These principles have been "fully established," and their correctness is "beyond doubt," states Maimonides, since "Aristotle and the Peripatetics who followed him have proved each of these propositions."[7] But the twenty-sixth proposition, the one which posits the eternity of the universe, Maimonides does not accept, but will admit for the sake of argument.[8]

Maimonides then introduces his first argument, the proof from motion. Too lengthy to quote verbatim, we may summarize the proof in this way: There must be a cause of the change in the transient sublunary world. This cause is itself caused by another. The series of moving causes cannot be infinite; it must ultimately derive from the heavenly sphere which causes all motion by its rotary locomotion. There must be a cause of the motion of this sphere, either within the sphere or without it. If the cause is without the sphere, it is either corporeal or incorporeal. If it is incorporeal, it is not properly 'without' the sphere, but 'separate' from the sphere. If the cause is within the sphere, it may be extended throughout it and be divisible, or it may be indivisible. Thus, we have four alternatives: the motion of the sphere may be caused by (1) a corporeal object without the sphere, (2) an incorporeal object separate from the sphere, (3) an internal force extended throughout the whole sphere, or (4) an indivisible force within the sphere. The first alternative is impossible because this cause would require another cause and so on, *ad infinitum*. But this would involve an infinite number of spheres, which is impossible. The third alternative is impossible because the sphere, being corporeal, must be finite. Therefore, the force it contains must be finite, and a finite force cannot cause eternal motion. The fourth alternative is impossible because then the soul of the sphere would be moved accidentally, and a thing moved accidentally must come to rest. Thus, it could not cause eternal motion. This means only the second alternative can be affirmed; Maimonides proclaims triumphantly, "This Prime Motor of the sphere is God, praised be His name!"[9] The reader will recognize the Aristotelian origin of the proof. According to Husik, the proof from motion was first introduced into Jewish philosophy by Abraham ibn Daud (d. 1180?), and Maimonides' version differs from that of his Jewish predecessor primarily in being more elaborate.[10] But Maimonides' thoughtful formulation of the argument historically marks him as the third great champion of the proof for God from motion; for, amazing as it may seem, during the nearly fourteen long centuries separating Maimonides and Aristotle, no truly great proponent of the prime mover argument except ibn Rushd ever arose.[11] Neoplatonic arguments for the One were much more in vogue, and the nearly millennium and a half between the Greek and Jewish philosophers saw only incidental use of the proof from motion. It must seem no less astounding to moderns to find Maimonides confidently expounding the same astronomical system of spheres as that propounded by Aristotle in the fourth century B.C. But this is testimony both to the overpowering influence of Aristotle's intellect and to the sluggish progress of a world lacking the scientific method of experimentation.

We may outline Maimonides' proof as follows:

1. There must be a cause for the motion or change of transient things in the sublunary world because:
   a. prop. 25.
2. There must be a cause of the motion of the cause.
3. This causal series of motions cannot be infinite and will cease at the first heavenly sphere, which is the source of all sublunary motion, because:
   a. prop. 3.
4. There must be a cause for the motion of this sphere because:
   a. prop. 17.
5. This cause may reside without the sphere or within it.
6. If it resides without the sphere it may be corporeal or incorporeal (in which case it is really separate from, not without, the sphere).
7. If it resides within the sphere, it may be extended throughout the sphere and be divisible, or it may be an indivisible force.
8. Therefore, the cause for the motion of this sphere must be either a corporeal object without the sphere, an incorporeal object separate from the sphere, a divisible force extended throughout the sphere, or an indivisible force within the sphere.
9. It cannot be a corporeal object without the sphere because:
   a. a corporeal object is itself moved when it sets another object in motion,
   b. and this corporeal object would need another corporeal object to set it in motion, and so on, *ad infinitum;*
   c. but this is impossible
      i. because of prop. 2.
10. It cannot be a divisible force extended through the sphere because:
    a. the sphere is finite
       i. because of prop. 1,
    b. and therefore the force it contains must be finite
       i. because of prop. 12;
    c. but a finite force cannot produce an eternal motion.

11. It cannot be an indivisible force within the sphere because:
    a. as the sphere moves, the force would be moved accidentally
       i. because of prop. 6,
    b. and things that move accidentally must come to rest
       i. because of prop. 8;
    c. therefore, it could not cause eternal motion.
12. Therefore, the cause for the motion of this sphere must be an incorporeal object separate from the sphere, or God.

Let us briefly analyze the proof step by step. First, *there must be a cause for the motion or change of transient things in the sublunary world.* Like Aristotle, Maimonides selects as his point of departure an empirically observable facet of experience, namely change. This marks the *a posteriori* character of the proof. The support for the first step is the twenty-fifth proposition, which is the Aristotelian analysis of change in terms of matter and form. Whenever change occurs, it is because the primary matter has been imbued with a new form. The proposition asserts that every such change requires a cause which moves the matter to receive the form. The analysis here ultimately reduces to Aristotle's actuality/potentiality distinction, for the form is the actuality that causes the pure potentiality of matter to be a certain thing. Being purely potential, matter cannot actualize itself; therefore, there must be some cause. Hence, there must be a cause for the motion or change of transient things in the sublunary world.

Second, *there must be a cause of the motion of this cause.* Maimonides assumes that the cause of motion in step 1 is itself in motion. For if it were an unmoved mover, his point would be proved. Therefore, he takes it to be in motion just like its effect. He adds that the motion of this cause will be either the same as the kind it causes or different, but he does not develop the point. Aristotle, it will be remembered, had argued that the kinds of motion are finite in number, and therefore there could not be infinite movers. But Maimonides has no need of this argument and lets it lie. Unlike Aristotle, Maimonides also includes substantial change, or generation and corruption, as a kind of motion right from the start of his proof. The same analysis of actuality and potentiality that required a cause of the motion in step 1 also requires that there must be a cause of the motion of this cause.

Step 3 asserts that *this causal series of motions cannot be infinite and will cease at the first heavenly sphere, which is the source of all sublunary motion.* Maimonides supports the step by use of proposition 3, that an infinite number of causes and effects is impossible, this being so because any infinite magnitude cannot actually exist (propositions 1 and 2). Now this is extremely interesting because it marks a sharp departure from the Aristotelian argument from motion. It will be remembered that Aristotle's *tour de force* against the infinite regress is that in a hierarchically arranged series of simultaneous causes of motion, the intermediate causes have no causal efficacy of their own, being mere instruments, and, thus, a first cause must exist to produce the given effect. Maimonides completely abandons this line of reasoning: he makes no mention of the impossibility of a so-called essential series of causes, arguing instead that an infinite number of actual existents cannot exist. He believed that an infinite series of causes and effects could exist extending back into the past, for it was his opinion that the eternity of the world is philosophically possible, even if not plausible. But in that case, the infinite number of entities do not co-exist, for they appear successively; it is the co-existence of an infinite number of finite things that is impossible. In arguing against an infinite series of causes of motion, Maimonides thus makes it evident that he, like Aristotle, is thinking of simultaneous causes of motion, for these all co-exist. The causes of motion cannot be infinite, not because of any analysis of the nature of essential causality, but because an actual infinite cannot exist. This step of the proof also brings into full view the Aristotelian system of the spheres. Maimonides asserts that the causes of sublunary motion can only go so far until they reach the motion of the fifth element, by which he apparently means the ether of which the spheres are composed in contrast to the four elements of the sublunary world, earth, water, air, and fire. The spheres are the source of all motion on earth, according to Maimonides, and he furnishes an exceedingly instructive example:

> The motion of the fifth element is the source of every force that moves and prepares any substance on earth for its combination with a certain form, and is connected with that force by a chain of intermediate motions. The celestial sphere [or the fifth element] performs the act of locomotion which is the first of the several kinds of motion (Prop. XIV), and all locomotion is found to be the indirect effect of the motion of this sphere; e.g., a stone is set in motion by a stick, the stick by a man's hand, the hand by the sinews, the sinews by the muscles, the muscles by the nerves, the nerves by the natural heat of the body, and the heat of the body by its form. This is undoubtedly the immediate motive cause, but the action of the immediate motive cause is due to a certain design, e.g., to bring the stone into a hole by striking against it with a stick in order to prevent the draught from coming through the crevice. The motion of the air that causes the draught is the effect of the motion of the celestial sphere. Similarly it may be shown that the ultimate cause of all generation and destruction can be traced to the motion of the sphere.[12]

One of the key moves in the prime mover argument is to get away from sublunary motion to astronomical motion. Otherwise, the human soul takes on the character of an unmoved mover. Here again Maimonides leaves Aristotle, referring to the Greek philosopher's argument in the passing mention of generation and destruction as ultimately assignable to the sphere. Maimonides instead argues that the soul (which is the form of the body) does indeed have a cause for its causal activity. The causes of the soul's activity are its motives, and its motives are determined by external factors. Thus, Maimonides moves from the world into the soul and back into the world again, which allows him to move up to the heavenly sphere as the cause of certain environmental factors. What is so interesting about this is that Maimonides seems to have unwittingly involved himself in total determinism for, as his example illustrates so clearly, even the 'free' acts of man are determined by purely physical factors. If he denies this, then every human soul may be an unmoved mover. For even if the soul causes certain effects because of determining external influences, it is nonetheless *unmoved.* We might say it is moved to action by some cause, but that is an equivocal use of the word 'moved', meaning 'motivated', for the soul does not move *per se.*[13] In what sense, then, does Maimonides contend that the sphere is the source of all sublunary motion, when clearly the soul is the unmoved source of at least some motion? The answer is that the sphere is the source of all sublunary motion in that it causes the external factors that determine the purposes of the soul. Thus, even the motion caused by the soul is ultimately caused by the sphere. Therefore, what Maimonides is really about is the demonstration of cosmic determinism. His argument is not a simple proof from motion, that z is moved by y, and y by x, and so on, back to a. This sort of chain is broken when one reaches the soul, for it is not moved at all. But Maimonides wants to show that when the soul causes motion, it does so because of the factors determined by the motion of the sphere.

The fourth step asserts that *there must be a cause for the motion of this sphere.* Maimonides cites proposition 17 as the basis of this step. The root analysis is the same as that found in step 1, the Aristotelian distinction of actuality and potentiality. Step 5 asserts a disjunction: *this cause may reside without the sphere or within it.* Step 6 posits a further disjunction within the first disjunct above: *if it resides without the sphere, it may be corporeal or incorporeal (in which case it is really separate from, not without, the sphere).* Step 7 posits a disjunction within the second disjunct of step 5: *if it resides within the sphere, it may be extended throughout the sphere and be divisible, or it may be an indivisible force.* The disjunction is based on proposition 11, which asserts that things existing through a material object may be extended and divisible (like color or heat) or it may be indivisible (like the intellect or soul). This means that there exist four alternatives: *the cause for the motion of this sphere must be either a corporeal object without the sphere, an incorporeal object separate from the sphere, a divisible force extended throughout the sphere, or an indivisible force within the sphere.* Maimonides now proceeds to eliminate three of the alternatives.

He argues in the ninth step that *it cannot be a corporeal object without the sphere.* Proposition 9 requires that when one corporeal object moves another, it can do so only by setting itself in motion. That means that if the sphere were set spinning by another enclosing sphere, this latter would also have to be revolving. But then it would require some cause of its motion as well. Thus, the initial problem is only encountered again at a later step. Because of the impossibility of an infinite number of actual existents, there cannot be an infinite number of spheres. Maimonides makes no reference to the Aristotelian argument against an infinite series in this step any more than he did in step 3. The argument here does not prove that there is only one heavenly sphere directly moved by God; Maimonides would have to admit that this sphere could be moved immediately by a corporeal object without the sphere, that is, another sphere, but he insists that this only delays the problem and cannot settle it.[14] Because no actual infinite can exist, the motion of the sphere cannot ultimately be caused by another sphere—there must be an outermost sphere not moved by another. Therefore, the cause of the motion of the sphere cannot be a corporeal object without the sphere.

Maimonides skips down to the third alternative and argues that *it cannot be a divisible force extended throughout the sphere.* The sphere being corporeal, it must also be finite, since proposition 1 declares that no actual infinite can exist. Since the sphere is finite, the force it contains must also be finite, for, according to proposition 12, a force that occupies all parts of a corporeal object is finite. And according to this alternative, the force does occupy all parts of the sphere, being extended throughout. No doubt Maimonides is reasoning that if each part contains a determinate quantum of force, then a finite number of parts will produce a finite quantum of force. But a finite force cannot produce an infinite, eternal motion, such as was assumed according to proposition 26. The argument harks back to Philoponus's proofs of the temporality of the universe, as we saw in the last chapter, and ultimately to Aristotle himself. It assumes that a finite force cannot do a finite amount of work for an infinite time. For these reasons, the cause of the sphere's motion cannot be a divisible force extended throughout the sphere.

Maimonides in step 11 dismisses the fourth alternative: *it cannot be an indivisible force within the sphere.* In other words, the sphere is not a self-mover moved by its own soul. Here Maimonides does employ the Aristotelian argument concerning the soul's accidental motion, but he does so with a twist. As the sphere turns, its soul would be moved accidentally, according to proposition 6. Maimonides illustrates accidental motion by the example of a nail in a boat; the nail itself is firmly fixed, but as the boat moves, so does the nail. A more modern example might be that of a stationary man standing in a lift; though he himself does not move, as the lift moves to the top floor, the man moves in a secondary or accidental sense. So also when a body/soul composite moves about, the body moves essentially, but the soul only accidentally.[15] Therefore, the soul of the sphere would be moved accidentally by the sphere's rotation. But according to proposition 8, things moved accidentally must come to rest. This is so because a thing moved accidentally "does not move of its own accord;"[16] for example, the soul moves only because of the body's motion. But since the soul causes the body's motion, could not the soul cause the body to move eternally, and so itself be moved accidentally forever? Here again, Maimonides' determinism comes to the fore; this is impossible, he contends, for the soul only moves the body at the instigation of external causes, and, according to this alternative, there are no external causes superior to the soul of the sphere.[17] Since there are no eternal entities other than the sphere, there would be nothing to move the sphere from eternity. The reasoning is reminiscent of Aristotle's unmoved mover, which eternally moves the spheres by acting as the eternal object of desire for their respective souls. If the sphere were moved by its soul, then either there must be some more ultimate cause of its motion in terms of external determining factors existent from eternity, or it would come to rest. In either case, the sphere does not ultimately cause its own motion. Thus, the cause of the sphere's motion cannot be an indivisible force within the sphere.

The conclusion is that alternative two must be affirmed and that *therefore, the cause for the motion of this sphere must be an incorporeal object separate from the sphere, or God.* There must exist a source of all motion which is incorporeal, separate from the material universe, unmoved either essentially and accidentally, and eternal. This, proclaims Maimonides, is God.

We may schematize Maimonides' first proof as follows:

1. There must be a cause for the motion of things in the sublunary world.
2. This causal series of motion cannot be infinite and will cease at the first heavenly sphere, which is the source of all sublunary motion.
   a. It cannot be infinite.
      i. In a series of the causes of motion, all the causes exist simultaneously.

      ii. An infinite number of things cannot actually exist.

      iii. Therefore, the number of causes and effects must be finite.

   b. It will cease at the first heavenly sphere.

      i. Things in motion are either moved by another or self-moved.

      ii. Things moved by another are ultimately moved by the sphere.

         a. Things moved by another ultimately derive their motion from environmental factors determined by the sphere.

      iii. Things self-moved are ultimately moved by the sphere.

         a. Self-movers move only at the stimulus of external factors.

         b. These factors are determined by the sphere.

         c. Thus, self-movers ultimately are caused to move by the sphere.

      iv. Therefore, all sublunary motion is ultimately caused by the sphere.

3. There must be a cause for the motion of this sphere.

4. This cause may be either a corporeal object without the sphere, an incorporeal object separate from the sphere, a divisible force extended throughout the sphere, or an indivisible force within the sphere.

5. It cannot be a corporeal object without the sphere.

   a. A corporeal object is itself moved when it sets another object in motion.

   b. This corporeal object must have another corporeal object as a cause of its motion, and so on.

   c. This causal series cannot be infinite (2.a.).

   d. Therefore, a corporeal object without the sphere cannot be the ultimate cause of motion of the sphere.

6. It cannot be a divisible force extended throughout the sphere.

   a. The sphere must be finite.

      i. For no actual infinite can exist.

   b. Therefore, the force it contains must be finite.

   c. And a finite force cannot cause eternal motion.

   d. But motion is eternal, according to the hypothesis.

   e. Therefore, a divisible force extended throughout the sphere cannot be the ultimate cause of the motion of the sphere.

7. It cannot be an indivisible force within the sphere.

   a. As the sphere moves, the soul of the sphere would move accidentally.

    b. Things that move accidentally must come to rest.
        i. They do not move of their own accord, but are caused to move by the stimulus of external factors.
        ii. But no external factors are eternal.
        iii. Therefore, things moved accidentally cannot be in motion forever.
    c. Therefore, the soul of the sphere could not cause eternal motion.
    d. But motion is eternal, according to the hypothesis.
    e. Therefore, an indivisible force within the sphere cannot be the ultimate cause of the motion of the sphere.
  8. Therefore, the cause for the motion of the sphere must be an incorporeal object separate from the sphere, or God.

What can be known of the nature of God? Maimonides has already in the proof itself called attention to God's incorporeality, separateness, utter immobility, and eternity. In addition to that, he argues, God must be indivisible and unchangeable. For according to proposition 7, whatever moves is divisible, and since God cannot move, he must be indivisible. And according to proposition 5, motion implies actuality and potentiality; God, not being able to move, must not possess any potentiality to change. Moreover, there is only one God, for, according to proposition 16, incorporeal beings cannot be counted. Finally, God transcends time because, according to proposition 15, things which do not move have no relation to time, as time cannot exist apart from motion. Thus, from the prime mover argument alone, Maimonides seeks to establish a God characterized by some of the traditional theistic attributes.

Maimonides' second argument, a more simple argument from motion, he ascribes to Aristotle:

> If there be a thing composed of two elements, and the one of them is known to exist also by itself, apart from that thing, then the other element is likewise found in existence by itself separate from that compound. For if the nature of the two elements were such that they could only exist together—as, e.g., matter and form—then neither of them could in any way exist separate from the other. The fact that the one component is found also in a separate existence proves that the two elements are not indissolubly connected and that the same must therefore be the case with the other component. Thus we infer from the existence of honey-vinegar and of honey by itself, that there exists also vinegar by itself. And after having explained this Proposition Aristotle continues thus: We notice many objects consisting of a *motor* and a *motum,* i.e., objects which set other things in motion, and whilst doing so are themselves set in motion by other things; such is clearly the case as regards all the middle members of a series of things in motion. We also

see a thing that is moved, but does not itself move anything, viz., the last member of the series; consequently a *motor* must exist without being at the same time a *motum*, and that is the Prime Motor, which, not being subject to motion, is indivisible, incorporeal, and independent of time, as has been shown in the preceding argument.[18]

The argument may be outlined as follows:

1. Given a thing composed of two elements, if one of the elements exists separately, then the other element does so as well because:
   a. the separate existence of one element proves that the two elements are not so indissolubly united that they cannot exist separately.
2. We see in experience objects that are in motion and move others and objects that are in motion but do not move others.
3. Therefore, there must be something that moves other things but is not itself in motion.
4. This is the Prime Mover, or God.

The argument is straightforward enough. Step 1 tells us that *given a thing composed of two elements, if one of the elements exists separately, then the other element does so as well.* Maimonides recognizes that not all composites are capable of being divided. Primary matter, for example, cannot exist alone, but only in conjunction with form. But, he argues, when we see one of the two elements existing alone and that same element existing in combination with another, it is a valid inference that when this element is extracted from the composite, the other element will continue to exist.

Step 2 continues: *we see in experience objects that are in motion and move others and objects that are in motion but do not move others.* Maimonides views motion and causing motion as a sort of composition in a being. For example, the stick is set in motion by the hand and moves the stone. The stone is in motion but moves nothing else. Thus, the stick has a combination of two elements, while in the stone only one element exists alone.

The conclusion is that *therefore, there must be something that moves other things but is not itself in motion.* Maimonides simply applies the reasoning of step 1 to motion. Since the element of being in motion can exist alone, then the element of causing motion can exist by itself.

This is the Prime Mover, or God. This assumes the cogency of the foregoing proof. For the human soul would fit quite nicely the description given in step 3. But Maimonides presupposes the ascription of sublunary motion to the causal efficacy of the spheres and the motion of the spheres themselves, which no one could seriously believe to be caused by the human soul.

Any schematization of the proof would be the same as the outline. The only real point of interest in the argument is that it is unusual in employing an analogical form of reasoning, which is more commonly associated with the teleological argument. There one argues that in the same way that we assume that products evidencing the adaptation of means to ends imply a designer, so we assume that the universe must have a designer; here Maimonides maintains that in the same way that we assume that the existence of a separate element from a composite implies that the other element can also exist alone, so we assume there must be a mover which is not in motion. Hence, this is a cosmological argument using analogical reasoning.

Maimonides' third proof is an extremely important version of the cosmological argument and may be summarized as follows: Many things actually exist, as is evident by the senses. There are three alternatives concerning these: (1) all things are without beginning and end, (2) all things have a beginning and end, or (3) some things have a beginning and end. The first is clearly refuted by the testimony of the senses. The second is inadmissable, because then everything could cease to exist, and that which is said of a whole class of things must actually happen. Everything, then, would cease to exist, and, since something cannot come from nothing, nothing would ever exist. But since we see things existing and we ourselves exist, we may conclude that since transitory things exist, there must be an eternal being not capable of ceasing to exist and whose existence is real, not just possible. This being is necessary, either on its own account or on account of some external force. If it is the latter, then its existence or nonexistence is equally possible in itself, but its existence is made necessary through the external force. That force, then, is the absolutely necessary being. This being possesses absolutely independent existence and is the source of the existence of all things. We may outline Maimonides' third proof in this way:

1. Many things exist because:
   a. we perceive them with the senses.
2. There are three alternatives: all things are without beginning and end, all things have beginning and end, or some things have beginning and end.
3. It is impossible that all things are without beginning and end because:
   a. we clearly perceive objects that come into and pass out of existence.
4. It is impossible that all things have beginning and end because:
   a. then all things might cease to exist,

    b. and whatever is said to be possible of a whole class of things must actually happen.

    c. Therefore, everything would cease to exist.

    d. But then nothing would exist now

        i. because there would be no being to cause things to exist.

    e. But this is not true

        i. because we perceive existing things,

        ii. and we ourselves exist.

5. Therefore, there must be an eternal, indestructible being, whose existence is real, not merely possible.

6. This being is necessary on its own account or on account of some external force.

7. If it is necessary on account of some external force, then it would be necessary because of that force, though it would be possible in itself.

8. The external force, therefore, is the absolutely necessary being, the source of the existence of all things.

Though Maimonides gives Aristotle the credit for this proof, the reader will immediately recognize the work of al-Fārābī and ibn Sīnā. According to Husik the argument from possible and necessary being is introduced into Jewish philosophy by Abraham ibn Daud.[19] Maimonides is too great a thinker, however, to simply parrot his Arabic and Jewish predecessors, and therefore a thorough analysis of his version of the proof should be rewarding.

The first step is characteristic of the cosmological argument from contingent being: *many things exist.* The justification is entirely *a posteriori;* we know things exist because we perceive them with our senses.

Second, *there are three alternatives: all things are without beginning and end, all things have beginning and end, or some things have beginning and end.* Maimonides states the alternatives poorly, for the compound predicate makes the statements confusing. We might ask why all things or something might not have a beginning but no end, or have an end but no beginning. But if all things had one of the conjuncts but not the other, then alternative 1 would cover it, since it can be stated, "no things have beginning and end." And if some things possessed just one of the conjuncts, alternative 3 would cover it, "some things have beginning and end." It is clear that Maimonides is taking the predicate as a unity, 'beginning-and-end'. Either no things have beginning-and-end, all things have beginning-and-end, or some things have beginning-and-end. A more simple way of putting it is to use the word 'eternal'. Thus, the alternatives would be: all things are eternal, no things are eternal, or some things are eternal.

This clearly covers all the possibilities. For consistency's sake, it is best for now to retain the original language of the proof: there are three alternatives: all things are without beginning and end, all things have beginning and end, or some things have beginning and end.

The first alternative is easily eliminated: *it is impossible that all things are without beginning and end* because we see objects in the world which come to exist and then are destroyed.

Next *it is impossible that all things have beginning and end.* In other words, not every thing can be transitory in existence, coming to be and passing away. He states,

> The second case is likewise inadmissible, for if everything had but a temporary existence all things might be destroyed, and that which is enunciated of a whole class of things as possible is necessarily actual. All things therefore must come to an end, and then nothing would ever be in existence, for there would not exist any being to produce anything. Consequently, nothing whatever would exist [if all things were transient]; but as we see things existing, and find ourselves in existence, we conclude as follows: — Since there are undoubtedly beings of a temporary existence, there must also be an eternal being that is not subject to destruction, and whose existence is real, not merely possible.[20]

In this very interesting argument, Maimonides contends that if no thing were eternal, then it would be possible for everything to simply lapse into non-existence. And once absolutely nothing existed, something could never re-appear, for nothing would exist to bring it into being. In other words, out of nothing, nothing comes. If there were nothing — no matter, no space, no time, no God — then nothing could ever come into existence, he argues. Maimonides must be assuming in the third proof that time is infinite, just as he did in the first proof. For he maintains that if nothing were eternal, then it would be possible that all things might cease to exist. But if time is not infinite, this is not necessarily so. For it is possible that the universe began *ex nihilo* at some point a finite number of years ago and will continue to exist indestructibly into the future. Similarly, Christianity holds that the human soul is immortal, but not eternal, unlike Plato, who believed in the pre-existence and eternity of soul. Hence, it is not strictly true to say that if no thing were eternal, then everything could lapse into non-existence: for a thing may be indestructible, but not eternal.[21] This realization would not be damaging, however, for it would simply force the insertion of an extra clause into the argument. Maimonides could have argued that if no things were eternal then either (1) all things came into existence from nothing or (2) it is possible that all things might cease to exist. In either case, the refutation is the same: out of nothing, nothing comes.[22]

Hence, nothing would exist now. And this is absurd on two counts: (1) we clearly perceive existing things all around us, and (2) we are aware of our own individual existence. Now the crucial premise in this argument is 4.b. For certainly 4.a. appears true enough: it must be remembered that even matter would be included in the 'things' Maimonides is talking about. If every thing had a beginning and an end (or even just an end), then it is possible that everything could simply cease to exist. The real problem concerns the existence of transitory beings whose life-spans overlap, such that before one ceases to be another comes into being. Could not such a series be eternal? Maimonides argues that it cannot: whatever is said to be possible of a whole class of beings must actually happen. In a letter to ibn Tibbon, Maimonides elucidates the point:

> When the possible is said of a species, it is necessary that it exists in reality in certain individuals of this species: for if it never existed in any individual, it would be *impossible* for the species, and what right would one have to say that it is *possible*? If, for example, we say that writing is a thing possible for the human race, it is necessary then that there be men who write at a certain time: for if one held that there is never any man who writes, that would be saying that writing is impossible for the human race. It is not the same for the *possible* which is said of an individual: for if we say that it is possible that this child writes or does not write, it does not follow from this possibility that the child must necessarily write at one particular moment. Therefore, the *possible* said of a species is not, properly speaking, in the category of the possible, but is in some ways *necessary*.[23]

Maimonides is arguing that every possible that really deserves the name must, if it is enunciated of a whole class of things, be actualized at some time. Therefore, given an infinite time, which would be presupposed by a beginning-less series of overlapping transitory beings, the possibility of everything's vanishing would have to be actualized. The root of this is probably grounded in Aristotle's contention that the possible is that which can be other than it is, and every possible *must* at some time be actual.[24] Thus, if it is possible for nothing to exist, then at some point in infinite time, nothing will exist. And, asserts Maimonides, that point having been reached nothing would ever exist again. Thus, because in infinite time everything would cease to exist if no eternal thing exists, it is impossible that all things have beginning and end.

Maimonides concludes, *therefore, there must be an eternal, indestructible being whose existence is real, not merely possible.* It is interesting that he contrasts the real with the possible; it is evident that he is speaking in terms of actual necessity and possibility, not logical necessity and possibility. It ought also to be kept in mind that he has not concluded to

God, but simply to some eternal thing(s), whether it be matter, or the spheres, or the Intelligences.

In the sixth step, Maimonides states that *this being is necessary on its own account or on account of some external force.* In this step Maimonides uses 'necessary' in the sense of eternal, just as al-Fārābī and ibn Sīnā do on occasion. It is further evident that the external force is the cause of the necessary being. Thus, we have the familiar distinction between necessary *per se* and necessary *ab alio* here repeated. Maimonides is inquiring whether the eternal being discovered in the first five steps is absolutely necessary or is derivatively necessary, that is, eternal but nonetheless dependent upon a cause for its existence.

Step 7 proceeds, *if it is necessary on account of some external force, then it would be necessary because of that force, though it would be possible in itself.* Maimonides puts it this way: ". . . its existence and nonexistence would be equally possible, because of its own properties, but its existence would be necessary on account of the external force."[25] This brings to mind the essence/existence distinction of al-Fārābī and ibn Sīnā. For in what sense can this being's existence and non-existence be said to be equally possible, when it has been proved to exist necessarily? The answer can only be that its existence is possible in itself; its essence does not involve existence, or as Maimonides says, its properties, that is, its essential attributes, do not require that it exist. Hence, it must have what we have called an existential cause which causes its existing by continually conjoining existence to its essence.[26] Although it is derivatively necessary on account of its existential cause, it is nonetheless possible in itself because its essence does not involve existence.

Maimonides then concludes in step 8, *the external force, therefore, is the absolutely necessary being, the source of the existence of all things.* This is the being whose essence involves existence and is therefore not merely necessary in the sense of eternal, but is absolutely necessary, that is, it possesses "absolutely independent existence" and is "the source of the existence of all things, whether transient or permanent."[27] It is necessary *per se* whereas all other beings are possible *per se*. It is of interest to note that for Maimonides the existence of a contingent being is apparently immediately caused by the absolutely necessary being, for he has no argument here against an infinite regress of contingent causes of existence. He proceeds without intermediary from the contingent being to the absolutely necessary external force. We may schematize Maimonides' proof in this fashion:

1. Many things exist.
    a. The testimony of our senses makes this undoubtable.

2. There are three alternatives concerning the existence of these things: all things are eternal, no things are eternal, or some things are eternal.
3. It is impossible that all things are eternal.
   a. We clearly perceive some things that come into and pass out of existence.
4. It is impossible that no things are eternal.
   a. If no thing were eternal, then it is possible that all things could cease to exist.
   b. What is said to be possible of a whole class of things must eventually actually happen, given sufficient time.
   c. Therefore, everything would have ceased to exist.
      i. Given infinite past time, all possibilities would have to have been actualized.
      ii. The existence of nothing is a possibility (4.a.).
      iii. Therefore, the possibility of the existence of nothing would have to have been actualized.
   d. But then nothing would exist now.
      i. Out of nothing, nothing comes.
   e. And this is absurd.
      i. We clearly perceive existing things.
      ii. We are aware of our own individual existence.
5. Therefore, some things are eternal.
6. This thing is eternal on its own account or on account of an external cause.
   a. If its essence includes existence, it is eternal on its own account.
   b. If its essence does not include existence, it is eternal on account of an external cause.
      i. There is a real distinction between essence and existence.
      ii. Thus, if the essence does not include existence, existence must be added to the essence in order for the thing to exist.
      iii. The being that adds existence to the essence is therefore the existential cause of that thing.
7. If this thing is eternal on account of some external cause, then this thing is contingent in itself, though eternal on account of its cause.
   a. If its essence does not include existence, it depends for its existence on a cause (6.b.).
   b. It is therefore contingent in itself, though it exists eternally.
8. The external cause is therefore the absolutely necessary being.
   a. Its essence includes existence.

> i. All things which have existence added to their essences are caused by a being whose essence involves existence.
>
> b. It is therefore necessary in itself and causes the existence of all other things.

Again we may ask what can be known of the nature of such a being. We have already seen that this being is eternal and utterly independent in existence. It is therefore uncaused (proposition 10); it does not include any plurality (proposition 21), that is, it is a simple being without composition; thus, it cannot be material or reside in a material object (proposition 22), for all corporeality involves composition. Hence, concludes Maimonides,

> It is now clear that there must be a being with absolutely independent existence, a being whose existence cannot be attributed to any external cause, and which does not include different elements; it cannot therefore be corporeal, or a force residing in a corporeal object; this being is God.[28]

Moreover, there is but one God. First if there were two absolutely independent beings, they would share the property of absolute existence. This property would thus be added to their respective essences. But that means that their essences do not involve existence, and they are not therefore absolutely necessary beings. Second, a being whose essence involved existence would be absolutely simple. It would therefore be the only member of its species and have nothing in common with other beings. Thus, there can only be one being whose essence involves existence, or only one God.

This is a sophisticated version of the cosmological argument and one destined to exercise great influence. Maimonides himself held it in high esteem: "This is a proof the correctness of which is not doubted, disputed, or rejected, except by those who have no knowledge of the method of proof."[29] The foundation stone of the argument is the real distinction between essence and existence.

Finally, we may turn to Maimonides' fourth argument, the proof from potentiality and actuality. He states,

> We constantly see things passing from a state of potentiality to that of actuality, but in every such case there is for that transition of a thing an agent separate from it (Prop. XVIII). It is likewise clear that the agent has also passed from potentiality to actuality. It has at first been potential, because it could not be actual, owing to some obstacle contained in itself, or on account of the absence of a certain relation between itself and the object of its action; it became an actual agent as soon as that relation was present. Whichever cause be assumed, an agent is again necessary to remove the ob-

stacle or to create the relation. The same can be argued respecting this last-mentioned agent. . . . This series of causes cannot go on *ad infinitum;* we must at last arrive at a cause of the transition of an object from the state of potentiality to that of actuality, which is constant, and admits of no potentiality whatever.[30]

The argument is clearly Aristotelian in character, and, when one remembers that motion is the transition from potentiality to actuality, it also becomes apparent that the proof is another version of the argument from motion. We may outline it as follows:

1. We see things passing from potentiality to actuality.
2. Every such transition requires a separate cause because:
   a. prop. 18.
3. This cause in turn requires a separate cause for its transition from potentiality to actuality.
4. This series of causes cannot be infinite.
5. Therefore, there must be a being which is wholly actual and causes constantly the transition from potentiality to actuality.

The first step, that *we see things passing from potentiality to actuality,* is based on sense experience. The change here referred to is all types of change mentioned in proposition 4.

Second, *every such transition requires a separate cause.* Here again Maimonides' implicit determinism pervades the argument. He wants to prove that nothing can be self-moved, that is, that it cannot bring itself from potentiality to actuality. For example, we might say that a man is self-moved and that his soul is unmoved. But then the soul becomes an unmoved mover, which is not the conclusion Maimonides seeks. Therefore, he argues in proposition 18 that even the soul is caused to act by external factors.[31] Maimonides informs us that in cases where the soul is the cause of the change, there are two alternatives with regard to that change: (1) If there is no external obstacle to the change, then there would be no change, but only the effected actual state. This clearly denies the exercise of free will. Maimonides argues that when we choose to effect some change, this causal activity takes place only because of external determining factors. Otherwise, we would have always effected the change. This presupposes that new motives cannot appear in the soul wholly of its own accord. (2) If the change occurs when an obstacle is removed, then it is this removal that is the true cause of the change. In other words, our choices are not the causes of our activities; our actions are wholly determined by causes outside ourselves, and our exercise of free will is entirely illusory.

It is difficult to see how Maimonides can avoid complete determinism. In effecting a transition from potentiality to actuality, the soul is determined to do so, and thus every such transition requires a separate cause.

But this still does not solve the difficulty. For even if the soul is determined to act as it does, it still is unmoved and would be a purely actual being. So in step 3 Maimonides asserts, *this cause in turn requires a separate cause for its transition from potentiality to actuality*. Maimonides is endeavoring to prove that even the soul in effecting change itself changes. He must prove that the soul changes when effecting change, or it could be the purely actual being. Hence, he argues that any cause of change, in effecting change, itself changes. It does so in changing from a potential cause to an actual cause. Before it effects the change, it is only a potential cause; but as it effects the change, it is an actual cause. Hence, it has moved from potentiality to actuality. Again Maimonides emphasizes that it does not change itself from potential to actual cause (i.e. by its own free will). Rather this change occurs when another external agent either removes the obstacle to change that exists in the potential cause itself or brings the potential cause into a relation that brings the potentiality of the cause to actuality. For example, perhaps a man cannot sleep because he is worried about losing his employment; but when the boss informs him that his job is secure, the internal obstacle to sleep (namely, the worry) is removed, and the change from waking to slumbering is blissfully effected. Or again, a captured soldier may be the potential cause of the signing of a false confession to his crimes; but he does not become the actual cause of such until he is brought into relation with the gun at his head. Thus, even the soul is not purely actual, for in effecting changes it moves from being a potential cause to being an actual cause, and it does this not on its own initiative but only at the instigation of some external cause. Therefore, every transition from actuality to potentiality requires a cause, and this cause in turn requires a separate cause for its transition from potentiality to actuality.

Fourth, *this series of causes cannot be infinite*. Presumably this is because an actual infinite cannot exist.

Finally, *therefore, there must be a being which is wholly actual and causes constantly the transition from potentiality to actuality*. The being in which this series terminates must be a being that constantly causes the same eternal effects, otherwise it would change from being a potential cause to being an actual cause. Now this is obviously not the conclusion Maimonides wants, for it would necessitate, among other things, an eternal creation. For God could not change from being potential creator to actual creator. God would cause the eternal rotation of the spheres, and these would cause certain specific effects that would mechanically occur like the motion of the gears of a clock as they are moved by the spring. We may provide the following schema of the proof:

1. We see things passing from potentiality to actuality.
2. Every such transition requires a separate cause.
   a. Nothing can cause itself to pass from potentiality to actuality.
      i. If a thing could change itself, then, given no obstacle to change, the change would have always already occurred; that is, there would be no change, only the actual effected state.
      ii. If a thing could change itself and does so when a given obstacle is removed, then the cause of the change is not the thing itself, strictly speaking, but the cause of the removal of the obstacle.
   b. Therefore, it must be caused to pass from potentiality to actuality by some external cause.
3. This separate cause in turn requires a separate cause for its transition from potentiality to actuality.
   a. In becoming a cause, it passes from potentiality to actuality.
      i. It changes from being a potential to an actual cause.
   b. Such a transition requires a separate cause (2.).
4. This series of causes cannot be infinite.
   a. An actual infinite cannot exist.
5. Therefore, the series must terminate in a being that is wholly actual and causes constantly the transition from potentiality to actuality.

What can we know about this being? First, it has no potentiality in its essence, that is, it cannot not-exist (proposition 23). Second, it cannot be corporeal because potentiality, which it lacks, is inextricably bound up with matter (proposition 24). At this point Maimonides announces that ". . . the immaterial being that includes no possibility whatever, but exists actually by His own essence, is God."[32] Third, since He is incorporeal, there can be only one God (proposition 16).[33]

Maimonides concludes his four proofs for the existence of God by stating: "Even if we were to admit the Eternity of the Universe, we could by any of these methods prove the existence of God; that He is One and incorporeal, and that He does not reside as a force in a corporeal object."[34] Although Maimonides believes we can prove that God exists, he does not think that this means that we have any positive knowledge of God's essence. Maimonides is a champion of the *via negativa* which accords us only knowledge of what God is not.[35] In his systematic presentation of arguments for God's existence and for the negative knowledge of God,

Maimonides greatly influenced the Christian scholastics who drew upon his work. The *Guide* was translated from Arabic to Hebrew during Maimonides' lifetime and into Latin within ten years of his death. His thought was thus readily available to Latin-speaking theologians, and Thomas Aquinas in particular used Maimonides as his "guide and model" in his systematic harmonization of Aristotle and Christianity.[36] This is especially significant for our purposes because, as J. O. Riedl explains, the greatest influence of Maimonides on Aquinas is precisely in the Five Ways, in which Thomas follows Maimonides closely, even utilizing identical phraseology in his arguments.[37]

NOTES

1. Isaac Husik, *A History of Medieval Jewish Philosophy* (Philadelphia: The Jewish Publication Society of America, 1940), p. 236. In the words of J. H. Hertz, "The popular Jewish estimate of him is reflected in the contemporary saying, . . . 'From Moses to Moses, there never arose a man like Moses'; while to the non-Jewish world, he has ever been *the* Jewish philosopher and *the* Jewish theologian" (J. H. Hertz, "Moses Maimonides: A General Estimate," in *Moses Maimonides: VIIIth Centenary Volume,* ed. I. Epstein [London: Socino Press, 1935], pp. 3–4).

2. Moses Maimonides, *The Guide for the Perplexed* I, 74. Guttmann states,

He proved the existence of God by purely Aristotelian arguments. . . . Taking his stand upon strict science — that is, the metaphysics of Aristotle — Maimonides repudiates the proof of the Kalam as superficial and tendentious (Julius Guttmann, *Philosophies of Judaism: The History of Jewish Philosophy from Biblical times to Franz Rosenzweig,* with an Introduction by R. J. Z. Werblowsky, trans. David W. Silverman [London: Routledge & Kegan Paul, 1964], p. 157).

3. Leo Strauss, "The Literary Character of the *Guide for the Perplexed,*" in *Essays on Maimonides: An Octocentennial Volume,* ed. Salo Wittmayer Baron (New York: Columbia University Press, 1941), p. 44; this volume, above, p. 35.

4. Ibid., p. 39; this volume, p. 32.

5. Maimonides, *Guide* II, Intro.

6. The propositions may be summarized:

1. An infinite magnitude cannot exist.
2. An infinite number of finite magnitudes cannot co-exist.
3. An infinite number of causes and effects cannot exist.
4. Change may be in substance, quantity, quality, or place.
5. Motion implies change and transition from potentiality to actuality.
6. Motion is either essential or accidental, the former being due to

an external force, the latter to its participation in the motion of another thing.

7. Changeable things are divisible and, hence, corporeal.
8. A thing moved accidentally must come to rest.
9. A thing that moves something else does so by setting itself in motion.
10. Anything in a corporeal body is either an accidental or essential property.
11. Some properties of a corporeal object (e.g. color) are divisible; others (e.g. soul) are not.
12. A force occupying all parts of a corporeal, finite object is finite.
13. Only circular locomotion can be continuous change.
14. Locomotion is the most basic motion.
15. Time and motion are inseparable.
16. Incorporeal beings cannot be numbered, unless they inhabit a corporeal body.
17. Everything in motion is moved by an agent, either external or internal.
18. Everything that passes from potentiality to actuality is caused to do so by an external agent.
19. A caused being is a possible being.
20. A necessary being has no cause.
21. The essence of a composed being does not necessitate existence, since its composition is the cause of its existence.
22. Material bodies are composed of substance and form and are subject to accidents.
23. Every possible being may at some time be without actual existence.
24. Potentiality implies corporeality.
25. Every composed being consists of matter and form and requires a cause for its existence.
26. Time and motion are eternal.

This wholesale borrowing on the part of Maimonides perfectly illustrates the point made earlier that the Jewish philosophers concentrated on religious problems, being content to simply adopt the philosophical backdrop of their Arabian predecessors.

7. Maimonides, *Guide* II, Intro. All quotations from the *Guide* will be from Moses Maimonides, *The Guide for the Perplexed,* 2nd ed. rev., trans. M. Friedländer (London: George Routledge & Sons, 1928).

8. Ibid. Maimonides believed that the doctrine of *creatio ex nihilo* was both religiously superior and philosophically more probable than the eternity of the universe (ibid., II, 22, 23). But all his proofs for God's existence take for granted the eternity of the universe. For more on this, see E. L. Fackenheim, "The Possibility of the Universe in Al-Farabi, Ibn Sina, and Maimonides," *Proceedings of the American Academy for Jewish Research* 16 (1946–47), 57–70; Majid Fakhry, "The 'Antinomy' of the Eternity of the World in Averroes, Maimonides, and Aquinas," *Le Museon* 66 (1953), 139–155; Georg Wieland, "Die Gottesbeweise des Moses

Maimonides und die Ewigkeit der Welt," *Philosophisches Jahrbuch* 82 (1975): 72–89. For a good overall discussion of Maimonides' four proofs, see George C. Papademetriou, "Moses Maimonides' Doctrine of God," *Philosophia* 4 (1974): 306–329; Wieland, "Gottesbeweise," pp. 77–84.

9. Maimonides, *Guide* II, 1.

10. Husik, *History,* p. 253; cf. 217.

11. See R. L. Sturch, "The Cosmological Argument," (Ph.D. thesis, Oxford University, 1970), pp. 19–27.

12. Maimonides, *Guide* II, 1.

13. Maimonides might say, with Aristotle, as he indeed later does, that the soul is moved accidentally, but he does not argue the point here.

14. In point of fact, Maimonides does accept a system of multiple spheres, souls, and intelligences. See Friedländer, Analysis to *Guide,* by Maimonides, p. 1.

15. Maimonides, *Guide* II, 1.

16. Ibid.

17. Ibid.

18. Ibid.

19. Husik, *History,* pp. 218–219, 253.

20. Maimonides, *Guide* II, 1.

21. This raises yet another fascinating question: Could the converse be true, that a thing could have an end and yet no beginning? It would not be eternal, yet it would exist for infinite time in the past, a sort of mirror-image of immortality. This would not damage Maimonides' case, however, for he would argue that in infinite time, this being would cease to exist, just like beings that have both beginning and end, and thus there would be nothing. The *mutakallimūn,* of course, would have said it is nonsensical to speak of a being's actually existing for infinite time and yet having an end to its existence. Thus, we can imagine them asking Maimonides why could not tomorrow or next year be the point at which the possibility of the non-existence of the world be realized? Should he counter that in the infinite time that has passed, all possibilities would have been actualized, they might rejoin that at *any* point on the series of past events, an infinite time would have already elapsed, and thus one could never reach a point at which the universe would have collapsed into non-being. What this really goes to show, they might conclude, is the absurdity of positing infinite past time, for at *any* point all previous possibilities would have been already realized, given that in infinite time every possible will be actualized.

22. Maimonides himself alludes to this additional clause which we have added to the argument when he later says,

> If the spheres were transient, then God is their Creator, for if anything comes into existence after a period of non-existence, it is self-evident that an agent exists which has effected this result. It would be absurd to contend that the thing itself effected it (Maimonides, *Guide* II, 2).

23. Moses Maimonides to R. Samuel ibn Tibbon, cited in Munk, Commentary to *Le Guide des Égarés* (Paris: A. Franck, 1861), p. 39.

24. Aristotle, *Metaphysica* IX, 8, 1050b5–25. In his commentary on Ibn Rushd's *Tahafut,* Simon Van den Bergh encounters the same line of reasoning and traces it to Aristotle:

> every potentiality will realize its actuality. . . . Averroës refers here to one of the problems most discussed in Islam, whether there can be possibles that are never realized. According to Aristotle, *Met.* Θ and init., you cannot say that a certain thing may possibly be but will never be, for this would destroy the definition of the impossible, since 'impossible' means what will never be . . . a possible cannot be infinitely unrealized . . . (Simon Van Den Bergh, Notes to *Tahafut al-Tahafut* [*The Incoherence of the Incoherence*], 2 vols., by Averroes [London: Luzac & Co., 1954] 2:36).

25. Maimonides, *Guide* II, 1.

26. Cf. ibid., I, 57. According to Copleston, Maimonides follows al-Fārābī in designating existence as an accident or accidental determination (Copleston, *Medieval Philosophy,* p. 139). But Fackenheim disputes this, asserting that although Maimonides calls existence an accident in all beings other than God, this only means that existence in created beings is given to them by God; accordingly, existence is "each being's mediated participation in the creative act of God" (Fackenheim, "Possibility," p. 68).

27. Maimonides, *Guide* II, 1. According to Wolfson,

> In Jewish philosophy the assertion that in God essence and existence are identical . . . was merely another way of saying that God is necessary existence out of which arises the eternity, unity, simplicity, and unknowability of God, and in fact all those negations which tend to make God an absolute and infinite being. It did not however mean that thereby God becomes a 'real' being (*ens reale*) as opposed to a being of reason or a fictitious being (*ens rationis, ens fictum*). Or, in other words, the fact that in the idea of God essence involved existence was not used to prove the actual existence of God, for in Jewish as well as in Arabic philosophy that mode of reasoning was not followed (Harry Austryn Wolfson, *The Philosophy of Spinoza,* 2 vols. [Cambridge, Mass.: Harvard University Press, 1934], p. 122). Hence we find no ontological argument in Maimonides.

28. Maimonides, *Guide* II, 1.
29. Ibid.
30. Ibid.
31. Ibid., II, Intro.
32. Ibid., II, 1.
33. Ibid.
34. Ibid.
35. For a further discussion on this aspect of Maimonides' thought, see T. L. Penido, "Les attributs de Dieu d'après Maïmonide," *Revue Néo-Scholastique de Philosophie* 26 (1924): 137–163; H. A. Wolfson, "The Amphibolous Terms in Aristotle, Arabic Philosophy, and Maimonides," *Harvard Theological Review* 31 (1938):

151-173; H. A. Wolfson, "Maimonides on Negative Attributes," in *Louis Ginzberg Jubilee Volume* (New York: Jewish Publications, 1945), pp. 419-446; Joseph A. Buijs, "Comments on Maimonides' Negative Theology," *New Scholasticism* 49 (1975): 87-93; Clyde Lee Miller, "Maimonides and Aquinas on Naming God," *Journal of Jewish Studies* 28 (1977): 65-71.

36. Husik, *History,* p. 306.

37. John O. Riedl, "Maimonides and Scholasticism" *New Scholasticism* 10 (1936): 27-28.

Essence and Existence in Maimonides[1]

ALEXANDER ALTMANN

Maimonides defines existence (*wudjūd*) as "an accident (*'araḍ*) affecting (lit. happening to) that which exists (*mawdjūd*), and therefore something (*ma'na*) superadded to the essence (*māhīya*) of that which exists." He immediately qualifies this definition by restricting it to "all beings the existence of which is due to a cause." The existence of such beings, and of such beings only, will be something superadded to their essence. But a being whose existence is not due to any cause will contain being in its very essence. The only such Being is God, the necessary Existent. In Him, therefore, essence and existence are perfectly identical. "The existence of such a Being is its essence and truth, and its essence is its existence" (*Guide* I, 57).

It can hardly be doubted that the above statement reflects Avicenna's famous theory concerning essence and existence, and the commentators of the *Guide* have not been slow in pointing out this fact. Moses of Narbonne and Shemtob ben Joseph take the opportunity of assailing Maimonides from the point of view of Averroes' critique of Avicenna's doctrine, while others (Shemtob Ibn Falaquera and Asher Crescas) are content to reproduce some of the arguments used by Avicenna and Averroes respectively.[2] Maimonides himself introduces his statement by referring to the theory he is about to explain as one "well-known" and, to all intents and purposes, commonly accepted. He has obviously not had an opportunity of becoming acquainted with Averroes' attack on Avicenna's doctrine.[3] He must also have had in mind the fact that Avicenna's theory of essence and existence had gained some currency in Jewish philosophical

Bulletin of the John Rylands Library 35 (1953): 294–315. The article also appeared with an updating of some references in A. Altmann, *Studies in Religious Philosophy and Mysticism* (Ithaca, N.Y.: Cornell University Press, 1969), pp. 108–127. Reprinted by permission of the John Rylands University Library of Manchester.

writings. Thus, among the Jewish Neoplatonists, Gabirol and Jehudah Hallevi clearly state that in the case of all beings except God existence is different from essence.[4] But the question arises in what sense Maimonides understood existence to be an "accident" to essence. Did he attribute to Avicenna the view which was made the target of Averroes' subsequent attack, or did he interpret him in a different manner? This question is of added interest in view of the fact that only recently an attempt has been made to re-interpret Avicenna's doctrine and to clear it of the criticisms levelled against it by Averroes.[5]

We shall best open our enquiry by examining Maimonides' notion of essence. Here Maimonides stands solidly on Aristotelian ground. Aristotle had defined essence as that which a thing is said to be *per se* and which has its formula in the definition (*Met.* VII, 4, 4–5). "Essence belongs to all things the account of which is a definition" (*Met.* VII, 4, 9). Maimonides says likewise that among the five Praedicabilia "species" constitutes the "essence" of the individuals to which it is common. Seeing that species itself contains genus and specific difference, essence coincides with the definition which is composed of the same elements (*Treatise on Logic* X, 1). Thus the terms "rational animal" which express the definition of man constitute the essence (*ḏāt*) and truth (*ḥaḳīḳ*) of man (*Guide* I, 51, 52). It may be noted that Maimonides is fond of calling the essence the "truth" of a thing (*Guide* I, 33, 51). He no doubt means thereby the true being of a thing in the same way in which Aristotle regards the essence as the very being of a thing. He does not seem to have noticed the difficulty of attributing essence to God which arises from his own concept of essence. Seeing that a definition consisting of the *genus* and the *differentia* is inapplicable to God, the term "essence" should be likewise inapplicable to God. Maimonides, like his Jewish predecessors, emphatically states that no definition can be given of God (*Guide* I, 52).[6] Yet he does not hesitate to speak of God's essence.[7] We are therefore compelled to assume that Maimonides uses the term "essence" in two *toto coelo* different senses when speaking of God and all other beings respectively. From his statement that the *Tetragrammaton* "includes nothing but His essense" one might infer that "essence" in the case of God is identical with "necessary existence"; for this, he says, is the meaning of that proper name (*Guide* I, 61). The *Tetragrammaton,* he says in another place, implies nothing except God's existence (I, 53, end). It expresses the notion of God as the necessary Existent, and is identical with the name "I AM THAT I AM" (Ex. 3:14) which God revealed to Moses (I, 63).[8] In God, essence and existence are one (I, 57). Maimonides prefers this formula rather than the more radical one of the Jewish Neoplatonists and of Ghazālī who had described God as existence without essence.[9]

What kind of existence does Maimonides attribute to essence? Here again he is a strict Aristotelian. Form or essence, Aristotle had said, does not exist independently. It is not a self-subsistent substance, for otherwise it could not be contained in an actually existing substance (*Met.* VII, 8, 6). On the other hand, neither form nor essence are generated. The concrete whole is generated, for generation means inducing form or essence into particular matter (*Met.* VII, 8, 3–5). Maimonides likewise holds that, as a universal, essence has no independent existence. "It is an established fact that species have no existence outside our minds, and that species and other universals are concepts appertaining to the intellect, while everything that exists outside our minds is an individual or an aggregate of individuals" (*Guide* III, 18). At the same time, forms, unlike the combinations of the elements, do not change. They remain in their self-same natures, and appear and disappear instantaneously according to the ability of matter to receive them (II, 12). Maimonides does not further analyze the peculiar mode of being that attaches to essence or form as something existing only in concrete individuals and yet transcending them. He might have assigned to essence the character of something mid-way between being and non-being which certain schools of Kalām had attributed to the universals. Maimonides does indeed make reference to this particular theory, but only to reject it. Speaking about the attributes of God, he mentions the Kalām doctrine according to which the attributes of God are neither His essence nor anything extraneous to His essence. "This," he adds, "is like the assertion of others that the 'states' (*aḥwāl*), i.e. universal concepts, are neither existing nor non-existent." This view he strongly repudiates. There is, he says, no mean between existence and non-existence (*Guide* I, 51). Both the theological doctrine referred to and the *ḥāl* theory belong to the same school of thought. Abū Hāshim introduced the *ḥāl* theory as a means of reconciling the concept of the unity of God, which implies simplicity of essence, with the affirmation of distinct attributes. Do the latter not constitute accidental qualities in God? The answer put forward is to the effect that there is a *tertium quid* between essence and accidental attributes, i.e. the "states" such as wisdom, power, life which are one with the essence and yet conceptually different.[10] This doctrine was accepted also by members of the Ash'arite school. Al-Djuwainī, the teacher of Ghazālī, defined a "state" (*ḥāl*) as an attribute of an existing thing, being itself neither existent nor non-existent.[11] It would appear that Maimonides referred to this formula when rejecting the theory of *aḥwāl*.[12] It is obvious that it could not solve for him the problem of the mode of being attached to essence seeing that the *ḥāl*, according to this theory, stands in between the essence and the accident. It is a notion specifically designed to fit a theological requirement. But it should be borne in mind that the concept of *ḥāl* has also a wider significance in the thinking of Kalām, and re-echoes, as Dr. van den Bergh has shown, the Stoical concept of "states" (*pōs échon*) under which the Stoics, to the displeasure of Plotinus, had subsumed most of the accidental categories.[13] The facts designated under this term constitute a something "neither corporeal nor non-corporeal," i.e. a "meaning" (*ennóēma*) in an objective sense and akin to the Platonic Forms.[14] This realm of "meaning" includes not only universals and essences but also illusions and errors. Maimonides, however, does not avail himself of this notion. He says of fictitious beings such as the griffin, the centaur, and similar figments of the imagination, simply that they are non-existent. On the other hand, a true essence exists only in the concrete individual. Its universality arises from the intellectual process of abstraction. Maimonides is thus a true Aristotelian.[15] It follows that essences do not exist in an ideal realm of their own but "appear" in individual substances in which alone they have their being.

This brings us to the important question of the relationship between essence and substance. A clarification of this issue will help us to appreciate Maimonides' view-point concerning essence and existence.

What emerges from Aristotle's discussion of substance is the fact that substance has two fundamentally different meanings. In one sense substance is identical with the "what" of a thing, i.e. its essence. In another sense, it is the concrete particular thing. Aristotle does not always clearly distinguish between these two distinct senses of substance. But that he was fully aware of their difference cannot be doubted. Substance, he says, has two senses: "the ultimate subject, which cannot be further predicated of something else; and whatever has an individual and separate existence," i.e. the essence of a thing (V, 3, 4). "Substance," he says in another context, "is of two kinds, the concrete thing and the formula" (VII, 15, 1). This broadly corresponds with the distinction between primary and secondary substance laid down in the *Categories* (ch. 5). Aristotle designates as "primary substances" the things "which are neither predicated of a substrate nor found in a substrate, e.g. this man or this horse." He describes as "secondary substances" the genera and species. The designation of the concrete thing as "primary substance" makes it clear that being attaches primarily to the particular thing, not to essence. In the *Metaphysics* too, Aristotle speaks of the concrete individual as "substance in the highest degree" (VII, 6, 2). On the other hand, he regards the concrete thing as inferior in being to the essence. It admits of generation and destruction while essence does not. "The essence of house is not generated, but only the essence of *this* house" (VII, 15, 1). He adds that for this reason there is no definition or demonstration of particular sensible substances, because they contain matter "whose nature is such that it can both exist and not exist" (VII, 15,

2). One has therefore to realize the paradoxical fact that the primary substance, i.e. the concrete thing, exists and has its being by virtue of its endowment with secondary substance, i.e. essence. Concrete individuals are perishable (VII, 15, 2). "Once they have passed from the sphere of actuality it is uncertain whether they exist or not, but they are always spoken of and apprehended by the universal formula" (VII, 10, 18). We may, therefore say of essence that while it exists only in concrete things and never by itself, it has nevertheless being and unity in a higher degree than the concrete thing. On the other hand, the concrete thing is substance in the truest sense, and existence belongs to it absolutely and primarily. Yet its existence is but the result of a particular matter achieving its form, and therefore dependent upon a specific set of causes. It is due to a process of generation which means "inducing form or essence into particular matter" (VII, 8, 4).

If one bears in mind Aristotle's dual approach to the problem of substance, one will not be surprised by Maimonides' definition of the relationship between essence and existence as stated in the opening paragraph of this paper. It has to be noted that Maimonides describes existence as an accident not to essence – no statement is made as to the being or nonbeing of essence *qua* essence – but to "that which exists," i.e. the concrete thing. This we interpret to mean that the existence of a concrete thing composed of matter and form is due to the fact that, as a result of a causal process, a certain form has been induced into a certain matter. The term "accident" merely expresses the fact that the thing "happens" to exist. In a certain sense it also means that the essence "happens" to appear in this particular matter. It does not indicate that a non-existent or ideal essence has become "existent" by the grace of the accidental attribute of existence. Nor does it obliterate the recognition of concrete substances as having existence in a primary and absolute sense. It merely defines existence as being due to factors outside the essence, and for this reason uses the term "accident." As Dr. Rahman has suggested, Avicenna employed the same term in a similar sense, and it is not unlikely that this is the way in which Maimonides understood Avicenna.

A closer analysis of Maimonides' definition of existence will bear out the correctness of our interpretation. From the statement quoted it is obvious that to exist is, in Maimonides' view, tantamount to being caused. Only in the case of God is existence uncaused. But precisely for this reason the term "existence" is used homonymously of God and all other beings (*Guide* I, 56). The efficient cause, Maimonides states in his *Treatise on Logic* (IX, 3), is He who causes form to exist in matter, that is to say God. The philosophers, he adds, are in agreement with this, except that they regard God as a remote agent and seek for every existing being that is created its proximate agent. Seeing that the efficient cause is invariably outside the essence,[16] it is understandable that existence is described as an "accident superadded to the essence of that which exists." The proximity of this view to Alfārābī's and Avicenna's is too obvious to need much emphasis. The "that," says Alfārābī, does not derive from the "what" but from something external to the "what."[17] In other words, existence is due to an external agent. It does not derive from the essence as such. Both Alfārābī and Avicenna use the phrase that "considered in themselves and apart from their relation to the necessary Being, essences deserve privation of being."[18] Maimonides does not go as far as that. He does not designate essence as a mere possible in itself, but he agrees that existence in the sense of an "instantiation" of essence is a happening due to an agent outside the essence.

There is another aspect to the accidentality which Maimonides attributes to existence. To exist means to be actual. But everything that passes from a state of potentiality to that of actuality is caused to do so by some external agent (*Guide* II, Introduction, Prop. XVIII). It follows that existence is due to some external agent, and therefore accidental to the thing itself. We may also say that existence is merely potential being as long as certain conditions are as yet unfulfilled. Maimonides calls this element of uncertainty surrounding the actualization of the potential a "possibility." "Everything that exists," he says, "and whose essence includes a certain state of possibility (*'imkān*) may at some time be without actual existence" (Prop. XXIII). In his Letter to Samuel Ibn Tibbon, he explains that there is a difference between potentiality and possibility which to grasp requires great subtlety and is a matter of utmost difficulty even to trained philosophers.[19] It appears that the possibility of which he speaks refers to the as yet unrealized presence of the conditions necessary for the actualization of a potential being. What Avicenna and the Latin schoolmen called *potentiae remotae* as distinct from *potentiae proximae* lies in the same direction.[20] But neither Aristotle nor Avicenna differentiates between potentiality and possibility.[21] According to Maimonides—if we understand him correctly—the element of possibility is bound up with external causation, whereas potentiality is the as yet unrealized being of the thing as such. Maimonides says distinctly, "A thing which owes its existence to certain causes has in itself (lit. in consideration of its essence) merely the possibility of existence" (Prop. XIX). Again, existence is seen to be purely accidental from the aspect of essence. In the case of God, existence is not merely actual but necessary. This is brought out in Maimonides' Fourth Argument for the existence of God, which from the impossibility of an infinite regress postulates the existence of a cause which is pure actuality and admits of no potentiality whatever (*Guide* II, 1). "In the essence of this Cause nothing exists potentially, for if its essence included any possibility of existence it would not exist at all." It should be noted that Maimonides is not content to exclude from God potentiality but that he excludes possibility as well. A being devoid of potentiality is actual—such is the God of Aristotle—but a Being free from possibility as well must be necessarily existent. Maimonides defines it as Being "that includes no possibility whatever but exists actually by its own essence." In God, therefore, essence and existence are one.

There is yet a third aspect to Maimonides' view concerning the nature of existence. To exist is to be willed by God. It is not enough to say that existence is caused by God. For that might imply an existence which necessarily derives from Him in the same manner "as the shadow is caused by a body, or heat by fire, or light by the sun" (*Guide* II, 2).[22] But Maimonides holds the world to be created by design (*kaṣd*) and determination (*taḥṣīṣ*) (ibid.). The best proof for design in the universe he finds in the different motions of the spheres which cannot be explained as the necessary results of differences in their substance. One substance is common to all spheres, and yet each one has its own particular form, i.e. kind of movement and velocity. Who then, he asks, determined and pre-disposed these spheres to receive different forms? The answer he puts forward is: The Will of God (*Guide* II, 19). If one assumed "Nature" as such to operate without any voluntary determination, the "Wisdom" of God would be equivalent to Nature, and the essences of things would achieve existence in accordance with causal necessity. But the fact is that existence does not follow a plain and intelligible pattern. It contains an opaque, irrational element, as we might say. It points to "Will" as a determining factor besides "Wisdom." It appears that on the whole Maimonides related essence to the Wisdom, and existence to the Will of God, although he is rather vague in his utterances on the subject. He sometimes speaks of God's Wisdom as responsible for determinations which are rationally inexplicable (II, 19), sometimes of "the Will of God or his Wisdom" (III, 13), but it is clear that what he really means is Will, voluntary determination (cf. II, 19). In God there is, of course, no duality of Will and Wisdom. They are both identical with His essence (I, 69; III, 13). But the distinction is a valid one from the aspect of existing things. Their analysis reveals two distinct elements, i.e. essence which represents the realm of nature in the timelessness and constancy of being, and existence by which essence is thrown into combination with matter beyond the strict confines of causal necessity. Existence is thus from yet another angle accidental to essence. But its accidental nature is now seen to derive from the Will of God. The final causes which Aristotle found in nature, Maimonides declares to terminate in the Will of God (I, 69; III, 13). But God's Will is not arbitrary;

it is guided by His Wisdom. "The object of His Will is only that which is possible, and of the things possible only such as His Wisdom decrees upon" (III, 25). The duality of essence and existence in all created beings therefore corresponds in a way to the Wisdom and Will of God.

Maimonides' concept of God's essence as the Unity of Wisdom and Will marks his standpoint in the great controversy between Ash'ariya and Mu'tazila as to whether Will or Wisdom operates in the workings of Divine Providence (cf. *Guide* III, 17). It seems to imply a compromise solution combining both features. But its real purport must be seen in the stand Maimonides takes in the larger controversy between Kalām and the philosophers. There the issue is that of creation. As Isaac Abrabanel has pointed out, the issue is not between creation and non-creation but between creation by will and design or creation by necessity.[23] Creation by will and design as conceived by Kalām left no room for a realm of essence, and, vice versa, creation by necessity as conceived by the philosophers seemed to ignore the nature of existence. The theologians of Kalām refused to call God the First Cause and designated Him either as Agent (*fā'il*) or Determinant (*muḥaṣṣiṣ*).[24] Maimonides assumes an intermediate position. He does not share the rejection of the term "Cause" for God (I, 69), and, at the same time, adopts the Kalām notion of *taḥṣīṣ* which expresses the concept of will and design. He recognizes most clearly that the denial by Kalām of the "true nature," i.e. the essences, of things stems from a desire to prove the determination (*taḥṣīṣ*) of things (II, 19). He, on his part, accepts the theory of *taḥṣīṣ* but wishes to demonstrate the operation of this principle in the natural universe. He does not wish to disregard the "nature of things," i.e. their essences. In the view of Kalām, the principle of *taḥṣīṣ* determines the composition, size, place, accident, and time of the spheres and the sublunar beings (cf. *Guide* I, 74, Fifth Argument). Maimonides restricts the operation of *taḥṣīṣ* to the spheres and admits it only indirectly to the sublunar world.[25] But once the principle of voluntary determination is established, the universe as a whole is proved to be created.

Moses of Narbonne, in his *Commentary* on the *Guide*, passes the remark that Maimonides' arguments for creation by will and design were taken over from Ghazālī; moreover, that they did not represent Maimonides' esoteric view but were meant merely to please the religionists. In his own generation one could safely agree with Averroes that all causality was determined by the nature of existing things, i.e. by the pure causality of form in the case of simple bodies, and by a combination of formal and efficient causes in the case of composite bodies.[26] Averroes does indeed eliminate the voluntaristic concept of final causes. He defines the Will of God as "the process of necessary action accompanied by knowledge."[27]

Spinoza went even beyond that by denying both the Will and Intellect of God. He thus eliminated the final causes, and reduced the formal cause to the efficient cause.[28] Maimonides, on the other hand, upholds efficient, formal and final causes. There is no justification for the view expressed by Moses of Narbonne that Maimonides' arguments for creation by design were not meant seriously. As we have seen, there is a close correspondence between Maimonides' ontology of essence and existence on the one hand, and his theology of Wisdom and Will on the other.

How far Maimonides succeeded in establishing the voluntaristic principle is another matter. The question is: To what extent is the Will of God free to operate in a world already determined by essences, i.e. formal causes? Moses of Narbonne had said that Maimonides' arguments for the principle of *taḥṣīṣ* were borrowed from Ghazālī. Abrabanel strongly repudiates this contention. Ghazālī, he asserts, furnished only the first of Maimonides' arguments.[29] But this is beside the point. The question is: Does Maimonides follow the whole trend of Ghazālī's argumentation? The answer to this is in the negative. Ghazālī wished to disprove causality altogether, and to replace it by the causality of Will alone. In full accord with Ash'arite Kalām, he denies the concept of essence and all it implies, i.e. formal causality and the reality of the potential. There is no such thing as a natural process of change, of becoming, and of matter receiving successive forms as a result of a predisposition to receive them. Existence is not the result of a series of formal and material determinations but arises from discrete acts of Will on the part of God. This position is a renewal of the Megaric doctrine which Aristotle had taken pains to repudiate (*Met.* IX, 3). Maimonides' Aristotelianism has no use for such a radical application of the voluntaristic principle. He firmly upholds the concept of essence and formal causality but admits for the translunar sphere, and thus indirectly also for the sublunar world, the principle of *taḥṣīṣ*. Existence thus becomes something both caused and willed. It is caught in a nexus of causality which has its First Cause in God. Existence is therefore, metaphysically speaking, an "accident," something that "happens" to occur, and not something determined by essence as such.

In the light of the afore-going interpretation of Maimonides' concept of essence and existence, the criticisms levelled against it by the commentators will be seen to fall to the ground.

(1) Shemtob Ibn Falaquera (*Moreh Ha-Moreh,* p. 28) does not expressly criticize Maimonides but adduces by way of comment Averroes' critique of Avicenna and obviously wishes to apply it to Maimonides. He quotes Averroes as saying that "Our statement that a thing exists does not indicate something superadded to its essence *extra mentem* as would be the case in our stating that the thing is white. We found, however, that

Avicenna mistakenly believed that unity is something superadded to the essence, and likewise existence, whenever we say that a thing exists; and that, moreover, an existing thing has no existence by virtue of its essence. This statement is most misleading, for it implies that the term 'existent' signifies an accident common to all categories *extra mentem,* which is the opinion of Avicenna. Concerning this 'accident' the question is asked whether in saying that it (*sc.* this accident) exists, we refer to the truth of the matter or to another accident existing in that (first) accident, in which case there would be an infinite series of accidents, which is absurd."

It is obvious that the target of Averroes' attack is the view supposedly held by Avicenna that existence is an accident like whiteness. The fallacy of this assumption has been demonstrated by Dr. Rahman. The concrete individual thing "happens" to exist, but its existence is not an "accident" like quality or quantity. Averroes' argument that such an "accident" would be common to all categories does not therefore apply.[30] The other argument from the impossibility of an infinite series of accidents is a favorite one, and occurs in a number of medieval Jewish authors such as Joseph ben Jehudah ibn Aknīn, Isaac Albalag, Gersonides and Ḥasdai Crescas.[31] Aristotle employs a similar argument to prove the absurdity of separating a thing from its essence (*Met.* VII, 6, 11-12). Again, the argument has no *locus standi* if the "accidental" nature of existence is interpreted as a "happening" due to a causal process.

(2) Moses of Narbonne (*Bi'ūr Narbonī,* p. 9a) reproaches Maimonides for having failed to distinguish between two fundamentally different senses of "being" to which Aristotle had already drawn attention, and which had been stressed anew by Averroes. Unfortunately, he says, Avicenna had ignored this distinction, and Maimonides had blindly followed him. "To be" and "is" may, according to Aristotle, sometimes mean that a thing is true, and "not to be" that it is false (*Met.* V, 7; VI, 2). In another sense, being attaches to the "what" of a thing, that is to say, primarily to substance and in a secondary sense to the other categories as well. For in asking what quality "is," we are using the term "is" in a different sense. We may even say that not-being *is* not-being (*Met.* IV, 2, 3; VII, 4, 12-13). "The senses of essential being are those which are indicated by the figures of predication (i.e. the categories): for being has as many senses as there are ways of predication" (*Met.* V, 7, 4).[32] Likewise, Averroes says that "being" is a term "used for the true, i.e. that which being *in mente* agrees with what is *extra mentem,*" and is used also "for that which has quiddity and essence *extra mentem,* irrespective as to whether this essence is conceived or not." "Hence the term 'being' is reducible to these two senses, i.e. the true and that which is *extra mentem*" (*Epitome,* ed. v.d. Bergh, p. 7; cf. *Met.* VI, 4).

Moses of Narbonne makes the point that Maimonides' failure to distinguish between the uses of the term "is" in the sense of "being true" on the one hand and of the being of the categories on the other prevented him from realizing the essential character of categorial being. For only when using the term "is" in the sense of "being true" do we separate being from essence, whilst in the other case essence and existence are inseparable. Aristotle does indeed say that "existent man" and "man" are the same thing. The duplication in the statement "He is a man and an existent man" yields no fresh meaning (*Met.* IV, 2, 7). Essence has intrinsic being. But Maimonides nowhere disputes this view. He is not concerned with the mode of being that attaches to essence but with the existence of concrete things.

(3) Asher ben Abraham Crescas, in his *Commentary* on the *Guide* (I, 57), identifies Maimonides' view with Avicenna's and quotes Averroes' refutation of it. "Avicenna supposed existence to be an accident, his argument being as follows: If existence signified the essence (*'aẓmūt*), the statement, 'substance exists' would be equivalent to the statement, 'substance is substance'. Averroes, however, argued against him that 'existence' is spoken of in regard to essence and to being true, as e.g. in the statement, 'The man is existent or non-existent', as well as in the sense of the copula (*ḳesher*), as e.g. in the statement 'The man is (*nimẓa'*) righteous. Hence 'being' applies to substance essentially (*bĕ-'aẓmūt*) and to the other categories *secundum prius et posterius* (*bi-ḳĕdīmah we-'iḥūr*); not homonymously (*bĕ-shitūf*) nor as a *nomen appellativum* (*bĕ-haskamah*) but *secundum prius et posterius*. It applies to substance absolutely (*bĕ-'amitūt*) and to each other category according to the nature thereof."

Avicenna's argument quoted in the above context occurs, as Dr. Rahman was good enough to inform the present writer, in the *Kitāb al-Shifā', Met.,* Maḳala, 1, Faṣl, 5, and reads as follows: "It is certain that the peculiar essence of everything is different from its being, i.e. its determinate existence. This is the case because if you say, 'such and such an essence exists' . . . your statement yields a definite and intelligible meaning; but if you say (which you *would* say if you equated essence and existence), 'essence is essence', it would be a superfluous and unprofitable talk." What Avicenna means to convey is, according to Dr. Rahman, the following: (1) In asserting existential propositions of individual objects, we add nothing to the subject of which existence is asserted, and hence any such affirmation is "unprofitable." (2) If, however, we assert existence of quiddities such as "elephant" by saying, "elephant exist," the affirmation of existence is "profitable" because it yields some fresh information about reality. The proposition, "elephant exists," is equivalent to the proposition, "there exists an instance (or there exist instances) of elephant." Existence in such cases means "instantiation." The distinction between essence and existence does, however, not imply that existence is an accident in the logical sense of accident as opposed to substance and attached to it, as it were, from the outside.[33]

While Crescas offers a correct version of Avicenna's argument, Averroes seems to present it in a slightly different form. In the *Epitome* of Aristotle's *Metaphysics* (ed. S. van den Bergh, p. 8) we read as follows: "It was argued that if the term 'being' signified the essence, the statement, 'substance exists' would be self-contradictory." The same version of the argument occurs also in Moses Ibn Tibbon's Hebrew translation,[34] from which Jacob Mantinus made his Latin translation in the sixteenth century. Unfortunately, the present writer was unable to consult the editions of the two Arabic mss. (Cairo and Madrid) used by Dr. van den Bergh. It is, however, generally agreed that the Hebrew translation is more reliable than the Cairo ms.[35] It broadly corresponds with the Madrid ms. This would lead us to assume that the text before us is genuine, and that Averroes in fact misrepresented the true meaning of Avicenna. On the other hand, the statement by Asher Crescas of Avicenna's and Averroes' respective arguments appears to be a paraphrase of the relevant passages in the *Epitome* (cf. pp. 8, 28–29 in van den Bergh's edition). This would indicate that he had before him an Averroes text offering the correct version of Avicenna's argument.

Crescas also presents a brief summary of Averroes' statement that existence applies to substance essentially and to the other categories *secundum prius et posterius,* i.e. *analogice* as distinct from *aequivoce* and *univoce* (*Epitome,* p. 28). This view goes back to Aristotle who, speaking of the senses of "being" as related to the categories, made it clear that that which *is* primarily and absolutely is substance, and that the "being" of the other categories, whilst still essential, is not primary. How then was it permissible to use the term "being" in such a variety of senses? Aristotle's answer is that "we use the terms neither equivocally nor in the same sense, but just as we use the term 'medical' in *relation* to one and the same thing; but not *of* one and the same thing, nor yet equivocally. The term 'medical' is applied to a body and a function and an instrument, neither equivocally nor in one sense, but in relation to one thing" (*Met.* VII, 4, 12–16; IV, 2, 2). Essential being thus has "ten ultimate meanings or colourings answering to the ten ultimate kinds of things" (cf. Sir W. D. Ross, *ibid.*). But it has to be borne in mind that whilst "to be a quality" is indeed an essential mode of being, "to be white" is accidental being. Likewise, the concrete individual thing, with which Maimonides is concerned, has not essential but accidental being.

(4) Shemtob ben Joseph, in his *Commentary* on the *Guide* (I, 57),

mentions four arguments which, in his view, induced Maimonides to hold the opinion that existence is an accident:

(*a*) We conceive the quiddity of things and may still remain in doubt as to their existence. Hence existence is something additional to essence. This argument reflects a line of thought pursued by Alfārābī in his *Ring-stones of Wisdom* (ed. Dieterici, pp. 108–109).

(*b*) Essence is not caused, but we say *that* man exists, and ask *why* he exists. Hence existence cannot belong to essential things. In other words, the questions "why?" and "whether?" do not properly belong to essence. They apply only to existence. It follows that existence cannot be essential. This argument reflects Aristotle's distinction as to the four possible questions: *Whether* a thing is such and such; *why* it is such and such; *whether it exists*; and *what* it is (*Anal. Post.* 2. 1). "After the existence of a thing is known to us, we enquire as to its whatness in asking, e.g. 'What, then, is God?' or, 'What is man?'" (*loc cit.*). Here Aristotle himself distinguishes between essence and existence as related to two different kinds of questions.[36] But in the same way in which Aristotle fails to draw the inference that existence must be accidental, Maimonides, too, may have left it at that.

(*c*) "Existence" is a term which can be used neither as a *nomen appelativum,* i.e. *secundum prius et posterius,* nor homonymously. Hence it must be used as a hybrid term (i.e. one denoting common accidental characteristics).[37] But seeing that hybrid terms denote accidental characteristics, and no accidental characteristics apply to God, it follows that the term "existence" which is applied to all beings cannot be used of God. This argument need not be taken seriously at all, since it begs the question. It pre-supposes the accidental character of existence instead of proving it. On the other hand, it does reflect Maimonides' view that the term "existence" cannot be used *analogice* of God and all other beings. But Maimonides describes the term as a homonymous one, and not merely as a hybrid.

(*d*) "Know thou that every agent, especially one endowed with intellect, must necessarily conceive the essence of the thing (i.e. which he produces) before it comes into existence. Take, e.g., a house which existed in the mind of the architect: it is the cause of the existence of the house existing *extra mentem*. Now, since all things exist by virtue of the First Cause who knows them, it follows that the quiddity of the thing exists prior to its existence. Hence existence is an accident to quiddity." This argument merely proves that the essences of things, i.e. the universals exist in the Mind of God, a view which is totally different from the one which describes existence as an accident. That the Platonic Forms exist in the Mind of God was already stated in Middle-Platonism, Neo-Pythagoreanism, and Philo of Alexandria. But it did not there carry the connotation of existence as a mere accident of essence.

Shemtob completely fails to produce evidence that the above arguments had in fact weighed with Maimonides. He himself brushes these arguments aside by declaring that essence and existence are one. Like his predecessors, he joins the camp of Averroes. Like them, he seems to have misunderstood the real purport of Maimonides' concept. As we have seen, Maimonides remains firmly planted on Aristotelian ground.

In his *Aristotle, Fundamentals of the History of his Development* (Oxford, 1934), Werner Jaeger has suggested that there are three different conceptions of the nature of metaphysics underlying the different strata of the corpus of Aristotelian writings to which, probably by Andronicus, the name of *Metaphysics* was given in some complete edition in the Hellenistic age. They are (1) the earliest "theological" concept which replaces Plato's supersensible Forms by the unmoved Mover, and sees the problems of metaphysics against a Platonic background; (2) the concept of metaphysics as the science of Being as such in the sense that it enquires into the kinds of Being uncritically assumed by the sciences; (3) metaphysics as ontology, describing the various senses of Being, including sensible as well as supersensible substance, and aiming at a morphology of Being (*loc. cit.,* p. 387).

The medieval definitions of the aims of metaphysics faithfully reflect these levels of meaning. Thus Alfārābī's "Catalogue of Sciences" (*Iḥsā' al-ulūm*)[38] subdivides metaphysics into (1) the science which investigates Being *qua* Being; (2) the science which investigates the principles of the particular sciences; and (3) the science which investigates the supersensible beings. Similarly, Averroes assigns to metaphysics the threefold task of examining (1) the sensible beings *qua* beings; (2) the supersensible beings, including God; and (3) the principles of the particular sciences (cf. *Epitome,* pp. 4–5). Amongst Jewish authors, Shemtob ibn Falaquera lists the same three branches of metaphysics (cf. *Reshit Ḥokmah,* ed. M. David, Berlin, 1902, p. 53).[39] Maimonides, on the other hand, divides metaphysics into two parts only: (1) into an investigation of all beings which are supersensible, i.e. God and the angels; (2) into an inquiry into the principles (lit. remote causes) of the sciences (cf. *Treatise on Logic,* ch. 14). He entirely omits the ontological task of metaphysics, i.e. the investigation of Being *qua* Being. Whilst Aristotle had moved away from the theological concept of metaphysics towards the ontological one, Maimonides, in common with most of the Jewish metaphysicians, is primarily concerned with the theological aspect of metaphysics. The ontological elements of Aristotle's *Metaphysics,* insofar as they are made use of, now serve the purposes of theology. The concepts of matter and form, potentiality and actuality are employed to this end. But Maimonides seems entirely to ignore Aristotle's investigation into the manifold senses of essential being. This central part of the Aristotelian ontology is left out of account altogether. It is here that Maimonides parts company with Aristotle. He does not repudiate the notion of a gradation of being according to the categories, but, being interested primarily in the theological angle, the different shades of being in all created beings are neutralized, as it were, and reduced to one single level compared with the totally other Being of God. The only ontological distinction which matters from the theological point of view is the one between created and uncreated being. All created existence is caused, actualized from potentiality, and willed by God. The term "being" is therefore used homonymously of God and the created beings. Maimonides makes no use whatever of Aristotle's concept of the analogy of being on which Averroes laid such great stress, and which Alfārābī had already used to theological advantage. Both Alfārābī and Averroes had conceded the admissibility of applying the term "being" to God and created existence *secundum prius et posterius.* They held that God has being primarily and essentially while all other beings possess existence only in a derivative sense, i.e. derived from God. Alfārābī's view is clearly stated in his "The political Governments," a work well known to Maimonides and highly praised by him in his Letter to Samuel Ibn Tibbon.[40] It is all the more remarkable that Maimonides refrained from using Aristotle's concept of the analogy of being and insisted on the homonymous nature of the term. The reason for this attitude must be sought in his neoplatonic orientation which he shared with Avicenna. It was left to his more radically Aristotelian successor Gersonides to introduce the analogical concept of Being into Jewish theology, and thus to follow the lead given by Averroes. But even then the issue was not fully settled, as is apparent from Ḥasdai Crescas' attack on both Avicenna and Averroes, and his compromise suggestion that existence is neither accidental to essence nor identical with it but "essential" to it.

NOTES

1. The present article was one of a series presented to Dr. S. van den Bergh, the distinguished scholar, philosopher, and teacher, on the occasion of his seventieth birthday.

2. We learn incidentally that Shemtob ben Joseph composed a treatise on this particular subject which, unfortunately, appears to be lost. Two other treatises of his, one on Matter and its Relation to Form, and one on Final Causes are extant in manuscripts. Cf. *Jewish Encyclopedia, s.v.* Ibn Shemtob.

3. This corroborates the prevalent assumption that, at the time of his writing the *Guide*, Maimonides was as yet unacquainted with the work of Averroes. Cf. H. A. Wolfson, *Crescas' Critique of Aristotle* (1929), p. 323. The famous Letter to Samuel Ibn Tibbon in which Maimonides reviews the contemporary philosophical literature and mentions Averroes twice was written after the completion of the *Guide*. Cf. J. Sonne, *Tarbiz*, ed. J. N. Epstein (Jerusalem, 1939), X, p. 147. The Verona ms. of the Letter published by Sonne does not contain the relevant paragraph but merely alludes to it. Another version of the Letter published by Alexander Marx from Codex Adler 2031 proves again inconclusive by virtue of the fact that the ms. is mutilated just where the reference to Averroes occurs in the Constantinople edition. Cf. *Jewish Quarterly Review*, N.S. 25 (1934–35): 375. A critical edition of the Letter has been announced by D. H. Baneth in *Tarbiz* 23 (1952): 171. From a Letter written by Maimonides to his favourite disciple, Joseph ben Jehudah ibn Aknīn and dated 1190, more definite conclusions can be drawn. There he mentions the fact that he had just received all the writings of Averroes except one and praises Averroes as "hitting the mark." He expresses regret at not having as yet had an opportunity of going over all his books. Cf. D. H. Baneth, *'Iggĕrot Ha-Rambam*, ed. Meḳiẓe Nirdamīm (Jerusalem, 1946), pp. 33, 70. Seeing that the *Guide* had been completed by 1190, it is obvious that he had not been able to draw on Averroes' writings at the time of its composition. Shemtob Ibn Falaquera's assertion to the contrary cannot be substantiated. Cf. *Moreh Ha-Moreh* (1837), p. 8.

4. Cf. *Fons Vitae*, ed. C. Baumker, V, 24; *Kuzari*, IV, 25 (Cassel, p. 354).

5. As Dr. F. Rahman has shown, Averroes' reading of Avicenna is not borne out by the relevant texts of the *Kitāb al-Shifā'*. Unfortunately, it has misled all subsequent interpretations of Avicenna's doctrine. Dr. Rahman's thesis has been presented in a paper on "Essence and Existence in Avicenna" read before the Scottish Society for Ancient Philosophy, and kindly made available to the present writer. Since published in *Mediaeval and Renaissance Studies*, ed. Richard Hunt, Raymond Klibansky, Lotte Labowsky, IV (London, 1958), pp. 1–16.

6. Cf. Jehudah Hallevi, *Kuzari*, IV, 25 (Cassel, p. 354); Abraham Ibn Daud, *Emunah Ramah*, ed. Weil, pp. 46, 52.

7. God is "a simple essence" (I, 53); Will and Wisdom are one with His essence (I, 69; III, 13); His essence is unknowable (I, 54, 58); and *passim*.

8. The Latin schoolmen too, interpreted the name "I am that I am" as denoting the very essence of God. Cf. Etienne Gilson, *The Spirit of Medieval Philosophy* (1950), pp. 51ff. This interpretation goes back to Philo of Alexandria. Cf. H. A. Wolfson, *Philo* (1947), I, pp. 19, 210; II, pp. 120–121.

9. Cf. Gabirol, *Fons Vitae*, V, 24; Shemtob Ibn Falaquera, *Moreh Ha-Moreh*, pp. 28f.; Joseph Ibn Ẓaddiḳ, *Microcosm*, ed. Horovitz, p. 48; Asher Crescas' Commentary on the *Guide* I, 57. As to Ghazāli, see T. de Boer, *Die Widersprüche der Philosophie nach Al-Gazāli und ihr Ausgleich durch Ibn Rošd* (1894), pp. 53f.; H. A. Wolfson, "Crescas on the Problem of Divine Attributes," *Jewish Quarterly Review*, N.S. 7 (1916): 189–191. Avicenna's view has met with a twofold interpretation. Ghazāli understood him to suggest that God is existence without essence; Averroes attributed to him the view that in God essence and existence are one. Cf. Wolfson, *ibid*.

10. Al-Shahrastānī, *Milal,* translated by Haarbrücker, I, pp. 83ff.; David Kaufmann, *Geschichte der Attributenlehre in der jüdischen Religionsphilosophie* (1877), p. 35, n. 65; S. Horovitz, *Ueber den Einfluss der griechischen Philosophie auf die Entwicklung des Kalam* (Breslau, 1909), p. 54–69. See now Harry A. Wolfson, *Religious Philosophy: A Group of Essays* (1961), p. 52, and his book *The Philosophy of the Kalam* in which the concept of the "modes" (*ahwāl*) is fully discussed [1976].

11. Cf. *Kitāb al-Irshād,* ed. Luciani, p. 48 (81).

12. Neither Munk (*Guide* I, 185, n. 2) nor Friedländer (*Guide* I, 176, n. 1) seems to have understood this reference.

13. Cf. H. von Arnim, *Stoicorum Veterum Fragmenta* II, 131, 124.

14. Op. cit. I, 19, 117.

15. Cf. Shemtob Ibn Falaquera, *Moreh Ha-Moreh,* pp. 129–130, where this point is made in the clearest possible terms. S. B. Scheyer, in his *Das Psychologische System des Maimonides* (1845), pp. 41ff., suggests that Maimonides' rejection of the objective existence of the universals (*Guide* III, 18) refers only to logical and mathematical concepts. This interpretation cannot be upheld.

16. Cf. *Met.* VII, 8; Gabirol, *Fons Vitae,* V, 24.

17. Cf. Alfārābī, *Ringstones of Wisdom,* ed. Dieterici, p. 67 (110). As for the Aristotelian origin of the distinction between essence and existence, see I. Madkour, *L'Organon d'Aristote dans le monde arabe* (Paris, 1934); and H. A. Wolfson, *The Philosophy of Spinoza* (1934), I, 124.

18. Cf. Alfārābī, loc. cit.; Avicenna, *Metaphysics,* VIII, 6, quoted by E. Gilson, *Being and Some Philosophers* (1949), p. 78.

19. Cf. *Ḳobeẓ Tĕshuḇot Ha-Rambam wĕ- 'Iggĕrotaw,* II, 27b.

20. For the Aristotelian source of this distinction, cf. H. A. Wolfson, *Crescas' Critique of Aristotle,* pp. 691–692. Hillel of Verona, in his Commentary on the Twenty-Five Propositions of Maimonides (Tagmulē Ha-Nefesh [Lyck, 1874], pp. 38a–39a) offers a different interpretation. He explains that the potentiality of a substratum to become X implies (a) a natural disposition, (b) a general possibility, whilst (c) the potentiality of X (e.g. the man being potentially in the seed) is pure potentiality; being as yet non-existent, the X has neither disposition nor possibility.

21. The term *dunamis* in Aristotle denotes both potentiality and possibility. As to Avicenna, cf. M. Horten, *Metaphysik des Avicenna,* p. 25.

22. Two of these examples occur also in Maimonides' *Aphorisms (Fuṣul Mūsā).* Cf. M. Steinschneider, *Al-Farabi* (1869), p. 236.

23. Cf. *Shamayim Ḥadashīm,* ed. Heidenheimer (1828), p. 1b.

24. *Guide* I, 69; S. Pines, *Beiträge zur Islamischen Atomenlehre* (1936), p. 38.

25. Abrabanel, loc. cit., pp. 2b–3.

26. Cf. Moses of Narbonne, *Bi' ūr lĕ-Sefer Moreh Nĕḇuḵim,* ed. J. Goldenthal (1852), pp. 34a–b.

27. Cf. S. van den Bergh, *Die Epitome der Metaphysik des Averroes* (Leiden, 1924), p. 270.

28. Cf. H. A. Wolfson, *Spinoza,* pp. 316ff.

29. Cf. Abrabanel, loc. cit., p. 3a. The argument referred to is based on the fact that certain spheres move from east to west, others in the opposite direction. Cf. *Tahāfut* I, 12.

30. For a more elaborate account of this particular argument cf. *Die Epitome der Metaphysik des Averroes,* ed. S. van den Bergh, pp. 8–9.

31. Cf. H. A. Wolfson, "Crescas on Divine Attributes."

32. Cf. Franz Brentano, *Von der mannigfachen Bedeutung des Seienden nach Aristotles* (1862), p. 85; "Die Kategorien sind verschiedene Bedeutungen des ὄv." [The categories are different meanings of Being — ed.] See also Sir W. D. Ross, *Aristotle's Metaphysics,* I, 307: "Thus Being is not a genus common to the various senses of being but has a different meaning in the various categories."

33. The above summary of Dr. Rahman's interpretation follows closely the text of his paper on "Essence and Existence in Avicenna."

34. Cf. Bodleian Library, ms. Can. Or. 63 (Neubauer 1377.3), fol. 154a.

35. Cf. *Philosophical Essays* by Isaac Husik, ed. by Milton C. Nahm and Leo Strauss (1952), pp. 162–163.

36. This fourfold division is used by Gabirol for a fourfold classification of ontological levels. Cf. *Fons Vitae,* V, 24. For a discussion of Aristotle's four types of inquiry in early Arabic and Jewish philosophy, see now A. Altmann and S. M. Stern, *Isaac Israeli* (1958), pp. 10–23.

37. Cf. Maimonides' *Treatise on Logic,* ch. 13; *Guide,* Introduction.

38. Quoted in L. Gardet-M. M. Anawati, *Introduction à la Théologie Musulmane* (Paris, 1948), p. 103.

39. This definition of the objects of metaphysics forms part of the classification of sciences introduced into Arabic philosophy through the translation of John Philoponus' Commentary on Porphyry's *Isagoge.* Sometimes, the Aristotelian scheme is mixed with the Platonic classification which identifies metaphysics with logic. Cf. H. A. Wolfson, "The Classification of Sciences in Medieval Jewish Philosophy," *Hebrew Union College Annual,* Jubilee Volume (1925): 263–315; Leo Strauss, "Farabi's Plato," *Louis Ginzberg Jubilee Volume,* American Academy for Jewish Research (New York, 1945), pp. 389ff.

40. Alfārābī's "The political Governments" was edited in Hyderabad in 1346, and appeared in a German translation ("Die Staatsleitung von Alfarabi") by Brömle (Leiden, 1904). We possess the work also in Samuel Ibn Tibbon's Hebrew translation under the title, *Sefer Hatĕhalōt Ha-Nimẓa'ōt* (ed. Zebi Filipowski [Leipzig, 1849], in *Sefer Ha-'Asīf*). The passage referred to in the text is found on p. 16 of this Hebrew edition. As to the significance of the work for an appraisal *of* Maimonides, cf. Leo Strauss, "Farabi's Plato," pp. 357ff.

Maimonides on
Modes and Universals

HARRY A. WOLFSON

In a passage dealing with the problem of divine attributes, Maimonides says: "You must know that God has no essential attributes in any manner (*wajh: panim*) and in any mode (*ḥāl: 'inyan*) whatsoever."[1]

At the time of Maimonides, the problem of attributes did not present itself simply as a contrast between the affirmation of attributes and the negation of attributes. Between these two contrasting theories there was a third theory, known as the theory of *modes*. The Arabic term for mode in this technical sense is *ḥāl*, which the Modalists say is used by them as the equivalent of the term *wajh*.[2] A few salient points in the history of the theory of modes, as I have reconstructed it in my work *The Philosophy of the Kalam,* are necessary as prefatory to the discussion as to the use of these terms in the passage quoted.

The theory of modes originally appeared as a theory of universals, and it was the culmination of a discussion of the problem of universals which had arisen about a century earlier, in an attempt to answer the question posed by Porphyry as to the nature of *genera* and species. From a theory of universals, which is also a theory of predication, the theory of modes was applied to divine attributes; and it resulted in a view which was at once opposed to both the orthodox affirmation of attributes and to the Mu'tazilite denial of them. In the course of time, however, certain orthodox Attributists harmonized modes in the sense of divine predicates with their own affirmation of attributes, and certain Mu'tazilites harmonized them with their own denial of attributes.

Harry A. Wolfson, "Maimonides on Modes and Universals," pp. 311–321 in *Studies in Rationalism, Judaism, and Universalism; in memory of Leon Roth,* edited by Raphael Loewe (London: Routledge and Kegan Paul, 1966). Reprinted by permission of Routledge and Kegan Paul Ltd.

166

Although, on the whole, various distinctive formulae were used by exponents of these three theories in the description of their respective views, sometimes the same formula was used by them in different senses. The most common formula used for modes in the sense of both universals and divine predicates was that modes are neither existent nor non-existent. The most common formula for modes in the sense of only divine predicates was that modes are neither the same as God nor other than God. A stock objection to the theory of modes was that it infringed upon the Law of Excluded Middle. The answer to this stock objection was that modes have a conceptual existence and that a conceptual existence is a special kind of existence, which is intermediate between the existence of things which correspond to words and the non-existence of mere words for which there is no correspondence in things; and, since the existence of modes is an intermediate between two extremes, the negation of both the extremes is no infringement upon the Law of Excluded Middle.

In view of the fact then, that by the time of Maimonides modes had already been harmonized with either the affirmation of attributes or the denial of attributes, when Maimonides says here that "God has no essential attributes in any *wajh* and in any *ḥāl* whatsoever," the following question arises: Does his rejection of attributes here include also a rejection of modes or does it not include a rejection of modes? In the former case, the phrase "in any *wajh* and in any *ḥāl*" will have been used by him significantly, in order to emphasize the inclusion of modes among the attributes rejected by him; in the latter case, the phrase will have been used by him to emphasize merely that attributes are to be rejected, no matter how their real meaning may be disguised by the use of some evasive formula.

The same question with regard to Maimonides' attitude toward modes arises also in connection with another passage, which reads as follows: "Some people of speculation got to the point where they said that the attributes of God are neither His essence nor anything extraneous to His essence."[3]

This type of formula, though usually associated with the name of Abū Hāshim[4] and the theory of modes of which he is the founder, was used long before him in the sense of the affirmation of attributes, first by Sulaymān b. Jarīr and his followers[5] and then by Ibn Kullāb and his followers.[6] Subsequently among the Ash'arites it was used by some in the sense of the affirmation of attributes[7] and by others in the sense of the affirmation of modes.[8] Accordingly, in Maimonides' ascription here of this type of formula to "some people of speculation," the following question arises: Does he use this type of formula in the sense of an expression of a belief in attributes only, or does he use it in the sense of an expression of a belief in modes?

In his refutation of this formula, Maimonides goes on to say as follows:

> But this is similar to the saying of some others that the modes (*al-aḥwāl:* *ha-'inyanim*), that is, the universal concepts (*al-ma'ānī al-kulliyyah: ha-* *'inyanim hak-kelaliyyim*), are neither existent nor non-existent and similar to the saying of still others that the atom is not in a place (*makān: maqom*) but it occupies space (*yushghal al-ḥayyiz: yaṭridh hag-gebhul*) and that man has no action at all but he has acquisition (*al-iktisāb: haq-qeniyyah*). All these are sentences (*aqāwil: debharim*) which are only said, so that they exist in words (*alfāz: milloth*) and not in rational judgments (*adhhān: de'oth*), and all the more, they have no existence outside the mind (*dhihn: sekhel*).⁹

At first sight, his statement that the formula which he has previously ascribed to "some people of speculation" is similar "to the saying of some others" about "modes," would seem to indicate that the "some people of speculation" to whom he ascribed the aforementioned formula were not those who believed in modes. But when, right after mentioning the term "modes," he explains that he means by it "the universal concepts," he clearly indicates that he is aware of the distinction between modes as universal concepts and modes as divine predicates. The same question with regard to Maimonides' attitude towards modes thus arises again: Do the "men of speculation," to whom Maimonides ascribes the formula which he compares to the formula used for modes in the sense of universals, include those who used the same formula for modes in the sense of divine predicates, or do they not include them? In the former case, it would indicate that Maimonides agreed with those who harmonized modes in the sense of divine predicates with the affirmation of attributes; in the latter case, it would indicate that he agreed with those who harmonized modes in the sense of divine predicates with the denial of attributes.

But then there is another question in connection with this refutation. Why should Maimonides object to the formula that modes in the sense of universals are neither existent nor nonexistent? Those who considered universals as modes held, as said above in the prefatory remarks, that universals have a conceptual existence, and that a conceptual existence is a kind of existence which is intermediate between the existence of things and the non-existence of words; and that, because universals are intermediate between existence and non-existence, to say of them that they are neither existent nor non-existent is not a violation of the Law of Excluded Middle. Now Maimonides himself admits that universals, while they are not extra-mental things, are mental things (*ma'ānī dhihniyyah: debharim* *sikhliyyim*).¹⁰ Moreover, from his contention that a definition implies that the *definiendum* is composed of genus and specific difference which are causes of the *definiendum*,[11] it is to be inferred that universals, described by him as "mental things," do have some kind of existence. The kind of existence which, according to him, universals could have would be, we may assume, like that ascribed to them by Avicenna in his triple stage theory in the existence of universals, namely, before multiplicity (*qabl al-kathrah*), in multiplicity (*fī al-kathrah*), and after multiplicity (*ba'd al-kathrah*), which, as I have shown, is traceable to Ammonius Hermiae.[12] Now, according to this theory, universals in their after-multiplicity stage, that is, the stage during which they exist in the human mind, may be said to have a conceptual existence[13] analogous to that ascribed to them by the Muslim Modalists, and may thus be described as being neither existent like extra-mental things nor non-existent like mere words. In view of this, why should Maimonides object to the formula that universals are neither existent nor non-existent, when that formula can be interpreted as not being an infringement upon the Law of Excluded Middle?

Let us see how Maimonides would answer this question as to why he objects to the modalistic formula about universals, and from his answer to this question we shall try to find out what his answer would be to the questions we have raised with regard to his view on modes in the sense of divine predicates.

In his answer to this question, Maimonides, I imagine, would say that although he was willing to admit that the formula could be interpreted so as not to infringe upon the Law of Excluded Middle, he still objected to it on the ground that in its form, in its phrasing, it does infringe upon that Law. To him, he would argue, for a formula to be right it must be one which, both in form and in substance, is logically sound. By such a logically sound formula, he would go on to explain, he meant a formula which conforms to what Aristotle calls an "enunciative sentence" (λόγος ἀποφαντικός: *al-qaul al-jāzim*), by which Aristotle means a logical proposition which is subject to the description of being either true or false[14]: and the test as to whether it is true or false is, according to him, its correspondence or non-correspondence to something outside the mind.[15]

It is in accordance with this conception of his as to what constitutes the right kind of formula that Maimonides goes on to reject as unsound the four formulae under consideration. The formula that "the atom is not in a place (*makān*) but occupies space (*yushghal al-ḥayyiz*)" may, indeed, in its external form be a well constructed logical proposition; for externally it appears that the predicate that is negated in the first part of the proposition is not the same as the predicate that is affirmed in its second part. Still, in meaning the proposition infringes upon the Law of Contradiction; for, inasmuch as by definition "place" (*makān*) is that which is occupied by an extended body only,[16] the statement in the first part of the proposition, namely, that "the atom is not in place," implies that the atom is not an extended body; but, inasmuch as only those who believe that the atom is an extended body say that the atom occupies space,[17] the statement in the second part of the proposition, namely, that the atom "occupies space," implies that the atom *is* an extended body. Similarly the formula that "man has no action at all but he has acquisition" may, again, be a well-constructed logical proposition in its external form. Still, in meaning it is an infringement upon the Law of Contradiction, for the "acquisition" affirmed in its second part is itself an "action," and thus it is contradictory to the denial of "action" in the first part. As for the formula quoted by Maimonides from certain Attributists, we may assume that he knew that Ibn Kullāb and the others after him had used it, as can be shown, in such a way that, by their denying that attributes are "His essence," they meant to deny the Mu'tazilite view that the attributes of God are "His essence"; and that by their denying that attributes are "extraneous to His essence," they meant to deny the view of the Zurariyyah and Karrāmiyyah that the attributes are created, and hence are "extraneous to His essence": so that in meaning the formula does not infringe upon the Law of Excluded Middle. Still, in its external form it is an infringement upon that Law, since it denies both that the attributes are "His essence" and that they are "extraneous to His essence," that is to say, they are neither the *same* as His essence nor *other* than His essence. Similarly, we may assume that he knew that the Modalists by their denying that universals are "existent" meant to deny that they are existent like extra-mental real things, and that by their denying that universals are "non-existent" meant to deny that they are non-existent like mere words; so that the formula is no infringement upon the Law of Excluded Middle. Still, in its external form it is an infringement upon that Law. What, according to Maimonides, would be the right formula for conceptual universals is suggested by him in his statement that "no species exist outside the mind, but species and other universals are mental things."[18] The right formula would thus be that "universals are non-existent outside the mind, but they are existent in the mind."

That Maimonides' criticism here is aimed exclusively at the formulae used in the four theories he mentions, and not at the theories themselves, is evidenced by his use of the term *aqāwil* in his opening statement, namely, "these are all *aqāwil* (Hebrew: *debharim*)."[19] The term *aqāwil* is the plural of *qaul*, which in the Arabic translation of *De Interpretatione*[20] translates the Greek term λόγος in the passage quoted above. In that passage Aristotle, starting with an explanation of the general meaning of the term λόγος, "sentence" (of which he subsequently says that it may be either enunciative, which conveys judgment as to truth and falsehood, or verbal, which does not convey judgment as to truth and falsehood), goes on to say that "a word" (φάσις, *lafẓah*), such as the word "man," which is part of a sentence, never does convey "affirmation or negation,"[21] that is, it never conveys judgment as to truth and falsehood. Thus Maimonides' opening statement means to say that all these formulae are only what Aristotle would consider as mere verbal sentences, for, as he goes on to explain, "they are only said and consequently they exist only in words (*alfāẓ: milloth*) and not in rational judgments (*adhhān: de'oth*)."[22] By this he means to say that they are combinations of words which form only verbal sentences that convey no judgments as to truth and falsehood. He then adds: "and all the more, they have no existence outside the mind (*dhihn: sekhel*)."[23] By this he means to say that, more than merely being sentences which *do not* convey judgments as to truth and falsehoods, these formulae are like words which, according to Aristotle, *never* convey judgments as to truth and falsehood,[24] seeing that there can never exist outside the mind anything to correspond to any of those formulae.

Finally, in trying to explain in concrete terms what his objections really are against the four formulae he has mentioned, he makes two statements. First: anyone who uses these formulae, he says, "endeavors to make exist something that does not exist."[25] By this he refers to two of the four formulae quoted by him, namely, those used by some Atomists and the Acquisitionists, both of which, as I have tried to explain, are in meaning infringements upon the Law of Contradiction which, as quoted by Aristotle in the name of Heraclitus, reads: "It is impossible for anyone to suppose that the same thing exists and does not exist."[26] Second: anyone who uses these formulae, he says again, "endeavors . . . to create an intermediate between two contraries (*ḍiddāni: shenē hephekhim*) between which there is no intermediate"[27] — that is, they infringe upon the Law of Excluded Middle. Here Maimonides himself indicates that this criticism is aimed at the other two of the four formulae quoted by him, namely those used by some of the Attributists and by Modalists in their conception of universals; for immediately after this criticism he goes on to say that there is no intermediate between the contraries "existent" and "non-existent" and between the contraries "same" and "other"[28]: that is, the two pairs of contraries denied respectively in the formula of the Modalists in their conception of universals, and in the formula of some of the Attributists. Maimonides' carefully phrased statement that the contraries between which the users of these formulae endeavor to create intermediates are those "between which there is no intermediate," reflects Aristotle's statement that, with respect to opposites which are "by way of contraries (ὡς τὰ ἐναντία: *'alā ṭarīq al-muḍāddah*)," some have intermediates and some have no intermediates; and that those which have no intermediates are "such that the subject in which they naturally exist, or of which they are predicated, must necessarily contain either the one or the other of them,"[29] the implication being that the subject cannot be said to contain neither the one nor the other.

The upshot of our discussion is that, with respect to modes in the sense of universals, Maimonides agrees with the Modalists that they have a conceptual existence which is neither existent like things nor non-existent like words, but he disagrees with them as to the logical propriety of the use of their formula. With regard to the use of modes as an interpretation of divine predicates, inasmuch as in his discussion of divine attributes Maimonides has made it clear that no term predicated of God can be a universal,[30] it follows that no term predicated of God can be a mode. Consequently, with regard to divine predicates, he not only disagrees with the Modalists in the use of their formula: he disagrees with them also in their interpretation of divine predicates as modes.

By this we are now able to answer the other questions we have raised. The terms *ḥāl* and *wajh* in the first passage are quite definitely used by him in the technical sense of "mode," and similarly "some men of speculation," to whom he ascribes the formula that "the attributes of God are neither His essence nor anything extraneous to His essence," include both those who use this formula in the sense of attributes and those who use it in the sense of modes, for to him modes as an interpretation of divine predicates are not to be distinguished from attributes; the former, no less than the latter, being to him incompatible with the conception of the absolute simplicity of God.

The conclusion we have arrived at in our interpretation of these vague passages also throws light on a third vague passage in the *Moreh Nebukhim*. In that passage, dealing with those who believe in attributes, Maimonides says: "Some of them express themselves clearly on the existence of attributes, enumerating them as things superadded to the essence."[31] This quite evidently refers to those Ash'arites whose formulation of the doctrine of attributes contains the expression "superadded to the essence."[32]

Maimonides then goes on to say: "Others among them do not state this clearly, but that this is their belief is quite clear, even though they do not express themselves in clear-cut language, as is the case of some of them who say that God is powerful in virtue of His essence, He is knowing in virtue of His essence, He is living in virtue of His essence, He is willing in virtue of His essence."[33] Now the expression "in virtue of His essence" as a description of terms predicated of God has been used in various senses. According to Ash'arī, the formula that "the names and attributes of God are in virtue of His essence" was used by Ibn Kullāb, together with his formula that "they are not God and they are not other than God," as an expression of his belief that "they subsist in God,"[34] by which he means, as he makes even more clear elsewhere,[35] that God possesses real attributes. According to Shahrastānī, the expression "in virtue of essence" was used by Jubbā'ī in the sense of the denial of attributes and by Abu Hāshim in the sense of the affirmation of modes.[36] From the context of the passage, which deals directly with Attributists, it is not clear whether "the others among them" who use the expression "in virtue of His essence" include Attributists only or also Modalists. In the light, however, of our conclusion that Maimonides was opposed to modes no less than to attributes, it is quite certain that "the others among them" include also Modalists. But although in this passage the use of the expression "in virtue of His essence" is rejected by Maimonides with reference only to its use as an affirmation of either attributes or modes, it may be inferred from other passages, as I have shown elsewhere,[37] that Maimonides would not use it even in the sense of the absolute denial of attributes; and one of the reasons for his not using it is the fact of its being used by others in the sense of the affirmation of either attributes or modes. To him, any formula describing the meaning of terms predicated of God must be free of any vagueness and ambiguity.

NOTES

1. *Moreh Nebhukhim* I, 50, Arabic, ed. Joel, p. 75, ll. 5–6.

2. Shahrastānī, *Nihāyat*, ed. Guillaume, p. 137, l. 18.

3. *Moreh,* I, 51, p. 76, ll. 24–26.

4. Baghdādī, *Farq,* ed. Badr, p. 182, l. 14.

5. Ash'arī, *Maqālāt,* ed. Ritter, p. 70, ll. 8–10; p. 514, ll. 15–16; p. 547, l. 13.

6. Ibid., p. 169, ll. 10–13; p. 514, ll. 15–16; p. 546, l. 11.

7. Ibn Ḥaldun, *Muqaddimah,* ed. Quatremère, III, p. 38, ll. 16–17; cf. discussion in my *Religious Philosophy,* pp. 182–183.

8. Ibn Ḥazm, *Fiṣal,* ed. Cairo, 1317–1327, V, p. 49, ll. 2–4.

9. *Moreh* I, 51, p. 76, l. 26–p. 77, l. 2.

10. Ibid., III, 18, p. 343, ll. 9–10.

11. Ibid., I, 52, p. 77, ll. 19–25.

12. Cf. my paper "Avicenna, Algazali, and Averroes on Divine Attributes," *Homenaje a Millás-Vallicrosa,* vol. 2 (1956), pp. 547–550.

13. Cf. my interpretation of Maimonides' theory of universals in terms of Avicenna's triple stage theory of universals in my paper "Crescas on the Problem of Divine Attributes," *Jewish Quarterly Review* N.S., 7 (1916): 11–13. At that time I thought of Maimonides' triple stage theory of universals as a sort of moderate realism, and hence I described his criticism of the modalistic formula for universals in *Moreh* I, 51, as a criticism of conceptualism. According to my present way of thinking, however, all theories of universals between extreme realism and ex-

treme nominalism are to be considered as various shades of conceptualism. Maimonides' theory of universals is, therefore, one of the various shades of conceptualism. His criticism, as I now try to show, is only of the phrasing of the formula.

14. *De Interpr.* 4, 17a, 1-3.

15. *Metaph.* IV, 7, 10111b, 27.

16. Jurjānī, *Kitāb al-Taʿrifāt,* ed. Flügel, p. 244, l. 20-p. 245, l. 1; cf. Munk, *Guide* I, 51, p. 186, n.

17. Abū Rashīd, *Masāʾil,* ed. Biram, p. 38, l. 15, and p. 41, l. 18-p. 42, l. 2 (German, pp. 46 and 49).

18. *Moreh* III, 18, p. 343, ll. 9-10.

19. Ibid., I, 51, p. 76, l. 29.

20. Cf. I. Pollak's edition of the Arabic translation of the *De Interpretatione* and Badawi's edition of the *Organon.*

21. *De Interpr.* 4, 16b, 27-28.

22. *Moreh* I, 51, p. 77, l. 1. For my translation of *adhhān* by "rational judgments," see Avicenna's descriptions of *dhihn* quoted by Goichon in *Lexique,* §263, pp. 132-134. This explains also why Ibn Ṭibbon translated it by *deʿoth.*

23. *Moreh* I, 51, p. 77, ll. 1-2.

24. *De Interpr.,* 4, 16b, 26-30.

25. *Moreh,* I, 51, p. 77, l. 6.

26. *Metaphys.* IV, 3, 1005b, 23-24.

27. *Moreh* I, 51, p. 77, l. 6.

28. Ibid., ll. 7-8.

29. *Categ.,* 10, 11b, 33-12a, 3.

30. *Moreh,* I, 52, p. 77, l. 19-p. 78, l. 1.

31. Ibid., I, 53, p. 82, ll. 1-2.

32. *Nihāyat,* p. 181, ll. 1-4; Averroes, *Kashf,* ed. Müller, p. 56, ll. 3 and 7.

33. *Moreh* I, 53, p. 82, ll. 2-4.

34. *Maqālāt,* p. 169, ll. 12-13.

35. Ibid., ll. 10-12.

36. *Milal,* p. 55, l. 19-p. 56, l. 3.

37. Cf. my paper "Maimonides on Negative Attributes," *Louis Ginzberg Jubilee Volume* (1945), pp. 415-418.

Providence, Divine Omniscience, and Possibility: The Case of Maimonides

ALFRED L. IVRY

1. MAIMONIDES' EXOTERIC POSITION STATED

As in practically every area of Maimonides' discourse, his position on the issue of providence, divine omniscience, and possibility is not obvious on a first reading of the material. Or rather, it is too obvious, obvious twice over, the difficulty being that on the face of it Maimonides contradicts himself on these issues, as he does on many others. Here too it would seem that he has both an exoteric and esoteric position. Taking the *Guide of the Perplexed* as the main source for our study, it is the esoteric position mostly which I should like to attempt to describe. My thesis is that this is Maimonides' true position, as shown by the philosophical coherence it possesses.

We may begin with Maimonides' statement in *Guide* III, 20, which offers what I see as his exoteric position.

> To sum up the notion that I have stated in résumé: Just as we do not apprehend the true reality of His essence, but know withal that His existence is the most perfect of existences and not commingled in any way with any deficiency or change or being acted upon, so although we do not know the true reality of His knowledge because it is His essence, we do know that He does not apprehend at certain times while being ignorant at others. I mean to say that no new knowledge comes to Him in any way; that His knowledge is neither multiple nor finite; that nothing among all the beings

From *Divine Omniscience and Omnipotence in Medieval Philosophy*, edited by T. Rudavsky, pp. 143–159. Copyright © 1985 by D. Reidel Publishing Company. Reprinted by permission of D. Reidel Publishing Company.

is hidden from Him; and that His knowledge of them does not abolish their natures, for the possible remains as it was with the nature of possibility. All the contradictions that may appear in the union of these assertions are due to their being considered in relation to our knowledge, which has only its name in common with His knowledge. Similarly the word "purpose" is used equivocally when applied to what is purposed by us and to what is said to be His purpose, may He be exalted. Similarly the word "providence" is used equivocally when applied to what we are provident about and to that of which it is said that He, may He be exalted, is provident with regard to it. It is accordingly true that the meaning of knowledge, the meaning of purpose, and the meaning of providence, when ascribed to us, are different from the meanings of these terms when ascribed to Him. When, therefore, the two providences or knowledges or purposes are taken to have one and the same meaning, the above-mentioned difficulties and doubts arise. When, on the other hand, it is known that everything that is ascribed to us is different from everything that is ascribed to Him, truth becomes manifest. The differences between the things ascribed to Him and those ascribed to us have been explicitly stated, as have been mentioned above, in its dictum *Neither are your ways My ways.*[1]

With this quotation from Isaiah we could well draw our discussion to a pious and mercifully brief close, taking refuge in the equivocal nature of language about God, which ostensibly permits us to make assertions of a traditional sort, even though we do not understand the meaning of what we say. As Maimonides has said, "When . . . it is known that everything that is ascribed to us is different from everything ascribed to Him, truth becomes manifest."

Maimonides, however, has not said that everthing ascribed to us is *totally* different from everything ascribed to God, just that everything is different. He would probably have liked to make the stronger claim, as he has elsewhere (I, 56), but his very discussion of the issues belies that. There are a necessary similarity and a univocal core of meaning in the concepts mentioned which serve as a base for discussion and comparison, even if that comparison leads to tremendous disparities. Maimonides clearly believes in the essential difference between God and man, but that does not necessarily imply a total difference, as we shall see, his protestations to the contrary notwithstanding.

Maimonides himself, in the passage just quoted, intially makes some definitive and presumably comprehensible statements about God's existence and knowledge, to which the Divine purpose and providence are related; and he surrounds this chapter with further intelligible discussion, analysis actually, of these themes. It is not, therefore, unwarranted to follow "the master" in examining these concepts critically, beginning, as Maimonides does here, with God's essence and existence.

2. THE CREATOR AND HIS CREATION: THE NATURE OF GOD, MATTER, AND FORM

The concepts of essence and existence are identical in God, both for Maimonides as well as for Avicenna, whom Maimonides joins in describing God as the Necessary Existent, *wājib al-wujūd,* he whose essence is existence *simpliciter.* As such, God's existence is uncaused, having no reason or reality other than itself, its essence absolutely self-contained and pure being.[2] All the customary Divine attributes — life, power and knowledge, for example — must necessarily be identified with this simple essence, as Maimonides makes clear in I, 57; for to introduce distinctions in God's being would entail multiplicity and require explanation. It was felt that this would deprive the Necessary Existent of its singular status as pure being.

The Necessary Existent is, however, for Maimonides even more than for Avicenna, also regarded as solely responsible ultimately for the being of the world, that is, for the many and diverse beings in the world.[3] The uncaused One is thus the cause (in whatever sense we use the term) of the many, and the Necessary Existent, supposedly without losing its essential unity and absolute autonomy of being, functions as though it indeed is the source of those properties of life, power and knowledge which, among others, exist in the world.

Though Maimonides insists upon the identification of the multiplicity of Divine attributes with the single Divine essence, the basic problem of the simple One being the source of the many and thus putatively multiple itself is a conundrum he cannot resolve. It is a mystery of being for Maimonides similar to that whereby the One is said to know all, i.e., the many, in a single way.[4] Lacking other necessary independent principles of being besides the Necessary Existent, Maimonides has no principle of multiplicity which can account for its initial appearance. It is not for nothing that the world is created from nothing, for Maimonides, and neither is it negligent on his part that matter, the requisite principle, never receives the full status it enjoys in Aristotle's thought, where it may be seen as the eternal live-in partner of form.[5]

Far from regarding it as a spouse or partner of form, however, Maimonides calls matter a "harlot," likening it to Satan, darkness, and evil.[6] Its fatal flaw, for Maimonides, is its inherent transiency, its impermanent and corruptible nature. Originating in the absence of all beings, created from nothing, matter remains impressed in Maimonides' consciousness as related to privation, to the absence of forms associated with specific beings. Such forms are potentially present in the matter, but it itself is void of all but the disposition to receive them. Matter comes as close as one can get to non-being, where being is identified with permanent substance.

Of course, Maimonides makes it clear in numerous places, and particularly in his discussion of Aristotle's description of the nature of the universe, with which he explicitly concurs,[7] that he realizes that matter plays a necessary role in the physical world: it both provides a substratum for forms and individual existence, and serves as a principle of change and potentiality. As part of the way things are, with matter always specifically informed, Maimonides is even prepared to acknowledge that the world in its entirety, matter included, exhibits the wisdom and goodness of its Creator.[8]

This more generous and accepting attitude of Maimonides to matter does not, however, disguise his deeply felt aversion to material and corporeal things. For him, matter is basically a necessary evil, necessary as the condition for the realization of form in the world, evil because of its incipient insubstantiality. At the same time, however, matter is not viewed as essentially insubstantial, for it is created as a genuine substance, however elusive its origins or nature.

The non-being (or privation, al-'adam) which precedes the creation of the world is not for Maimonides a real substance: it is not Nothing. Similarly, the matter which serves as the substratum for form is not regarded as an independent principle of (non-) being, an autonomous counterforce to form. Matter so regarded could provide the rationale for viewing physical existence as a *real* "veil" (Maimonides' imagery, *Guide* III, 9), a veritable kingdom of evil to be overcome.

This would more than justify Maimonides' negative attitude to matter and matters physical, as well as provide a rational explanation for creation from nothing. Maimonides, however, does not avail himself of this option, which would have been familiar to him from both philosophical and mystical sources.[9] He prefers his creation to be purely "from nothing,"[10] and he remains irrationally set against matter. He is irrational, since the same Aristotelian reading of form and matter which precludes his accepting a basically dualistic world view, should have prepared him to accept with greater equanimity the necessary — and hence desirable — role of matter in being. Thus, what must be said here is that Maimonides accepts the Aristotelian definition of substance as including matter, but places it within a Neoplatonized value scheme in which the substantiality of matter is markedly inferior to that of form. It is form which is preeminently substance for Maimonides, form which is derived from the "form of forms," form with which the *donatur formarum* (wāhib al-ṣuwar) is necessarily and permanently involved.[11] Matter, unlike form, is neither with God from all eternity, nor close to him after its creation. It serves as a showcase and/or trial for form, but has little intrinsic worth. The best thing Maimonides can say of it is that it is good, in spite of being "a concomitant of privation entailing death and all evils," because of the "perpetuity of generation and the permanence of being through succession" in which it participates.[12] At every stage of this succession, however, it is form which dominates matter, even as it is form which is dominant in Maimonides' thinking.

The form which the Divine mostly takes, for Maimonides as well as for most medieval (and classical) philosophers, is of course Intelligence.[13] He *is* Intelligence itself, the source of order, proportion, and (proper) form. As Intelligence, or Intellect, God's being is a knowing, not just of itself as Aristotle would have it, but of all that is intelligible, the entire intelligible universe. He is the cause of this universe in all but the material mode of causation.[14] According to Maimonides, God's knowledge thus has to be "over all" in existence, that is over all that may be known, since his knowledge is an expression — our expression — of his creative activity in the world.

This action is, moreover, regarded as an expression of God's goodness; it is, indeed, identical with his goodness. For God is the "Pure Good" as well as the Intelligence and Form of the world (as well as its Necessary Existent), and all these terms are identical with his essence. Maimonides says in the opening of III, 19 of the *Guide*, that "it is a primary notion that all good things must exist in God," and that he has no deficiencies. Maimonides takes this to mean that God cannot be ignorant of anything, since "ignorance with regard to anything is a deficiency." That which God brings into existence and/or knows is therefore good. As he is the first cause or principle of all that exists, all in the universe must be good, a necessary consequence of his omniscience and omnipotence.

This summary of Maimonides' position is both right and wrong. He believes it to be the case, but only after offering serious, though discrete, qualification. For to accept this view literally would make the Deity already responsible for the evil in the world, which Maimonides acknowledges, however reluctantly, to be real.[15] The incorporeal nature of the Divine as well as his unity are also threatened by the literal view of omniscience, since the objects of God's knowledge, which knowledge is his essence, are and become that which exists in the world. The physical universe would then be the direct result of God's action, which is another term for his essence, so that the created world, with all its warts, would equal the Creator.

3. THE PROCESS OF EMANATION (AL-FAYḌ)

To avoid this pantheistic and materialist consequence, Maimonides adopts the originally Neoplatonic scheme of emanation, which is meant to provide just the mechanism desired to both bridge and maintain the gap between the One and the many, as well as between the spiritual and physical spheres of being.[16] Maimonides, we should note, utilizes the emanative idea for the first purpose only, his notion of creation from nothing offering an alternative description, if not explanation, for the origin of matter.

If matter does not emanate from the One, though, in Maimonides' scheme of things, the forms of this world do; and this emanation must include, paradoxically, the form of matter. It is known to God as an intelligible concept, an object of his intelligence, as everything else is known to him and exists with him. How God turns this intellection of matter into a physical reality is, Maimonides believes, totally beyond our comprehension.[17] It is no more comprehensible, however, than his mode of knowledge itself, which comprehends the identity of the One and the many.

Yet there is an important difference between the mystery of creation and the mystery of God's knowledge, as Maimonides treats them. He is very eager to establish the possibility of creation from nothing, but completely opposed to speculating about its nature; whereas he is not reticent in discussing God's omniscience, however problematic a topic it is. We are, therefore, on surer ground in describing the particular form his belief in this concept takes.

I do not wish to give the impression that Maimonides is really enlightening on the notion of emanation (al-fayḍ), the mechanism of providence in general. The term is used frequently, together with appropriate and conventional imagery, but without any of the actual ontic structures that normally accompany it and which render it comprehensible.[18] The Maimonidean world upon which the Divine One casts its light, "unfolding" its being, beauty, and goodness, is in its structure more of an Aristotelian place than anything else, a world divided into supra- and sub-lunar spheres, each with its hylomorphic constitution. It is not a world of universal substances, neither the World Mind and Soul, as in classic Neoplatonic thought, nor any other completely separately existing universal being.

The forms of the world which are one in God are, accordingly, many in the world itself, via emanation, though without a gradual unfolding of the many from the One. The world is not, and then suddenly it is, in its entirety, for Maimonides. Yet here he is very clear: there is no creation from nothing of these forms in the world, there is no hiatus in their being; they derive from God, in whom they are necessarily eternal, being "part" of his eternal essence.

God is present in the world, then, for Maimonides, through the forms of everything that exists. This presence is not equally found in all members of a given species, since the forms of individual bodies may not be well realized, of which we will soon have more to say. The Divine presence is found, rather, in the species itself, as the definitive form of that species, though Maimonides is quite explicit that species don't really exist independently of their constituent individual members.[19]

The forms of things do exist separately from matter, we have seen, in the mind of God, and have done so eternally. Though the mode of existence of these forms "there," as God, is beyond our comprehension, it is clear to Maimonides that it is just this eternal existence of theirs which gives us assurance of the stable, even permanent, nature of our universe. While the world as we know it, with its combination of material and formal elements, is created, the essential nature of beings, their ideal forms, are eternal.[20]

These ideal forms, the pure forms, are, then, the objects of God's knowledge, and constitute his being and that of the essential being of the universe. The two beings are one and the same in God, though not in the universe, through the mystery of emanation. The isolated sparks of the Divine in the world (to use a later image) are further removed from the totality of God's being by their association with matter, the very antithesis of form and permanence. Though created by God, matter is intelligible to him only and necessarily in its intelligible mode, as form. God therefore knows the principle of matter, which in good part is that matter itself—to the degree that it exists by itself—is free of God's knowledge.

Of course, since matter never exists "by itself," for Maimonides, it is never not known to God, to some degree. Yet, while matter does not exist by itself, it has a self of its own, which self is a real substance.[21] It is this irreducible physical core of an object, the material cause itself, which is beyond direct Divine knowledge and ministration. God has willed this to be so, for Maimonides: he has chosen to create a substance over which he has no immediate control, the concrete, individual instances of which he is ignorant.

4. MAIMONIDES' THEORY OF PROVIDENCE

To say that Maimonides considers God's knowledge to be confined to the form of things, and to the forms in general, as representative of the species, seems to contradict his frequent assertions to the contrary. God is not ignorant of anything, Maimonides says in a number of places, asserting that divine omniscience extends to all individual existents. Nor is God's knowledge limited to currently existing individuals, but he is said also to know everything that will occur in the future too.[22]

Maimonides explicitly qualifies this position, however, as soon as he develops his theory of providence.

> For I for one believe that in this lowly world—I mean that which is beneath the sphere of the moon—divine providence watches only over the individuals belonging to the human species and that in this species alone all the circumstances of the individuals and the good and evil that befall them are consequent upon the deserts, just as it says: *For all His ways are judgment* (Deut. 32:4). But regarding all the other animals and, all the more, the plants and other things, my opinion is that of Aristotle. For I do not by any means believe that this particular leaf has fallen because of a providence watching over it; nor that this spider has devoured this fly because God has now decreed and willed something concerning individuals; nor that the spittle spat by Zayd has moved till it came down in one particular place upon a gnat and killed it by a divine decree and judgment; nor that when this fish snatched this worm from the face of the water, this happened in virtue of a divine volition concerning individuals. For all this is in my opinion due to pure chance, just as Aristotle holds.[23]

The restriction of individual providence to human beings is not for Maimonides just a matter of scriptural fiat, though he is quick to cite chapter and verse in support of his position that, in regard to "animals other than man," the biblical texts "refer to providence watching over the species and not to individual providence."[24] It is logic, however, and not authority which dictates Maimonides' position, for as he says quite candidly in the continuation of the previously quoted citation:

> According to me, as I consider the matter, divine providence is consequent upon the divine overflow; and the species with which this intellectual overflow is united, so that it became endowed with intellect and so that everything that is disclosed to a being endowed with the intellect was disclosed to it, is the one accompanied by divine providence, which appraises all its actions from the point of view of reward and punishment.[23]

For Maimonides, then, providence is entailed by emanation: it "is consequent upon the divine overflow" (*al-'ināyah al-ilāhīyah . . . tābi'ah lil-fayḍ al-ilāhī*) which is immediately called an "intellectual" overflow (*al-fayḍ al-'aqlī*). "Providence" is the term primarily given to this intellectual overflow as it reaches the only species which has a faculty capable of receiving it directly, or "purely." Man's rational faculty alone is believed to be "conjoined" (*ittaṣala*) to this divine intellect, and in consequence of this unique natural endowment (though willed by God to be man's nature), shared by all members of the species, man alone is individually, and necessarily, the object of divine providence. As Maimonides says elsewhere, "this consideration follows necessarily (*lāzim*) from the point of view of speculation, provided that, as we have mentioned, providence is consequent upon the intellect."[25]

Maimonides then continues with the following significant remark:

> It would not be proper for us to say that providence watches over the species and not the individuals, as is the well-known opinion of some philosophic schools. For outside the mind nothing exists except the individuals; it is to these individuals that the divine intellect is united. Consequently providence watches only over these individuals.[25]

This last statement is puzzling, given the above quoted view of providence watching over the species of species other than ours. Maimonides could not mean to say here that just our species is non-existent; that is rather a categorical statement negating the ontological reality of all species. They all have a nominal reality only, for Maimonides, given identity by the common form which their individual members possess. The divine intellect relates to this specific form, being, in Maimonides' view, responsible for it.[26]

This form, together with all others, exists separately only in God's mind, though in a manner, Maimonides says, beyond our comprehension, so that we should not say even that "it" exists there either. From God, however, the entire formal aspect of the universe emanates in an order of his own devising. This order becomes the nature of the world,[27] understood through categorization into genera and species. The divine intellect or providence may, accordingly, be said to "watch over" the species,[28] i.e., over the specific form present in individual members of the species, and to do so for every species in nature.

Homo Sapiens may be said to receive individual treatment primarily in the sense that he alone is *aware* of the divine intellect, and only he is able to benefit from this awareness by modifying his behaviour in accordance with it. The rational faculty which is man's *proprium*, given to him by God, enables man to respond consciously and individually to the knowledge he acquires, and thus to become responsible for his own destiny in a way other creatures are not.

The emphasis on man's ability to control his destiny distinguishes for Maimonides his view of providence from that of Aristotle. Maimonides stresses the role chance (*ittifāq*) plays in Aristotle's scheme, in contrast to its absence, for the sage, in his own theory. The two men are not really far apart, as Maimonides tells it, on the issue of individual versus species providence, as a close inspection of Maimonides' presentation of Aristotle's view would reveal.[29] It is, accordingly, in the total control which the true philosopher can supposedly exercise over his environment that Maimonides feels providence is most fully expressed.

If, as he (Aristotle) states, the foundering of a ship and the drowning of those who were in it and the falling-down of a roof upon those who were in the house, are due to pure chance, the fact that the people in the ship went on board and that the people in the house were sitting in it is, according to our opinion, not due to chance, but to divine will in accordance with the deserts of those people as determined in His judgments, the rule of which cannot be attained by our intellects.[30]

Though the unsuspecting reader may well think passages of this sort affirm providence to be an action taken by God *ad personam,* willed specifically (for or) against a particular individual, this is not the case. The individual who acts on the basis of correct or incorrect knowledge is responsible for what happens to him in all circumstances, Maimonides is saying, and this is the will of God. It is a will which functions "in accordance with that which is deserved" (*bi-ḥasb al-istiḥqāq*), i.e., deserved for such a person, whoever he is. The divine judgments in these matters, Maimonides concludes, are beyond our understanding. We do know, however, that these are "judgments" (*aḥkām*), general determinations of the permanent, unchanging wisdom (*ḥikmah*) of God, and need not be taken personally, in the usual sense of that term.

It is we who appraise God's actions from the point of view of reward and punishment, we who personalize the actions of the divine overflow, which become individualized in the varied responses we — and all corporeal being — bring to it. This understanding of providence agrees with Maimonides' general theory of divine attributes, which restricts the legitimate predication of attributes to God to those of a negative or relational kind. The latter category considers events in this world as effects of God's actions, and consciously interprets his inscrutable being in terms of behavior familiar to us.[31]

We could say therefore that the divine intellect is essentially impersonal and functions of necessity, but for the element of will which Maimonides, as is customary in medieval philosophy, regards as essential to the divine being. What happens in the world is regarded as a necessary consequence, directly or indirectly, of God's will. He wills, ultimately, without any external constraint, to be himself, a Necessary Existent, all the actions of which are perfect and good, necessarily. God freely wills, likewise, to emanate "part" of his being onto the world; an emanation, like creation, which follows necessarily from his nature, being part of his eternal, unchanging plan. The will of God is thus synonymous with his wisdom, as Maimonides says often,[32] and his freedom, we may add, synonymous with necessity. The divine will is perhaps most successful a term when taken as representing the outwardly oriented and purposive nature of the divine being, a purpose which, for Maimonides, should be said to extend to individuals, though not intended in the personal way we like to believe.

Maimonides is actually quite open about God's knowledge being of a general sort, dealing with universal concepts and species. This follows necessarily from his nature, i.e., from his wisdom and will combined, which is to say, from his very being. Statements of a more personal and traditional kind are also to be found throughout the *Guide*, but on close analysis they yield readings consistent with the philosophical position I have outlined.[33] The social and political problems Maimonides would have faced in presenting his views unadorned, unreconciled to traditional Jewish belief in a personal God and providence, are obvious. Fortunately for him, both the political theory he embraced and his view of prophecy — topics beyond our present discussion — complemented his metaphysical theory and encourged him to believe in the legitimacy of traditional formulations of these issues. As he says at one point, the opinion of some thinkers and necessarily that of those who adhere to a religious law (*kullu muttasharri'in*) is that "(God's) knowledge has for its object the species, but in a certain sense (*bi-ma'nī mā*) (it) extends to all the individuals of the species."[34] For socio-political reasons Maimonides often dwells on the individual aspect of providence, but he does not reduce it to that. Nor could he, given that God's providence follows his essence, and that is fixed, necessary, and essentially universal.

5. DIVINE OMNISCIENCE AND POSSIBILITY

The necessity that encompasses the divine intellect reflects upon the world, for Maimonides, and is a reflection of it. Not only are certain things, viz., logically contradictory things, impossible even for God to affect; but also, and equally, only certain things are possible for him, viz., those which agree with his essence, being derived from it. As God is the ultimate principle of being, his essential will is to let things be, to bring into being whatever may exist, the limits of possible existence being dictated by his wisdom. That wisdom in turn is characterized by goodness, which "indubitably," Maimonides says, (to which we would add "preeminently"), includes existence.[35] It thus follows necessarily from God's nature that there be an existent world and that it include all that may possibly exist; for to exclude eternally a real possibility would be to deprive the world of a good being, an act inconsistent with the nature of the "Pure Good."

A real possibility for Maimonides thus turns out to be identical, after creation, with actual possibilities (mostly) familiar to us, and potentially existing in material beings. The purely logical possibility of something existing merely by not running afoul of the law of contradiction – the notion of possibility which appealed to the Islamic theologians[36] – is not for Maimonides a sufficient criterion of possibility. The truly possible for him is also that which God has eternally determined to be so, willing that which his wisdom dictates. As Maimonides says, "He wills only what is possible, and not everything that is possible, but only that which is required by His wisdom to be such."[37] (Lest one think this statement implies after all that Maimonides does accept the notion of an ontological category of purely theoretically existing possibilities, think of what this would entail: the existence of ideal entities neither willed nor necessitated by God! Nor does it help to image that these possibilities could actually exist and be necessary in another world, for Maimonides is referring here to a category of possibilities that never actually exists, a category that in his thought is self-contradictory, given the necessity of God's goodness and perfection.)

That which exists, then, is, for Maimonides, a necessary consequent of God's necessary existence, and is as such good. In his initial discussion of the presumed evil of mortality, Maimonides puts it this way:

> Everything that is capable of being generated from any matter whatever, is generated in the most perfect way in which it is possible to be generated out of that specific matter; the deficiency attaining the individuals of the species corresponds to the deficiency of the particular matter of the individual. Now the ultimate term and the most perfect thing that may be generated out of blood and sperm is the human species with its well-known nature consisting in man's being a living, rational, and moral being. Thus this species of evils must necessarily exist.[38]

In this passage Maimonides succinctly puts the paradoxical nature of God's omniscience. It encompasses deficiencies and evils of a sort, real enough and even necessary, but not ultimately or essentially significant. Ultimately, in fact, they are witnesses to God's perfection and goodness. This goodness is available to anyone willing to participate in it, both through actions which correctly nurture and sustain life, and even more so, through intellectual efforts to reunite with the divine overflow. Since the overflow is constant, this conjunction is possible for man; the overflow sustains all the forms of the world, including that of man, in their permanent order.

On the other hand, the constancy of God's emanation, the continuous unfolding of ideas or forms from his eternal being, allows Maimonides to say with conviction that God knows all things, both now and in the future. God knows all of them through the formal principles with which he endows them; and he knows the future, as the present, since for God there is neither past, future, or present, just an eternal now.[39] The permanent forms of nature which come from God are of course related always to particular matters in particular times and places; but these are the accidents of existence, concomitants of matter, itself known only in the broadest of terms. Time and place, as matter, are known to God in principle only, the principle being that forms require them. For God it is sufficient to know that although his forms will always have a "certain" concrete and temporal identification, a particular material manifestation of one sort or another, nevertheless they will necessarily exhibit, whatever the occasion, certain eternal properties. It is these forms which interest God, or as we should say, these which are intelligible to him.

Maimonides points a number of times to the difficulty of believing that the one divine being should know the species of many things, and yet he finds it necessary to assert this.[40] It would have been relatively easy for him to go further and posit the existence of individual souls prior to their birth, i.e., of particular forms eternally known to God. He is reluctant to do this, however, for reasons which he makes rather clear: such knowledge would deprive man of his freedom and God of his justice, two principles which Maimonides recognized as tenets of Judaism. This kind of omniscience would remove the contingent nature of the possible, that aspect of a material body which for Maimonides contains its various potential states of being, all equally real. In interpreting the actions of all bodies as strictly determined, this kind of omniscience would in effect deprive matter of its freedom, and with that its relative distance and residual autonomy from God. Matter would then be harnessed as completely to God's will as is form now, and this in turn would make God necessarily and totally responsible for all the evil and deficiencies with which matter is now associated. Divine foreknowledge of this kind threatens God's goodness, on the one hand, and the reality of the world as our senses and intuitions reveal it, on the other.

It is, accordingly, perfectly consistent of Maimonides to say that God's knowledge "that a certain possible thing (*mumkin mā*, literally, "something possible") will come into existence, does not in any way make that possible thing quit the nature of the possible,"[41] and other statements to that effect. They may be read in a way that seems to indicate God knows specifically which possibilities will be realized, and Maimonides does this deliberately. Yet he is actually making the point that God knows the possibilities—all the possibilities, including that which is realized—inherent in everything.

6. DIVINE PROVIDENCE AS
THE EXPERIENCING OF ULTIMATE FELICITY

That God allows man (and other animals) to be free is part, then, of the necessary order of being which he has created. It is a sign of his providential regard for man, and of his loving-kindness, judgment, and righteousness.[42] These attributes, which man is to emulate, are most in evidence, for Maimonides, in the providence which God bestowed on the patriarchs and Moses, traditional symbols in the Jewish tradition of righteous and deserving men. Yet the providence which Maimonides describes in regard to these figures, as in general, is not the traditional kind. It is a providence which disdains not only material possessions and wealth, but even physical life itself.[43] That the patriarchs and Moses succeeded materially and politically is a consequence of the providence they enjoyed, an unusual byproduct, usually unnecessary if not counterproductive to providence. For the true providence and perfection of man, as Maimonides states in a number of places and particularly towards the end of the *Guide*, is an intellectual (or intellectual *cum* psychic) experience which elevates the individual into the presence of the divine, offering him a rapturous participation in the eternal beauty and love of God.[44] This ultimate perfection has nothing to do with physical or social concerns; indeed Maimonides depicts man as able to free himself from such concerns entirely in the felicitous moment of conjunction.[45] In so doing, Maimonides says, man frees himself from evil, indeed, from evil "of any kind." Here the perfect man has achieved full control of his environment, for he has transcended it entirely. In connecting his intellect fully with that of the divine intellect, man assumes a new identity, at least for as long as he can maintain the conjunction. He is now like the angels: pure form, part of eternal being, savoring a taste of eternity. The natural evils which can befall all men cannot touch him, for he is no longer mortal—at least, not essentially so.[46] Should anything happen to his physical body while in this state, it will not affect his mind, his true being, which is with God.

The evil of this world, connected to its matter, thus has, in Maimonides' opinion, a lesser degree of substantial being than does the good, which is connected to form. If the latter may be compared to essential being, then the former comes close to being a kind of accidental being, albeit a necessary accident. Maimonides is too much the Aristotelian to relegate matter to the status of non-being and illusion, or to break the hylomorphic knot of Aristotelian physics. However, in his understanding of providence and the many issues connected with it (though not, interestingly, as regards the issue of freedom and determinism), Maimonides comes perilously close to abandoning his Aristotelian anchors and setting off on a Neoplatonic sea.

NOTES

1. Following the translation of S. Pines, *Moses Maimonides: The Guide of the Perplexed* (Chicago and London: University of Chicago Press, 1963), III,

20 (43a), p. 483. All translations except when otherwise noted will be taken by permission from this work. References in parentheses are to the page numbers of the Judaeo-Arabic edition, *Dalâlat al-Ḥâ'irîn,* ed. S. Munk (Jerusalem 1929).

2. See *Guide* I, 57, 63 (82a), p. 154; II, 1 (8a) p. 247. Avicenna's remarks on the Necessary Existent have been assembled, in translation, by G. Hourani, "Ibn Sina on Necessary and Possible Existence," *The Philosophical Forum* 4 (1972): 74–86. Cf. too A. Altmann, "Essence and Existence in Maimonides," in *Studies in Religious Philosophy and Mysticism* (Ithaca: Cornell University Press, 1969), pp. 108–120; reprinted in this volume.

3. Maimonides' Necessary Existent acts more "unilaterally" than does Avicenna's, since the Muslim philosopher explicitly recognizes the necessity to posit eternal supernal beings in addition to the Necessary Existent, accomplished through the mechanism of emanation. Cf. Ibn Sina, *Al-Shifâ': Al-Illâhiyyât,* ed. I. Madkhour, *et al.* (Cairo: Cultural Dept. of the Arab League, 1960), 9, 4, p. 402ff.; and see L. Gardet's discussion of these matters, *La Pensée Religieuse d'Avicenne* (Paris: J. Vrin, 1951), pp. 48ff. For Maimonides' view, cf. *Guide* I, 69 (89a), p. 167f.; I, 70 (91b), p. 172; II, 12 (26a), p. 279f.

4. See *Guide* III, 20 (42a), p. 482; and see too I, 60 (76a), p. 144f.

5. See *Metaphysics* VIII, 1ff.; XII, 2ff.

6. Maimonides' view of matter, and its relation to evil and privation has much in common with Avicenna's thought, the ideational roots of both being traceable to Plotinus. Cf. Avicenna's *Al-Shifâ'; al-Ilâhiyyât,* op. cit., 4, 2, pp. 171ff., found in the Latin edition of S. Van Riet, *Avicenna Latinus: Liber De Philosophia Prima sive Scientia Divina I–IV* (Louvain-Leiden 1977), pp. 200ff.; and *al-Ilâhiyyât* 9: 6, pp. 416ff., now translated by S. Inati, *An Examination of Ibn Sîna's Solution for the Problem of Evil* (Ph. D. Dissertation, University of Buffalo, 1979), pp. 222–238. For Plotinus, cf. *Enneads* I 8.3, 7, trans. by S. McKenna (New York: Pantheon Books, 1953); II, 4.4ff., 16; II, 5; and see J. Rist, "Plotinus on Matter and Evil," *Phronesis* 6 (1981): 154–166.

7. *Guide,* Introduction to the Second Part (4b), p. 239.

8. Ibid., III, 8 (12a), p. 431; 10 (17a), p. 440.

9. Such sources could be found in the diverse philosophical and theosophical literature present in the Egypt of Maimonides' day, particularly that of a Neoplatonic and gnostic bent. Possible sources are among those discussed by S. Pines in his introduction to the *Guide,* particularly pp. lix f., lxxv f., xciii ff., and cxxiii. See too Pines' article, "Shi'ite Terms and Conceptions in Judah Halevi's *Kuzari,*" *Jerusalem Studies in Arabic and Islam* 2 (1980): 196, 240ff.

10. See my article, "Maimonides on Possibility," *Mystics, Philosophers, and Politicians: Essays in Jewish Intellectual History in Honor of Alexander Altmann,* ed. J. Reinharz *et al.* (Durham: University of North Carolina Press, 1982), p. 77f.

11. Cf. particularly *Guide* I, 69, p. 166f.

12. Ibid., III, 10 (17a), p. 440.

13. Ibid., I, 2 (13b), p. 24; III, 19 (40b), p. 479 *et passim.*

14. Ibid., I, 69 (89a), p. 167.

15. Ibid., III, 16 (30b), p. 463.

16. See the Fifth and Sixth *Enneads* of Plotinus, a good portion of which was available to Maimonides in various Arabic abridgements, particularly that known as "The Theology of Aristotle." The Arabic Plotinian material has been translated by G. Lewis and may be found set against its probable Greek source in the edition of P. Henry and H. R. Schwyzer, *Plotini Opera* II, Desclée de Brower, Paris, 1959, and cf. particularly pp. 263ff., 291ff., 353, 393f., 439ff., 474ff.

17. Cf. *Guide* II, 17, pp. 294ff., and see above, note 10.

18. Cf. *Guide* I, 58 (71a), p. 136; 69 (90a), p. 169; II, 12 (25b), p. 279; III, 9 (15b), p. 279; III, 9 (15b), p. 437.

19. Ibid., III, 18, p. 474f.

20. Ibid., III, 19, 20.

21. Ibid., II, Introduction, Premises 21–25, pp. 238, 239; III, 10 (17a) p. 440.

22. Ibid., III, 16 (31a), p. 463; 20 (42b), p. 482; 21, p. 484f.

23. Ibid., III, 17 (35b, 36a), p. 471.

24. Ibid., 37a, p. 473.

25. Ibid., III, 18 (39a), p. 476.

26. Cf. A. Altmann, op. cit., p. 111f.; in this volume, above, p. 151–152f.

27. *Guide* III, 10 (40b), p. 479.

28. "Watching over" is the expression Pines uses to convey that which in the Arabic is given more neutrally, usually as a Providence which is simply "over" (*'alā*) its objects. Cf. *Guide* III, 51 (127a), p. 624f.

29. Ibid., III, 17, pp. 464–466; and see too III, 51, p. 625.

30. Ibid., III, 17 (36a) p. 472. An alternative translation of the last part of this passage could well be, ". . . but to divine will, in accordance with that which is deserved in His judgments, the canon of which our intellects cannot comprehend."

31. Cf. *Guide* I, 51ff., 58.

32. See *Guide* II, 22 (40b), p. 319; 25 (55b), p. 329; III, 13 (24a), p. 452f., p. 456, end of chapter.

33. See *Guide* III, 17 (36a), p. 471; 20 (41b), p. 480f.; 21 (44a) p. 485. These and other passages are presented in detail in my paper on "Neoplatonic Currents in Maimonides' Philosophy," part of the Proceedings of a symposium on "Maimonides in Egypt," held at Tel Aviv University (1982) edited by J. Kraemer.

34. *Guide* III, 20 (41b), p. 481.

35. Ibid., III, 25 (56b), p. 506.

36. Ibid., I, 73, Tenth Premise, p. 206; see too my article, "Maimonides on Possibility," op. cit., p. 68ff.

37. Cf. *Guide* III, 25 (56a), p. 505, and compare Maimonides' earlier remark (55b) in this chapter, "the entire purpose (of creation – A. I.) consists in bringing into existence the way you see it everything whose existence is possible; for His wisdom did not require in any way that it should be otherwise; for this is impossible, since matters take their course in accordance with what His wisdom requires".

38. Ibid., III, 12 (19b), p. 444.

39. Ibid., III, 20 (41b), p. 480f.; and see too I, 57 (69b), p. 133.

40. Ibid., III, 30 (41b), p. 481; and cf. I, 60 (76a), p. 144.

41. Ibid., III, 20 (42b), p. 482.

42. Ibid., III, 53, 54, pp. 630ff. These traits are, of course, not necessarily related to free choice, which some scholars believe Maimonides could not accept, on their interpretation of his view of strict causality. Cf. S. Pines, "Studies in Abul-Barakāt al-Baghdādī's Poetics and Metaphysics," *Studies in Philosophy, Scripta Hierosolymitana* 6 (1960): 195–198; A. Altmann, "The Religion of the Thinkers: Free will and Predestination in Saadia, Bahya, and Maimonides," *Religion in a Religious Age,* ed. S. D. Goitein (Cambridge, Mass.: Association for Jewish Studies, 1974), pp. 41–45.

43. Cf. *Guide* III, 24 (53a), p. 500f., and 51 (126b), p. 624.

44. Ibid., III, 51 (125a), p. 621.

45. Ibid., 128a, p. 625.

46. Ibid., 129a, p. 628.

SECTION III

Issues in Ethics, Law, and Politics

Maimonides, the Disciple of Alfārābī*

LAWRENCE V. BERMAN

Maimonides may be taken as the exemplar of a disciple. The term disciple here I take in a strict sense to mean an individual who follows a specific discipline, a doctrine or rule which has been laid down by a master. Here the emphasis is not on originality, but rather on adherence to a set of principles and the development of learning and thought within that framework. Ideally, of course, the adherence to a specific discipline ought to be based on a freely pledged allegiance founded on a judicious weighing of all factors involved.

In the area of law, Maimonides might be called both the disciple of the Rabbis and the systematic tendencies of later Greek thought, for in his code of Jewish law he accepted the fundamental principles of Rabbinic thought and arranged the material of Jewish law in accordance with the principles of systematic organization developed in later Greek thought and continued in medieval Middle Eastern civilization.[1] In medicine he was the disciple of Galen although at times offering criticism of the master in accordance with his own views.[2] In mathematics and astronomy he considered himself the disciple of the Greeks although he did not write any treatises in these areas except for, notably, his work on the *Sanctification of the New Moon*[3] which he included in his code of Jewish law. In philosophy, Maimonides was primarily the disciple of Aristotle, mainly through the commentaries of his interpreters, both later Greek and Middle Eastern. He was also influenced to a marked degree by certain Neoplatonic tendencies of Alfarabi and Avicenna.[4]

The point of my title is that Maimonides was also the disciple of Alfarabi in the area of the relationship between religion, jurisprudence, theology, and philosophy. I should like to argue as well and in conformity with the preceding that Maimonides did what no one else did explicitly

Israel Oriental Studies 4 (1974): 154–178. Reprinted by permission of *Israel Oriental Studies*.

in medieval Middle Eastern culture. He took the Alfarabian theory of the relationship between philosophy, religion, jurisprudence, and theology and applied it in a through-going manner to a particular religion, Judaism. His approach takes on new significance and greater clarity once we have put on our Alfarabian spectacles. Doubtless, there were many intellectuals who accepted the Alfarabian view and tried to understand Islam and Christianity from its perspective, but no one else in a major work attempted to apply his theory in detail to a particular religious tradition.[5]

In the remaining parts of this paper, I should like to discuss first Alfarabi's concept of the origin and relationship of philosophy and religion. Subsequently I take up Maimonides' concept of the origin of the Jewish religion and its relation to philosophy. In a concluding section, I sum up the results of the inquiry and speculate on the possible influence of Alfarabi on the life of Maimonides.

Finally, I should point out that it is only very recently that a fuller picture of the Alfarabian view has been available thanks mainly to a number of recently published texts. Two of them in particular are germane to the understanding of our subject, his *On Religion*[6] and the middle part of his *Book of Letters*.[7] It is especially to the latter, published in 1970, that I shall be referring.

I

The following passage occurs at the beginning of the section of the *Book of Letters* which concerns us:[8]

> Since it was natural that demonstrations be perceived after these [that is, dialectical and sophistical powers],[9] it followed necessarily that dialectical and sophistical powers, as well as philosophy based on opinion, or philosophy based on sophistical thinking, should have preceded in time certain philosophy,[10] that is, demonstrative philosophy. And religion, considered as a human matter, is later in time than philosophy in general,[11] since it is aimed at teaching the multitude theoretical and practical things which were deduced in philosophy through ways which facilitate the multitude's understanding of them, either through persuasion, or representation,[12] or through both of them together.
>
> The arts of theology[13] and jurisprudence are later in time than religion and are subordinate[14] to it. And if the religion is subordinate to an ancient philosophy, either based on opinion, or on sophistical thinking, then the theology and the jurisprudence which are subordinate to it accord with either of them,[15] but are below either of them.

Here we see quite clearly laid out the idea that dialectical and sophistical modes of thinking must have preceded the origin of demonstrative philosophy. The model Alfarabi has in mind is the development of Greek philosophy as he understood it.[16] From sophistical thinking, knowledge of dialectical thinking and gradually demonstrative thinking developed. The thought of Plato he identifies with a middle stage between dialectical and demonstrative modes of thought, whereas Aristotle, of course, represents the acme of demonstrative philosophy. The point is that there is an ascending hierarchy of forms of thought, conceived in a threefold progression. Religions corresponding to each of these three stages can come into existence.[17]

Religion comes after philosophy in time and its function is teaching the multitude theoretical and practical things, previously deduced philosophically, in ways which are consonant with the limited understanding of the mass. At the very beginning of his *On Religion*, Alfarabi gives a definition of religion which is unique in the literature of medieval Middle Eastern civilization:

> Religion consists of opinions and actions, determined and limited by conditions, which their first ruler[18] lays down to the group, seeking to achieve a specific goal which he has, either in them or by means of them, through their active utilization of these opinions and actions.

This general definition of religion underlies our text and all of the Alfarabian corpus of writings on religion and political science.

Coming after religion in time are the arts of jurisprudence and theology. Jurisprudence is defined as "an art by which man can derive and deduce soundly the determination of each matter which the lawgiver did not explicitly define from the matters which he did explicitly determine. He establishes that in accordance with the purpose of the lawgiver with respect to the religion which he laid down in the nation to whom it was laid down as law. And this is not possible unless he believes firmly in the opinions of that religion and has the virtues which are virtues in that religion. A person of such a nature is a jurisprudent."[19] Alfarabi goes on to remark that "since determination is related to two things, opinions and actions, it follows consequently that the art of jurisprudence will consist of two parts, one part concerning opinions and one part concerning actions."[20] Thus clearly the jurisprudent and jurisprudence are subordinate to religion and the founder of the religion. In his *Enumeration of the Sciences*, Alfarabi has the following definition of theology: "And the art of theology is a habit by which man is capable of defending through statements the defined opinions and actions which the founder of the religion enunciated and the falsification of everything opposed to it and this art also is divided into two parts: a part concerned with opinions and a part concerned with actions."[21] Alfarabi then proceeds to differentiate between theology as he has just defined it and jurisprudence in the following way:

> The jurisprudent takes the opinions and the actions which the founder of the religion enunciated as given and makes them fundamental principles from which he deduces those things which are necessary corollaries, but the theologian defends the things which the jurisprudent employs as fundamental principles without deriving from them other things. Therefore, whenever it happens that someone has the ability to perform both matters together, he is a jurisprudent and a theologian. He will defend them insofar as he is a theologian, and will deduce from them insofar as he is a jurisprudent.[22]

Here we see even more clearly that both jurisprudence and theology in Alfarabi's view are subordinate to religion.

Thus ideally you have a neatly symmetrical structure in threes. On the ascending side you have dialectical and sophistical thinking leading up to demonstrative philosophy and then demonstrative philosophy giving rise to virtuous religion which then produces jurisprudence and theology. The link between demonstrative philosophy and religion is the philosopher-statesman who has complete mastery of demonstrative philosophy and lays down the religion in accordance with it and the circumstances of his period.[23]

The principal matter to be kept in mind here is the temporal succession of the elements mentioned: dialectical, sophistical, and demonstrative philosophies, religion, jurisprudence, and theology.

The relationship between these elements comes out most clearly in another passage from the *Book of Letters.*

> In general, therefore, philosophy precedes religion in the way that the employer of instruments precedes the instruments in time. But dialectic and sophistic precede philosophy in the way that the food of the tree precedes the fruit, or in the way that the flower of the tree precedes its fruit. Religion precedes theology and jurisprudence in the way that the master who employs the servant precedes the servant and the one who employs the instrument, the instrument.[24]

Here we see clearly stated that religion is subordinate to philosophy, and is, in fact, the tool of philosophy. Religion in turn uses theology and jurisprudence as its tools, so that in the Alfarabian conception theology and jurisprudence are the tools of the tool of philosophy which is, of course, a far cry from the familiar slogan of philosophy being the handmaiden of theology thought to be characteristic of medieval thinking. Dialectic and sophistic also are subordinate to philosophy but by ways of preparation.[25] Alfarabi here wishes to intimate, it seems to me, that the precedence of dialectic and sophistic to philosophy per se does not imply any subordination of philosophy to them. Clearly here, philosophy is at the top of the hierarchy of ascending and descending matters, flanked on the one hand by dialectic and sophistic and on the other by religion, jurisprudence, and theology.

The picture sketched above seems to be a model for an ideal development. This is all very nice as long as matters develop in a logical manner, but we know that matter is recalcitrant. Is it then possible for religions to come into existence in a way different from the logical model? Is it possible for religions to develop in particular societies without being first preceded by philosophy? In a crucial passage, Alfarabi states:[26]

> But if a religion is transferred from a nation[27] which has that religion to a nation which does not have a religion, or a religion belonging to a nation is taken, then is reformed, through additions, or it is diminished, or some other change is made in it, and then it is given to another nation whose people are trained in it and are taught it and are governed by it, it is possible that religion will come to be in them before philosophy is realized in them and before dialectic and sophistic are realized. And if[28] philosophy does not originate in them from their native abilities, but is transferred to them from other people in whom it existed previously, it may come to originate in them after the religion which was transferred to them.

Here Alfarabi is dealing with two cases, one is that the religion of one nation is simply taken over by another nation, and the second case is that the borrowed religion has been changed in various ways by some person who is not mentioned, then it is given to a society which is devoid of philosophy. In these two cases, philosophy might come to exist after the acceptance of a particular religion. I must leave to another occasion, an attempt at suggesting concrete cases to which Alfarabi might be referring.

In general, the passages quoted previously, throw into question any simplistic identification of Alfarabi as a Muslim. Alfarabi appears here as a philosopher dealing with certain broad categories of existing society such as philosophy, religion, jurisprudence, and theology in terms of the system of thought he has accepted. If one were to ask him whether he were a Muslim, he might answer, "Yes, insofar as Islam embodies the philosophic point of view." From his point of view, Islam must be understood from the standpoint of his total systematic understanding of all facets of reality.

We have seen here that Alfarabi's attitude to religion is that of a philosopher and that he is interested in integrating his understanding of religion into a general theory of the development of philosophy, religion, jurisprudence, and theology which takes cognizance not only of the pure forms of this religious development, but also tries to account for hybrid forms. In the next section, I shall try to indicate the relationship of Maimonides' position to the preceding.

II

A fundamental difference between Alfarabi and Maimonides, at least as far as their published works are concerned, is that Alfarabi appears as a philosopher without being committed to any particular religious tradition, while Maimonides, except for his short *Treatise on the Art of Logic,*[29] has written no philosophic work. He appears as the commentator, the lawyer, the jurisprudent, the theologian, the communal leader, and the physician, but not as the philosopher.

In his *Guide of the Perplexed,*[30] he appears as a theologian in the Alfarabian sense and here the Alfarabian point of view is clearly felt. In the *Guide*, Maimonides applies the Alfarabian theory of the development of the virtuous religion to a specific religious tradition. In his role as theologian, Maimonides accepts the fundamental principles of a particular tradition, in this case Judaism, and uses all means at his disposal to defend the claim of religion to validity[31] and, consequently, to authority. The *Guide* is clearly set off from books of philosophy by Maimonides' admission that it will intentionally contain a type of contradiction which philosophic books do not contain.[32] In fact, Maimonides is stating that his book is necessarily dialectical,[33] rather than being demonstrative. It is important to point out that in a passage neglected up to now, Maimonides himself refers to his major theologico-political opus as one dealing with the principles of religion,[34] the designation of theology in Maimonides' time generally.

Alfarabi's influence may be discerned in Maimonides' theory of the development of the Jewish religion and his concept of prophecy. Maimonides states:[35]

> It is well known that *Abraham our Father,* peace be upon him, was brought up in the religious community of the Sabians,[36] whose doctrine it is that there is no deity but the stars. When I shall have made known to you in this chapter their books, translated into Arabic, which are in our hands today, and their ancient chronicles and I shall have revealed to you through them their doctrine and histories, it will become clear to you from this that they explicitly asserted that the stars are the deity and that the sun is the greatest deity[37]. . . . However, when *the pillar of the world* grew up and it became clear to him that there is a separate deity that is neither a body nor a force in a body and that all the stars and the spheres were made by him, and he

understood that the fables upon which he was brought up were absurd,[38] he began to refute their doctrine and to show up their opinions as false; he publicly manifested his disagreement with them and called *in the name of the Lord, God of the world*—both the existence of the deity and the creation of the world in time by that deity being comprised in that call. . . . We have already made it clear in our great compilation, *Mishneh Torah,*[39] that *Abraham our Father* began to refute these opinions by means of arguments and mild preaching,[40] conciliating people and drawing them to obedience by means of benefits. Then the master of the prophets received prophetic inspiration; thereupon he perfected the purpose in that he commanded killing these people, wiping out their traces, and tearing out their roots. . . .

Here we see clearly that a first stage in the religious evolution of mankind was the existence of a religious community based on sophistical notions. It was then that Abraham came on the scene. He demonstrated the falseness of the doctrine of the Sabians, and developed a more correct view of reality, based on rational proofs which undermined the basis of the Sabian religion. It remained for Moses, the master of the prophets to come and lay down the law which was to embody the ideas first promulgated by Abraham. In this passage we see therefore a scheme of the development of philosophy and religion which resembles the picture derived from the writings of Alfarabi. Moses however was not only the master of the prophets in Maimonides' terminology but also the master of those who know,[41] that is, a master of demonstrative philosophy, so that he corresponds to the position of the philosopher-statesman in the scheme of Alfarabi, the link between the highest attainments of speculative reason and the highest attainments of practical activity.[42] It is therefore Judaism, according to the Maimonidean scheme, which is the first and closest approximation to the ideal state of the philosophers within the limits imposed by time and place.

   Of course, historically, it is clearly impossible to conceive of Abraham and Moses as philosophers along with the rest of the prophets, as is the view of Maimonides. It is in order to answer this objection that Maimonides puts forth the following idea:

> Know that the many sciences devoted to establishing the truth regarding these matters that have existed in our religious community have perished because of our being dominated by the pagan nations, and because, as we have made clear, it is not permitted to divulge these matters to all people.[43]

This pronouncement should be understood as an attempt to answer a possible historical objection to the system of Alfarabi accepted by Maimonides. According to the Alfarabian scheme, demonstrative philosophy must have preceded the establishment of the virtuous religion in the Jewish nation. The religion of Moses represents the virtuous religion, yet we do not know of any tradition of philosophic knowledge among the Jews which is continuous from ancient times. Therefore, Maimonides must put forward a premise which accounts for the loss of this tradition.[44]

We have seen therefore a concept of development in history according to a logical scheme and Maimonides perhaps might argue that this is the only time the logical and the ontological have so completely coincided with respect to the development of a religion.

Furthermore, we see in the *Guide* that, in different historical periods, different means of accomplishing the purpose of the Torah are needed. In the time of Moses a refined sacrificial cult was needed in order to wean the people away from the cultic practices of the Sabians.[45] Maimonides intimates that were Moses to come in his time, he would not need to lay down the sacrificial cult[46] since the multitude in the time of Maimonides did not seem to be in need of this additional burden.[47] This accords perfectly with the Alfarabian notion that were a philosopher-statesman of the same rank to come after the first founder of the religion, he would have the right to change the prescriptions of the first founder in accordance with the different circumstances current in his day.[48] Here one receives an idea of religion which is flexible and seemingly malleable and responsive to the needs of the time.

In contrast with the *Guide*, in Maimonides' code of Jewish law, his *Mishneh Torah,* the feeling of rigidity and inflexibility is paramount. The Torah was given on Mount Sinai both in its written and oral form.[49] It was transmitted and then codified. It will never be abrogated or changed, and, in fact, the laws relating to the temple cult make up much of the bulk of the work. It is partially this difference in approach that has led to difficulty in understanding the unity of the Maimonidean oeuvre.[50] How can we explain the difference in tone between the two works?

In line with the thought of Alfarabi, the answer is clear, for the function of the two works and Maimonides' function in composing them are different. In the *Mishneh Torah,* Maimonides is taking the role of the jurisprudent in opinions and actions,[51] developing the implications of the words of the lawgiver in the areas of opinion and actions into coherent order. He must proceed according to the principles which have been laid down, not questioning them but rather developing the exposition of the law according to these principles. In the *Guide,* on the other hand, his function is that of the theologian, whose function it is to defend the fundamental principles of the religion against attack. In order to accomplish this purpose, Maimonides must use every means at his disposal. Since the danger against which he is trying to defend the law is that presented by philosophy, he must try by every means possible to defend his position dialectically. Therefore, Maimonides *qua* theologian can allow himself freedom which he cannot *qua* jurisprudent. And this is especially true of the sacrificial cult which was not a practical issue in his time. In fact, one can understand the *Mishneh Torah* and the *Guide* as two rungs on a dialectical ladder to the truth both in action and contemplation. The code represents a full blown position with respect to actions and opinions at one level of understanding. The *Guide* represents a more sophisticated position at a higher level of understanding.

The question then arises whether Maimonides would take a position higher on the dialectical ladder which would differ from the apparent positions he has taken in the *Guide*? What would those positions be and how radical might they be? The answer to these questions depends on how seriously one takes the remarks of Maimonides that his true doctrine has been concealed in contradictions in the *Guide*, and ultimately depends on the development of canons of interpretation of the *Guide*.[52] How far Maimonides accepted the Alfarabian philosophical stance and was not content to remain at the positions overtly described as his own is a question which cannot be discussed within the limits of the present paper. In any case, I think it is quite clear that in his *Guide* as well as the *Mishneh Torah,* Maimonides accepted the Alfarabian view of the development and functions of religion, jurisprudence and dialectical theology and their relationship to philosophy and tried to apply it to the Jewish religion. In this effort Maimonides was the disciple of Alfarabi.[53]

III

Up to now, I have tried to point out some aspects of the influence which the system of Alfarabi had on Maimonides in his works on theology and jurisprudence. It doesn't seem to me farfetched likewise to discern a possible influence on the life of Maimonides and his own self-image.

Here we have before us a man who from his youth on is obviously destined to play a great role in the intellectual life of his time. He completes his *Commentary on the Mishnah*[54] at an early age, and then goes on to complete his monumental code of Jewish law which is immediately recognized as either authoritative or as requiring an opposing stance. At a later stage, he is recognized as the head of the Jewish community in Egypt and is intimately concerned with the administration of that community. His leadership is recognized far beyond the confines of Egypt and letters with questions[55] for his decision are sent from most parts of the Jewish community outside Egypt. Finally, he composes his genial *Guide of the Perplexed* in which he sets forth his defense of the Jewish religion as a theologian operating on the highest level. His position at the reigning court of Egypt is also high and he is a recognized authority on medicine and composes works which are recognized as outstanding contributions.

Isn't it conceivable that Maimonides could have thought of himself as successively ascending in a series of Alfarabian steps to the highest pinnacle of achievement possible for him? That is, first Maimonides by writing his *Mishneh Torah* is fulfilling the function of *the* jurisprudent in actions and opinions. His statement that his *summa* of Jewish law will dispense for the need for other books besides the Hebrew bible reinforces this suggestion most clearly. By writing his *Guide* he is fulfilling the function of a theologian and in his role as a communal leader he fills the function of the prince of the law, in the Alfarabian terminology,[56] who follows the lead of the founder of the religion, but is not equal to him in authority. Finally, in his political function Maimonides was attempting to realize the ideal described at the end of the *Guide,* based in large part on the Alfarabian view that speculative perfection needs to be complemented by political action, by maintaining as perfect a society as possible in imitation[57] of the deity who provided the means for the world to exist.

NOTES

*A preliminary draft of this paper was read at the annual meeting of the American Academy of Religion on October 29, 1971. I wish to thank Mr. Elmer Grieder and the staff of the Stanford University Libraries, as well as the staffs of the other libraries mentioned below, for help in providing me with manuscript and book materials used in the preparation of this paper. The research here reported was assisted by a grant awarded by the Joint Committee on the Near and Middle East of the Social Science Research Council and the American Council of Learned Societies.

1. For criticism of the term "Islamic civilization," see S. D. Goitein, *Studies in Islamic History and Institutions* (Leiden: E. J. Brill, 1966), pp. 54–70.

2. See Maimonides' Introduction to the Twenty-Fifth Discourse of his *Medical Aphorisms*: "as he is the chief of this science and has to be followed in it (*idh huwa imām hādhihi al-ṣinā'a wa-huwa Ilādhi yuqtadā bihi fīhā*)" in J. Schacht and M. Meyerhof, "Maimonides against Galen, on Philosophy and Cosmogony," *Bulletin of the Faculty of Arts of the University of Egypt,* vol. 5, part 1 (1937), Arabic Section, p. 77 (Arabic text), p. 64 (English translation). For the medieval Hebrew translations of Nathan ha-Me'ati and Zeraḥyah ben Isaac ben Shaltiel Gracian (Ḥen), see Maimonides, *Pirqe moshe,* ed. S. Muntner (Jerusalem: Mosad Harav Kook, 1959), pp. 324–325.

3. See *The Code of Maimonides. Book Three. Treatise Eight. Sanctification of the New Moon,* translated from the Hebrew by S. Gandz with Supplemen-

tation and an Introduction by J. Obermann and an astronomical commentary by O. Neugebauer (New Haven: Yale University Press, 1956). Of specific interest here are the words of Neugebauer: "His work does not contain any new contribution, nor does he make any claim beyond that of having presented certain parts of the classical theory of the moon in a form most suitable for the practical computation of the visibility of the new moon. Yet the adaptation of a wider theory to one specific problem requires not only real skill but full mastery of the theory as a whole." (p. 147).

4. For the relationship of Maimonides to his predecessors in the area of philosophy, see S. Pines, "Translator's Introduction: The Philosophic Sources of *The Guide of the Perplexed,*" in Maimonides, *Guide of the Perplexed* (University of Chicago Press, 1963), pp. lvii–cxxxiv and the notes of S. Munk to his French translation, *Le guide des égarés* (Paris: G.-P. Maison-neuve et Larose, 1963; photographic reprint of 1856–66 edition), 3 volumes.

5. Within the Muslim community, notably Ibn Sīnā (Avicenna) and Ibn Rushd (Averroes), correspond most closely to Maimonides' position. See Ibn Sīnā, *Al-Shifā'*: *al-Ilāhiyyāt*, II (Cairo, 1960), eds. M. Y. Moussa, S. Dunya, and S. Zayed, pp. 441–455 (partial English translation by M. Marmura in M. Mahdi and R. Lerner, eds., *Medieval Political Philosophy: A Sourcebook* [The Free Press of Glencoe, 1963], pp. 99–111); idem, *Fī ithbāt al-nubuwwāt,* ed. M. Marmura (Beirut: Dār Nahār, 1968), esp. pp. 48–61 (English translation in Mahdi and Lerner, pp. 113–121), which is important for detailed philosophic interpretations of Qur'ānic passages; Ibn Rushd, *Kitāb faṣl al-maqāl,* ed. G. F. Hourani (Leiden: E. J. Brill, 1959) with English translation by Hourani in: Averroes, *On the Harmony of Religion and Philosophy* (London: Luzac and Co., 1961); idem, *Manāhij al-adilla fī 'aqā'id al-milla,* ed. M. Qāsim (Cairo, 1964), esp. p. 251 where Ibn Rushd expresses his unfulfilled desire to examine all of the statements in the Qur'ān and the Ḥadīth which are liable to interpretation with Pines, "Translator's Introduction," p. cxx who remarks on the similarity of this plan to the program of the *Guide;* idem, *Commentary on Plato's Republic,* ed. and tr. E. I. J. Rosenthal (Cambridge University Press, 1968; reprinted with corrections) with the detailed review of the present writer in *Oriens* 20 (1968– 69): 436–439. For the view of a Muslim of the generation between Alfarabi and Ibn Sīnā, see J. Kraemer, *Abū Sulaymān as-Sijistānī: A Muslim Philosopher of the Tenth Century* (diss. Yale University, 1967; copy issued by University Microfilms, 1968), pp. 204–233 and for a Christian view, see S. Pines, "La loi naturelle et la société: la doctrine politico-théologique d'Ibn Zur'a," in *Studies in Islamic History and Civilization,* Scripta Hierosolymitana 9 (1961): 154–190 (reprint). Among the works of Alfarabi himself is one concerned with collecting statements of the Prophet alluding to the art of logic; see M. Grignaschi, in Al-Fārābī, *Deux ouvrages inédits sur la réthorique* (Beirut: Dar El-Machreq, 1971), p. 130, n. 4 with J. van Ess, "The Logical Structure of Islamic Theology," in *Logic in Classical Islamic Culture,* ed. G. E. von Grunebaum (Wiesbaden: Harrassowitz, 1970), p. 22.

6. *Alfarabi's Book of Religion and Related Texts,* ed. with Introduction and Notes by Muhsin Mahdi (Beirut: Dar El-Machreq, 1968). The Arabic text of

On Religion (*Kitāb al-milla*) is to be found on pp. 43–66. In the Introduction to my translation of *On Religion* with commentary which I have in preparation I discuss the reasons for my translation of the title.

7. *Alfarabi's Book of Letters,* ed. with Introduction and Notes by Muhsin Mahdi (Beirut: Dar El-Machreq, 1970 [English title page, 1969]). The text related to our inquiry is to be found on pp. 131–161.

8. P. 131.4–12 (that is, p. 131, lines 4–12 and so throughout). For the context of this passage and others quoted, see the English translation originally published as an appendix to this article in *Israel Oriental Studies* 4 (1974): 171–178.

9. The explanatory material in brackets has been added by the present writer. Here we have one of the indications that our text may not be complete and perhaps had a different order originally. See Mahdi, *Book of Letters,* pp. 40–43 and p. 131.4 with note on p. 231.

10. Ar. *al-falsafa al-yaqīniyya.* For the meaning of *yaqīn,* see most recently G. Vajda, "Autour de la théorie de la connaissance chez Saadia," *Revue des études juives* 126 (1967): 141, 377 and n. 2, 385 n. 1, 391 n. 6; Alfarabi, *Sharā'iṭ al-yaqīn,* ed. by M. Türker, in *Araştirma* (Ankara) I (1963): 195–204; Alfarabi, *Kitāb al-ḥaṭāba,* ed. J. Langhade, in Al-Fārābī, *Deux ouvrages* (above, n. 5), pp. 33.11–35.2.

11. Reading *bi-'l-jumla,* omitting *wāw.* In checking the microfilm of the unique manuscript used by Mahdi to establish the text (Teheran University Central Library, Mishkāt 339), I see that the *wāw* clearly appears. It should be kept in mind that the *Book of Letters* has been preserved in a unique manuscript copied in a careless manner (see Mahdi, *Book of Letters,* pp. 51–53). Mahdi has done a superb job of restoration, but the text must still be considered somewhat fluid. See also the continuation of this same passage, p. 132.7: *fa-'l-falsafa bi-'l-jumla tataqaddam al-milla.*

I find the reading *wa-bi-'l-jumla* difficult. (1) If it is to be attached to the preceding *al-falsafa ,* it makes no sense. (2) If the *wāw* is to be taken as signalling the beginning of a coordinate sentence, then the *idh* clause has no main clause governing it. (3) If it is to be taken independently, as Mahdi seems to have done by setting it off with commas, then the translation would be: "And religion, considered as a human matter is later in time than philosophy, and in general, since. . . ." The meaning would be then that both religion considered as a human matter and the other types of religion also are later in time than philosophy. This is a conclusion which, it seems to me, conflicts with other Alfarabian texts mentioned below.

I suggest the following interpretation of this passage somewhat tentatively. Religion, considered as the product of human intellect ("considered as a human matter") generally comes after philosophy, since it is dependent on it. At times, however, religion, considered as the product of human intellect, may precede philosophy in time. This is the case of religion which is a product of cross cultural borrowing (see *Book of Letters,* p. 154.14–19, Appendix for English translation, and below at n. 26).

Religion, here considered as a human matter, would be opposed to religion transcending human powers of intellect. The distinction between two types of revelation is taken up in the greatest detail in Alfarabi, *Fuṣūl al-Madanī: Aphorisms* of the Statesman, ed. and tr. D. M. Dunlop (Cambridge University Press, 1961), Section 89, pp. 164ff., esp. p. 167 (Eng. tr., pp. 74–75, with some changes): "as for the man who is given the practical part by a revelation which guides him towards determining each separate detail of what should be chosen or avoided, that is a different way, and if they are both called 'knowers,' the name of knowledge is a homonym for both of them, just as it is a homonym for the possessor of natural science and the diviner (kāhin). . . . Similar is the case of him who has perfected speculative knowledge and him to whom the determination of the actions of the people of one or more cities has been revealed, without possessing any knowledge of speculative science. And between him to whom a revelation has been made, being perfect in speculative knowledge, and him to whom a revelation has been made, being imperfect in speculative knowledge there is in fact no relation or agreement. The agreement is one in name only." See also On Religion, p. 44.7–13; Alfarabi, Virtuous City, ed. F. Dieterici (Leiden, 1895; reprinted 1964), pp. 58.18ff; Maimonides, Guide II, 37 beginning. A religion which is the direct product of supernatural forces does not have any necessary relationship to philosophy. The attitude of Alfarabi to such a religion might be that only "human things" are in the purview of the philosopher. In this connection, it is interesting to note that both Judah ha-Levi (twice) and Ibn Rushd quote Socrates' ironic dictum that the divine things transcend the ability of the philosopher to deal with them. See Judah ha-Levi, Das Buch al-Chazari, ed. H. Hirschfeld (Leipzig, 1887), IV, 13, p. 254.6–9 and V, 14, p. 328.14–16 (to be corrected in the light of the Ibn Rushd text which follows) and Ibn Rushd, Talkhīṣ kitāb al-ḥiss wa-'l-maḥsūs, ed. H. Gaetje (Wiesbaden: Harrassowitz, 1961), p. 78 (Hebrew translation in Qiṣṣur sefer ha-ḥush ve-ha-muḥash li-Ibn Rushd, ed. H. Blumberg, Corpus Commentariorum Averrois in Aristotelem, vol. VII [Cambridge, Mass.: Mediaeval Academy of America, 1954], p. 48) with Plato, Apology 20 D-E with C and L. Strauss, Persecution and the Art of Writing (Glencoe, Ill.; 1952), p. 106–108.

For a new edition of the text of Alfarabi, Fuṣūl al-madanī, ed. D. M. Dunlop, see Alfarabi, Fuṣūl muntaza'a (Beirut: Dar el-Machreq, 1971), pp. 98–99. The differences between the two editions for the purpose of this paper are trivial.

12. Ar. bi-iqnā' aw takhyīl. Persuasion is the goal of rhetoric. See Alfarabi, Kitāb al-ḥaṭāba, ed. Langhade, pp. 31.3ff and passim. Representation (takhyīl) refers to formulating statements which imitate specific matters using figures of speech in order to present them to an audience and is a function of the poetic art. See Alfarabi, Kitāb al-shi'r, in Istanbul MS. Hamidiyye 812, 123a. I wish to thank Professor D. M. Dunlop for allowing me to use his photostats of this manuscript. I was unable to use the edition of this text by M. Mahdi, mentioned by J. Langhade in Alfarabi, Deux ouvrages (above n. 6), p. 6, n. 5. Cf. Alfarabi, Iḥṣā' al-'ulūm, ed. O. Amine, 2nd ed. (Cairo, 1949), pp. 67–68 which obviously depends on Kitāb al-shi'r. The text published by A. J. Arberry, "Farabi's Canons of Poetry," Rivista degli studi orientali 17 (1938): 267–272 does not contain this term. It uses instead tamthil. See further On Religion, p. 46.15–21; Virtuous City, pp. 69.19f.; Attainment of Happiness, Sec. 55 in Alfarabi, Philosophy of Plato and Aristotle, tr. M. Mahdi (The Free Press of Glencoe, 1962); Philosophy of Aristotle, Sec. 16 in Al-

farabi, *Philosophy of Plato and Aristotle*; and especially *Book of Letters*, p. 152.9–13.

13. Ar. *kalām*. I translate this term "theology" throughout. See further, *Shorter Encyclopaedia of Islam*, s.v.; L. Gardet and G.-C. Anawati, *Introduction à la théologie musulmane* (Paris, 1948); and J. van Ess, "The Logical Structure of Islamic Theology," (above n. 5), pp. 21–50, esp. pp. 21–26.

14. Ar. *tābi'atān*. Lit. "follow."

15. Ar. *bi-ḥasab dhālik*. The phrase is very vague.

16. See *Book of Letters*, pp. 150.1 to 153.11. Clearly, although Alfarabi is speaking as though he is developing a general theory of the development of discursive thought, he has in mind the Greek model. One of the problems involved in the interpretation of Alfarabi's thought is that often he seems to jump from the ideal, that is, theoretical plane, to the real, that is, historical plane. An important philological task would be to study Alfarabi's use of tenses in order to determine more accurately his style and usage.

17. For a discussion of lower types of religion, see *Book of Letters*, pp. 153f.

18. "First ruler" here is a technical term referring to the preeminent ruler of the group. See F. Rahman, *Prophecy in Islam* (London: Allen & Unwin, 1958), pp. 54–59; M. Mahdi, "Alfarabi," *History of Political Philosophy*, eds. L. Strauss and J. Cropsey (Chicago, 1963), pp. 166–170.

19. See *On Religion*, p. 50.10–15. For similar wording see Alfarabi, *Enumeration V*, in *On Religion*, p. 75.1–4 Mahdi (English translation in Mahdi and Lerner, eds., *Political Philosophy*, p. 27) except that the last two sentences, i.e., from "And this" to the end are left out. The relationship between *Enumeration* and *On Religion* is problematical. I think that they represent independent abbreviation-summaries of a longer text and I marshal the evidence to support my view in the introduction to my commentary to *On Religion* which I have in preparation. See also the review of *On Religion* by G. Endress to be published in *Zeitschrift der deutschen morgenlaendischen Gesellschaft*. I thank Dr. Endress for letting me see an advance copy of this review.

20. *On Religion*, p. 50.16–17 and see *Enumeration V*, p. 75.5–8 Mahdi which combines our text here with quotations from *On Religion*, pp. 43.1, 44.14f., 46.1, 46.7, and see next note (end).

21. *Enumeration V*, p. 75.9–11 Mahdi. In *On Religion*, "theology" is not mentioned, but the idea of using rhetoric and dialectic to defend the opinions of the religion is mentioned (p. 48.2–5) in terms very similar to those used in the passage quoted from *Enumeration* and its continuation in *Iḥṣā' al-'ulūm*, ed. Osman Amine, 2nd ed. (Cairo, 1949); English translation in Lerner and Mahdi, eds., *Political Philosophy*, pp. 27–30. It is to be regretted that Mahdi did not reedit as well the whole of *Enumeration V* or at least point out its relevance to *On Religion*. Cf. also *Book of Letters*, pp. 152.16–153.9 for a slightly different view. There the art of jurisprudence is restricted to making deductions from particular practical things, while the art of theology does deduce new things from the universal theoretical and practical matters of the religion as well as defending it. See also, ibid., p. 133.9–11.

22. *Enumeration V,* pp. 75.12–76.5 Mahdi. Cf. Gardet and Anawati, *Introduction à la théologie musulmane,* pp. 102–106, esp. the last paragraph on p. 105 which should be corrected in the light of our fuller knowledge of the works of Alfarabi. Alfarabi is looking at *kalām* from the perspective of philosophy; he himself is not a *mutakallim,* although he could easily assume that role were it necessary. See also G. Vajda in *Revue des études juives,* 126 (1967): 376, n. 1.

23. See note 18 above and the references quoted there.

24. P. 132.7–11. See Appendix for the translation of this passage in its context.

25. In the metaphors employed by Alfarabi to explain the relationship of dialectic and sophistic to philosophy, I take "the way the food of the tree precedes the fruit" to refer to the relationship of dialectic to demonstrative philosophy, since dialectic is of real use in discovering problems and suggesting solutions to them. On the other hand, "the way that the flower of the tree precedes the fruit" refers to the relationship of sophistic to demonstrative philosophy, since philosophy in the absolute meaning of the term derives no real benefit from sophistical thinking. See *Book of Letters,* p. 151.6 for the statement that sophistic is ultimately to be discarded and only used for testing and ibid., pp. 209.1–7 and 210.12–15. See further J. van Ess, "The Logical Structure of Islamic Theology," (above n. 5), p. 25 for the use of the term *jadal* in *kalām.* In sum, for Alfarabi the tree of philosophy in the true sense of the word always bears fruit; for a Judah ha-Levi in a famous line, Greek wisdom bears only flowers, but no fruit (See H. Schirman, *Ha-shirah ha-'ivrit bi-sefarad u-ve-provans,* 2 volumes [Jerusalem, 1954–56], I, 493 with commentary).

26. *Book of Letters,* p. 154.14–19. See n. 11 above.

27. Ar. *umma.* For usage of this term, see Alfarabi, *Political Regime,* ed. F. Najjar (Beirut Dar El-Machreq, 1968), pp. 70.5–7 with L. V. Berman, "Reexamination of Maimonides' Statement on Political Science," *Journal of the American Oriental Society* 89 (1969): 108, n. 8.

28. Supplying *idhā* instead of Mahdi's *allātī.*

29. For a characterization of this work and its relationship to the thought of Alfarabi, see L. V. Berman, "Reexamination," 106–111 (above n. 27).

30. All subsequent references are to Maimonides, *Guide of the Perplexed,* tr. S. Pines (University of Chicago Press, 1963) which contains references to the Judaeo-Arabic text published by S. Munk. In parentheses I have added references to the edition of the Munk text by I. Joel, *Dalālat al-ḥā'irīn* (Jerusalem, 1931). Although Maimonides does not mention the *Book of Letters* in the *Guide,* he does mention the *Book of Letters* in his *Medical Aphorisms.* See *Al-fuṣūl fī 'l-ṭibb,* Istanbul University MS. 1375 Arabic, 132b–133a with the two Hebrew translations in *Pirqe moshe* (above n. 2), p. 361; M. Steinschneider, *Alfarabi* (St.-Pétersbourg, 1869), p. 118; M. Mahdi in *Book of Letters,* p. 39 with note on p. 231 to pp. 135.6–139.5. Maimonides' reference to the *Book of Letters* is a very brief summary of the Alfarabian text (beginning p. 134.20 rather than 135.6 as Mahdi has it and ending on p. 139.5) interpreting it with the aid of the doctrine of the seven climes which Alfarabi does not mention explicitly, namely, that the different articulations of the letters of the alphabet of different languages and the different movements

of the external and internal organs of speech depend on the difference in climes, and temperate areas are better than non-temperate areas. In turn this is used to defend the statement of Galen that Greek is the best of languages which had been subjected to criticism on the ground that language is a product of convention. It should be pointed out that after Maimonides' statement "Alfarabi has already mentioned that in his *Book of Letters*" the Istanbul manuscript has *fa-qāl* which the two Hebrew translations omit. Further, the *fa-qāl* would refer to a continuation of Maimonides' explanation of the Galenic statement rather than a statement by Galen (which one might conclude from Mahdi's remarks in the *Book of Letters*, p. 39 bottom). I wish to thank Mrs. Makbüle Ohri of Istanbul University Library for her efforts in supplying me with a microfilm of the Arabic manuscript of Maimonides' work. See further S. Pines, "Translator's Introduction," in *Guide*, pp. lxxviii–xcii for a general discussion of Maimonides' relationship to Alfarabi and the literature quoted there and H. Davidson, "Maimonides' *Shemonah Peraqim* and Alfarabi's *Fuṣūl al-Madanī,*" *Proceedings of the American Academy for Jewish Research* 31 (1963): 33–50 (offprint).

31. See *Guide*, Introduction, pp. 5–6 (Joel, p. 2). It is, of course, true also that by showing the compatibility of Judaism with philosophy Maimonides is asserting the legitimacy of philosophy from the point of view of Judaism. This he has done quite boldly in his code by including *pardes* (philosophical physics and metaphysics) within *talmud* (intellectual activities beyond the study of the written and oral laws). Maimonides' redefinition of the terms *pardes* and *talmud* represent a classical example of the process of revolution by redefinition within Rabbinic Judaism. The attempted revolution was too radical and failed for reasons which cannot be taken up within the limits of the present article. See Maimonides, *Mishneh Torah: the Book of Knowledge*, ed. and tr. M. Hyamson (Jerusalem, 1965), *Hilkhot yesode ha-torah*, IV, 13, p. 39b and *Hilkhot talmud torah*, I, 12, p. 58a (hereafter *Book of Knowledge*) with the brilliant commentary of I. Twersky, "Some Non-Halakic Aspects of the Mishneh Torah," in *Jewish Medieval and Renaissance Studies*, ed. A. Altmann (Cambridge, Mass., 1967), pp. 106–118 and n. 44 below.

32. See *Guide*, Introduction, pp. 19–20 (Joel, pp. 12–13).

33. One is tempted to say sophistical. See Alfarabi, *Iḥṣa' al-'ulūm*, ed. O. Amine, p. 65.1–7: "and sophistical statements are those whose nature is to cause mistakes, mislead, deceive and cause one to imagine with respect to that which is not the truth that it is the truth . . . (*wa-'l-aqāwīl al-sūfisṭā'iyya hiya llatī sha'nuhā an tughalliṭ wa-tuḍalil wa-tulabbis wa-tūhim fimā laysa bi-ḥaqq annahu ḥaqq . . .*)." Maimonides might argue in response that his use of contradictions is intended to lead those who are able upwards in a dialectical ascent to the truth and that it is a given of human nature in general that there are levels of capacity of understanding; certain levels are not capable of grasping the truth in any simple sense. See further *Book of Letters*, p. 210.16–21.

34. See Schacht and Meyerhof, "Maimonides against Galen," (above n. 2), p. 85.10–11 (Arabic), p. 72.3 bot. -73.2 (English translation): "but Moses . . . has plainly stated that God does not do anything without purpose and by chance, but that he creates very well with justice and equity all which he creates, as I have explained in my exposition of the principles of religion (*wa-mithluh ṣaraḥ mūsā 'alayhi*

al-salām ann allāh lā yaf'al shay'an 'abathan wa-lā kayf ittifāq bal kull mā khalaq ḥasanan jiddan khalaqahu bi-'adl wa-taqsīṭ kamā bayyantu fīmā takallamtu bihi fī uṣūl al-dīn). For the Hebrew translation, see *Pirqe moshe,* ed. Muntner (above n. 2), p. 381. For the passage in the *Guide,* see *Guide* III, 25, pp. 502f. and 503 bot. (Joel. pp. 365.5f. and 366.1f.) and above nn. 21 and 22. It is theoretically possible to think that Maimonides is referring to *Hilkhot yesode ha-torah* which might correspond to *uṣūl al-dīn,* but such a topic is not mentioned there. In fact, I think that *yesode ha-torah* is a translation of *qawā'id al-sharī'a* which is much more suitable; but cf. *Guide* III, 35, p. 535 (Joel, pp. 391.1–392.2).

35. *Guide* III, 29, pp. 514 (Joel, p. 374.24f.), 516 (Joel, pp. 376.15f.), 517 (Joel, pp. 377.5f.)

36. Ar. *millat al-ṣāba.* Here the term translated as "religious community" is the same word I translated as religion, in the passages from Alfarabi given above. For the Sabians see *Shorter Encyclopaedia of Islam,* s.v. *al-Ṣābi'a* (R. Strothmann) and the literature quoted there; S. Munk, tr., *Le guide des égarés,* III, 217, n. 1 and 231, n. 2; and S. Pines, "Translator's Introduction," in *Guide,* pp. cxxiii f.

37. According to Maimonides, there was also a more sophisticated Sabian conception which he quotes in the name of Ibn Bājja (*Guide* III, 29, p. 515; Joel, p. 375.23–27). See also Maimonides, *Book of Knowledge. Hilkhot 'avodah zarah,* I, for a more highly developed historical account of the origin of idolatry. See further L. Strauss, "Notes of Maimonides' Book of Knowledge," in *Studies in Mysticism and Religion Presented to Gershom G. Scholem,* eds. E. E. Urbach et al. (Jerusalem, 1968), pp. 279–280.

38. Another possible translation: "when he understood that the myths upon which he was brought up were impossible." The term *khurāfāt* means fable, story, or myth and is used in a pejorative sense. See the expression *khurāfāt al-'ajā'iz* in Maimonides, *Treatise on the Resurrection,* ed. J. Finkel (New York: American Academy for Jewish Research, 1939), p. 3 (Judaeo-Arabic) and p. 94 (English). See also Plato, *Gorgias* 527A5; F. Buffiere, *Mythes d'Homère et la pensée grecque* (Paris, 1956), p. 33, n. 2; Pines, "Translator's Introduction," in *Guide,* p. lxxx.

39. See *Book of Knowledge. Hilkhot 'avodah zarah,* I, 2 and n. 37 above.

40. Ar. *da'wa ḍa'īfa.* Pines translates "feeble preaching." Munk, *Guide des égarés,* III, 229 has "une prédication pleine de douceur." Both Samuel Ibn Tibbon and al-Ḥarizi have *qeri'ah ḥalushah* (cf. Ex. xxxii 18). Abraham did not lead from a position of strength.

41. The use of these two epithets to describe Moses is not uncommon in the *Guide.* Maimonides uses the epithet "master of those who know (*sayyid al-'ālimīn*)" with reference to Moses in a philosophic context (see *Guide* I, 54, p. 123, Joel, p. 83.21; II, 28, p. 336.9, Joel, p. 235.7; III, 12, p. 448.8, Joel, p. 323.15; III, 54, p. 637.27, Joel, p. 470.24) whereas "master of the prophets (*sayyid al-nabī'īn*)" he uses in a political or religious context (see *Guide* II, 19, p. 311.2 [Pines translates here "chief of the prophets"], Joel, p. 217.1; II, 31, p. 359.12, Joel, p. 252.19; III, 18, p. 475.33, Joel, p. 344.2; III, 29, p. 517.18, Joel, p. 377.8). See also Pines, "Translator's Introduction," in *Guide,* p. lxi, n. 8.

42. For Maimonides' concept of Moses and some of the difficulties involved, see L. Strauss, "How to Begin to Study the Guide of the Perplexed," in *Guide,*

p. xxxvi; idem, "On Abravanel's Philosophic Tendency and Political Teaching," in *Isaac Abravanel* (Cambridge University Press, 1937), p. 98 with references quoted; S. Pines, "Translator's Introduction," in *Guide*, p. xci. I hope to deal exhaustively with Maimonides' concept of Moses and its relationship to the Arabic sources elsewhere.

43. *Guide* I, 71 beginning. The Maimonidean formulation is much more moderate than the position taken by Shem-Ṭobh Falaquera who argues that the wisdom of the Greeks and of other nations had its source among the Jews along with certain Muslims and Christians; see H. Malter, "Shem Tob ben Joseph Palquera," *Jewish Quarterly Review*, N.S. I (1910): 167, n. 29 with I. Twersky, "Some Non-Halakic Aspects of the Mishneh Torah," (above n. 31), pp. 114–115. Incidentally, Falaquera knew the *Book of Letters* quite well and quoted excerpts from it in his *Reshit Ḥokhmah*, ed. M. David (Berlin, 1902). See Mahdi, *Book of Letters*, p. 40 and p. 231. Mahdi notes the passages from *Reshit Ḥokhmah*, pp. 28.26–31.8 corresponding to *Book of Letters*, pp. 142.6–145.1 and 150.2–153.10 in his apparatus (to be corrected in some details). Mahdi has neglected to notice that Falaquera has excerpted another passage from *Book of Letters*. Compare *Reshit Ḥokhmah*, pp. 21.19–23.13 with *Book of Letters*, pp. 135.6–138.17. An urgent desideratum of Alfarabi studies is the detailed examination of all of the works of Falaquera, both published and unpublished, for the quotations of this excellent historian of philosophy from the corpus of Alfarabian writings. See also Maimonides, *Mishneh Torah: Sanctification of the New Moon*, tr. S. Gandz (above n. 3), p. xxvii (Obermann) with *Sanctification of the New Moon*, XVII, 25 where Maimonides takes the same position as in the *Guide*. For references to the *Khazarī* of Judah ha-Levi, see J. Kraemer in *Jewish Quarterly Review* 62 (1971): 68, n. 19.

44. It is in the same light that Maimonides' "back projection" of philosophy into Rabbinic expressions must be understood. The interpretation of *ma'aseh merkabhah* and *ma'aseh bereshit* as referring to philosophical physics and metaphysics, both of them included in the term *pardes*, is a result of the same general outlook (for precise references, see above n. 31). Maimonides, in his view, is continuing the tradition of the Rabbis who continued the line of philosophic investigation which started with Moses. It is fortunate indeed for the Maimonidean reinterpretation of these doctrines that detailed information about the esoteric concepts of the Rabbis was lost. For a historical understanding of the esoteric concerns of the Rabbis, see G. G. Scholem, *Major Trends in Jewish Mysticism* (New York: Schocken Paperback, 1965), pp. 40–79; idem, *Jewish Gnosticism, Merkabah Mysticism, and Talmudic Tradition* (New York: Jewish Theological Seminary, 1965); E. E. Urbach, *"Hamesorot 'al torat ha-sod bi-tequfat ha-tanna'im,"* *Studies in Mysticism and Religion Presented to Gershom G. Scholem*, eds. E. E. Urbach et al. (Jerusalem, 1968), pp. 1–28 (Hebrew Section). The question of how seriously Maimonides took this point of view (see Pines, "Translator's Introduction," in *Guide*, p. cxx with L. V. Berman, in *Journal of the American Oriental Society* 85 [1965]: 412–413) cannot be discussed within the limits of the present paper.

45. See *Guide* III, 32 on the wily graciousness of God with S. Pines. "Translator's Introduction", in *Guide*, pp. lxxii–lxxiv and cxxiii–cxxiv.

46. See *Guide* III, 32, p. 526.21–29 (Joel, p. 384.25–385.2).

47. See *Guide* III, 47, p. 592 (Joel, p. 435.1–10). The consciousness of the unpleasantness or burden (*mashaqqa aw kulfa*) entailed in the performance of the obligations of the Torah is very prominent in the *Guide*. It would seem that one of the tasks which Maimonides takes upon himself is to counter the feeling that the law of Moses is overly concerned with ritual actions, one of the perennial themes of Jewish-Muslim-Christian polemics. Maimonides tries to show that the religious system against which the Torah was reacting was even more of a burden.

48. See *On Religion,* pp. 49.9–50.2; *Political Regime,* ed. Najjar, pp. 80.15–81.2; M. Mahdi, "Alfarabi," (above n. 18), p. 172.

49. See *Book of Knowledge,* p. 1b.

50. See I. Twersky, "Some Non-Halakic Aspects of the *Mishneh Torah,*" (above, n. 31) pp. 95–118, esp. pp. 97–98; and G. Vajda, "La pensée religieuse de Moïse Maïmonide: unité ou dualité?" *Cahiers de civilisation médiévale* 9 (1966): 29–49 (not mentioned by Twersky). Vajda's conclusions need to be sharpened by the results of the present investigation, although the thrust of his argument is impeccable in my view.

51. It is because of Maimonides' acceptance of the Alfarabian definition of the function of the *faqīh* (jurisprudent) in his *Enumeration* (see above at nn. 21 and 22) which differs so radically from the ordinary Rabbinic conception of the Talmudist that Maimonides begins his *Mishneh Torah* with the *Book of Knowledge.* The lack of understanding of this radically different concept is the source of the view that holds that "Maimonides . . . begins the *Mishneh Torah* . . . with a philosophical chapter which has no relationship whatever to the Halakhah itself." See G. G. Scholem, *Major Trends in Jewish Mysticism,* pp. 28–29. I. Twersky comes to an understanding of Maimonides' view of *fiqh* (jurisprudence) which is essentially identical to the one outlined here on the basis of a "phenomenological" study of certain passages of the *Mishneh Torah.* In looking for the source of this view within the Jewish tradition, Twersky is not successful. I hope to have supplied the source here. See I. Twersky, "Some Non-Halakic Aspects of the *Mishneh Torah,*" (above n. 31), pp. 116–118.

52. An important start in the interpretation of the *Guide* has been made by Leo Strauss in a number of the works mentioned in the notes to this paper. However, Strauss' views merit a full scale exposition and critique which I hope to undertake on another occasion.

53. I cannot within the limits of the present paper go into a detailed *exposé* of Maimonides' view of other religions; see in the meantime Maimonides, *Epistle to Yemen,* ed. by S. Halkin with English translation by B. Cohen (New York: American Academy for Jewish Research, 1952), pp. 6–19 (Judaeo-Arabic and Hebrew translation) and pp. [ii]–[iv] (English translation) and the text quoted in L. V. Berman, "Reexamination . . . ," (above n. 27), p. 111.

54. For an edition of the Judaeo-Arabic text with Hebrew translation, see *Mishnah 'im perush rabbenu moshe ben maymon,* ed. J. Kapaḥ (Jerusalem: Mosad Harav Kook, 1963–1968), 7 volumes.

55. See his *Responsa,* ed. J. Blau (Jerusalem: Mekize Nirdamim, 1957–61), 3 volumes.

56. See *On Religion,* p. 56.12–14; ibid., p. 60.13–14; *Aphorisms,* ed. Dun-

lop, pp. 137–138 (Section 54); *Political Regime,* ed. Najjār, p. 81.2–5; *Virtuous City,* ed. Dieterici, p. 60.15–61.15; and also Mahdi, "Alfarabi," (above n. 18), p. 172. In my commentary to *On Religion* I discuss the problems involved in the relationship of these passages in detail.

57. See L. V. Berman, "The Political Interpretation of the Maxim: The Purpose of Philosophy is the Imitation of God," *Studia Islamica* 15 (1961): 53–61 with S. Pines, "Translator's Introduction," in *Guide,* pp. xci, xcvii, cxxii; idem, "Un texte inconnu d'Aristote en version arabe," *Archives d'histoire doctrinale et littéraire du Moyen Age* 23 (1956): 5–43; and J. L. Kraemer, *Abū Sulaymān as-Sijistānī* (above n. 5), pp. 234–236 for the view of a representative thinker in the generation after Alfarabi. For the Hellenistic and Byzantine background, see Francis Dvornik, *Early Christian and Byzantine Political Philosophy,* 2 volumes (Washington, D.C.: Dumbarton Oaks Center of Byzantine Studies, 1966), II, 624, 627, 661, 667, 691, 709, 713 and passim. It is significant that an epistle of Themistius was translated from Syriac into Arabic by Ibn Zur'a, see Dvornik, ibid., pp. 666–667 and above n. 5 end. The interesting and provocative article of G. E. von Grunebaum, "Parallelism, Convergence, and Influence in the Relations of Arab and Byzantine Philosophy, Literature, and Piety," in *Dumbarton Oaks Papers* 18 (1964): 89–111 does not contain a discussion of the imitation theme. For a general discussion of the imitation theme and its relationship to the motif of man as the image of God in Greek literature, see H. Merki, "ΟΜΟΙΩΣΙΣ ΘΕΩ der platonischen Angleichung an Gott zur Gottaehnlichkeit bei Gregor von Nyssa," *Paradosis* 7 (Freiburg in der Schweiz: Paulusverlag, 1952). For a good summary of Rabbinic doctrine and a Kabbalistic concept of the imitation of God as applied to ethical theory, see the introduction of L. Jacobs to his translation of *The Palm Tree of Deborah,* by M. Cordovero (London: Valentine, Mitchell, 1960), pp. 18–38.

The Purpose of the Law according to Maimonides

MIRIAM GALSTON

The importance that Maimonides attached to the Jewish law[1] is evident from his sustained interest in legal matters throughout his life. The majority of his writings are devoted to explaining, systematizing, and defending the Torah and the Rabbinic works that complete it. Even those who would accuse him of attempting to reformulate Jewish law surreptitiously would be forced to concede that the massiveness of his effort is itself the most persuasive proof that he considered the law indispensable for human life. In view of the centrality of law, therefore, for Maimonides' life and thought, persistent attempts to clarify his political thought need no defense. The present study will contribute to this effort by examining Maimonides' discussion of the law in what is considered his most philosophic work, the *Guide of the Perplexed*.[2] The purpose is to qualify the view usually attributed to Maimonides, namely, that the (revealed) law aims both at the perfection of man's reason and at the well-being of political life, in contradistinction to (nonrevealed) laws or *nomoi,* which make political well-being their sole concern.[3] Although not wholly inaccurate, statements of this kind tend to mislead by failing to distinguish the many kinds of political and spiritual well-being discussed by Maimonides, by not making precise the connection between each of the political well-beings and the spiritual well-beings, and by failing to clarify the relation between the spiritual well-being that a perfect law promotes and the ultimate spiritual well-being available to man.

The law is discussed thematically in three places in the *Guide*: (1) in the section devoted to belief in creation (II, 25–31); (2) in the section devoted to belief in prophecy (II, 39–40); and (3) in the section devoted

---

The Jewish Quarterly Review 69 (1978): 27–51. Reprinted by permission of Dropsie College, Merion, Penn.

to the rationality and utility of the actions commanded by God (III, 27–34).[4] What follows is an analysis of several of the most critical chapters in the latter two sections, which taken together form the core of Maimonides' teaching about the purpose of the law. These chapters provide several distinct accounts of the end or purpose of the law. Although discrepancies abound, the several accounts ultimately supplement one another, the discrepancies being occasioned by the differences in perspective of the respective chapters. The effort to disentangle and correlate the various formulations of the law's purpose is hampered by Maimonides' habit of shifting almost imperceptibly from "the law" to "the law in general," "the divine law," "the law of Moses," "governance," and "*nomoi.*" The purpose of this study will be to identify the strands of his discussions and to distill his teaching about each of the core notions.

REVEALED V. DIVINE LAW (II, 39)

The theme of Chapter II, 39 is the uniqueness of the law of Moses. The stipulation of the law itself regarding its own uniqueness is that there will never be another law after it. This is said to be a fundamental (*qāʿidah, yesōd*) of the law (416:2–3/268:7–8): the law asserts — without proving and without seeking to prove — the basis of its authority. Maimonides, on the other hand, undertakes to defend this fundamental, first on the basis of Scripture (416:4–417:12/268:9–269:6) and subsequently on the basis of reason (417:13–418:5/269:6–16). In the process of reformulating the fundamental, he changes its meaning: the fundamental of the law is that there will never be another law; the fundamental that Maimonides maintains is that there has never been another law and that there will never be another law.

To support *his* fundamental on the basis of Scripture, Maimonides distinguishes between the activities of teaching, instruction, guidance, and injunction on the one hand and legislating or giving commands on the other (416:5–417:6/268:10–29). He claims that Moses alone issued commands; the prophets who preceded Moses either imparted opinions to people or induced people to perform particular actions through persuasion ("beautiful speeches").[5] Those who came after Moses he likens to preachers: they took as their starting point the law as it was given, and then sought to insure people's adherence to that law by means of threats and promises (417:8–12/269:2–6).

However, in order to maintain this distinction between the legislative activity of Moses and the nonlegislative activity of all other prophets, Maimonides is forced to alter Scripture. According to Gen. 18:19, Abraham in fact *commanded* circumcision to his sons and relatives.[6] That Scripture should attribute commands to someone prior to Moses is not surprising, since the law's fundamental circumscribes only the activities of his successors. It is Maimonides who extends its restriction to prophets prior to Moses. What induced him to tamper with a sacred text comes to light in the second half of the chapter — Maimonides' defense of the uniqueness of the law on rational grounds. Here he has recourse to the principle that "when something is as perfect as is possible within a species, it is impossible that there should be within that species something else which does not fall short of that perfection because of excess or deficiency" (417:13–16/269:6–10). In other words, logically speaking, in any species there can only be one absolutely perfect member; everything else must be lacking in some respect when compared to it.

Maimonides makes two moves in relation to the perfection of the law of Moses. First, after announcing that in comparison with what is perfect, everything else will be excessive or deficient, he deduces the perfection of the law from the fact that it prescribes the mean between excesses and deficiencies in ritual matters (417:16–418:5/269:10–17).[7] The argument is questionable because it shifts without explanation from the assertion of perfection in a single respect to perfection in general. Excess or deficiency in ritual matters can, he claims, lessen a person's ability to achieve moral and speculative perfection; and this, we are told, was what occurred with the *nomoi* of previous religious communities (418:1–4/269:13–15). The superiority of the Mosaic law over all other laws, then, is that it avoids distracting people from speculation with unnecessary religious obligations at the same time that it prevents them from immoderate indulgence in bodily pleasures. For the move from the law's perfection in this respect to its absolute perfection to be valid, the primary or highest function of the law would have to be commanding things that are not themselves the highest good, but are the condition of, lead to, or are otherwise instrumental in, realizing that good. Moreover, it would require subordinating all the other provisions of the law, such as the opinions it imparts about God, to the end of ritual perfection.[8]

Maimonides introduces a second consideration in connection with the perfection of the law, namely, its "aim" (*maqṣūd, kawwānāh*). The divine law is the law which aims at every person becoming perfect (418:15–16/269:26–27). This is the first time the expression "divine law" occurs in this section, and it is noteworthy that the context is the law's end and not its agent. By speaking of the *aim* of the law, Maimonides makes clear that to warrant the name "divine," it is not enough for a law to include provisions of a certain kind; its goal must be promoting human perfection. A law that accidentally contains provisions which lead to human perfection, or one that contains provisions which accidentally lead to human perfection, is not divine. His formulation in terms of intention has the additional consequence that a law that fails to perfect all men may nonetheless be divine, for it is only stipulated that this be the aim and not necessarily the result. And in view of the uniqueness of anything perfect within a species, by speaking of the aim of the law over against the result, Maimonides saves the law from charges of ignorance or absurdity in addressing itself to the perfection of all men.

In sum, the theme of Chapter II, 39 is the uniqueness of the Mosaic law. Initially it dwells on the question of the *agent* of the law, Moses, whose prophecy is unique by virtue of being legislative, i.e., issuing in commands. It moves to a discussion of the *content* of the law — the law's provisions in relation to ritual matters. Maimonides here speaks first of the "balance" of "this law" (the Mosaic law) in matters of ritual observance, and subsequently of the "balance and wisdom" of "the laws" (*sharā'i'*), without any qualification. The chapter concludes with a statement about the *aim* of the law: to be divine the law must aim at the perfection of all. Revealed law and divine law are not, therefore, equivalent expressions, and it is not precluded that a *nomos* may be divine.

THE COMMUNITY AS SUCH; THE CITY RULED BY *NOMOS;* DIVINE LAW (II, 40)

In Chapter II, 40 Maimonides begins to flesh out the distinction between divine and human law, in the course of which *nomos* becomes the technical term to denote human law that is not divine. Three types of community are taken up: the community as such (*jam', ijtimā'*), communities constituted by divine law, and communities whose laws are a product of human imagination uninformed by reason (419:15–420:2, 421:1–10, 11–15/270:17–26, 271:16–24, 24–29).

The community as such answers a need that arises out of the unparalleled diversity among individual human natures, as contrasted with the members of other species: owing to the conflicts human diversity renders likely, if not inevitable, mankind needs to rule to standarize individuals' behavior, if the species as a whole is to endure.[9] Maimonides refrains from imparting to this code of behavior any specific content. Rather, its distinguishing characteristic is purely formal — uniformity of actions and morals. It is a condition of group activity as such, regardless of its goal, that all the members observe at least a minimal set of restraints and guidelines in their relations with one another. A group so constituted is prepolitical: it is a community or association, not a city (419:17, 19–20; cf.

421:3-4/270:18, 21-22; cf. 271:17-18), and the rules it observes are traditions, which lack the formal character of promulgated laws (419:18/270:20). Maimonides' community as such may be viewed less as a concrete but primitive form of social organization than as the lowest common denominator of concrete political communities which, by definition, pursue some species of good (real or imaginary) in addition to survival. The community as such, then, is part of all actual communities; hence its ruler can be either a prophet or someone who institutes a *nomos* (420:1-2/270:25-26). It is neither simply natural nor contrary to nature; it is rather grounded in nature (*la-hā madkhal fī' al-amr al-ṭabī'ī*), inasmuch as the goal is natural while the means transcend nature.

Both the nomoitic community and the divine community have goals beyond mere cooperation or harmony. The former takes its bearings from a false view of happiness advocated by the head of the community (421:7-8/271:22); the latter aims at making people wise, possessed of understanding, and alert (421:13-14/271:27-28). The disparity in goals is mirrored by a disparity in method: the community ruled by a *nomos* is preoccupied with protecting its members from bodily harm, to the exclusion of any theoretical concerns, while the community ruled by a divine law seeks to assure for its members both physical well-being and sound opinions about theoretical subjects (421:3-7, 11-12/271:18-20, 26-27). We can say that a *nomos* functions as a policeman, achieving its objectives through punishment or the threat of punishment. Divine law, on the other hand, undertakes to create an internal mechanism of restraint through education, as well as to provide its adherents with an introduction to the contemplative life.

II, 40 thus clarifies the character of the gap separating the two poles of law mentioned in II, 39. The law that aims at perfection — the divine law — attends to the individual's bodily health and the possibility of intellectual development; the law[10] that is man-made — *nomos* in the technical sense — confines itself to creating an orderly society, one in which people can be said to treat each other "justly" within the horizon of that community's (false) goals. Two features of this chapter are noteworthy. First, Maimonides distinguishes prophecy, true prophecy, and the pretense of prophecy. As expected, true prophecy characterizes the founder of a divine law, and the pretense of prophecy the founder of a *nomos* which claims divine inspiration. Prophecy without any qualification, however, denotes whoever grasps directly the conditions of the survival of the human species (419:21-420:2/270:23-26). Achieving this seemingly minimal political goal is said to partake of "the wisdom of the deity." As a consequence of the dignity Maimonides confers on securing mankind's survival, the founders of communities governed by man-made *nomoi* are prophetic impostors when measured against their specific and false understandings of the end of man, but are genuine prophets when viewed as contributing to the low but indispensable good of preservation. This tension recalls the Aristotelian formulation of the dual nature of political communities: their original existence is for the sake of mere life, their continuance for the sake of the good life (*Politics*, 1.2, 1252b, 29–30). Aristotle also singles out the agent of the lower of these two goals for special praise (*ibid.*, 1253a, 31–32).

Second, the physical goals of divine and nomoitic law are not equivalent, the nomoitic law having as its object healthy relations among men, the divine law having as its object healthy bodies (*aḥwāl al-madīnah* and *aḥwāl al-nās* versus *al-aḥwāl al-badanīyah*). In contrast to the social focus of nomoitic law, the physical intent of divine law is strikingly individualistic. [11]

By stipulating that each of the two poles of governance be totally devoted to the the end specified, Maimonides imposes on the chapter a kind of abstractness. This is a skeletal understanding of the law, at best, since most if not all the laws we encounter fall somewhere between the two extremes. In general, the discussion of law in II, 39 and II, 40 is programmatic: it occurs in the course of Maimonides' thematic treatment of prophecy. The account of the law in the context of the law's architect must be supplemented by a more thorough-going consideration of its purpose, content, and outcome.

THE LAW IN GENERAL; HUMAN PERFECTION; THE LAW PAR EXCELLENCE

Chapter III, 27 offers two accounts of the end of law, one of "the law in general," and one of "the law *par excellence*," which is equated with "the law of Moses," (579:2–16, 580:11–16/371:17–30, 372:16–21). The discussion of the law in general is divided into two parts, the first dealing with the health of body and soul, the second treating of their perfection (579:12–16, 16–580:10/371:17–30, 30–372:16). Only the health of body and soul is explicitly attributed to the effects of the law in general. The discussion of perfection can be seen as an elaboration of the passage on health or as an alternative to it.

The health of the soul consists in "the multitude acquiring correct opinions" insofar as they have the capacity to do so. The body's health consists in improving people's way of living with one another; and this, in turn, comes about when (1) reciprocal wrongdoing is eliminated and people perform actions "useful for all," and (2) there is realized in "every human individual moral habits useful for social intercourse, so that the city will be well-ordered." Instrumental, therefore, to the health that the law in general promotes are correct opinions for the multitude, actions useful for all on the part of individuals, and morals useful for society or the city on the part of each individual.

The perfection of the soul and of the body bear a superficial resemblance to their healthy condition: in each case the body must reach its objective before the soul can do the same, and the perfection of the soul consists in opinions – not morals – as does the soul's health. However, "bodily health" describes the quality of social interactions, whereas "bodily perfection" denotes the fitness of individual bodies. The "health of the body" that the law in general intends is therefore primarily societal well-being, characterized as bodily, no doubt, because it ordinarily consists in the distribution of physical goods and services according to some principle acceptable to most members of the community. To be sure, bodily perfection requires that individuals possess the necessities of life, and hence that they inhabit a community self-sufficient enough to fulfill their needs (579:19–22/372:3–6). The difference is not that bodily health presupposes political life, while bodily perfection does not. The difference is rather that in one case the health of the body is a function of the health of the community, while in the other the health of the body is a function of an individual's personal fitness. In the former case, bodily health is in the service of the community; in the latter, it is the community that is in the service of bodily health.

Maimonides alludes to this reversal of priorities by speaking of a "city" in connection with bodily health (421:4–5, 579:10, 13/271:17–18, 371:25, 27–28) but not in connection with bodily perfection. In the context of perfection, he concedes that individuals need a "political community" to achieve their goals (579:21–22/372:5–6); and "political" (madanī) is derived from "city" (madīnah). However, "political" here depends for its principle or organization on the noun it modifies, and Maimonides earlier established a contrast between communities unified for survival alone and cities whose inhabitants cooperate to achieve some form of happiness beyond mere survival (419:15–20, 421:2–8/270:17–22, 271:17–22). Bodily perfection thus has as its precondition a society whose members have solely negative obligations towards one another. The members of the community that bodily health presupposes, on the other hand, are required to perform actions "useful to all." In short, the minimal community that makes bodily perfection possible makes fewer and less rigorous demands on its members than the city directed to bodily health. The gulf which separates the two communities is identical to the gulf which separates "a political association" from "a well-ordered city."

The seemingly paradoxical conclusion is that bodily perfection requires an association of a lower order than does bodily health. One consequence of this is that the community linked to bodily perfection admits of greater individualism than the city that bodily health presupposes — a possibility hinted at in II, 40.[12] There may be a tension between bodily perfection and bodily health, inasmuch as actions useful to all the members of a city — military service, for example — threaten the bodily perfection of particular individuals. The law in general, we may say, is indifferent to bodily perfection as such, owing to its lack of concern for individuals as ends in themselves. Since the perfection of the soul was said to depend on the perfection of the body, the law in general would seem to be indifferent to the perfection of the soul as well, and in some instances even antithetical to it.

The disjunction between bodily health and bodily perfection forces us to examine the relationship between the perfection of the soul and its healthy condition, given that the law in general aims only at the latter. The perfection of the soul, also referred to as man's ultimate perfection (579:17/372:1), consists in "becoming rational in actuality, i.e., having an intellect in actuality," which is further explained as "knowing everything about the beings which it is in man's capacity to know" (580:1–3/372:6–9). Ultimate perfection, so understood, amounts to possessing "opinions arrived at through speculation and found to be necessary by investigation (*baḥth*)" (580:4–5/372:10). Both the health of the soul and its perfection, therefore, consist in opinions. The health of the soul, however, entails "correct opinions," whereas in the case of the perfection of the soul Maimonides stipulates not their correctness but the manner in which they are acquired, through speculation and investigation. On the face of it, the health and the perfection of the soul are less opposed than were the health and perfection of the body. Although Maimonides does not explicitly label the opinions which comprise the souls' perfection "correct," it is implied that they are at least correct, if not correct and something more. And despite the fact that he links the health of the soul to the multitude (*jumhūr*), while the perfection of the soul is presumably confined to an élite, Maimonides considers all people prior to the exercise of reason as belonging to the multitude. Thus even philosophers belonged to the multitude when they were young, so that a healthy soul seems to be necessary for all people at some stage of life. In some health will be superseded by perfection as the rational faculty becomes actualized. At the same time, the soul's health does not seem to threaten the possibility of the soul's perfection, as was the case with the health and perfection of the body. In fact, the soul's health is designed to encourage the emergence of its perfection, as Maimonides makes clear in the next chapter.

To sum up, in the first half of III, 27 Maimonides takes up two relationships, the body's health vis-à-vis its perfection and the soul's perfection vis-à-vis its health. He claims that his remarks about the two perfections have been demonstrated, whereas we can only conjecture that what he says about the two kinds of health are either mere assertions or are deduced from what has been demonstrated about the two perfections. The two kinds of health include opinions, actions, and morals; the two perfections comprise only opinions and actions. The relation between the two kinds of health and between the two perfections is not developed beyond the suggestion that bodily perfection is not dependent on bodily health and may even conflict with it, while the perfection of the soul is either dependent on, or harmonious with, its health. The difficulties raised by the latter relationship are the theme of III, 28.

The remainder of III, 27 deals with the law *par excellence* (*al-sharī'ah al-ḥāqqah, ha-tōrāh ha-amittīt*):

> [The law *par excellence*,] namely, the law of Moses our master, . . . has come to give us both perfections — I mean the health of the states of people in their relations with one another through the removal of reciprocal wrong doing and through the adoption of noble and virtuous moral character, so that the preservation of the inhabitants of the land and their perpetuation under a single order will be possible, so that every one of them will achieve his first [bodily] perfection; [and this law has come] for the soundness of beliefs and giving correct opinions, through which ultimate perfection is achieved (580:11–16/372:16–21).

From this description it appears that in the case of the law *par excellence*, healthy social relations (equated with bodily health in 579:5–7, 13–14/371: 20–22, 27–28) are a precondition of bodily perfection, and the health of the soul (sound beliefs and correct opinions) is a precondition of its perfection.[13] The superiority of the law *par excellence* to the law in general would then be that it achieves a greater harmony between bodily and spiritual health and their corresponding perfections, or even that the law *par excellence* is the sole law in which the two kinds of health are a preparation for the two kinds of perfection. But this formula needs to be qualified, first, in light of the new meaning Maimonides gives to societal well-being in the discussion of the law *par excellence*. Although cast in terms reminiscent of the description of societal well-being in III, 27, the stated objective of societal well-being in this chapter is survival, the goal of the minimal pre-political community introduced in II, 40. Thus the analogue to bodily health as conceived by the law *par excellence* is to be found not in the provisions of the law in general, but in the lower order community which is common to nomoitic as well as divine communities. In other words, in addition to distinguishing between bodily health and bodily perfection, one must also separate the two modes of societal well-being that are preludes to them. The law *par excellence* does not resolve the potential conflict between bodily health and bodily perfection as much as bypass it, by substituting a political community of a different order than law in general establishes. Second, the moral habits inculcated by the law in general are acquired for their *utility* in social interactions, while the law *par excellence* instills "noble and virtuous moral character." In short, the bodily health sought by the law *par excellence* resembles the parallel concern of the minimal community, as contrasted with the bodily health pursued by cities, while it differs from the bodily health of the minimal community by providing for the growth of "noble and virtuous character."

Maimonides postpones his systematic treatment of the effects of the various kinds of law on the soul until III, 28. III, 27 merely adds to the accumulation of raw data with which III, 28 will deal. The health of the soul at which the law *par excellence* aims consists in healthy beliefs and opinions (*ṣalāḥ al-i'tiqādāt wa-i'ṭā' arā' ṣaḥīḥah*). It must be distinguished, therefore, not only from the nomoitic law that neglects opinions altogether (421:5–6/271:20), but also from the law in general which limits itself to sound opinions (579:12/371:26–27) or sound opinions for the masses (579:3/371:17–18). The law *par excellence* hearkens back to the divine law of II, 40, which also displayed concern for both opinions and beliefs (421:12–13/271:25–26).

The teaching of III, 27 regarding the difference between the law in general and the law *par excellence* is not that the former is concerned with the health of body and soul and the latter with their perfection. For the provisions of both laws are designed to promote a kind of health. However, the health of the body and the health of the soul can each be conceived in different ways, some (or one) of which are more conducive to the attainment of ultimate perfection than the others. The law in general promotes the kind of health that is either indifferent or hostile to the two perfections. The law *par excellence* promotes the kind of health that either makes possible or facilitates the attainment of the two perfections. It is a difference of kind, not merely of degree, but a difference that is elusive nonetheless because of Maimonides' use of a wide range of seemingly synonymous expressions. What this chapter leaves unanswered is, first, what "sound beliefs" are and how they differ from "correct opinions," and second, what "noble and virtuous character" is and how it differs from "morals useful for social interaction." The first of these is taken up in III, 28.

OPINION AND BELIEF (III, 28)

According to III, 28, there are three classes of opinions and beliefs. To the first belong correct opinions which the law has conveyed to people in a summary way. Examples of such opinions are the Deity's existence,

His unity, His power, His will, and His eternity. It is possible to gain detailed and precise clarification of such opinions only after a person knows many other opinions (581:10–14/373:7–11). In this sense summary opinions are really conclusions which the law presents summarily as axioms. If, as Maimonides implies, these are the correct opinions referred to in the previous chapter which make ultimate perfection possible, then adopting them provisionally as axioms on the authority of the law would seem to be a condition of, or to facilitate the process of, arriving at the same opinions on the basis of reason, in detail, and with precision. The second class is made up of "necessary beliefs," presented as a prerequisite for "healthy political conditions." An example of this class is the belief that God becomes angry at anyone who disobeys Him, which belief promotes fear and hence obedience on the part of the believer (581:15–17/373:11–13). The third class consists of "all the other correct opinions concerning the whole of this existence – opinions that constitute the theoretical sciences in their many kinds, by means of which those opinions which constitute the ultimate end are validated" (581:17–19/373:14–21).

The law conveys correct opinions of the first class in a summary way, but is explicit in summoning people to believe them. The opinions of the third class, on the other hand, are not conveyed by the law at all, and it only summons people to believe in them implicitly or summarily. It does this by calling upon them to *love the Lord thy God with all thy heart, and with all thy soul, and with all thy might* (Deut. 6:5). This clarifies a notion alluded to in previous chapters, namely, that even when the law aims at human perfection, it promotes this goal in an indirect manner. In the sphere of actions, in contrast, it can command directly what produces bodily health or bodily perfection, and the latter is a necessary precursor of the perfection of the soul. In the sphere of opinions, the law can at most command *belief* in opinions the *knowledge* of which would constitute perfection. And it cannot even command belief in the opinions that are the grounds of the opinions the knowledge of which constitutes perfection, but is limited to alluding to the need to acquire them. The reason for this is not made clear until III, 34.

The threefold classification of opinions and beliefs, set forth in the first half of III, 28, is thus determined by the manner in which each is commanded by the law: explicitly but summarily; explicitly and in detail; implicitly. The opinions in the third class have to do with "this existence," i.e., visible or sensible existence, whereas the opinions in the first class have to do with things which cannot be perceived by the senses. Opinions about nonsensible things only become fully known on the basis of the conclusions of the theoretical sciences, that is, on the basis of reasoned opinions about sensible things. To use the terminology of the discussion of prophecy, the correct opinions of the third class are the province of the men of science or theoretical men, while the correct opinions of the first class are known with precision and in detail to prophets alone.[14] The opinions in the first class are the completion of the opinions in the third class, and the opinions of the third class are the means to, and the verification of, those in the first class, just as the prophet's knowledge was said to include, and be, the completion of the knowledge of men of science, at the same time that the theoretical sciences were said to be the avenue to the attainment of prophecy (II, 36, 404:14-18, 406:17-18, 408:1/260:24-27, 262:5-10, 28-29).

The epistemological status of the central class — the necessary beliefs that healthy political conditions presuppose — is not stated. According to the second half of the chapter, the object of politically salutary beliefs is the elimination of injustice in men's relations with each other and the acquisition of noble moral habits. Discovery of the means to these ends is traditionally the province of deliberation or practical wisdom. In II, 36, however, insights of this kind appear to depend on theoretical knowledge and a grasp of metaphysics (406:17-407:2, 407:20-408:4/262:5-10, 27-263:1), although their immediate locus may be the imaginative faculty (407:21, 410:8-11/262:27-28, 264:13-15).

In the second half of III, 28 the first classification is replaced by a second, and the new classification designates both the opinions and the beliefs of the earlier classification as "beliefs." These are then divided into (1) correct beliefs — those that should be believed for their own sake, and (2) beliefs that are necessary (a) for the removal of reciprocal wrongdoing, or (b) for the acquisition of noble moral habits (583:11-17/373:24-26). Clearly all the necessary political beliefs of the first classification would fall under the necessary beliefs of the second. Some of the axiomatic opinions of the first classification would also be believed because of their political utility in addition to their possible theoretical interest. For example, if belief in God's anger is a necessary political belief to insure obedience to the law, then belief in the Deity's existence — one of the axiomatic and summary opinions of class one — would also be a necessary political belief. What the second classification excludes is the possibility of opinions that should be acquired for the sake of other *opinions,* if the latter are sought for their own sake. In other words, there is no room in the new classification for the summary and axiomatic opinions of the first class of the earlier classification when these have no utility for political life. It would seem, therefore, that there is no such thing as approximate or summary knowledge acquired for its own sake by people incapable of, or not disposed to, philosophy.

This last inference is not, however, necessary, since the second classification does not claim to be exhaustive. Rather, it occurs in the context of determining which commandments are, or should be, a source of perplexity. Maimonides maintains that correct opinions which ought to be believed for their own sake, or for the sake of removing reciprocal wrongdoing or acquiring noble morals, are not inherently perplexing, because their utility is obvious. Since most people do not recognize that axiomatic and summary opinions are merely summary, and so assume that such opinions are to be believed for their own sake, these opinions will not be a source of perplexity to them. From the vantage point of people in general, therefore, there is no conflict between the two classifications of opinions and beliefs in III, 28.

At the same time Maimonides vacillates between speaking about commandments which have been a source of perplexity at some time in the past and those concerning which questions ought to be posed. He thus tacitly acknowledges that some of the axiomatic and summary opinions, when properly understood, should be a source of perplexity; in particular, commandments to believe in opinions whose sole utility is in connection with man's ultimate perfection are in and of themselves problematic. The *Guide* has thus come full circle: now it appears that those aspects of the law which are useful only for encouraging speculation are the real sources of perplexity, whereas in the introduction to the *Guide* perplexity appeared to be linked to occasions when speculation and the law were in conflict (9:15–10:4/2:14–19).

To summarize Maimonides' teaching about opinions or beliefs and the law, we can say that according to the beginning of III, 27, the things that ought to be believed are called "correct opinions" and appear to be sought for their own sake. In the course of that chapter and III, 28, Maimonides introduces the notion of beliefs acquired for their political utility. At first these appear to comprise less than half of what the law commands people to believe (581:10–582:1/373:7–17); subsequently they are revealed to make up the majority of such commands (583:7–10/374:12–14). Finally he makes clear that even those things which ought to be believed and which are connected to man's ultimate perfection, i.e., the actualization of his intellect, do not themselves constitute that perfection in the form in which the law imparts them. Maimonides thus moves the reader from the impression that all the beliefs which the law commands are to be believed for their own sake, to the realization that some of these beliefs are necessary because of their usefulness for other things, and to the possibility that none of the beliefs commanded by the law are to be believed for their own sake. This movement is epitomized by Maimonides' shift from speaking about correct opinions to speaking about correct beliefs. We can say that beliefs are not opinions, even when they are correct, because they are adopted on the authority of someone or something else. Correct opinions, in the rigorous sense of the expression, cannot be imparted by the law because they must be acquired through an individual's own efforts by means of inquiry and study. These chapters in the *Guide* thus explain why, in the *Treatise on Logic,* Maimonides never claims that the law has rendered scientific philosophy superfluous, not even that part of metaphysics which inquires into the Deity and the angels. Far from replacing scientific philosophy, the law in fact reaches its completion through scientific philosophy, which turns the axiomatic and summary opinions into precise and reasoned conclusions.

Further, the initial superiority of the health of the soul over the health of the body has been significantly qualified. The law in general aims at the health of both. Our first impression was that bodily health is sought for the sake of the soul's health, while the latter is sought for its own sake. III, 28 reveals that correct opinions—which are properly called correct beliefs, and which constitute the soul's health—are mere approximations of the opinions which make up the perfection of the soul, man's ultimate perfection. The soul's health is thus sought not for its own sake, but as the cognitive forerunner of the perfection of the soul. This second impression was, in turn, undermined by the introduction of the notion of politically necessary beliefs, sought for the sake of the health of the community as a political entity, and by Maimonides' identification of the health of the soul with "beliefs," not "opinions." There is, then, an aspect of the *soul's* health, i.e., politically salutary beliefs, that is sought for the sake of *bodily* health—the reverse of the relationship between the two forms of health as they first appeared. Not only are such beliefs not sought for the sake of the perfection of the soul; they are antagonistic to it, to the extent that the health of the body is at odds with the body's perfection (above, pp. 221–223, 224).

It is "the law in general," according to Maimonides, that is made up of beliefs of this sort exclusively, although he does not preclude the possibility that some such beliefs may accidentally promote the soul's perfection as well. The law *par excellence* is to be distinguished from the law in general in that it contains some beliefs which have no political utility, but which are conducive to the acquisition of correct opinions through speculation. At the end of III, 28 Maimonides suggests that one such "correct opinion" is the belief in the incorporeality of the Deity, which does not contribute to political stability. Insistence on this belief is one of the features of the Jewish law that distinguishes it from all other laws and that confirms its claim to be the law *par excellence,* the law without equal (583:11–15/374:19).[15]

MORALITY AND LAW

The subject of moral habits, not treated systematically in the chapters on law, must be clarified by recourse to individual statements scattered throughout the chapters. This structural feature of the *Guide* is mirrored by the relative lack of independence attributed to the moral sphere in the individual statements themselves. In II, 39 one of the consequences of the perfection of the law of Moses in ritual matters was set forth as the moderation it encourages in regard to bodily pleasures (417:16–418:3/269:10–15). Moral habits are not there characterized as simply noble or desirable in their own right. They appear to be choiceworthy by virtue of their ability to reduce the number of distractions that keep people from desiring to engage in speculation or from engaging in it successfully.

II, 40 dwelt on the great natural diversity among people's moral habits due to differences in temperament and environment (419:2–22/270:5–24). The disparity among the moral characters of individuals was depicted as so great that people might appear to belong to distinct species of animals. Governance came to light as the means of neutralizing these differences so that people could live together in an "orderly community." Since communal life is as integral a part of people's nature as the diversity of their actions and morals, laws that eliminate the heterogeneity among them are in accordance with nature and are necessary. Here too, then, moral habits are subservient to a larger goal, the orderly rule of men, which is linked in turn to the preservation of the human species. Although the mere preservation of mankind is a lofty enough goal to warrant inclusion in "the Deity's wisdom," such minimal associations are usually directed to other ends as well: one or more of the false forms of happiness (421:6–8/271:21–22). In this respect, the actions the law commands and the morals which it establishes serve a two-fold function: the perpetuation of mankind and the acquisition of apparent happiness. The second half of II, 40 continues this depreciation of morals by failing to mention them explicitly in the account of the divine law, although, as we saw, a certain level of moral habits is implied in the notion of the "health of bodily states."

Morals fare somewhat better in the third part of the *Guide.* According to III, 27, the law in general inculcates morals useful to society in order to bring about a well-ordered city (579:9–10/371:24–25). As far as the law in general goes, then, the position of morals in relation to man's perfection is as ambiguous as was the position of the well-ordered city to man's first perfection. The law *par excellence,* on the other hand — the law of Moses — provides for "noble and virtuous moral character" in the name of the continuation of orderly life among the inhabitants of a country (580:12-14/372:17-19). Since this form of political stability—linked not to a city or nation, but to a country—is presented as the means to bodily perfection, which is the precondition of man's highest perfection, morals here can be said to be in the service, at least indirectly, of the highest human good (579:11-16/371:25-30).[16]

What emerges from III, 27 and III, 28, taken together, is that there are two broad classes of moral habits corresponding to two kinds of political goods: the good of the association as such and the good of the individuals who live in the association. Morals giving rise to actions that promote an association's well-being are "noble" morals; morals which result in actions above and beyond those useful for the association are excellent or virtuous. According to II, 40, a ruler determines the morals and actions of those he rules with a view to dulling the force of people's natural diversity by creating a body of shared beliefs and practices. In the terminology of II, 40, then, morals which have no utility for the city as such, but which are conducive to philosophy or other private activities, increase the diversity among men and hence may contribute to political instability. Such morals would be virtuous but not noble. The law *par excellence,* according to Maimonides, is the only law which gives rise to both kinds of morals; to be precise, it gives rise to those morals that are simply noble and those that are both noble and virtuous.[17] From the perspective of the law, according to Maimonides, virtuous morals *per se* (i.e., as contrasted with morals both noble and virtuous) and the end to which they lead are, and should be, a source of perplexity because of their indifference to political concerns.

In conclusion, the difference between ancient *nomoi* or regimes and revealed laws is not one of goals but of method. Both aim at bodily goods —preservation and imaginary forms of happiness. Unique to revealed laws is the awareness of the power that opinions can have in reinforcing the actions commanded by nonrevealed laws and thus in insuring the perpetuation and stability of the political order. In terms of this criterion, the laws of Plato's *Laws* partake of a "revelation" in no way inferior to those at the origin of the more generally accepted revealed religions.[18] The contribution of any of these laws, as well as of admittedly nonrevealed laws, to man's intellectual development is directly proportionate to the moderation they teach in regard to physical appetites. However large this contribution, it is incidental to their primary purpose, and so the role such governances play in man's ultimate perfection is necessarily accidental.

Two things distinguish the law of Moses. First, it excels beyond the other laws, revealed or man-made, in promoting moderation in physical desires and in matters of ritual worship. Second, in addition to containing opinions parallel to those contained in inferior laws, it contains some opinions with no utility other than encouraging the attainment of intellectual perfection. Maimonides does not make light of the potential conflict between these two kinds of opinions. Opinions of the second kind comprise only a fragment of the provisions of the Jewish law. For when properly understood, the law must, according to Maimonides, attend to the welfare of the majority of men (III, 34). What distinguishes the law of Moses is not that it abandons ordinary men for the sake of exceptional ones, but that it permits the fullest development of each in the highest and most complete way possible.

NOTES

The research for this study was made possible by a grant from the Memorial Foundation for Jewish Culture. I would also like to thank the Center for Middle Eastern Studies at the University of Texas in Austin for their generous support and their encouragement over the years.

1. The word "law" will be used to translate the Arabic *sharī'ah* and Hebrew *tōrāh*, both of which are usually understood as signifying revealed law in contradistinction to *nomos* (Arabic *nāmūs*, Hebrew *nimōs*), which signifies man-made or conventional law. Maimonides gives these expressions a new content, as will become clear in what follows.

2. All references to the *Guide* are to Part and Chapter (for example, III, 27), followed by page and line references in Atay's Arabic edition and the Munk-Joel Judaeo-Arabic edition (*Delâletül-Hâirîn*, ed. Hüseyin Atay [Ankara, 1972]; *Dalālat al-hā'irīn*, ed. Solomon Munk and revised by Issachar Joel [Jerusalem, 5691/1930-31]). Page references in the body of the paper are to the *Guide* unless otherwise noted.

3. See, for example, E. I. J. Rosenthal, "Maimonides' Conception of State and Society," in his *Studia Semitica I: Jewish Themes* (Cambridge, 1971), pp. 282–284; Julius Guttmann, *Philosophies of Judaism,* English translation by D. W. Silverman (New York, 1973), pp. 203–204; Arthur Hyman, "Maimonides' 'Thirteen Principles'," *Jewish Medieval and Renaissance Studies,* ed. A. Altmann (Cambridge, Mass., 1967), p. 119. In reaching his conclusion that the law aims at the development of the intellect, Hyman overlooks the fact that Maimonides defines the welfare of the soul (at which the law in general aims) as sound opinions *for the multitude* proportionate to their ability (*Guide* III, 27, 579:3/371:17–18). To maintain Hyman's thesis one would have to argue a necessary connection between "sound opinions for the multitude" and "the development of the human intellect."

4. See the outline of the plan of the *Guide* in the Pines translation, pp. xi–xiii.

5. More than 95 percent of the instances of *ṣiwwah* (and other verbal forms) have Moses or God as their subject (*Veteris Testamenti Concordantiae Hebraicae atque Chaldaicae,* ed. Solomon Mandelkern, pp. 988–990).

6. Maimonides was of course aware of this verse; he quotes the first half of it in II, 39.

7. Maimonides deduces the uniqueness of Moses' prophecy from the uniqueness of the law, and not the reverse. The traditional understanding considers the law unique because the prophecy was unique, because God singled Moses out for a special revelation. Tradition evaluates the law by its agent; Maimonides evaluates Moses by his handicraft.

8. Since Maimonides derives the uniqueness of the prophecy of Moses from the uniqueness of the law, and not the reverse, the case for Moses stands or falls with the case Maimonides makes for the perfection of the Jewish law.

9. Contrast Aristotle (*Politics,* I.2), where the suggestion is that nature has insured the survival of the species by instilling in male and female the desire to mate, while the need for a ruler is connected with a less abstract concern—the survival of individuals.

10. Maimonides uses "law" (*sharī‘ah*) to refer to man-made laws which claim to be revealed as well as to truly prophetic or divine laws. He likewise uses "regimens" (*tadbīrāt*) in connection with divine as well as man-made laws.

11. See below, pp. 221–222.

12. See above, pp. 219–220.

13. Maimonides avoids the actual expression "health of the body" in the passage on the law *par excellence,* probably in order to acknowledge that the societal well-being there described is closer to the pre-political harmony of the community as such than it is to the previous descriptions of societal well-being (compare II, 40, 421:3–4, 6–7/271:17–18, 21 and III, 27, 579:6–9, 13–14/371:21–25, 27–28 with III, 27, 579:18–20, 580:12–15/372:2–4, 17–19). It seems that "prevention of injustice and wrongdoing" in the two passages just cited is the provision for assuring life, while the regulations dealing with order are directed toward the "good" life—"good" because the ruler is mistaken in his view of the human good.

14. In II, 36, 406:17–407:2/262:5–10, understanding seems to include two stages, the perfection of human wisdom and the attainment of divine wisdom. The second arises after, and perhaps out of, the first.

15. Several Muslim philosophers believed that the doctrine of God's incorporeality was unnecessary for ordinary believers (Averroes, *Kitāb faṣl al-maqāl/Decisive Treatise,* ed. G. Hourani [Leiden, 1959], 25:3–8) or positively harmful (Avicenna, *Al-Shifā’ al-ilāhīyāt,* eds. Moussa, Dunya, Zayed, and Madkour [Cairo, 1960], X.2, 442:13–443:2).

16. See 580:12–14/371:25–30, where Maimonides divides bodily well-being into (1) the governance of the city, and (2) the health of the inhabitants' conditions, according to their capacity. He seems to be referring to the latter when he says "*this* second aim" is the more certain one, and not at all of bodily well-being, which would be "*the* second aim."

17. That is, it is the only law that achieves the homogeneity necessary for

orderly political life by training people in moral habits that are means between extremes. Only moral habits of this kind are both noble, when shared in common, and virtuous (see *Eight Chapters,* IV).

18. Thus, according to Avicenna, the standard works on prophecy and (re-vealed) law are the books Plato and Aristotle wrote on *nomoi* (*Fī aqsām al-'ulūm al-'aqlīyah/Divisions of the Rational Sciences* [Cairo, 1908], 108:2–3).

The Doctrine of the Mean in Aristotle and Maimonides: A Comparative Study

MARVIN FOX

The scholarly literature dealing with the interpretation of the philosophy of Maimonides moves between two poles. There are those who insist that Maimonides was in all significant respects a true and faithful disciple of Aristotle, or of the Aristotelianism which he knew through the Arabic sources. At the other extreme there are those who argue that the Aristotelianism of Maimonides is only a surface appearance but that he is, in fact, not an Aristotelian at all in his actual philosophical and theological doctrines.

The difference of opinion is especially sharp in the discussions of Maimonides' ethics, particularly with respect to his doctrine of the mean. Many writers take the position that the Aristotelianism of Maimonides' doctrine of the mean is so obvious that it does not even require discussion or evidence. Writing about Shem Tov ben Joseph Palqera, Malter says that "the Aristotelian ethics of the golden mean found in Palquera a disciple scarcely less devoted than his master Maimonides."[1] Gorfinkle, in his edition of the *Eight Chapters of Maimonides* speaks of the chapter "in which the Aristotelian doctrine of the *Mean* . . . is applied to Jewish ethics." He adds that "Although Maimonides follows Aristotle in defining virtue as a state intermediate between two extremes, . . . he still remains on Jewish ground as there are biblical and talmudical passages expressing such a thought."[2] Harry S. Lewis speaks of "the famous attempt of Maimonides to equate Jewish ethics with the Aristotelian doctrine of the mean." He

From *Studies in Jewish Religious and Intellectual History,* edited by Siegfried Stein and Raphael Loewe (University, Ala.: University of Alabama Press, 1980), pp. 93–120. Reprinted by permission of the University of Alabama Press.
Translations added to the text in brackets are those of the editor with the help of David Louch.

goes on to affirm that "Maimonides derived his doctrine of the Mean from Greek sources, but it was quite congenial to the native hebraic spirit."[3] Rosin, in his basic study of the ethics of Maimonides, sees the doctrine of the mean as essentially Aristotelian in origin and character, despite some of Maimonides' deviations from the Aristotelian pattern. "Handlungen, sagt M. in Übereinstimmung mit Aristoteles, sind gut, wenn sie angemessen sind indem sie in der Mitte zwischen zwei Extremen liegen . . . " [Actions, says Maimonides in agreement with Aristotle, are good whenever they are suitable because they lie in the mean between two extremes.][4] Even those writers, like Rosin, who seek also in rabbinic literature for the sources of Maimonides' doctrine of the mean, take the position that these are supports which legitimate the Jewishness of the doctrine, but they do not claim that they are the actual sources from which Maimonides derived his position.

Opposed to these writers are those who deny that Maimonides' ethics are Aristotelian in any significant respect. A typical voice from the traditional camp, that of Rabbi Ya'akov Mosheh Harlap, affirms with the greatest passion that no non-Jewish source can make any contribution to Jewish doctrine. After having discussed at great length various aspects of Maimonides' doctrine of the mean, Harlap is concerned to protect his readers from the mistake of supposing that this doctrine has any non-Jewish origin. If it appears to be similar to the teachings of Aristotle, this is no more than an appearance, and we must understand it properly. Such a doctrine can enter Jewish teaching from the outside only if it is first thoroughly Judaized, only if, like the convert, it is reborn and acquires a new, specifically Jewish, nature. "Whatever is taught by others cannot be presented as Jewish teaching unless it has first undergone conversion (geruth). Just as it is possible to convert souls, so is it possible to convert doctrines."[5] Harlap claims that this is what happened with Maimonides' doctrine of the mean. It may appear to be similar to Aristotle's doctrine, but after having been converted, it is a totally new and uniquely Jewish creation.

Coming to the materials from a different background and perspective, Hermann Cohen also argues fiercely against the Aristotelianism of Maimonides' ethics. Cohen holds that for purposes of tactical effectiveness Maimonides chose to give the appearance that he was agreeing with Aristotle since otherwise he would open himself to endless attack.[6] In fact, says Cohen, his doctrine is not Aristotelian at all. It is independent of Aristotle and not in agreement with him. If we were forced to affirm that Maimonides derived his ethics from Aristotle and was in agreement with him, "so wäre die Ethik Maimunis nicht nur keine philosophische Ethik mit einem selbstständigen und einheitlichen Prinzip, sondern auch als religiöse Ethik wäre sie widerspruchsvoll in sich; auch als ein Anhang zum

Moreh als eine Art von Homilie, würde sie sich nicht anpassen; und selbst als ein Glied in seinem System der Theologie wäre sie unorganisch und exoterisch" [then not only would the ethics of Maimonides not be a philosophical ethics based on an independent and unified principle, but as a religious ethics it would also be self-contradictory; neither would it fit as an appendix to the *Guide*, nor as a sort of homily; and even as an element in his system of theology it would be unsystematic and exoteric].[7] Cohen goes on later to delineate carefully and in detail the ways in which Maimonides' doctrine of the mean differs from that of Aristotle.[8]

Our aim in the present paper is to present a fresh investigation of the question. We shall focus our attention specifically on the doctrine of the mean as it is treated by Maimonides in his various works. It is one of our main contentions, however, that no responsible treatment can be offered of the relationships between Maimonides' and Aristotle's doctrines unless we are first clear about what it was that Aristotle actually taught. In our view, conventional representations of the doctrine of the mean in Aristotle fail to grasp the fundamental philosophical ground on which that doctrine rests. We shall, therefore, attempt in this study to set forth a careful interpretation of the Aristotelian position as the basis on which to make the comparison. Our interpretation of Maimonides will then be directed to the double task of understanding him in his own right and of seeing him in comparison to Aristotle.

I

Although the doctrine of the mean is among the most familiar and popular of Aristotle's teachings, it has been widely misunderstood and misrepresented. This failure to grasp the essential elements in Aristotle's doctrine is evident in the standard criticisms to which it has been subjected, as a brief survey will reveal.

Some writers have argued that the mean is no more than Aristotle's adaptation of the long established Greek folk rule, *mēden agan,* nothing to excess. They deny that it is or is based on a philosophical principle but see instead in Aristotle's doctrine nothing but a restatement of the common sense of the ages. A related, but a more pointed and more serious charge, is that the Aristotelian mean is, in the last analysis, nothing more than an affirmation of the proprieties of social convention. Typical of this approach is the statement of Gomperz in which he charges that Aristotle's ethics rest on the view that "Current opinion, when purged or corroborated by the settlement of real or apparent contradictions, is identified with absolute truth so far as concerns questions relating to the conduct of life."[9]

Hans Kelsen has expressed the criticism even more vigorously in charging that "Although the ethics of the *mesotēs* doctrine pretends to establish in an authoritative way the moral value, it leaves the solution of its very problem to another authority. . . . It is the authority of the positive morality and positive law — it is the established social order. By presupposing in its *mesotēs* formula the established social order, the ethics of Aristotle justifies the positive morality and the positive law. . . . In this justification of the established social order lies the true function of the tautology which a critical analysis of the *mesotēs* formula reveals."[10] This criticism gains support from Aristotle's admission that all judgment concerning the application of the doctrine of the mean to particular cases depends completely on the insight of the man of practical wisdom; but, the critics argue, that man has no standard to which he can appeal other than the accepted conventional attitudes and values of his society.

The absence of any objective standard appears to be underscored by the fact that the Aristotelian mean is not determined arithmetically and is thus not the same for all men. It is, rather, a rule which must be applied only with full cognizance of the particular circumstances and the characteristic peculiarities of the individual in question. It is *pros hēmas*, determined in relation to the individual moral agent. This compounds the difficulty, since it would now appear that in the doctrine of the mean we have merely social convention adjusted to individual differences — a far cry indeed, so it seems, from a serious philosophical principle.

Perhaps the most contemptuous of all the criticisms was made by Kant, when he wrote:

> The proposition that one should never do too much or do too little says nothing for it is tautological. What is it to do too much? Answer: More than is good. What is it to do too little? Answer: To do less than is good. What is meant by I ought (to do someting or forbear doing something)? Answer: It is not good (contrary to duty) to do more or less than is good. If this is the wisdom we are to seek by returning to the ancients (Aristotle) as being precisely those who were nearer to the source of wisdom, then we have chosen badly to turn to their oracle. . . . For to be much too virtuous, i.e., to adhere too closely to one's duty, would be like making a circle much too round or a straight line much too straight.[11]

If these charges are justified, they are grave indeed, since they challenge what Aristotle himself claims explicitly. In his definition of moral virtue he includes the proviso that the choice in accordance with the mean is *hōrismenē logō*, determined by a *logos,* that is by a rule or principle of reason.[12] It is clear that in his view what he is offering is a principle of reason, not just the arbitrariness of convention.

Yet the charges against him do not appear to be totally without foundation. Does he not himself inform us early in the *Nicomachaean Ethics* that the actions which are the subject matter of ethical reflection and choice "admit of much variety and fluctuation of opinion, so that they may be thought to exist only by convention (*nomos*), and not by nature (*physis*)?"[13] Does he not, near the end of the same book, express the view that, "what all think to be good, that, we assert, is good?"[14] Moreover, he regularly invokes common opinion about moral matters and the good life as if it were clearly worthy of being considered authoritative. In all this he seems to be admitting the very criticisms that are thought by many to be fatal to his position. What can we make out of the doctrine of the mean in the light of these critical attacks? In what follows I seek to answer that question by offering an interpretation of the doctrine of the mean which takes account of and copes with the difficulties that have been raised.

To grasp the doctrine correctly it is extremely useful to take full account of the medical model which Aristotle uses repeatedly, the recurring comparison that he draws between the process of attaining moral virtue and the work of the physician who brings his patients to a state of physical health. At almost every important point in his exposition of the way to moral virtue, Aristotle employs the practice of medicine as a paradigm which illuminates and clarifies his basic points. The subject has been treated carefully and convincingly by Jaeger, who concludes on the basis of his study of the *Nicomachaean Ethics* that the appeal to the medical pattern is so deep and pervasive that "in the light of it Aristotle tries to justify almost every step he takes in his ethical philosophy."[15]

The essential elements in that medical model are easy to discern. The practice of medicine has as its end the attainment of health for the patient. That end is given in and defined by the physical nature of the human patient. There is nothing arbitrary about what physical health is in general. It is the proper excellence of the body which is gained when the body is brought to its highest degree of natural perfection. Insofar as it concerns the treatment of bodies in general, the practice of medicine involves a knowledge of principles that are fixed because they are the principles of a type of being which exists by nature and has its own nature. Yet, these general principles alone are insufficient for the practice of medicine. The physician's art requires him to deal with particular cases, to make practical decisions, and to offer practical guidance for each individual case. His prescriptions can be approximately correct only, at best, never absolutely precise. Even when he knows what foods are healthful, he is ineffective unless he is able to prescribe for each particular case a diet which is adjusted to the special needs and specific circumstances of the patient before him. It is here that his special art comes into play, for anyone who is modestly educated might be expected to know general rules of health, but only the skilled physician can be relied upon to diagnose individual cases and to apply the general rules to the particular needs of each patient. In his medical practice the doctor must use the rule of the mean as Aristotle repeatedly notes. As the work *On Ancient Medicine* (sometimes attributed to Hippocrates) expresses it, in the treatment of human ailments "it is necessary to aim at some measure."[16]

If we follow Aristotle in thinking about ethics on the model of medical practice, then we can solve most of the problems which his critics raise concerning the doctrine of the mean. Like medicine, ethics rests on a natural base. If there were not this base in the nature of man, a nature which is fixed, there could be no talk of ethics as a practical *science*. It would be at best a fairly sophisticated art, but even as an art it could not proceed successfully if it had no fixed points of reference. Like medicine, ethics is concerned not with knowledge for its own sake but for the sake of action. This is what makes it *practical*. This practical element is carried out primarily with respect to particular men in particular circumstances, as is the case with medicine. To achieve this, the moral teacher (the *phronimos*) cannot rely only on his knowledge of the nature of man in general. He must have the capacity to deal with particular cases, and that is done finally through *aisthēsis,* a kind of immediate perception of what is required in order to apply the general rules to the particular individual before him. In this sitution he cannot expect to achieve demonstrative certainty. At best he can offer the kind of informed judgment which emerges from the total combination of his theoretical understanding, his practical experience, and the special intelligence of the practically wise man, which is a capacity to deliberate well about such moral issues. Finally, his judgment will depend, in some degree, on *nomos,* on the accepted patterns and attitudes of the society in which the individual lives. The doctor prescribes for his patient taking account both of his particular situation with respect to physical health and development and of his particular needs. Thus, when he prescribes for Milo, he must know not only that this patient has such and such specific complaints and that his physical condition is so and so, but also that he is a wrestler and wants to be restored to the state of health which is requisite for a successful wrestler. Similarly, the moral guide must know not only what the particular moral situation of his client is, but also what his place is in society and what the norms are of the society in which he must function. The norm of courage for a soldier at the battle front is likely to be different from that which is proper for a professional baby sitter.

Where the critics have gone wrong is in supposing that all Aristotle offers us is the social framework and the individual peculiarities of the moral agent. They have utterly ignored the crucial fact that his moral philosophy and his doctrine of the mean, in particular, are rooted in principles of nature. They have failed to see that Aristotle carefully introduces qualifications whenever he speaks of the conventional aspects of morality. The earliest passage in the *Nicomachaean Ethics* which deals with this topic is a case in point. Aristotle stresses that we must not expect in ethics the same kind of precision and the same degree of certainty that we expect in the demonstrative sciences. The subject matter of ethics and politics are *ta kala kai ta dikaia,* the fine or noble and the just, "but these conceptions involve much difference of opinion and uncertainty, so that they may be thought to exist only by convention and not by nature."[17] The stress is on the fact that "they may be *thought*" to be nothing more than convention, but those who think this are mistaken. For while they are, of course, in some measure dependent on convention, that is not the whole of the content or foundation of moral virtue. Let us, then, examine that natural foundation of moral virtue which has escaped the attention of Aristotle's critics.

Moral virtue, like any virtue (*aretē*), is concerned with the proper excellence of its subject, in this case man, and this is determined by his proper end as it is given in nature. This is standard doctrine for Aristotle, to be found consistently in those of his works which deal with the question in any way at all. The principle is stated in *Metaphysics* v, 1021b 21ff., where he says that virtue (*aretē*) is a *telos,* the perfection of a thing by achieving its proper end. "And excellence is a completion (*telos*); for each thing is complete and every substance is complete (*teleion*), when in respect of the form of its proper excellence it lacks no natural part of its excellence." Note that the *aretē,* the excellence of virtue, is natural, it is determined by the nature of the thing. The same point is made in *Physics* vii, 246a 10–247a 20. "Excellence (*aretē,* i.e., virtue) is a kind of perfection (*teleiōsis*), since a thing is said to be perfect (*teleion*) when it has acquired its proper excellence, for it is then in most complete conformity to its own nature. . . . Excellence and defect are in every case concerned with the influences whereby their possessor is, according to its natural constitution, liable to be modified. . . . The same is true of the moral habits (*tēs psychēs hexeōn,* the states of the soul), for they, too, consist in conditions determined by certain relations, and the virtues are perfections of nature, the vices departures from it." These passages speak for themselves and merely reinforce what is stated in the *N.E.* on the same subject. The stress is on the nature of a thing, since for all things that exist by nature there can be no knowledge of their virtue except in terms of their nature.

That ethics is closely tied to nature is eminently clear, since man's virtue is determined by his nature, and this, in turn, requires a knowledge of psychology, the principles of the human soul. Aristotle sets out some of these principles in *N.E.* as a first step in defining human virtue. Lest there be any doubt that psychology is a subject matter that is natural, one need only turn to the opening of *De Anima,* where Aristotle says explicitly that the knowledge of the soul admittedly contributes greatly to the advance of truth in general and, above all, to our understanding of nature. The particular problems of ethics arise because of the complex nature of man. To the extent that man is truly rational, it is easy for Aristotle to specify what his proper end is. Here the nature of rationality itself determines the end, namely, the use of reason for the knowledge and contemplation of that which is highest and most perfect. The most virtuous life for man would be one in which he would engage most completely in that supreme contemplative activity which is philosophical wisdom.

However, man is not a purely and perfectly rational being. He is a rational animal, an animal that has the capacity for being rational. This animal aspect of his nature must be given its due but must not be allowed to control him, otherwise man will be only animal and not rational at all. The problem then is to determine what it would be like for man's animal nature to be subject, to the fullest possible degree, to the rule of reason, and to discover the practical means by which this end might be achieved. True virtue for man will be the fullest realization of his *telos,* his proper end as a rational being, a life in which not only his contemplative powers, but also his actions and passions are directed and controlled by reason. But what exactly does it mean to say that action and passion are controlled by reason? Aristotle's answer is that formally such a state can be defined as that in which action and passion are directed in accordance with the rule of the mean, and this is what we call moral virtue.

The crucial question is, then, why should we consider the rule of the mean to be a rule of reason? Aristotle's answer is that the mean is the way in which nature and art normally achieve their goals of proper excellence, the realization of the proper end of each thing which exists by nature or is the product of art. To the extent that moral virtue has its foundations in nature, reason requires that it accord with nature. Otherwise it will not be virtue, i.e., the proper excellence of man (in this case). If the end is to fulfill our proper nature as men, then virtue will consist in the fullest completion of that nature. If the nature of all things is to find their proper completion, *qua* natural, in the mean or the middle way, then this is also the way which reason requires us to choose in order to achieve moral virtue. For it is a rule, according to Aristotle, that a rational being acts always with an end in view, and that he must choose the means which are requisite to that end.[18]

The principle that all things that exist by nature tend toward the mean, or middle way, in order to attain their proper perfection is common to various areas of Aristotle's thought and is by no means peculiar to his ethics only. The simplest version of this point may be found in his discussions of the anatomical structure of animals. Over and over again he stresses that the middle is the best. "Eyes may be large or small, or medium-sized (*mesoi*). The medium-sized are the best."[19] "Ears may be smooth, or hairy, or intermediate; the last are the best for hearing. . . . They may stand well out, or not stand out at all, or intermediately. The last are a sign of the finest disposition."[20] "Now the tongue can be broad, or narrow, or intermediate; and the last is the best and gives the clearest perception."[21] The principle that nature always seeks the middle way is set forth in more complex cases as well. For example, Aristotle holds that all motions of sensation begin and end in the heart. This is as it should properly be he says, since reason requires that, if possible, there should be only a single source, "and the best of places in accordance with nature is the middle." (*euphuestatos de tōn topōn ho mesos*).[22] In this passage we see clearly how Aristotle ties together the way of reason with the normal way of nature, which tends always toward the mean.

He further expands and generalizes this doctrine when he propounds the view that nature always aims at the mean, always strives to overcome excess of every sort by counterbalancing it in such way that the mean is achieved. That is why the brain, which is cold, is continuous with the spinal marrow, which is hot. "Nature is always contriving to set next to anything that is excessive a reinforcement of the opposite substance, so that the one may level out (*anisazē*) the excess of the other."[23] Moreover, whatever comes into existence does so by way of the mean. In the process of generation opposites meet and are balanced, and in that way form new creatures by way of the mean. "It is thus, then, that in the first place the 'elements' are transformed; and that out of the 'elements' there come to be flesh and bones and the like – the hot becoming cold and the cold becoming hot when they have been brought to the mean (*pros to meson*). . . . Similarly, it is *qua* reduced to a mean condition that the dry and the moist produce flesh and bone and the remaining compounds."[24] This principle that nature always follows the middle way is explicitly viewed by Aristotle as a rule of reason. This might be expected in view of the relationship between *logos* and *ratio,* between reason and proportion or due measure. As Aristotle puts it, "Everything needs an opposite to counterbalance it so that it may hit at the mark of proper measure and the mean (*tou metriou kai tou mesou*). The mean, and not any of the extremes alone, has being (*ousia*) and reason (*logos*)."[25]

Since "art imitates nature," it is to be expected that the product of art will also conform with the rule of the mean. For art is defined by Aristotle as "concerned with making involving a true course of reasoning."[26] Consequently, it too must follow the rule of reason that all things achieve their proper realization when they have been formed in accordance with the right measure, that is, with the mean which stands at the proper point between excess and defect. The point is expressed charmingly by Aristotle in his discussion of the proper speed for narration in ceremonial oratory. "Nowadays it is said, absurdly enough, that the narration should be rapid. Remember what the man said to the baker who asked whether he was to make the cake hard or soft: 'What, can't you make it *right*?' Just so here. We are not to make long narrations, just as we are not to make long introductions or long arguments. Here, again, rightness does not consist either in rapidity or in conciseness, but in the happy mean."[27]

The principle is carried through consistently by Aristotle when he deals with what may be thought of as the highest products of art working in conjunction with nature, namely, virtuous men and good states. In his discussions of the various aspects of life in the city-state and of the constitution of such a state, he always considers the mean or the middle way to be the model which is most desirable. The structure and order of the state, which is, like the order of the life of the individual man, the combined work of art and nature, must be in accordance with the mean if it is to achieve its own proper perfection. Men would do well as individuals also to seek no more than moderate amounts of all desirable things. For since the mean is always best, "it is manifest that the middle amount of all of the good things of fortune is the best amount to possess. For this degree of wealth is the readiest to obey reason."[28]

We have now established clearly that Aristotle's doctrine of the mean is not peculiar to moral virtue. In his system of though it is an over-arching principle that encompasses the operations of the world of nature and the world of art. One cannot properly understand his treatment of moral virtue without seeing the mean in this wider context. Given this context, we can now turn to a specific examination of the way in which the doctrine of the mean is conceived by Aristotle as the pattern in accordance with which moral virtue is brought about. As a first step, we must note that he is quite explicit about the fact that there is a natural foundation for moral virtue. We indicated this earlier in a general way when we noted that our knowledge of the proper end of man depends on the science of psychology. In introducing the discussion of moral virtue, Aristotle makes the point that it exists neither fully by nature nor fully contrary to nature but is a combination of nature and art. Virtue arises in us through habit as its efficient cause. This process of deliberate habituation, however, could not occur at all unless there were a natural medium in which it took place and to which it was adapted. "The virtues therefore are engendered in us neither by nature nor yet in violation of nature; nature gives us the capacity to receive them, and this capacity is brought to its proper completion by habit."[29]

In a later discussion in *N.E.* he expands his treatment of this topic. There he makes it clear that while all virtue is the product of a certain deliberate effort on man's part, nevertheless it has its origin and base in what is natural. For there is that which Aristotle calls natural virtue, and it is this natural virtue which is the initial source of all true moral virtue. Natural virtue is our inborn capacity for those states of character which become, when properly developed, the moral virtues. Without this inborn capacity we could not become morally virtuous. For it is that aspect alone of our nature which makes moral virtue possible. Just as cleverness is the natural base which, when developed properly, becomes practical wisdom, so, says Aristotle, is "natural virtue (*hē physikē aretē*) to true virtue (or virtue in the strict sense). It is generally agreed that the various kinds of character are present in man by nature, for we are just, and capable of temperance, and brave, or have the other virtues from the very moment of our birth. Nevertheless, we expect to find that true goodness is something different, and that the virtues in the true sense come to belong to us in another way."[30] There are, then, two types of virtue in us; natural virtue, which has a potentiality for development in a way which is appropriate to man, and true moral virtue, which is the actualization of that natural potentiality. The model for the development of that potentiality is the model which is followed by all natures seeking their own perfection, and that is, of course, the doctrine of the mean. Aristotle's insistence that moral virtue follows the rule of the mean is, thus, in no sense arbitrary. It is, following his own principles, a rule of reason. If the proper perfection of the moral part of our nature is specified by nature in accordance with its general rule that the middle is best and most complete, then reason requires that in seeking moral virtue we must employ as our guide and criterion that pattern which is the only appropriate instrument for attaining the end which we desire.

If this is so evident, how shall we understand all those criticisms which accuse Aristotle of offering us nothing more than a formalized approval of social convention? The answer, I believe, lies in the fact that the critics have ignored the natural foundations of moral virtue, despite the trouble Aristotle took to make his position clear. They have been further misled by two other considerations to which we must now turn our attention. The first is that there is, of course, a social-conventional aspect to moral virtue, as we already noted earlier. About this there can be no issue or difference of opinion. What is at issue is the question of how we should understand this dimension of moral virtue, what its nature is, what function it serves, and what weight we should put on it. Man is not an animal who ever achieves his goal of self-development in isolation or solitude. For Aristotle, man is a being whose development, whose excellence, whose true humanity, in fact, depends on society. By himself, detached from all social relations and structures, he is barely, if at all human. Man is by nature a political animal, a creature whose nature requires the association of community with other men of which the *polis* is a model. For this reason Aristotle considers the *polis,* or more widely the forms of human society, to exist by nature. Whatever the elements of human art that account for and cause the diversity of societies, society itself is natural, and only in society can man fulfill himself. Only in society, his natural setting, can he be humanly virtuous.

Aristotle is fully aware that, despite the natural basis on which human society rests, societies differ in their customs and value patterns. To the extent that there is such difference, moral virtue will always reflect the particular characteristics of the community in which a given man lives. Yet, this is not to say that moral virtue is only *nomos,* only convention and nothing more. Moral virtue is, rather, the result of the development of natural virtue toward its proper end in the context of a particular social setting. In fact, the existence of society is dependent on man's natural capacity for moral virtue. "For it is the special property of man, in distinction from the other animals, that he alone has the perception of good and bad and right and wrong and the other moral qualities, and it is partnership (community) in these things that makes a household and a city-state."[31] Without the natural capacity for morality there could be no human community at all. Given this capacity, there emerges a community in which moral virtue is possible for men. That virtue exhibits both the fixed elements which its nature determines and the varying elements which derive from the diverse characteristics of particular societies. When the man of practical wisdom deals with moral issues, he is guided by his knowledge of the natural character of moral virtue tempered by his knowledge of the standards of the society in which he lives. He is a model precisely because he has developed to its ideal level this combination of the natural and the socially conditioned. To understand Aristotle's conception of moral virtue one must give full weight both to the natural and the social elements. Those who say that morality is merely *nomos* are mistaken. Those who say that it is merely *physis* are equally mistaken.

The second factor which has led Aristotle's critics astray is the inescapable particularity of each moral situation. If the rule of the mean is to be applied to an individual with full cognizance of his own particular level of development and with equal cognizance of the circumstances in which he finds himself and of the special characteristics of his society, how can there be anything more than just individual and private judgments? To the extent to which this is a sound criticism it would appear to apply with equal force to any moral philosophy. The problem of moving from general moral principles to particular moral judgments is hardly peculiar to Aristotle. One need only think, as a classic example, of the agonies which interpreters of Kant suffer when they try to give an account of how he moves from the categorical imperative to particular moral judgments. The troubles that Kant's famous four examples have caused the commentators are sufficient to make the case.

Yet it seems that Aristotle is not without resources for dealing even with this aggravating problem. To begin with, let us note that he is fully aware of the problem. In the first chapter of *Book* vi of the *N.E.* he explicitly expresses his dissatisfaction with a moral rule which is general, unless one can show how to go about making it applicable to particular cases. In many places in the *N.E.* he repeats the same point, that judgments about conduct always deal with particular cases, and that it is especially difficult to apply the rule of the mean in an exact way to particular cases. Having laid down some procedural cautions for anyone who is trying to hit the mark of the mean, Aristotle recognizes that even if they are heeded, they offer no guarantee of success. One should aim at the mean, guided by these rules, "But no doubt it is a difficult thing to do, and especially in particular cases; for instance, it is not easy to define in what manner and with what people and on what sort of grounds and how long one ought to be angry."[32]

The difficulty of applying the rule to particular cases results in judgments which can never claim to be absolute or exact. They are, at best, approximations, guidelines for conduct leading to proper self-development, never demonstrated certainties. The lack of precision is compounded by the dependence on social circumstances as well as individual particularities. It is this that caused Aristotle to remark early in the *N.E.* that one should expect in ethics no more precision than the subject matter is capable of yielding. He stresses at several points that inquiry in this field can only be carried out successfully if one recognizes as a condition of the inquiry that he can expect conclusions which are far from certain or precise. "This must be agreed upon beforehand (i.e., before beginning to inquire into moral philosophy), that the whole account of matters of conduct must be given in outline and not precisely . . . matters concerned with conduct and questions of what is good for us have no fixity, any more than matters of health. The general account being of this nature, the account of particular cases is yet more lacking in exactness; for they do not fall under any art or set of rules, but the agents themselves must in each case consider what is appropriate to the occasion. . . ."[33] Nowhere does Aristotle claim that he is offering us a system which will result in precise and absolutely fixed and reliable moral judgments. In fact, he says exactly the contrary over and over again, so that it is difficult to understand why his critics think that they have discovered some secret dark failure in his treatment of these matters. Even general moral rules cannot be laid down, he believes, with precision, much less so judgments in particular cases.

Such judgments rest, according to him, with perception. The term used consistently is *aisthēsis,* which refers to a kind of immediate intuitive grasp of the particulars and a capacity to make a judgment concerning them. *Aisthēsis* is the only way in which we know particulars. It is one of the essential components of practical wisdom, which unlike scientific knowledge is concerned with particular cases. "Practical wisdom is concerned with the ultimate particular, which is the object not of scientific knowledge but of perception (*aisthēsis*) — not the perception of qualities peculiar to one sense but a perception akin to that by which we perceive that the particular figure before us is a triangle."[34] Here again Aristotle claims no certainty. On the contrary, he is fully aware of the fact that what he offers is both less than exact and less than certain. The development of the capacity of moral perception depends upon maturity and experience. There is no other source. Practical wisdom, though an intellectual virtue, is that part of the intellect that deals with opinion, not demonstrated knowledge. Its subject matter is not fixed but varies with individual and social circumstance. Yet it is capable of making judgments and offering guidance, precisely because it brings together the range of knowledge, experience, and perception out of which alone any reasonably sound moral judgment might emerge.

The problem which men face in their effort to attain moral virtue can now be readily formulated. Like all things that exist by nature, man has a fixed nature. This confers upon him certain fixed ends, the realization of which constitute his proper excellence. Unlike man, other things that exist by nature are without any independent power of choice and are moved by their internal principle of development in the direction of their proper ends only. It is outside forces or internal defects that prevent their attaining their end. The healthy acorn will become a full grown oak if nothing prevents it from the outside. Its nature, its internal principle of development, is fixed, and it can go only one way. Things are not nearly so simple for human beings. While they have a nature, they also have the capacity to choose their own actions. They can, by their choice, either advance or frustrate their development in accordance with their nature. If man had no fixed natural disposition toward moral virtue, such virtue would not be possible for him at all. If he had only a fixed natural disposition, moral virtue would be unnecessary; for he would achieve his end automatically. However, he is in the middle. He has a nature, but he must choose to bring it to its full actuality. He must develop his own character in accordance with his true nature, if he chooses to be a man in the full and proper meaning of the term. It is at this point that he must cope with the problem of knowing exactly what kind of action to choose. Nature specifies his end in a general way. It also specifies the criterion of virtuous character in a general way, namely, by the rule of the mean. However, this is insufficient as a guide to action in particular cases, and all action is particular. The components of the social framework, individual differences, and the special circumstances must all play a role in the decision. Here no precise rule can be specified. One can only appeal, within the context of a rule of reason determined by nature, to the perception and judgment of the man of practical wisdom.

Does it follow from all this that the doctrine of the mean is, as the critics claim, no more than an appeal to social convention, or that it is utterly useless as a guide to moral action, or that it is merely an empty tautology? I believe that we have shown otherwise. The doctrine of the mean is not a matter of social convention. It is a rational rule, which derives from nature and shows us the general way to actualize a deeply fixed principle of nature. It is not a fixed or precise rule, because it involves varying social circumstances and deals with a diversity of individuals, each of whom must be considered in the context of his special personal and social conditions. Even this is not arbitrary, however, since man is by nature a social animal, and action is by nature always particular.

Perhaps the matter can be made clear and the argument persuasive by returning to the medical model. The work of the physician, seeking the physical health of his patient, deals to a large extent with what is natural. No one wants to deny the natural aspect of the body and of bodily health. However, this is only part of the story. Health has to be achieved for each individual patient in the light of his special circumstances and conditions, and in the light of his particular constitution and its special possibilities. No diagnosis is foolproof. It can only claim to be probable, and it is never absolutely exact and absolutely certain. Similarly, no prescription is ever absolutely precise, nor is its anticipated effectiveness more than probable. All this is the case, just because medicine must take account of the particular. As Aristotle never tires of saying, a proper diet for Milo may be all wrong for the local chess champion. Despite its inexactness and uncertainty, we do not ordinarily condemn all medical practice as pointless. On the contrary, we see in it the very best we can achieve, considering the built-in limitations of the subject matter. Even if we doubt the soundness of a particular doctor's diagnosis, or if we fail to be helped by his prescriptions, we do not conclude that the practice of medicine is a fraud. We do know what good health is, and we do recognize that, with limitations, there are men of special knowledge and experience who can help us achieve that desirable goal. Similarly, Aristotle argues, we do know what a virtuous character is, for that is specified by our nature. Physicians of the soul may be harder to find than physicians of the body. It may also be more difficult for the former to lay out and justify their general principles and their rules of practice, to say nothing of their judgments in individual cases. It is our contention, nevertheless, that we have explained why Aristotle believes that this difficult task is not impossible and that his critics have misunderstood him.

II

As we reflect on the relationship of Maimonides' doctrine of the mean to Aristotle's, we are confronted by puzzles which demand resolution. Of all the areas concerning which Maimonides wrote, the ordering of human behavior should have presented him with the fewest problems. As an expositor of Jewish tradition and as a master of the law, he had a complete system of behavioral rules and norms ready-made for him in the *halakah*. It would seem, then, that there should have been no need to seek beyond the *halakah* itself for the principles and the specific patterns of virtue and the good life, all the more since Maimonides himself denied that there is any independent rational ground for morality. He rejected all claims that there is a natural moral law, holding rather that morality derives either from social convention or divine command. It is obvious that for Judaism the latter source only can be decisive.[35] Why, then, was it necessary for Maimonides to appeal to the doctrine of the mean at all? The elaborate and detailed principles and directions for the life of the Jew which he codified in his *Mishneh Torah* would seem to be sufficient to answer every need for guidance toward the virtuous life.

Furthermore, with respect to this subject matter in particular, an appeal to non-Jewish sources would seem to be singularly inappropriate. It might be argued plausibly that to the extent that his Jewish theology required principles of natural science or metaphysics as a foundation, these might appropriately have been drawn from non-Jewish sources, since the biblical and rabbinic literatures are relatively poor in these areas. This is surely not the case with regard to the area of human conduct. How strange, then, that in a treatise devoted to setting forth the principles and the end of the good life, Maimonides begins by telling us explicitly that he drew his materials from non-Jewish as well as Jewish sources. In his Foreword to *Shemonah Peraqim* he makes a special point of denying that the work contains any original ideas. All that is of consequence in the treatise has been gleaned, says Maimonides, "from the words of the wise occurring in the *Midrashim,* in the Talmud, and in other of their works, as well as from the words of the philosophers, ancient and recent, and also from the works of various authors." He immediately goes on to justify this procedure by invoking the principle that "one should accept the truth from whatever source it proceeds."[36]

The force of this open appeal to non-Jewish sources is even greater when we remember that these statements are contained in the introduction to a commentary on *'Avoth,* a treatise that takes great pains to establish its legitimacy (in its opening words) by associating itself with the tradition whose source is in the Torah which "Moses received at Sinai."[37] Our analysis of Maimonides' version of the doctrine of the mean will seek to resolve some of these puzzles. Our primary concern is to understand the doctrine precisely, to see it in relationship to the Aristotelian doctrine, and to determine how it fits into the Jewish tradition.

With respect to the general nature of ethical inquiry, Maimonides holds views which are similar to those of Aristotle. Like Aristotle, he makes clear at the very outset that he is concerned above all with the truly good life for man and that his interest in individual actions and states of character is primarily because they are instrumental to the realization of the ultimate good. In his foreword to *Shemonah Peraqim* he makes a point of explaining that the treatise on which he is commenting contains a rule of life which "leads to great perfection and true happiness." In fact, one who puts into practice the teachings of *'Avoth* can hope to be led even to prophecy. This ultimate human felicity comes to one who attains the knowledge of God "as far as it is possible for man to know Him" and the truly good life is that in which all of man's effort, thought, and activity are directed toward the realization of that goal.[38] The same ideal is developed in *H. De'oth,* iii, and of course it constitutes a central theme which reaches its climax in the final chapters of the *Guide of the Perplexed.*

Maimonides also follows Aristotle in his view that the ultimate aim, the contemplative life, presupposes the achievement of moral virtue. Man is so constituted that he can only devote himself to the highest intellectual activity if he has first achieved that personal and social discipline which is included under the heading of moral virtue. The crucial question then emerges, namely, what specifically is the character and shape of the morally virtuous life. Here, too, in his initial approach Maimonides remains faithful to the Aristotelian pattern. His primary concern, like that of Aristotle, is with states of character, not with individual acts. Thus, in *Shemonah Peraqim* he introduces his discussion of the rule of the mean by distinguishing between good acts and good states of character. "Good deeds are such as are equibalanced, maintaining the mean between two equally bad extremes. . . . Virtues are psychic conditions and dispositions (*tekhunoth nafshiyyoth we-qinyanim*) which are midway between two reprehensible extremes. . . . "[39] The very title of the section of the *Mishneh Torah* which deals with the mean is *De'oth,* and it is beyond any question that the term is used to refer to states of character. This is obvious enough from the way the term is used in its context and is confirmed in a passage in which Maimonides explicitly distinguishes *de'oth,* as states of character, from particular actions. In *H. Teshuvah,* vii, 3, Maimonides tells us that just as one must repent for those sins which involve a particular action, such as robbery or theft, so is one obligated "to search out his evil *de'oth* and repent of them, i.e., from such states as anger, etc."

Aristotle had already defined virtue as a state of character, or, according to another translation, "a settled disposition of the mind" which observes the mean.[40] Maimonides follows him here, as he does with respect to his view that our actions follow from the fixed states of our character, so that what must concern us most is the development of the appropriate states of character, since that is the best assurance that our acts will also be virtuous. Finally, in what appears to be a thoroughly Aristotelian fashion, Maimonides also defines the good character as one which is determined by the mean and avoids the extremes. Given these general similarities, we must now ask just exactly what the main elements are of Maimonides' doctrine of the mean and how they compare with Aristotle's views as we set them forth above.

The most fundamental distinction of all is in the ground on which the mean rests. It is striking that both in *Shemonah Peraqim* and in the *Mishneh Torah* Maimonides introduces the rule of the mean without any discussion as to its origins or justification. He treats it rather as an established truth to which one need only refer but which does not require any evidence to support it. In both works he proceeds as if it were an established fact that good deeds and good states of character follow the mean between extremes. In the *Mishneh Torah* he opens the discussion with some empirical observations about the diversity of states of character that are to be found among men and then informs us that "the two extremes which are at the farthest distance from each other with respect to each state of character are not the good way . . . while the right way is the middle way."[41] Not only does he offer no defense of this claim, but he goes on to say that because it is the case that the mean is the right way, "therefore the early sages (*ḥakhamim ha-rishonim*) commanded that man should always make an estimate of his various states of character and direct them toward the middle way." If we accept the view of most commentators, that the reference is to the sages of Israel, a view which seems plausible enough in this context, then we have the remarkable situation that Maimonides appears to be telling us that the principle that the middle way is good is known as an independent truth and that because it is known to be true the Jewish religious authorities accepted it as their rule of conduct and character development. So far he would seem to be doing exactly what he says in his introduction to *Shemonah Peraqim,* namely, relying on established knowledge without regard to its source.

There is evidence to support the view that Maimonides was convinced that the rule of the mean was a well established basic principle of explanation in the sciences and in philosophy. In the *Guide of the Perplexed* he was explicit about this point. In thoroughly Aristotelian fashion, he strongly supports the view that the order of nature is such that all things achieve their proper excellence when they reach the mean which suffers from neither excess nor deficiency. The highest praise that he can pay to the divine creation of the world is that it has been formed in accordance with the mean, from which it follows that in the created world there can be no change in the fixed order of nature. "The thing that is changed, is changed because of a deficiency in it that should be made good or because of some excess that is not needed and should be got rid of. Now the works of the Deity are most perfect, and with regard to them there is no possibility of an excess or a deficiency. Accordingly, they are of necessity permanently established as they are, for there is no possibility of something calling for a change in them. . . . *'The Rock, his work is perfect'* . . . means that all his works . . . are most perfect, that no deficiency at all is commingled with them, that there is no superfluity in them and nothing that is not needed."[42]

Viewing the doctrine of the mean as a scientific principle, Maimonides treats it as fully established and needing no further evidence. He is explicit about the general rule that whatever is scientifically known, whatever is demonstrated, must command our assent. For such matters we do not need to look for confirmation in the official Jewish literature, nor should we be uneasy if on such matters the views of the sages of Israel are contradicted by our contemporary knowledge. Here the sages spoke not with the authority of the prophetic tradition but only as students of physics or metaphysics who were bound by the limits of their own knowledge and the general state of knowledge at their time.[43] It seems clear enough that this is one of the points that Maimonides had in mind when he informed his readers in the foreword to *Shemonah Peraqim* that he would seek the truth from whatever source it could be found. Even with respect to the standards and rules of virtuous behavior, good character, and the good life for the faithful Jew, we need certain general principles of explanation, a general theoretical framework, in order to give a philosophical account of the subject. We also need a sound psychology on which to base our understanding of human character and its development. Without these theoretical foundations, our account of moral virtue, even of specifically Jewish moral virtue, will be incomplete and will lack an essential dimension. Moreover, no practical guidance toward the achievement of good character and the performance of good acts is possible, unless we first have sound theoretical understanding of human nature and of the nature of the good in general. These are universal truths, in no way peculiar to the Jewish religious community, and for them we may, nay we must turn to the most reliable scientific authority that we can find. This is the point of Maimonides' elaborate announcement that he seeks guidance wherever he can find it.

So far we might say without hesitation that Maimonides has followed Aristotle or the Aristotelian tradition faithfully. However, when we move away from the general theoretical foundations to his specific way of understanding and applying the doctrine of the mean the differences emerge sharply and clearly. Perhaps the most significant single difference is that while Aristotle construes moral virtue as a case of art imitating nature, Maimonides has as his standard the imitation of God. The first of the eleven *mişwoth* set forth in *H. De'oth* is *le-hiddamoth bi-derakhaw,* and it is to this commandment of *imitatio Dei* that the first five of the seven chapters of *H. De'oth* are devoted. The imitation of nature was for Aristotle nothing more than a general indication that the good life for man, like the pattern of all natural excellence, should be one of perfect measure. Nature does not itself give us specific norms or standards of behavior, nor does it tell us what a virtuous character is, apart from its general principle that the middle way is the best. Thus, given the imitation of nature as the only ideal, Aristotle has no choice but to fill out the specific details of the good life for man by appealing to the norms of society and to the judgment of the man of practical wisdom. Nature gives us only the form, i.e., the mean but not the content. It does not, and cannot teach us what the rule of the mean is in concrete cases of human action or human character development.

In striking contrast, Maimonides works here fully inside the Jewish tradition. He readily adopts the outer form of the mean as his theoretical base and principle of explanation, but the specific contents of the good life are defined not by way of nature but by way of the imitation of God. Now, viewed as metaphysically ultimate, Maimonides' God is not truly knowable, except by way of negative attributes; however, Maimonides does permit us knowledge of God through the attributes of action. We can know Him indirectly through his works in the world, and in this way we can speak meaningfully of *imitatio Dei* as the human ideal. This is why Maimonides is so careful to formulate the commandment as *le-hiddamoth bi-derakhaw,* since strictly speaking we can imitate his ways only, but not his nature. The God who is represented as Creator, who continues in some manner to make his presence felt in history as well as in nature, is a being whom man can meaningfully hold before himself as an ideal to follow.

As in the case of Aristotle's prescription for the imitation of nature, the general rule is insufficient as a guide to man. It must be made specific and concrete. For Maimonides this is achieved simply enough. The commandments of the Torah are, in fact, according to his view, the specification of ideal behavior in accordance with the rule of the mean, and this is what is meant when we are told to imitate the ways of God. The structure of his argument is clear and unambiguous, though it has often been ignored or misunderstood. First he gives us the theoretical principle which is generally known and acknowledged. Good action and good states of character are those which follow the middle way. So far we are in accord with all men who follow the way of scientific knowledge. Next we face the question of what it means specifically to act in accordance with the mean, and here Maimonides answers, unlike Aristotle (for whom such an answer would have been meaningless), that we should imitate God. Finally, he faces the question of what divine behavior is like, so that we can have a concrete model for imitation; and he answers that it is the rule of the Torah that is the divine paradigm and therefore also the concretization of the middle way. Maimonides is absolutely consistent in his adherence to this principle that the rule of the Torah is in actual fact the rule of the mean, that is, whatever the Torah commands is the middle way. There is no external standard which measures the commandments in order to determine whether they accord with the mean. This is impossible, precisely because the only standard we have is that given by the commandments. In *Shemonah Peraqim* he writes that "The Law did not lay down its prohibitions, or enjoin its commandments, except for just this purpose, namely, that by its disciplinary effects we may persistently maintain the proper distance from either extreme."[44] He goes on to stress that since *"the Law of the Lord is perfect,"* (*Ps.* 19:9) it is its injunctions and prohibitions alone that give us the proper standard. To impose upon ourselves ascetic practices or disciplines of self-denial that go beyond what the Torah commands is vice and not virtue.

The same principle is set forth in *H. De'oth*[45] and receives full expression in the *Guide,* where he argues that the Mosaic Law is absolutely perfect, the ideal and exact embodiment of true measure, the middle way in all regards. Thus, every law which deviates from it suffers from the fact that it moves away from the mean toward one of the extremes. "For when a thing is as perfect as it is possible to be within its species, it is impossible that within that species there should be found another thing that does

not fall short of that perfection either because of excess or deficiency.
. . . Things are similar with regard to this Law, as is clear from its equibalance. For it says: '*Just statutes and judgments*' (*Deut.* 4:8); now you
know that the meaning of 'just' is equibalanced. For these are manners
of worship in which there is no burden and excess . . . nor a deficiency.
. . . When we shall speak in this treatise about the reasons accounting for
the commandments, their equibalance and wisdom will be made clear to
you insofar as this is necessary. For this reason it is said with reference
to them: '*The Law of the Lord is perfect*'."[46] For the Aristotelian reliance
on *nomos* as interpreted and applied by the *phronimos*, Maimonides has
substituted the law of the Torah. The divine origin of this Law guarantees
its perfection as a standard of behavior. All others fall short. Only the
Torah "is called by us divine Law, whereas the other political regimens —
such as the *nomoi* of the Greeks and the ravings of the Sabians and of
others — are due, as I have explained several times, to the action of groups
of rulers who were not prophets."[47] The Torah alone, according to Maimonides, can give us the true standard of the mean.

There is, however, more to be considered. We recall that the main
interest in ethics is the development of virtuous states of character, not
merely the performance of virtuous actions. The latter are derived from
the former and are significant especially as outer evidences of a stable moral
character. The passages we cited make the Torah the standard of the mean
in action, but it is obvious that Maimonides must also provide for the
Torah as the standard of the mean with respect to states of character. This
is, in fact, precisely what he does in *H. De'oth*. The idea of *imitatio Dei*
is concerned primarily with states of character, and these are dispositions
which are described as generally in accordance with the middle way. "We
are commanded to follow these middle ways which are the paths that are
good and right, as is written, '*And you shall walk in His ways*' (*Deut.* 28:9).
Thus have they taught with respect to this *miṣwah*: Just as He is called
hannun (gracious), so shall you be *hannun*; just as He is called *rahum*
(merciful), so shall you be *rahum*."[48]

In the case of states of character Maimonides does not simply make
a rule that the Torah standard specifies the mean in every case, but rather
that whatever standard the Torah sets is the standard that we are obligated
to use as our norm, even in those cases where it clearly deviates from the
mean toward one of the extremes. Thus, in the very discussion in which
he takes the mean as the ideal Torah model of virtuous states of character,
Maimonides proceeds to rule that "there are certain states of character with
respect to which it is forbidden for a man to pursue the middle way."[49]
Pride and anger are dispositions which should be avoided completely, as
we have been specifically commanded. Aristotle also spoke of actions and

passions for which the mean is an inappropriate rule. They are those, as he puts it, whose very names imply evil.[50] The problems which this passage has posed for the commentators are familiar, and this is not the place to review them. What is significant for our purposes is the fact that here again Maimonides has a different ground on which he rests his cases of deviation from the mean. Not the name itself, or some other self-evident ground, but the commandments of the Torah determine which are the cases in which we are required to abandon the mean. We know that there can be no proper moderation with respect to pride and anger, simply because we are so taught by various biblical verses and the explicit rulings of the rabbis.

With this background we can also appreciate the difference between the medical analogy which is used by Maimonides and that of Aristotle. On the surface both seem very similar, yet the foundations on which they rest differ very significantly. In his various ethical writings Maimonides, like Aristotle, recommends that those who are in need of moral guidance seek out physicians of the soul. Moral decay is viewed by him as a sickness of the soul, and those who treat it do so on the analogy of the therapy of the physicians of the sick body. So far all is similar to Aristotle. Yet here, too, we find very important differences that result from the basically distinct foundations on which the doctrine of the mean rests in each case.[51]

Both Aristotle and Maimonides require the physician of the soul to be one who knows how to take account of individual circumstances and to advise in accordance with those circumstances. Both require their physicians of the soul to have a sound understanding of human psychology, otherwise they will be incompetent to give guidance. Both agree on the practical rule that the morally sick soul is to be treated by being directed toward the extreme opposite of his present state; and both agree that the aim should be to arrive at a stable state of character determined by the mean. Both consider the true physician of the soul to be a wise man. For Aristotle, he is the *phronimos,* the man of practical wisdom, and for Maimonides he is the *ḥakham,* the model Jewish scholar-teacher-man of piety. He advises that the proper way for sick souls to be healed is to "go to the *ḥakhamim,* who are the healers of souls, and they will cure the illness by teaching them to achieve the proper states of character, thereby bringing them back to the virtuous way."[52] Despite all these similarities, the differences are of crucial importance. While Aristotle's *phronimos* has only shifting conventional standards to guide him, Maimonides' *ḥakham* has the fixed discipline of the Torah as his standard. Of course, he must take account of the special condition of each individual and must tailor his particular advice to fit the special needs and circumstances in which he finds himself. Nevertheless, he is bound not by a conventional *nomos* but by a fixed law, by commandments, and by principles which are held to be divine and thus unchanging. The divine-human ideal is set, and to be virtuous a man must direct himself to that ideal. Maimonides is fully aware of the variations and diversity of human temperament and of social conditions. Nevertheless, his physician of the soul carries out his function by adhering rigorously to the fixed Law. He only varies his advice for each individual in order to move that individual closer to the one common ideal. Aristotle's mean, even when viewed as a principle of nature, always reflects something of the attitudes and values of the particular society in which it is invoked as the principle of moral virtue. Maimonides' mean permits no such variation, because it is controlled by the ideal of *imitatio Dei*, and this, in turn, is concretized and fixed in the commandments and principles of the Torah.

It is revealing that this point, which is evident enough in the earlier works, comes out with striking force and clarity in the *Guide*. Here, where he deals with the law as a primary force for the ordering of society, Maimonides shows openly his deviation from the Aristotelian norm. He first argues that men differ from each other in their temperaments and moral habits far more than any other living creatures, yet man, being by nature a political animal, must live in society. He then goes on: "Now as the nature of the human species requires that there be those differences among the individuals belonging to it and as in addition society is a necessity for this nature, it is by no means possible that this society should be perfected except — and this is necessarily so — through a ruler who gauges the actions of the individuals, perfecting that which is deficient and reducing that which is excessive, and who prescribes actions and moral habits that all of them must always practice in the same way, so that the natural diversity is hidden through the multiple points of conventional accord and so that the community becomes well ordered."[53] With this background he subsequently goes on to distinguish the application of the Law from the model of medical treatment. The Law is, he says, a divine thing, a perfect ideal which is not necessarily actualized in the life of each individual. He argues, therefore, against Aristotle, that "in view of this consideration, it also will not be possible that the laws be dependent on changes in the circumstances of the individuals and of the times, *as is the case with regard to medical treatment*, which is particularized for every individual in conformity with his present temperament. On the contrary, governance of the Law ought to be absolute and universal, including everyone, even if it is suitable only for certain individuals and not suitable for others; for if it were to be made to fit individuals, the whole world would be corrupted 'and you would make out of it something that varies' (*we-nathatta devarekha le-shi'urin*)."[54]

With all the seeming similarities between Aristotle's and Maimonides' doctrine of the mean, and with the especially striking similarity between the medical analogies of both thinkers, there is at the core a most fundamental difference. On these matters, Maimonides is finally controlled by the Jewish tradition, rather than by the principles of Greek philosophy. *Nomos* has about it an inescapable element of changing convention, while Torah has an equally inescapable element of fixity and permanence. For this reason Maimonides holds that a Jewish thinker may freely adopt general theoretical structures and principles of explanation which come to him from the world of Greek thought, if he finds them to be scientifically sound and useful in setting the foundations for his own doctrine. If, however, he is to remain loyal to his religious community, then he cannot substitute for the permanence of the Law and its divine-human ideal the shifting conventions of any society. (This is certainly true for Jewish thinkers of the middle ages, although it might well be challenged by our contemporaries.) Whatever the extent of Maimonides' possible deviation from orthodox Jewish theological norms, when he dealt with the world of practice, with the ordering of individual human life, and with the life of society, he was consistently faithful to Jewish law. At this point he is no longer an Aristotelian, but a Jew who stands fully inside the tradition.

The depth of this difference between Maimonides and Aristotle is underscored by the fact that even with respect to their understanding of psychology and the nature of man they diverge very significantly. For Aristotle, those faculties of the soul which man shares with other animals are essentially the same in man as in animals. Speaking of the nutritive faculty, Aristotle says that "The excellence of this faculty . . . appears to be common to all animate things and not peculiar to man." For this reason he concludes that in his discussion he "may omit from consideration the nutritive part of the soul, since it exhibits no specifically human excellence."[55] Maimonides categorically opposes this view. In his discussion of the faculties of the soul he makes a special point of emphasizing the fact that the human faculties, even when they carry the same name and exercise the same functions as the parallel animal faculties, are absolutely distinct and essentially different. As he puts it, "Our words concern themselves only with the human soul; for the nutritive faculty by which man is nourished is not the same, for instance, as that of the ass or the horse. . . . Although we apply the same term *nutrition* to all of them indiscriminately, nevertheless, its signification is by no means the same. In the same way, the term *sensation* is used homonymously for man and beast. . . . Mark this point well, for it is very important, as many so-called philosophers have fallen into error regarding it. . . ."[56] Little attention has been paid to this passage, but it seems to be of great importance. Maimonides is here saying explicitly that the standard psychology deriving from Aristotle (with whatever variations) is in error on a basic point. Man is not simply an animal, in all respects, with the addition of the faculty of reason. Man is absolutely distinct from animals, even with regard to those faculties that constitute what we usually call his animal nature. It is not our task here to take up the historical question of which "so-called philosophers" he had in mind.[57] We may wonder whether it was possible that Maimonides, with all his regard for Aristotle, should have included him among the "so-called philosophers."[58] However troubling it may be for Maimonides to have included Aristotle in this unflattering category of thinkers, it is certainly clear that he contradicts his great Greek predecessor directly and rejects his views. In the last analysis, it could not be otherwise; for if man is conceived as created in the image of God, he can no longer be understood as one more animal living in the order of nature. This affects the moral ideal and the medical analogy directly. In all respects man is now viewed as different from animals, and his ideal end, i.e., *imitatio Dei,* encompasses not only his reason, but all of his peculiarly human faculties. With such an understanding of man, the physician of the soul must be controlled by the divine norms. He is not training man on the analogy of training a dog or a horse. He is rather directing a human soul, in its totality, toward the divine ideal.

As a result of this difference we can understand why it is that Maimonides is so ready to deviate from the ideal of the middle way, while Aristotle holds to it firmly. Both acknowledge that moral virtue is only a propaedeutic to intellectual virtue and thus to the life of ultimate felicity. For Aristotle, however, the life of moral virtue, as he describes it in the *Nicomachaean Ethics,* is, with minor exceptions, a life in accordance with the mean. Maimonides, on the other hand, regularly invokes the rule of the mean but just as regularly deviates from it. In the foreword to his *Shemonah Peraqim* he reminds us that the treatise to which this is a commentary is concerned with *ḥasiduth,* with the life of special saintliness, and that such saintliness "paves the way to prophecy." If, therefore, one practises the teachings of *'Avoth,* one may hope to acquire prophecy. In short, the ultimate felicity is open to all who practise saintliness, and this is the subject under discussion in the treatise before us. Now saintliness is not simply a life in accordance with the mean but rather a deviation towards one of the extremes. Maimonides both recommends and defends this deviation at various points in those of his writings that deal with the good life in general and even in those that deal specifically with the mean. What is especially significant, however, is the fact that he sets forth an ideal which is, in principle, no longer in any way similar to the balanced life of the Aristotelian middle way. In *Shemonah Peraqim,* in *H. De'oth,* and in the *Guide* he repeats essentially the same line, namely, that all of a man's thought and activity, all of his striving, and all of his concern must be directed exclusively to one single goal of the knowledge of God and fellowship with Him. It is especially revealing that Maimonides sets out this ideal immediately after having discussed the doctrine of the mean, as if to make clear that the mean is not the true ideal at all. He considers it man's proper duty to devote himself to one single goal only, namely, "the attainment of the knowledge of God as far as it is possible for man to know Him. Consequently one must so adjust all his actions, his whole conduct, and even his very words, that they lead to this goal. . . . So, his only design in eating, drinking, cohabiting, sleeping, waking, moving about, and resting should be . . . all to the end that man may reach the highest goal in his endeavors."[59]

It may well be that, as some scholars hold, Maimonides is here betraying Neo-Platonic influences on his thought. Our interest is not in tracing out the possible sources and lines of influence but in recognizing how far Maimonides has moved from the Aristotelian line. He has, in effect, rejected the mean as a guiding principle and criterion of the good life and has substituted for it a single controlling ideal; the good is that which leads to true knowledge and continuing contemplation of the divine being. Though Aristotle agrees, he does not counsel, as does Maimonides, that in ordering his life man should have this one concern only, that every activity, every choice, every state of character should be such as will move him effectively toward the ideal end. Maimonides holds that the mean may be a good general rule for this purpose, but it is not in and of itself the controlling consideration. In both *Shemonah Peraqim* and *H. De'oth,* Maimonides cites in this connection the rule of the sages, "Let all your deeds be done for the sake of God," and the verse which teaches, "*In all thy ways know Him.*" This, rather than the mean, is decisive. Unlike Aristotle, Maimonides wants this extreme to be the practical rule for all men.

* * *

We can now see that the extreme opinions on both sides of the question with which we have been dealing are equally mistaken. There are both Aristotelian and non-Aristotelian aspects to Maimonides' treatment of the doctrine of the mean. It is impossible to support the view that there is nothing whatsoever of Aristotle in him, since it is clear that the general form of his doctrine of the mean and much of his psychology are Aristotelian. It is just as impossible to defend the view that there is in Maimonides' version nothing more than a repetition of the Aristotelian teachings. As we have seen, there are deep and important differences. As heir, interpreter, and creative contributor to two traditions, Maimonides could not have been a pure Aristotelian in these matters. If Greek philosophy lived in him, and it did, the Jewish tradition and its Law never departed from the center of his concerns. In dealing with the nature of man, the ideal of human existence and the practical patterns by which human life should be ordered, Maimonides learned much from Aristotle but even more from the Torah.

NOTES

1. Henry Malter, "Shem Tob ben Joseph Palquer," *Jewish Quarterly Review* n.s., 1 (1910–11): 160. See his extended footnote on pp. 160–161. See also Henry Malter, *Saadia Gaon: His Life and Works* (New York: 1926), p. 257.

2. Joseph I. Gorfinkle (ed.), *The Eight Chapters of Maimonides on Ethics* (New York, 1966, Reprint of 1912 edition), p. 54.

3. Harry S. Lewis, "The 'Golden Mean' in Judaism," *Jewish Studies in Memory of Israel Abrahams* (New York, 1927), p. 283.

4. David Rosin, *Die Ethik des Maimonides* (Breslau, 1876), p. 79. Throughout the book, and particularly in his discussion of the mean, Rosin repeatedly cites the Aristotelian sources of Maimonides' doctrine. For similar views with respect to the mean, see M. Wolff, *Musa Maimunis Acht Capitel* (Leiden, 1903), pp. xiii, ff.

5. Ya'akov Mosheh Harlap, *Mey Marom: Mi-Saviv li-Shemonah Peraqim le-ha-Rambam* (Jerusalem, 5705), pp. 85–86. An even stronger statement is made by Shem Ṭov ben Abraham ibn Ga'on in his *Migdal 'Oz*. Commenting on the passage in *H. De'oth*, i. 4, in which Maimonides attributes the doctrine of the mean to the *ḥakhamim ha-rishonim* (presumably, though not necessarily the earlier rabbinic authorities), the *Migdal 'Oz* makes the following observation: "All the moralists (*ḥakhmey ha-Musar*) have taught this principle, which they stole from the teachings of our sages (*genuvah hi 'ittam me-asher dareshu z"l*). Additional sources which make similar extreme attempts to find the doctrine of the mean in Jewish literature are cited in S. Rawidowicz, "*Sefer ha-Petiḥah le-Mishneh Torah*," in his *Iyyunim be-maḥasheveth yisra'el*, p. 429, n. 113. Reprinted from *Metsudah*, 7 (1954). See also M. D. Rabinowitch (ed.), *Shemonah Peraqim le-ha-rambam* (Jerusalem, 1968), pp. 20–21, n. 9, and especially the quotation there from Holzberg.

6. Hermann Cohen, "Charakteristik der Ethik Maimunis," *Moses ben Maimon,* i (Leipzig, 1908), p. 109. This important study by Cohen (reprinted in his *Jüdische Schriften*, iii) has as one of its main purposes the development of evidence that Maimonides was not an Aristotelian. In striking contrast is the view of Husik, who asserts without any qualification that in his ethics "Maimonides is an Aristotelian, and he endeavors to harmonize the intellectualism and theorism of the Stagirite with the diametrically opposed ethics and religion of the Hebrew Bible. And he is apparently unaware of the yawning gulf extending between them. . . . It is so absolutely clear and evident that one wonders how so clear-sighted a thinker like Maimonides could have been misled by the authority of Aristotle

and the intellectual atmosphere of the days to imagine otherwise." Isaac Husik, *A History of Mediaeval Jewish Philosophy* (Philadelphia, 1944), p. 300.

7. Cohen, op. cit., p. 85.

8. Ibid., especially pp. 113–115.

9. Theodor Gomperz, *Greek Thinkers* (London, 1929), iv, p. 274.

10. "Aristotle's Doctrine of Justice," Walsh and Shapiro, *Aristotle's Ethics* (Belmont, California, 1967), p. 109.

11. *Metaphysical Principles of Virtue* (Indianapolis, 1968), p. 95, n. 10.

12. *Nicomachaean Ethics* (hereafter *N.E.*), 1107a,1.

13. *N.E.* 1094b, 15–17.

14. *N.E.* 1173a, 1f.

15. Werner Jaeger, "Aristotle's Use of Medicine as a Model of Method in his Ethics," *Journal of Hellenic Studies* 77 (1952): 57.

16. *De Vet. Med.* ix.

17. *N.E.* 1094a, 16.

18. Cf., *N.E.* vi, 1139a, 32f.

19. *Historia Animalium* i, 492a, 7f.

20. Ibid., 492a, 33f.

21. Ibid., 492b, 31f.

22. *Part. Animalium,* iii, 666a, 15.

23. Ibid., ii, 652a,31f.

24. *De Gen. et Corr.* ii, 334b, 25–30.

25. *Part. Animalium,* ii, 652b, 17–20.

26. *N.E.* vi, 1140a, 20.

27. *Rhet.* iii, 1416b, 30ff.

28. *Pol.* iv, 1295b, 3–7.

29. *N.E.* ii, 1103a,24.

30. *N.E.* vi, 1144b,1f.

31. *Pol.* i, 1253a, 16–19.

32. *N.E.* ii, 1109b, 13f.

33. *N.E.* ii, 1104a, 1f.

34. *N.E.* vi, 1142a, 25f.

35. For an extended discussion of this point see, M. Fox, "Maimonides and Aquinas on Natural Law," *Diney Yisra'el* iii, (1972): v–xxxvi; reprinted in J. I. Dienstag (ed.), *Maimonides and Aquinas* (New York, 1975), pp. 75–106.

36. Joseph I. Gorfinkle (ed.), *The Eight Chapters* (see *supra,* n. 2), pp. 35–36.

37. For the attitudes of traditional commentators who see this first mishnah as an attempt to underscore the independence of Jewish ethics from all external sources, see the comments of Bertinoro and *Tosefoth Yom Ṭov,* ad loc.

38. *Shemonah Peraqim,* v.

39. Ibid., iv, Gorfinkle, pp. 54–55.

40. *N.E.* ii, 6, 1106b, 36f.

41. *H. De'oth,* i, 3, 4.

42. *Guide of the Perplexed* II, 28; ed. Pines, pp. 335–336.

43. For explicit comments on this point see *Guide* II, 8 and III, 14; *Letter*

on *Astrology*, ed. A. Marx, *Hebrew Union College Annual* III (1926): 356 and *Qobeṣ teshuvoth ha-rambam* (Leipzig, 1859), ii, f. 26a.

44. Gorfinkle, p. 64.

45. iii, 1.

46. *Guide* II, 39, ed. Pines, p. 380.

47. Ibid., p. 381.

48. *H. De'oth* i, 5, 6. (From the manuscripts it seems clear that the end of i, 5, as we have cited it here from the printed versions, should really be the beginning of i, 6).

49. Ibid., ii, 3.

50. *N.E.* ii, 6, 1107a, 9f.

51. The main sources for the moral-medical analogy in Maimonides are: *Shemonah Peraqim*, i, ed. Gorfinkle, p. 38; iii, iv, Gorfinkle, pp. 62f; *H. De'oth*, especially ii; *Guide* III, 34.

52. *H. De'oth*, ii, 1.

53. *Guide* II, 40; ed. Pines, p. 382.

54. *Guide* III, 34; ed. Pines, pp. 534–535 (my italics).

55. *N.E.* i, 13, 1102b, 2–12.

56. *Shemonah Peraqim*, i, ed. Gorfinkle, pp. 39–40.

57. An inadequate comment on this question is made by D. Rosin in *Die Ethik des Maimonides* (Breslau, 1876), p. 48, n. 1.

58. The usual printed Hebrew texts read *harbeh min ha-Pilosofim*, but there is no doubt, as is evident from the Arabic text, that the reading should be *mithpal-sefim*. On this point, see the editions of Gorfinkle and Kafiḥ.

59. *Shemonah Peraqim*, v, ed. Gorfinkle, p. 69ff; for almost identical language see H. *De'oth* iii, 2, 3; the very same idea is set forth elaborately in the *Guide* III, 51.

SECTION IV

The Influence of Maimonides

A Scholastic Misinterpretation of Maimonides' Doctrine of Divine Attributes

SEYMOUR FELDMAN

It is well established fact that Maimonides' *Guide to The Perplexed* had a significant influence upon Christian medieval thought. Such giants of scholastic philosophy as Albertus Magnus, Thomas Aquinas, and Duns Scotus all felt the philosophical impact of Maimonides' *magnum opus* and responded to it.[1] One particular philosophical doctrine in the *Guide* elicited considerable comment from the Scholastics — Maimonides' doctrine of divine attributes.[2] Some aspects of Maimonides' theory were welcomed, others criticized. But regardless of their ultimate judgment the Scholastics considered Maimonides' views to be worthy of discussion. In this paper I wish to raise the question: Did the Scholastics accurately understand Maimonides' doctrine of divine attributes?[3]

In his *Errores Philosophorum,* Giles of Rome gives a list of various errors committed by Maimonides, among which are two doctrines concerned with the problem of divine attributes.[4] After having stated that Maimonides maintained that the divine attributes are absolutely equivocal, Giles goes on to say that the only kinds of attributes permitted by Maimonides are negative attributes and attributes "by way of causality." As an example of the former Giles gives "God lives but not through life" (*vivat non in vita*); as an example of the latter he gives "God is said to be living, not because there is life in Him, but because He is the cause of living things."[5] This summary of Maimonides' doctrine of attributes is puzzling, for although Giles cites a specific chapter from the *Guide*, he

Journal of Jewish Studies 19 (1968): 23–39. Reprinted by permission of the author and of *Journal of Jewish Studies.*
Translations following Latin extracts are those of the editor.

does not accurately render Maimonides' doctrine of divine attributes. Indeed, his version of Maimonides' theory is mistaken or misleading in two respects; for Maimonides' theory of negative attributes is not usually formulated in the way Giles renders it, and attributes "by way of causality" are not part of Maimonides' doctrine at all. It is the purpose of this study to show that the imputation of the causal interpretation of divine attributes to Maimonides is mistaken.[6]

We shall see that Giles was by no means unique in his error and that he is a member of a class having some very notable representatives. The common mistake committed by these philosophers is the belief that Maimonides allowed attributes to be positively affirmed of God when such attributes are interpreted causally: "God is wise insofar as He causes wisdom in creatures." I maintain that Maimonides did not permit such attributions. Before I examine in detail some key texts exemplifying this misconception I shall consider some of the aspects of Maimonides' theory of attributes relevant to this particular problem.

The problem of divine attributes stems from the belief in divine simplicity. The latter thesis forbids any kind of description of God that would imply or even suggest a real plurality in God, or that God's essence is a composite. This demand rules out, for example, any of the Aristotelian analytical distinctions between form-matter, genus-species, substance-accident, with respect to God. This problem becomes aggravated if a realist theory of universals is adopted; for if expressions for properties designate real and distinct features of things, then a plurality within the internal structure of the substance results.[7] Now Maimonides was committed to at least a conceptualist theory of universals, according to which universals had a *fundamentum in re* although they exist in the mind; he therefore regarded any positive predication of a property to God as threatening His simplicity.[8] Yet in spite of these philosophical demands Scripture and liturgy are replete with language ascribing to God various properties. Some kind of adjustment between philosophical rigour and religious practice had to be found, and Maimonides thought he had succeeded in finding one.

Of crucial importance is his list of positive attributes and his critical analysis of such attributes with reference to God.[9] According to Wolfson this list constitutes a new classification of the predicables, since it departs both from Aristotle's tables and from Porphyry's.[10] And the differences are especially important for the purpose of this study. Of the five distinct predicates, or possible predications, only one is permissible with respect to God — actions. The first two classes — the definition or a part of a definition — are eliminated, since in either case a tautology would result and God would become definable.[11] But since tautologies are empty and God is not definable (which is ruled out by His simplicity), such attributions are not permitted. Nor are qualities (moral or psychological traits, natural capacities, affections, or quantitative properties) of any kind legitimate attributes of God; for all such properties are accidents, and no accident can be predicated of God. Not only would an accident destroy God's simplicity but it would also imply that God is subject to change, since an "accident" is a property that can belong and not belong to a substance at different times. [12]

Maimonides' discussion of the fourth and fifth classes of attributes — relations and actions — is more complicated, and yet constitutes not only an original feature of his overall theory of attributes, but also the essential point of his theory that the Scholastics failed either to recognize at all or to appreciate fully. From a historical point of view it can be said that Maimonides' distinction between relational and actional attributes of God was a departure from tradition, and in two senses. For his predecessors did not sharply distinguish actions from relational attributes; and, moreover, they permitted both types of predications as divine attributes. In Abraham ben David, for example, there is a general category of relations in which are included properties that Maimonides would regard as actions, e.g. creation, and which are permitted as attributes of God. [13] This treatment is also characteristic of Avicenna, who also considers actions to be relations, which are for Avicenna permissible attributes of God. [14] Now, Maimonides sharply distinguishes between these two types of predications and allows only one of them to be ascribed to God. Why?

In answering this question it will be useful to consider each of the types of relations considered by Maimonides and his reasons for rejecting them as divine attributes. In this way the contrast between relations and actions will be seen. Maimonides divides all relations into four classes: (1) spatial, (2) temporal, (3) reciprocal, and (4) comparative. [15] The first two classes are unexceptionable and present no difficulty. Since only bodies have spatial and temporal relations, God *qua* incorporeal has no such relations. The fourth class (יחס) also requires no extensive explanation. For here we compare two substances in terms of some respect such that they are similar or dissimilar in this respect; e.g. a particular color. To do this, however, is to subsume these items under a species or genus; e.g. color. But God is not subsumable under *any* species or genus; hence no comparative relation is permissible. [16]

The third class of relations (מצטרפים) is somewhat more complicated and needs explication. In these relations some kind of mutual *dependency* between the *relata* is implied. For example, a father and his son are so related that given one of these *relata* the other is implied. [17] But this necessary mutual dependency between the terms related is the reason why such relational characteristics cannot be applied to God. For if we were to ascribe such a relation to God we would then imply that some other entity necessarily exists. But since God alone possesses absolutely necessary existence and creatures have only contingent existence, no such relation between God and creature exists. Such a relation would bind God to some other thing, but God's absolute necessity precludes such a tie.[18] In general these relations make the related terms dependent upon each other. But God is not dependent upon anything; therefore He has no such relation to anything else.

Actually, Maimonides, and the Aristotelian tradition in general, construed relations as some kind of accidental quality that inheres in each of the related terms.[19] The implications of this metaphysical conception of relations are many, and one aspect of it will be explored later. Here it will be sufficient to observe that since any accident is a supervenient attribute subjecting its bearer to change, God is not subject to relations *qua* accidents.[20]

Maimonides claims that actions, or actional attributes, are not relations and are permissible descriptions of God. Now there are two difficulties with this claim: (1) in what way do actions differ from relations, and (2) why are actions permissible predications? Although it is not the purpose of this paper to construct an argument in behalf of Maimonides' theory of attributes, certain observations will be of use in the analysis of the texts that are the objects of this study. From a formal, or logical, point of view, actional attributions have, Maimonides claims, a different syntactical structure from that possessed by non-actional attributions. For, whereas the latter is of the type "Moses is φ," where φ is some property, essential, qualitative, or relational, the former has a verb instead of the copula and the adjective or noun. This is the Aristotelian-medieval logical distinction between trinary and binary propositions.[21] From the point of view of modern logic, however, this distinction is, as it stands, merely grammatical; for any verb can be put into adjectival form as a gerundive or participle, e.g. "Moses speaks" or "Moses is speaking." But there is a genuine logical difference between relational predicates and non-relational predicates, particularly actional predicates, that ought to be appreciated, and the difference does illuminate the distinction between relational and actional predicates. A relational characteristic is, logically speaking, a polyadic predicate that is asserted to be true of two or more individuals. An actional predicate is a monadic predicate asserted to be true of one individual. As has been already indicated, if a relational predicate were asserted of God, another individual or entity would then be implied. This implication, Maimonides believed, makes God dependent and impairs His absolute existence; for God exists without any ontological dependence upon anything else.

But from this logical point of view actional predicates have not been distinguished from other non-relational properties, which Maimonides excludes as possible divine attributes, since the latter are also monadic predicates. Maimonides himself is very much concerned in making the difference clear. He tells us that actions are not qualities, or accidents, i.e. they are not characteristics that are supervenient upon or inhere in their subjects.[22] Accidents have already been shown to be illegitimate attributes of God. He tries to explain this somewhat obscure point by means of several examples. The philosophical moral of these examples is that, unlike qualities, actions do not imply a plurality within the agent: the power of fire to burn wood, melt wax, harden mud, etc. is one and the same power. All the actions of God stem from His essence, which admits of no internal plurality. In God's case we do not know His essence, and so this power remains a mystery to us. But these actions are not, nor do they derive from distinct properties in or qualities of God. They are unique deeds or events, not qualities, habits, or traits.

Indeed, Maimonides suggests that the actions of God are coextensive with the course of nature, which men describe in anthropomorphic terms.[23] As long as we observe certain conditions we are permitted to speak of certain natural occurrences, or divine acts, in human terms. Firstly, no such description of a natural event as a divine act should be construed as implying in God any change or passion. Secondly, any similarity between these acts and human actions on the basis of which we describe these natural processes must be rejected, in spite of appearances and the needs of human expression. That is, all expressions, even of God's acts, are absolutely equivocal.[24] Thirdly, this level of religious language is inferior to negative attributes, which Maimonides maintains are the only true attributes of God. Actional attributes are merely a grudging concession to human needs and tendencies. The true believer knows better, and speaks the language of negative theology.[25]

It has been suggested by Wolfson that the actional attributes of God correspond to *propria* in Aristotle's scheme of predicables.[26] A *proprium* is, according to Aristotle, a property that distinguishes a substance from any other substance. Although it is not a defining, or essential property, the *proprium* is always true of substances of this species. In other words, the *proprium* is always true of members of a particular species but does not define the species, and it is not true of any member of another species. This initial definition of a *proprium*, however, is too general to capture Maimonides' notion of an action. Elsewhere in the *Topics* Aristotle distinguishes several kinds of *propria*, of which one type seems to correspond to actions. Certain kinds of *propria* are "temporary," such as "a particular man walking about in the market place."[27] Now, a temporary *proprium* is not only restricted in its temporal range, but is, as Aristotle's example shows, restricted to a definite individual. Thus, in this sense a *proprium* could be a unique action of a particular individual. Such descriptions would neither define the individual nor constitute an accidental quality that could be shared by other individuals. The actions of God, then, are neither essential nor accidental qualities; they are deeds or events exhibited in nature.[28]

Having established the relevant features of Maimonides' theory of attributes we are now prepared to return to our initial question, did Maimonides believe in attributes "by way of causality"? Such an attribute asserts that God is wise *because* He creates wisdom in creatures. As Scotus puts it . . . *ut sapientia* [applied to God] *quia sapientiam facit.*[29] Implicit in this account is the belief that we apply attributes to God insofar only as He causes us to have them. I now propose to examine several texts from certain scholastic philosophers in order to show that their conception of Maimonides' theory of attributes was not accurate.

In the passage just cited from Scotus, Maimonides and Avicenna are cited together as advocating a view of divine attributes according to which the only legitimate attributes are either negations or attributes of efficient causality:

> rationibus omnibus attributorum (quae scilicet dicunt perfectionem in Deo et in creaturis) correspondet in Deo unitas essentiae, non secundum esse quod absolute habet – ut dictum est – sed secundum respectum quem habet ad creaturam; non in genere causae efficientis (sic nullum sumitur attributorum, ut sapientia quia sapientiam facit), nec etiam ad removendum aliquid a Deo – quos duos modos videntur dicere Avicenna et Rabbi Moyses.[30]

> to all the reasons for attributes (that is, what they call a perfection in God and in creatures), there corresponds in God the unity of His essence, not according to a being which it [His essence] has absolutely – as it has been said – but according to a relation which it has to a creature; not in the category of efficient causality (none of the attributes are thus predicated, as wisdom because He creates wisdom) nor even to remove something from God – these two ways Avicenna and Rabbi Moses seem to mention.

In this passage Scotus is paraphrasing the *Quodlibet* of Henry of Ghent, who gives a more extensive discussion of Maimonides in his *Summa Theologiae.*[31] I shall now examine in some detail the discussion in the latter work.

According to Henry of Ghent, Avicenna and Maimonides admit two kinds of divine attribute only – negations and relations:

> immo omnia [*sc.* attributes] (ut dicit Rabbi Moyses) imposita sunt ad negandum aliquid ab eo; aut ad indicandum aliquem respectum in eo.[32]

> indeed, all attributes (as Rabbi Moses says) are predicated in order to negate something of Him or to indicate some relation to Him.

As the text indicates Henry employs the category of relations to characterize Maimonides' notion of an actional attribute. He defines these relations as a real, as distinct from a merely conceptual, or subjective, tie between God and creature.[33] Then Henry goes on to provide some examples and a description of these relations:

> Primo modo triplici [sc. real relations] modo attributa significant sub ratione respectus ad creaturas: ut *divina opera*: secundum quod dicit Rabi Moyses lib. 1 cap lii. . . . Exemplum de primo modo est quod deus dicitur misericors quia facit nos misericordes: et iustus quia facit nos iustos: et iuxta hunc modum cognoscitur deus *per causalitatem*.[34]

> In the first of three ways, attributes have meaning on the basis of a relation to creatures, as *divine deeds*: according to what Rabbi Moses says in Bk. 1, ch. 52 . . . An example of this first way is that God is called merciful because he makes us merciful, and just because He makes us just; and in this way God is known *through causality*.

The text clearly reveals that although Henry correctly includes actions as divine attributes, he incorrectly construes them as relations; indeed he characterizes them as attributes "by way of causality." This account is mistaken in both respects: actions for Maimonides are not relations, and hence they cannot be interpreted causally, since causality is a relation. Nor did we find in Maimonides any examples of the *schema* "God is φ because He causes φ in creatures." The latter mode of expression suggests that the alleged attribute is only secondarily true of God.[35] The actions of God, however, are His acts, not properties that we ascribe to Him in a derivative sense. (I shall discuss this point later in connection with Thomas.) Indeed, as has been pointed out, actional attributes are always expressed in a binary proposition with the purpose of suggesting the illegitimacy of ascribing to God properties, essential or accidental. On the other hand, Henry's account does represent the doctrine of Avicenna, whom he also discusses in this context.[36] As we shall see later, Avicenna and Maimonides were frequently mentioned together as representing a certain theory of divine attributes. But we have seen that this report is partially mistaken.

When we turn to Thomas Aquinas we encounter several difficulties, textual and philosophical; for the various passages where Thomas discusses Maimonides' theory of attributes are not internally consistent, or at least not entirely similar. Each text therefore deserves separate treatment. In the early *De veritate* Thomas mentions the following theory of attributes:

> For this reason others have asserted that when we attribute knowledge or something of the same sort to God, we postulate nothing positive in Him but merely designate Him as the cause of knowledge in created things.[37]

The translator, R. Mulligan, attributes this view to Maimonides and cites chapter 60 of Part I of the *Guide*. Although this chapter supports the contention that for Maimonides no attribute signifies anything "positive" in God, neither that chapter nor any other supports the view that attributes are causal in nature. In fact, in the next passage Thomas mentions another view, which is closer to Maimonides' theory than the former account:

> Still others have said that knowledge and the like are attributed to God in a certain proportionate likeness, as anger, mercy . . . For God is said to be angry in so far as He does something similar to what an angry man does, for He punishes. Properly speaking, of course, the passion of anger cannot be in Him . . . But according to this view, knowledge is attributed, merely metaphorically to God, as are anger and other like things — an opinion contrary to the words of Dionysius and other saints.[38]

This passage is both interesting, yet puzzling; it mentions examples of divine actions that Maimonides himself gives, but it does not give a wholly correct description of such actions. For, Maimonides does not admit any "proportionate likeness" between God and man. Nor is it clear that divine actions are merely "metaphorical." (I shall return to the latter point.)

In the *Summa Theologiae* Maimonides is explicitly mentioned several times in connection with the problem of divine attributes. One passage is especially important for our purposes, for in this context Thomas mentions two theories of divine attributes concerning which he has several reservations:

> Names which are said of God negatively or which signify His relation to creatures manifestly do not at all signify His substance . . . But as regard names of God said absolutely and affirmatively, as good, wise and the like, various and many opinions have been held. For some have said that all such names, although they are applied to God affirmatively, nevertheless have been brought into use more to remove something from Him . . . This was taught by Rabbi Moses. Others say that these names applied to God signify His relationship towards creatures: thus in the words, 'God is good', we mean, 'God is the cause of goodness in things.'[39]

Now, it is interesting to note that Maimonides is not mentioned here as advocating the causal interpretation of attributes. Indeed, the editors cite Alan of Lille as representing this latter theory, thus reversing Mulligan's interpretation of the passages previously cited from *De veritate*. In the passage from the *Summa* Thomas refrains from foisting upon Maimonides a theory which the latter philosopher does not accept.[40] On the other hand, some of Thomas' contemporary interpreters have not been equally scrupulous, for they attribute the causal theory to Maimonides and support their interpretation with this very passage from the *Summa*. R. Garrigou-Lagrange, for example, maintains that

> These absolutely simple perfections are said to be formally in God inasmuch as they are in Him substantially and in a literal sense. Substantially, indeed, and not merely causally, as if 'God is good' meant, as Maimonides contends, merely 'God is the cause of good things.'[41]

Perhaps the explanation for this latter misinterpretation can be found in Thomas himself, in another work, where indeed this mistaken interpretation is in fact attributed to Maimonides. We find in the *Commentary on the Sentences* the following passage:

> Quidam enim dicunt, ut Avicenna (lib. de Intelligent. cap 1) et Rabbi Moyses (lib. 1 cap 57 et 58) . . . quod Omnia autem alia quae Deo attribuuntur, verificantur de Deo dupliciter, secundum eos: vel per modum negationis, vel per modum causalitatis . . . Item per modum causalitatis dupliciter; vel inquantum producit ista in creaturis, ut dicatur Deus bonus, quia bonitatem creaturis influit et sic de aliis; vel inquantum ad modum creaturae se habet, ut dicatur Deus volens vel pius, inquantum se habet ad modum volentis vel pii in modo producendi effectum, sicut dicitur iratus, quia ad modum irati se habet.[42]

> For some say, as Avicenna (On Intelligibles, ch. 1) and Rabbi Moses (Bk. 1, ch. 57 and 58), that . . . [other than subsistent being] everything else which is attributed to God, is true of God in a two-fold way, according to them: either by way of negation, or by way of causality. . . . Likewise by way of causality in a two-fold way: either insofar as He produces those things in creatures, as God may be called good because He diffuses goodness in creatures and so for other attributes; or insofar as He is related to the way [of acting] of a creature, as God may be called willing or pious, insofar as He is related to the way [of acting] of one who wills or is pious in the way of producing an effect, just as He is called angry because He is related to the way [of acting] of one who is angry.

This passage is interesting for several reasons. Firstly, it subsumes divine actions under the category of causality, which for Thomas is a relation. Secondly, Thomas imputes this account of divine attributes to Maimonides, as well as Avicenna, without making a distinction between the two subclasses he recognizes such that actions alone, but not causal attributes, are admitted by Maimonides. Thirdly, the specific chapters mentioned by Thomas—c. 57–58—(Harizi's enumeration)—do not at all justify the causal interpretation of Maimonides' conception of actional attributes, although they do support a further contention of Thomas' that according to Maimonides all attributes are predicated of God equivocally. It is now comprehensible how Garrigou-Lagrange read Thomas' critique of the causal conception of attributes in the *Summa Theologiae* as applying to Maimonides.

One final point. A few sentences later Thomas concludes his argument with the statement that

> Unde sequitur quod rationes istorum nominum non sunt in Deo, quasi fundamentum proximum habeant in ipso, sed remotum . . . hujusmodi enim relationes in Deo secundum rem non sunt, sed sequuntur modum intelligendi . . . Et sic, secundum hanc opinionem, rationes horum attributorum sunt *tantum in intellectu,* et non in re, quae Deus est; et intellectus eas adinvenit ex consideratione creaturarum vel per negationem vel per causalitatem, ut dictum est.[43]

> From this it follows that the reasons for those names are not in God, as if they had a proximate foundation in God Himself, but are removed from Him . . . for relations of this kind are not in God according to reality but follow from a way of understanding. . . . And thus, according to this opinion, the reasons for these attributes are *only in the intellect,* and not in the reality which God is; and the intellect discovers them from a consideration of creatures either by way of negation or by way of causality, as it has been said.

Here Thomas says that according to Maimonides (and Avicenna) the divine attributes construed as relations are merely subjective. This is contrary to the analysis we found in Henry of Ghent. I suspect, however, that Henry is a bit closer to the truth; since for Maimonides actional attributes are real occurrences in nature, although our descriptions of these events do stem from human analogies, and hence are in this sense subjective. On the other hand, since Thomas construes Maimonides' actional attributes as relations and since there is the suggestion in Maimonides that relations are subjective, we can understand how Thomas could make this claim. It would seem that Henry and Thomas have captured only parts of the story.

In *De potentia dei* there are two specific references to Maimonides that are particularly relevant to our topic. The first passage is especially interesting since it gives an almost *correct* account of Maimonides' theory:

> dicit Rabbi . . . hujusmodi nomina de Deo dupliciter esse intelligenda. Uno modo per similitudinem effectus, ut dicatur Deus sapiens non quia sapientia aliquid sit in ipso, sed quia ad modum sapientis in suis effectibus operatur . . . Alio modo per modum negationis.[44]

> the Rabbi says . . . that names of this kind must be understood of God in two ways. One way is through the similarity of an effect, as God may be called wise, not because wisdom is something in God Himself but because He operates in His effects in the way of one who is wise. . . . The other way is by way of negation.

Here Thomas does not construe Maimonides' actional attributes as causal attributes in the sense in which he did so in the *Commentary on the Sentences,* although he does employ language that suggests such an interpretation. On the other hand, one of Thomas' criticisms of Maimonides shows that he has not read carefully the relevant chapters of the *Guide.* For he claims that on this view there would be no criterion for determining *which* actions are legitimately ascribable to God:

> quia secundum expositionem nulla differentia esset inter hoc quod dicitur, Deus est sapiens, Deus est iratus, Deus ignis est . . . Hoc autem est contra positionem sanctorum et prophetarum loquentium de Deo, qui quaedam de Deo probant, et quaedam ab eo removent.[45]

> because according to this exposition [i.e., of Maimonides] there would be no difference among these statements: God is wise, God is angry, God is fire. . . . However, this is contrary to the position of saints and prophets when speaking of God, who do attribute some things to God and remove other things from Him.

As we have already indicated Maimonides does place at least two important restrictions upon such ascriptions: they cannot imply that God is corporeal or that He is subject to change, conditions that Thomas himself puts upon such ascriptions.[46]

The second passage from *De potentia* is concerned with the legitimacy of describing God by means of relational terms. As we have shown, Maimonides rejects such predications. Thomas, however, does allow certain kinds of relational attributes, and he criticizes Maimonides for not being so tolerant. His discussion is especially revealing:

> In hoc autem deficit multipliciter Rabbi, qui voluit probare quod non esset relatio inter Deum et creaturam, quia cum Deus non sit corpus, non habet relationem ad tempus nec ad locum. Consideravit enim solam relationem quae consequitur quantitatem, non eam quae consequitur actionem et passionem.[47]

> In this, however, the Rabbi failed in many ways, in wanting to prove that there was no relation between God and creature, because God is neither related to time nor place since He is not a body. For he considered only that relation which follows from quantity, not a relation that follows from action and passion.

Here Thomas correctly describes Maimonides' position as rejecting relational attributes of God, but he unjustifiably criticizes him for not considering relations other than those that are concerned with quantity. This is obviously wrong, since Maimonides explicitly mentions not only comparative relations but the particular class of relations—actions and passions —that Thomas accuses him of not considering. Indeed, one of the examples Thomas elsewhere gives of this class is a relation that Maimonides himself mentions as an example of reciprocal relations—the relation of father to son. Moreover, the analysis Thomas gives of this type of relation justifies Maimonides' rejection of them as divine attributes. According to Thomas, in this kind of relation the terms are related because of some real property —the *fundamentum*—in both of the terms that grounds the relation. Such a relation is a real relation, as distinct from an ideal relation, which is constructed by the mind, e.g. the relation of genus to species.[48] In many cases these properties are accidents, or supervenient properties, e.g. the legal arrangements that govern the relationship between master and slave. Yet, insofar as they are accidents, such properties cannot be predicated of God; for God is not a subject of accidents. Finally, as Aristotle already indicated, such relations imply some kind of potentiality in the related terms.[49] For this reason, too, God could not be described by relations of action and passion. Thomas himself admits this point, and he refuses to countenance real relations of this sort between God and creature.

Nevertheless, Thomas does introduce a different kind of relation that he believes can be correctly applicable to God and creature. If the relation is real between the creature and God but only ideal between God and creature, then such a relation is an admissible attribute of God. As an example of such a relation Thomas cites the third type of relation discussed by Aristotle in *Metaphysics* v, 15. Aristotle describes a type of relation that is true of one term only because some other term is related to it; it is, so to speak, a one-sided relation. For example, the object of knowledge is logically independent of any knower, although a knower is logically dependent upon some object of cognition.[50] Thomas argues that all the relations between God and creature are of this sort: they are real only between the creature and God, whereas they are ideal between God and creature. Now among these "mixed" relations Thomas includes creation, which Maimonides construes as an act, indeed the supreme act of God. This suggests that for Thomas divine action is a "mixed relation," a relation that is real in one direction but ideal in the other.[51] Maimonides, however, did not recognize this type of relation; and perhaps for this reason he had to introduce a new category of predicates to accommodate actional attributes. Moreover, as we have already seen, any kind of relation was for Maimonides an accident, and no accident can be predicated of God.[52]

It is tempting to think that there is a close similarity between Maimonides' doctrine of actional attributes and Thomas' theory of analogical predication. Indeed, in one of the passages cited above Thomas reports Maimonides' position as permitting an analogy between divine action and human action.[53] God can be said to be merciful because certain natural events that are ascribed to God are beneficial to man and are similar to those events that we bring about when we are merciful. Before this comparison can be assessed it is important to appreciate several basic points about the notion of analogical predication.

Firstly, analogical predication in Thomas differs from the causal interpretation of attributes. For, whereas the latter ascribes to God an attribute insofar only as it is alleged to be found in creatures, the former ascribes this attribute first to God and then to His creatures. As Thomas says, these names are applied to God in a "primary" sense, whereas on the causal view they are applied to God only secondarily.[54] Indeed, Thomas' theory of analogical predication is the theory of amphiboly found in Aristotle, Alfarabi, Avicenna, and Averroes — the theory of amphiboly *per prius et posterius,* or the one-one analogy. According to this view a property is applied to God in a more fundamental sense than when it is applied to creature, just as the being of substance is prior to the being of any accident.[55] In other words, on this theory God is truly and essentially wise and good, not merely derivatively because He creates wise and good men.

Secondly, Maimonides rejects this theory of amphiboly with respect to divine attributes. There is no similarity *whatever* between God and creature.[56] He does however, admit a weaker kind of amphibolous predication between creatures, wherein some *accidental* feature is found amongst various entities. For example, a live man, a statue of a man, and a corpse may have the same shape.[57] But since God can sustain no accidents, there is no analogy, even of this kind, between Him and any creature. There is no common core to the concept of wisdom such that it could apply to both God and man in a wholly non-equivocal way. For Thomas there is some such core that enables us to make an analogy between human wisdom and divine wisdom.[58]

Now, there are several passages in the *Guide* that might be construed as suggesting something like Thomas' theory of analogy. In chapters 26, 46, and 47 of Part I Maimonides discusses the rabbinic principle that the Torah speaks in the language of men. He points out how Scripture often uses language that is anthropomorphic and hence philosophically objectionable. In particular, he shows how men attribute to God properties that they consider to be perfections in themselves but are with respect to God really "the highest degree of imperfection."[59] Some such properties are corporeal, e.g. physical strength, and are therefore impermissible as attributes of God. They can only be used metaphorically, and intelligent people do not construe them literally. However, there are other expressions that do not imply corporeality, e.g. wisdom, and for that reason some people are inclined to attribute such a property to God in a literal and nonequivocal sense. But we are mistaken in doing this, for these perfections are *completely* equivocal and bear no analogy with their "counterparts" in creatures. Indeed, the true path to God is the *via negativa,* which brings us closer to God than any other type of knowledge.[60] In the latter type of attribute the infirmities of human language are explicitly revealed and the almost inevitable tendencies to make analogies with human and natural phenomena are resisted. Actional attributes for Maimonides seem to be a concession to the psychologically explicable, but philosophically unjustifiable demand for humanizing the divine. God does act, but our descriptions of these acts can never be taken at face value. The inevitable hiatus between God and man is always stressed by Maimonides, and the best way to contemplate the divine is to remain silent.[61]

The texts we have examined have revealed that Maimonides' doctrine of actional attributes was not correctly understood by some of the Christian scholastic philosophers. It has also been suggested that the failure to recognize or appreciate Maimonides' distinction between relational and actional attributes might have led to this misinterpretation. Its elusiveness should perhaps cause us no wonder, since Maimonides' distinction was, for better or worse, quite subtle and even novel. And, after all, this is what we ought to expect from the *Rav Ha-Moreh.*

NOTES

1. Jakob Guttmann, *Das verhältniss des Thomas von Aquino zum Judenthum und zur jüdische Literatur* (Gottingen, 1891); *Die Scholastik des 13 Jahrhunderts in ihre Beziehungen zum Judenthum und zur jüdischen Literatur* (Breslau, 1902); "Über einige Theologen des Franziskanerordens und ihre Beziehungen zum Judenthum," *Monatsschrift für Geschichte und Wissenschaft des Judenthums* 40:314–329; "Die Beziehungen des Johannes Duns Scotus zum Judenthum", 38:26–39.

2. Harry A. Wolfson claims that the problem of divine attributes was not indigenous to Christianity and that one of the chief stimuli for the development of this problem in Christianity was the *Guide To The Perplexed;* see his *Religious Philosophy* (Cambridge, Mass., 1961), pp. 49–60.

3. The historical and textual aspects of the transmission of the *Guide* into the Latin world have been explored. The following works should be consulted: W. Kluxen, "Literargeschichtliches zum lateinischen Moses Maimonides," *Recherches de théologie ancienne et médiévale* 21 (1954): 23–50; "Maimonides und die Hochscholastik," *Philosophisches Jahrbuch* 63 (1955): 151–165; J. O. Riedl, "Maimonides and Scholasticism," *The New Scholasticism* 10 (1936): 18–28.

4. Giles of Rome (Egidio Colonna), *Errores Philosophorum,* ed. J. Koch and trans. J. O. Riedl (Miwaukee, 1944), pp. 60–61. The English text is also avail-

able in H. Shapiro (ed.), *Medieval Philosophy* (New York, 1964), pp. 409–410. I shall quote from the former source.

5. Article 3, p. 61.

6. I shall not here discuss the doctrine of negative attributes. It is sufficient to observe that Maimonides' customary examples of such attributes satisfy one or other of the following three *schemata;* (1) "God is not weak," where we are negating not only weakness but strength taken in its ordinary sense; (2) "God is incorporeal," or (3) "God is 'living'," where "living" is equivocal and equivalent to the first *schema.* (H. Wolfson, "Maimonides on Negative Attributes," *Louis Ginzberg Jubilee Volume* [New York, 1945], pp. 411–466 [English Section].) The example used by Giles of Rome, however, is formulated differently and follows the pattern of the negation of accidents or modes added to God which Maimonides discusses in chapter 57, not chapter 61 which is cited by Giles. In fact Maimonides does not mention negative attributes at all in chapter 57.

7. Wolfson, "Crescas on the Problem of Divine Attributes," *Jewish Quarterly Review* 7 (1916): 1–44, 175–221.

8. Wolfson, ibid.; "Maimonides on Modes and Universals," *Studies in Rationalism, Judaism and Universalism in Memory of Leon Roth,* ed. R. Loewe (London, 1966), p. 311–322; reprinted in this volume.

9. Moses Maimonides, *The Guide of The Perplexed,* trans. S. Pines (Chicago, 1963), I, 52.

10. Wolfson, "The Aristotelian Predicables and Maimonides' Division of Attributes," *Essays and Studies in Memory of Linda Miller,* ed. I. Davidson (New York, 1938), pp. 201–234.

11. That definitional attributes, either complete or partial, result in tautologies can be seen as follows: Let us say that the definition of "triangle" is "a trilateral plane figure." The sentence "A triangle is a trilateral plane figure", however, merely explains the term "triangle" and gives us no new information about triangles. (Maimonides, *Guide* I, 52. I. Kant, *The Critique of Pure Reason,* B 11.)

12. Aristotle, *Topics* 102b, 4–10.

13. Abraham ben David, *'Emunah Ramah,* ed. S. Weil (Frankfurt, 1852), p. 54.

14. Max Horten, *Die Metaphysik Avicennas* (Halle, 1907), pp. 537–538. Averroes, *Tahafut al Tahafut,* trans. S. van der Bergh (Oxford, 1954), i, Fifth Discussion, Paragraph 306. Wolfson, "Avicenna, Algazali and Averroes on Divine Attributes," *Homenajes a Millas-Vallicrosa* (Barcelona, 1956) II, 545–571.

15. Wolfson, "Crescas on Divine Attributes" (see note 7). Note that Maimonides, unlike Aristotle, considers space and time to be relational categories. Aristotle, *Categories* iv.

16. Maimonides, *Guide* I, 52 and 56.

17. Maimonides, *Treatise on Logic,* trans. I. Efros (New York, 1938), 11. Aristotle, *Categories* vii.

18. Aristotle, *Metaphysics* v, 15, especially 1021a, 27–29.

19. Aristotle, *Categories* ii and v; Maimonides, *Guide* I, 52; Julius Weinberg, *Abstraction, Relation and Induction* (Madison, 1965), pp. 75ff.

20. It is interesting to note that Thomas Aquinas had to construct a different theory of relations to account for the relations of the members of the Trinity. These relations are not "ordinary" relations, and thus are not accidental. *Summa Theologiae* I, Q. 28, a. 1–4.

21. Maimonides, *Treatise on Logic*, 3, p. 37. H. W. B. Joseph, *An Introduction to Logic* (Oxford, 1957), p. 162, n. 1.

22. Maimonides, *Guide* I, 53–54.

23. Ibid., I, 54 and III, 32.

24. Ibid., I, 54–56.

25. Ibid., I, 58–59.

26. Wolfson, *Philo* (Cambridge, Mass., 1948), II, 131ff; Aristotle, *Topics* 101b, 18ff, 102a, 17ff.

27. Aristotle, *Topics* 128b, 15ff.

28. Some of Maimonides' Jewish successors had difficulty in accepting the distinction between actions and relations. Crescas, for example, rejected it. (Hasdai Crescas, *'Or 'Adonai* [Ferrara, 1755], I, iii, 3.) Joseph Kaspi, on the other hand, was puzzled by it and tried to assimilate actions to relations. (J. Kaspi, *'Ammudey Kesef u-maskiyyoth Kesef* [Frankfurt, 1848], pp. 58–59.) Isaac Abarbanel's remarks are instructive, especially his warning not to construe actions as Aristotle's category of action and passion; for the latter implies some potentiality in the agent, but God has no potentialities (*Commentary* to the *Guide* I, 52.)

29. John Duns Scotus, *Opera Omnia,* ed. C. Balic (Vatican City, 1950), 4, d. 8, pars. 1, q. 4, n. 162.

30. Op. cit.

31. Henry of Ghent, *Quodlibeta* V, Q. 1; *Summa Theologiae* (St. Bonaventure, 1953), a. 32, q. 4. The original statement in the *Quodlibeta* is more informative than Scotus' paraphrase: after *"sapientiam"* it adds *"in nobis."* This is the *schema* that we found in Giles of Rome.

32. Henry of Ghent, *Summa Theologiae,* a. 32, q. 4 N.

33. Ibid., R. This is somewhat puzzling, since Maimonides suggests that relations are subjective (*Guide* I, 53). Moreover, Henry's account is incompatible with Thomas' representation of Maimonides' and Avicenna's theory that attributes are "only in the mind" (Thomas Aquinas, *Super libros sententiarum Magistri Petri Lombardi* (Parma, 1862–70) d. 2, q. 1, a. 3.). I shall return to Thomas' account later.

34. Henry of Ghent, *Summa Theologiae,* a. 32, q. 4 R. (My italics.)

35. Thomas Aquinas, *Summa Theologiae* I, Q. 13, a. 6.

36. In his *Henri de Gand,* Jean Paulus uncritically relies upon Henry and Thomas, and thus imputes to Maimonides the view that only negations and relational attributes are admissible descriptions of God (J. Paulus, *Henri de Gand* [Paris, 1948], p. 201, n. 1 and p. 245.).

37. Thomas Aquinas, *On Truth,* trans. R. Mulligan (Chicago, 1952) Vol. I, Q. 2, a. 1.

38. Ibid. The translator cites Alan of Lille as a representative of this view.

39. Thomas Aquinas, *Summa Theologiae* I, Q. 13, a. 2. I have used the translation published in the *Basic Writings of Thomas Aquinas,* ed. A. Pegis (New York, 1945), vol. 1.

40. Wolfson, "St. Thomas on Divine attributes," *Mélanges Offerts à Etienne Gilson* (Toronto, 1959), pp. 673–700.

41. R. Garrigou-Lagrange, *The One God* (St. Louis, 1944), p. 404. M. T. L. Penido, "Le rôle d'analogie en théologie dogmatique," *Bibliotheque Thomiste* 15 (1931): 149, 169.

42. Thomas Aquinas, *Super libros sententiarum* i, d. 2, q. 1, a. 3, *ad* 3. The chapters from the *Guide* cited by Thomas are numbered according to the Harizi Hebrew translation, from which Thomas' Latin version of the *Guide* was made. The Harizi enumeration of chapters is one less than the Ibn Tibbon enumeration.

43. Ibid.

44. Thomas Aquinas, *De potentia dei* (Parma, 1862–70), Q. 7, a. 5.

45. Ibid.

46. Maimonides, *Guide* I, 54–55.

47. Thomas Aquinas, *De potentia dei*, Q. 7, a. 10.

48. Thomas Aquinas, *Summa Theologiae* I, Q. 13, a. 7.

49. Aristotle, *Metaphysics,* 1021a, 15.

50. Metaphysics, 1021a, 27ff. Thomas Aquinas, *Summa Theologiae* I, Q. 13, a. 7; *Summa Contra Gentiles* II, 12-14.

51. Thomas Aquinas, *Summa Theologiae* I, Q. 13, a. 7, especially *ad* 1 and *ad* 3.

52. For Thomas some relations are essential properties, e.g. the relations of the Trinity. These relations are real in both directions. *Summa Theologiae* I, Q. 28, a. 1-4.

53. See above p. 276. Thomas, *De potentia dei,* Q. 7, a. 5.

54. Thomas Aquinas, *Summa Theologiae* I, Q. 13, a. 6.

55. Wolfson, "The Amphibolous Terms in Aristotle, Arabic Philosophy, and Maimonides," *Harvard Theological Review* 31 (1938): 151–173. Thomas Aquinas, *Summa Theologiae* I, Q. 13, a. 5.

56. Maimonides, *Guide* I, 56.

57. Maimonides, *Treatise on Logic,* 13.

58. Thomas Aquinas, *Summa Theologiae* I, Q. 13, a. 2-3, 5-6.

59. Maimonides, *Guide* I, 26.

60. Ibid., I, 59.

61. Ibid.

Maimonides and Aquinas on Man's Knowledge of God: A Twentieth-Century Perspective

ISAAC FRANCK

I

In the opening chapter of his book, *Eclipse of God,* Martin Buber recalls the hesitant but passionate reaction of a friend, an elderly scholar, against the author's repeated use of the word "God" in one of his writings:

> "How can you bring yourself to say 'God' time after time?" the old scholar asked. "How can you expect that your readers will take the word in the sense in which you wish it to be taken? What you mean by the name of God is something above all human grasp and comprehension, but in speaking about it you have lowered it to human conceptualization. What word of human speech is so misused, so defiled, so desecrated as this!"[1]

A long, backward leap in time is undertaken in this essay, from the idea of God as adumbrated in the words of Buber's aging friend to the "negative theology" of Moses Maimonides and Thomas Aquinas. On the question, "Can man have knowledge of God?" neither the simple statement by Buber's friend that "God is something above all human grasp and comprehension," nor the more complex views propounded by Maimonides and Aquinas, seem to have wide acceptance among philosophers and theologians today. Indeed, in the past two or three decades several sharp attacks have appeared against negative theology and its doctrine of the *unknowability of God.*

It would thus seem appropriate at this time to set forth some of the

The Review of Metaphysics 38 (1985): 591–615.
Reprinted by permission of *The Review of Metaphysics.*

elements of a radical negative theology, the principal tenet of which is that while we do know *that God is,* on the other hand, *what* God is, i.e., God's *nature* or *essence,* in the words of Thomas Aquinas, "remains absolutely unknown" (*penitus manet ignotum*).[2] With some significant deviations or modifications, the doctrine outlined here of the utter unknowability of God is derived from Rabbi Moses ben Maimon, the towering twelfth-century Jewish philosopher and theologian, more widely known as Moses Maimonides, and from Saint Thomas Aquinas, who was thoroughly familiar with Maimonides' major philosophical work, the *Guide of the Perplexed,* and was clearly influenced by it.

Before presenting an extended consideration of the views of Maimonides and Aquinas on man's knowledge of God, it will be of value to note that much of the contemporary criticism of negative theology and of the doctrine of the unknowability of God has concentrated, as we shall see below, on exposing alleged logical flaws in its reasoning. These criticisms require and deserve attention, and such comments as need to be made on some of them by way of rejoinder will be reserved for the second half of this paper. However, part of the analysis by one of these critics will be helpful at this point in the pursuit of the question of God's knowability.

In his acute and instructive essay entitled, "What We Can Say About God," Fred Sommers provides the reader with a distillation of essentially five views, or doctrines, classified according to their claims as to what attributes we may predicate of the divine being:[3]

1. That which Sommers calls "the naive, anthropomorphic view" according to which everything predicable of a human being is also predicable of the divine being
2. The "standard or sophisticated conception," rooted in Cartesian ontology and in the theology seemingly entailed by Descartes' ontology, namely, that no *material* predicates may be predicated of God
3. The view which rejects Descartes' dualistic ontology, but also rejects the naive anthropomorphic theology (referred to in doctrine 1 above), and therefore must, according to Sommers, end up with an animistic or panpsychistic metaphysics like that of Alfred North Whitehead, and a theology that speaks of God as a bodiless spirit
4. The view, which has been called "negative theology," but which falls short of being thoroughgoingly negative, namely, the view that nothing predicable of man is predicable of God
5. The doctrine that no affirmative or *positive attributes of any kind* are predicable of God, that God is completely unknown and unknowable, that we can meaningfully say about God only *what*

he is not (to speak of Him in *negative attributes*); the doctrine that man's highest knowledge of God is to know that we are *unable to know Him.*

We need be concerned here only with doctrines 4 and 5, since the views of both Maimonides and Aquinas are clearly at this end of Sommers's spectrum of possible positions. The differences between these two philosophers (albeit minimal on the main issue), and the apparent ambivalence discernible both in Aquinas and in Maimonides, make it perhaps a little risky to ascribe to them categorically doctrine 5 rather than 4, for fear of projecting on them the *extreme* view espoused in this paper. But at this point we had best let the two philosophers and some of their texts speak for themselves.

II

Maimonides' incisive and striking treatment of the problem of divine attributes, and of man's knowledge of God, is developed principally in Chapters 51 through 60 of Book 1 of the *Guide of the Perplexed.*[4] His conclusion is that no positive attributes may be predicated of God. The only affirmative attributes that may be employed in speaking about God are those that in fact refer to God's *actions* and their *effects* but "do not mean that He possesses qualities" or that such attributes are "notions subsisting within the essence of the agent" — meaning God — or are superadded to God's essence. (This modification of his negative theology is surely a Maimonidean equivocation. It is noted by Aquinas in his *De potentia Dei* and is properly criticized by him.)

Moreover, the ascription of positive attributes to God either constitutes in fact a definition by genus and differentia which would function merely as a stipulative, nominal definition of a term, and would thus tell us nothing about God. On the other hand, it may be a *real* or *essential* definition. But this would entail the assumption of a higher genus than God, under which God could be subsumed, and would thus imply an assumed cause for the *definiendum.* But God, who has no causes anterior to Him, and for Whom there is no higher genus, cannot be thus defined. Another kind of predication of attributes would constitute a *partial* definition because it would offer only a partial *definiens* — for example, in the case of man, the assertion that man is a living thing. This kind of predication would suggest that if we could properly ascribe to God *part* of an essence, then His essence would have to be composite. This we must reject as we reject any notion of plurality within God. The rejection of plurality also requires the rejection of a multiplicity of all kinds of qualities, and thus also a rejection of quantity, as belonging to the nature or essence of God. Finally, any affirmative attributes that might be proposed as predicable of God are *human conceptions,* and it is an error to assume that there is a relation or a correlation between God and these human conceptions or the referents for which they stand. There cannot be any such correlation between God's existence and the existence of things and their qualities, since God

> has a necessary existence while that which is other than He has a possible or contingent existence. . . . There accordingly can be no correlation between them. . . . For it is impossible to represent to oneself that a relation subsists between the intellect and color . . . although both of them are comprised by the same "existence." How then can a relation be represented between Him and what is other than He when there is no notion comprising in any respect both of the two, inasmuch as existence is . . . affirmed of Him . . . and of what is other than He merely by way of absolute equivocation . . . How could there subsist a relation between Him . . . and any of the things created by Him, given the immense difference between them with regard to the true reality of their existence, than which there is no greater difference?[5]

This exclusive and absolute distinction between God and what is not God logically rules out for Maimonides even any analogical predication. Aquinas, however, does allow it, though apparently with some reservations. The logic of Maimonides' rejection of analogical predication is clearly based on one or both of two considerations that are corollaries of his negative theology:

(1) For an attribute X (e.g., "good") to be predicated analogically of two entities (e.g., God and man), it would be necessary first to know that the attribute under discussion as it applies to one of the entities in the analogy is the same as, similar to, or overlaps with the attribute as it applies to the other entity in the analogy. There can be no analogy unless at least such similarity or overlapping exists. However, since we cannot possibly know what the attribute X would mean in its application to God, we have nothing on which to base an analogical ascription of attribute X to both God and man.

(2) The doctrine of the absolute and irreducible difference between God and what is not God means that any attribute X when predicated of God, if such predication were possible, would be completely and utterly different from the predicate carrying the same name when it is predicated of man, and therefore, no analogy would be possible.

Predicating positive attributes of God would thus result in unavoidable equivocation, not because, as Aristotle maintained, things of different types can *never* have the same attributes. Indeed, as Sommers has shown, when *comparisons* are admissible between two things of different types with respect to a given attribute, that attribute *can* be predicated *univocally* of both things, as, for example, when it makes sense to say that the duration in time of the solar eclipse was less, or more, or about the same as the duration in time of my working out this algebraic equation.[6] Rather, the unavoidability of equivocation when positive attributes are predicated of God results precisely because the radical otherness of God makes all comparisons between God and other things utterly impossible, and any terms used both about God and about other things therefore cannot be used univocally. There indeed is no middle ground here between univocity and equivocity.

What then can we know or say about the nature or essence of God? We can only speak in terms of *negative* predications. *We do not know what God is,* but we can and must only say *what God is not.* This is the doctrine of "negative attributes," or of the knowledge of God through the *via negativa.* When we say that God exists, the only meaning this can have is that non-existence is impossible for Him. When we say that God is living, the only possible meaning of the statement is that He is not dead or not mortal. When we say that He is eternal, what it means is that no cause has brought Him into existence. When we say "that He is powerful and knowing and willing" this is only to signify "that He is neither powerless, nor inattentive, nor negligent."[7] Or, to restate it once more in one of Rabbi Moses' own succinct formulations:

> Consequently, He exists, but not through an existence other than His essence; and similarly He lives, but not through life; He is powerful, but not through power; He knows, but not through knowledge.[8]

By way of anticipation of the next section, on Aquinas' negative theology, it is worth noting here that, whereas in other texts Aquinas states this Maimonidean doctrine as his own, in *De potentia Dei* (q. 7, a. 2) he quotes in the name of Maimonides, giving an almost exact translation of the above:

> Rabbi Moses says that God is a being but not in an essence, is living but not with life, is powerful but not with power, wise but not with wisdom.

It is not the case, Maimonides insists, that God's existence, or knowledge, or life, or power are more permanent, more durable, greater, or more perfect than ours. "The matter is not so in any respect," Maimonides emphasizes.[9]

God is utterly different. When we say that God is *one,* what is meant is not numerical oneness. "The meaning is that He has no equal and not that the notion of oneness attaches to His essence."[10] God is unique; He is *sui generis*; He is, to borrow a phrase from Rudolf Otto, "*wholly other.*"[11] It is this doctrine of God's otherness, of His uniqueness, that dictates the doctrine of negative attributes. That human descriptions cannot express the essence of God, that the human mind cannot know what God's nature is, is only another way of saying that God is non-human. "We are only able to apprehend the fact that He is, and cannot apprehend his quiddity," says Maimonides.[12] Only God can apprehend or know His own essence. God's knowledge and man's knowledge are heterotypical, and in God, in Whom there is no plurality, His knowledge and His essence are one and the same. Accordingly, man cannot even desire or try to know God's essence.

For man to desire or endeavor to know God's essence would be as if man wished or endeavored to have *God's apprehension* or *God's knowledge*. But "we cannot comprehend God's knowledge . . . for He is His knowledge and His knowledge is He," hence our desire to know Him would be "as if we desired that we be He and our apprehension His apprehension."[13] What is known to man is necessarily known in terms of *human* knowledge. God's essence cannot be known to man because knowledge of God is available only to God himself—His knowledge and His essence being one and the same—and not to man. For man to try to *know* God would be as if man tried to *be* God. Thus, the formulation of this doctrine by some commentators in the form of the epigrammatic apothegm, "If I knew Him, I would be He" (*Ilu y'dativ, he'yitiv*),[14] is clearly in full consonance with the Maimonidean spirit.

Let us then conclude this less than fully adequate account of the negative theology of Moses ben Maimon, by summarizing in his own words:

> It is not possible, except through negation, to achieve even that [limited] apprehension of God which it is in our power to achieve, . . . on the other hand, negation does not give knowledge in any respect of the true reality of the thing with regard to which the particular matter in question has been negated. . . . God cannot be apprehended by the human intellect, and none but He himself can apprehend what He is, and our knowledge [of Him] consists in our knowledge that we are unable truly to apprehend Him.[15]

It is interesting to note the slight variations in the rendering of the concluding clause by various translators. However, the core meaning is unambiguously clear. Shlomo Pines's version is: "our apprehension of Him consists in our inability to attain the ultimate term in apprehending Him."[16] Friedlander's rendition is "our knowledge of Him consists in knowing that we are unable truly to comprehend Him."[17] Jacob B. Agus's translation is: "We understand Him in the measure in which we grasp His final incomprehensibility."[18]

III

Let us now turn to the negative theology of Thomas Aquinas. We cannot be diverted for more than a paragraph or two to the interesting *historical* matter of Maimonides' influence on Aquinas. One need only refer to such scholars as Richard McKeon[19] and Etienne Gilson[20] for some of the evidence. However, the following should be noted here, in addition to what has already been said. The works of other medieval Christian philosophers and theologians immediately before and after Thomas contain numerous references to Maimonides' *Guide*. Among them, probably the most notable was Albertus Magnus (ca. 1200–1280). A German monograph on the relationship between Albert the Great and Maimonides, published in 1863, exhibits many extensive passages from Albert and Rabbi Moses, in parallel columns, which show them to be either completely or almost completely identical. The author of the monograph, M. Joel, stated:

> Es handelt sich nämlich nicht um einzelne Stellen, sondern um ganze Abhandlungen des Maimonidischen Werkes . . . die in den Schriften Alberts reproduziert sind.[21]

Albert was Aquinas' teacher. The very distinguished scholar in medieval philosophy, the late Anton C. Pegis, with whom it was this author's privilege to discuss the subject of this essay (and from whose insights and erudition he profited greatly), expressed the belief that the great influence of Albert on Aquinas has not been sufficiently researched, and is still far from being fully understood and appreciated. There is clearly good reason to suppose that it was Albert who introduced St. Thomas to Maimonides' *Guide*.

On numerous occasions Aquinas quotes directly from the *Guide*. Locations and concepts from the *Guide* are often reflected in Aquinas' two *Summas*. In *De potentia,* and in other works, he frequently refers to Maimonides by name, calling him Rabbi Moyses, or Moyses Egyptius, and on occasion voices disagreement with him. Without a doubt Aquinas was significantly influenced by Maimonides' ideas. As Emile Saisset, a Catholic professor of philosophy, said in 1862:

> Maimonide est le précurseur de Saint Thomas d'Aquin, et le *Moré Neboukhim* annonce et prépare la *Summa Theologiae.*[22]

Accordingly, the discovery that so much of Aquinas' negative theology bears a close resemblance to that of Maimonides should occasion no surprise.

What follows relies heavily on the work of Professor Anton C. Pegis, and especially on his definitive and instructive paper entitled *"Penitus Manet*

Ignotum," which appeared some nineteen years ago, in *Medieval Studies.*[23] Aquinas shares with Maimonides the doctrine of negative attributes. Affirmative attributes cannot be predicated of God. We can talk about God only by negating any attributes ascribed to Him. It is interesting to note, however, that in some respects Aquinas is more thorough and more consistent than Maimonides on the matter of ascribing affirmative attributes to God, whereas in other respects he is less consistent and less thorough in his rejection of them. The following discussion will provide some instructive examples.

On the one hand, as was pointed out earlier, in *De potentia Dei* Aquinas disagrees with Maimonides' view that, in talking about God, it is proper to use *some* positive attributes, because they indicate only God's actions and their effects, rather than purporting to signify the divine essence. In his strictures against Maimonides here, Aquinas points out that if, because God's actions have produced *wisdom* in man, it were proper to speak of God as being *wise,* then, since God's action also produces, as one of its effects, *anger* in man, or *fire* in combustible things, why would it not be proper to say that God is *angry,* or that God is *fire?* He repeats this argument in the *Summa Theologiae,* again referring directly to Rabbi Moses, by saying that no reason could be assigned

> why some names more than others should be applied to God. For He is assuredly the cause of bodies in the same way as He is the cause of good things; therefore if *God is good* signified no more than *God is the cause of good things,* it might in like manner be said that God is a body, inasmuch as he is the cause of bodies.[24]

On the other hand, however, Aquinas is less than consistent and thoroughgoing in his rejection of positive attributes, when he allows that some names, or attributes, "signify the divine substance, but in an imperfect manner. . . . We cannot know the essence of God as He really is in Himself, but we know Him according as He is represented in the perfections of creatures."[25]

This is part of the evidence of the ambivalences referred to at the beginning, in the negative theology of both Maimonides and Aquinas. An additional comment on these ambivalences will appear later. However, it is, I think, quite clear that the main thrust of Aquinas' doctrine is that the essence, the nature, of God is unknowable. Early in the *Summa Theologiae* he asserts categorically that

> since we cannot know what God is, but rather what he is not, we cannot consider how He is but how He is not. . . . We can show how God is not, by denying of Him whatever is opposed to the idea of Him.[26]

We cannot know the nature of God from knowledge of creatures, because this would be claiming to have knowledge from effect to cause. But, says Aquinas, "it is not possible in any of these ways to know from the effect what the cause is, unless the effect be adequate to the cause, one in which the entire virtuality of the cause is expressed."[27] In Book I of the *Summa Contra Gentiles* Aquinas establishes that we must use the negative way in our investigations about God, because God surpasses anything that our intellect can know and is completely and utterly different. Thus, "through negations, when we have a proper knowledge of a thing, we know that it is distinct from other things, yet what it is remains unknown."[28] Accordingly, to quote again, "while we know of God what He is not, what God is *penitus manet ignotum, remains completely unknown.*"[29]

This *via negativa,* as Professor Pegis pointed out, has momentous consequences. Nothing positive can be said about God's quiddity. Everything positive that *is* said about God is a distortion, it is a reduction of God to human terms. We can achieve the highest knowledge about God when we realize that we do not and can not know Him.

> Then only do we know God truly when we believe Him to be above everything that is possible for men to think about God; . . . for the divine substance transcends the natural knowledge of men. Hence, by the fact that some truths are proposed to man about God, that exceed his reason, the opinion that God is something above that which he can think is strengthened in man.[30]

And, to quote once more:

> It is because human intelligence is not equal to the divine essence that this same divine essence surpasses our intelligence and is unknown to us; wherefore man reaches the highest point in his knowledge about God when he knows that he knows Him not, inasmuch as he knows that that which is God transcends whatever he conceives of Him.[31]

And finally these words of Thomas:

> To know God consists in this for us here and now: that we do not know what God is.[32]

Can we possibly be in error when we hear in this significant statement by Aquinas a direct echo of the words of Maimonides quoted earlier: "Our knowledge of God consists in knowing that we are unable truly to comprehend Him?"

Anton C. Pegis distilled out of Thomistic negative theology consequences which seem most faithful to Thomas, theologically and philosophically sound, and very moving in emotional impact. He called the Thomistic doctrine "a radical doctrine . . . that has not escaped controversy."[33] (Let me say parenthetically that Maimonides' doctrine, too, was radical, and that it too has not escaped controversy.) Aquinas' doctrine requires us, according to Professor Pegis, to insist that in fact nothing can be said affirmatively about the nature of God. "Man must come to *unsay* the whole universe in order to say *God exists* properly."[34] Nothing in the universe is in any way God or like God, and man must *unsay* and *unknow* everything with reference to any God-talk. Pegis's closing paragraph says it better than any summary possibly could:

> God transcends anything and everything that we can think about Him. But to be true to Him we must unknow Him rather than simply be ignorant of Him. We must seek Him in all His creation, we must unsay everything that His creatures are, in order thereby to stand nearer and nearer to His transcendence. When St. Thomas said that God was utterly unknown, what was he saying but that man should seek the divine transcendence by a total unknowing?[35]

IV

The doctrine of the utter unknowability of God, or of radical negative theology, has encountered much criticism and resistance. This is not surprising. A relationship of congeniality between this doctrine and many of the traditional assumptions of popular religion, or even of the more sophisticated theologies that are based on the assumption of a personal God, is hardly to be expected. Numerous objectionable or even pernicious implications and consequences have been imputed to the negative theology of Maimonides and Aquinas in the controversies triggered by this doctrine both recently and in earlier days. I single out six such critical imputations for brief analysis, discussion, and attempted rejoinder:

1. God, the unknown and unknowable subject in such a theology, is "no subject at all," and therefore negative theology can not even claim to have knowledge that He exists.
2. This negative theology leads to and entails *mysticism.*
3. This negative theology leads to and entails *agnosticism.*
4. This negative theology is subversive of *religious doctrine,* of "The Law."
5. This doctrine leads "directly to the theology of silence."
6. This negative theology is a *reductio ad absurdum* of rational theology.

(1) *If God is unknowable, then there can not even be knowledge that He exists.* The first of these animadversions has received various formulations. For example, the question is asked, "If God is unknowable, then how could Maimonides and Aquinas know that God exists?" In an article on "The Logic of Negative Theology," George Englebretsen said:

> If all we ever know of a subject is that certain attributes are denied of it . . . we will never know anything about that subject (an uncircumscribed subject is an unknown subject and thus no subject at all).[36]

And in the same journal, two years later, Joseph A. Buijs concluded his "Comments on Maimonides' Negative Theology" with the assertion,

> How we can know the fact that God exists without thereby knowing anything positive about His nature is an epistemic and metaphysical issue.[37]

In its extreme form, this criticism alleges that one of the consequences entailed by negative theology is the denial of God's existence:

> But if we finally succeed in negating every attribute, we may well ask, what have we left at all. Not only can we not describe what God is, but we must define Him by the very negation of description. The conclusion of the whole matter would seem to be that God is pure negation, not only non-describable, but non-existent.[38]

In rejoinder to this last version of the allegation, the late Leon Roth, who had formulated it in these words more than half a century before, hastened to point to "the characteristic view of Maimonides that this consequence does not follow."[39] However, before reviewing Roth's reading of Maimonides on this matter, it seems proper to go back and note the contrast between Buijs's moderate contention that there is "an epistemic and metaphysical issue" in the doctrine (a cautious admonition from which one can hardly dissent), and Englebretsen's assertion that an uncircumscribed or unknown subject is "no subject at all." It is, of course, less than axiomatic that "an uncircumscribed subject," or an "unknown subject," is synonymous with "no subject at all." The claim that only the known, or only the knowable, exists, or even that only the knowable can be a subject of discourse, seems far from self-evident.

Leon Roth's explication of Maimonides on the ascription of attributes to God, properly emphasized the frequently neglected point that the doctrine does not deny that God has a "nature."

> That human descriptions are inadequate to express the nature of God does not mean that God has no nature . . . each negation of inadequate conceptions of God's being reaffirms the fact that He exists. Existence in the case of God is not an accident; it is identical with His essence. The more we ne-

gate the attributes the more we affirm the essence, and we are left finally with the idea of God as absolute existence.[40]

Without knowing the nature or essence of God, we know that God exists because we know from our experience that things, contingent things exist. If *anything* exists, and obviously finite, contingent things, such as you and I, do exist, then it cannot be the case that *everything* that exists is *contingent*. To be contingent means that the existence of the contingent thing is *contingent upon, depends upon,* some *other thing* or being. But *not everything* can be dependent on something else, i.e., *not everything* can have been *caused by,* or brought into being by, something else. At least *one entity* must be in existence *by itself, independent of anything else,* must have come into being (if it did not exist eternally) by itself, must be *its own cause,* i.e., must *exist necessarily not contingently,* and its non-existence is inconceivable. This *necessarily existent being* is what we call God. Some may call it *existence itself* (whatever this may mean), or *the totality of existence.* What we call God is thus the non-contingent, that which is *causa sui.* God is the absolute existent, to whom existence is so essential as to be His very essence. Accordingly, His very existence is different from the existence of contingent things. The very term "existence" "can only be applied equivocally to His existence and to the existence of things other than He."[41] We *know that* God exists, that His absolute, essential existence is radically different from our existence, and our knowledge *that He exists* is utterly independent of any affirmative attributes we may be tempted to ascribe to Him.

(2) *Negative theology leads to and entails mysticism.* To say that God is unknowable is not to propound or imply a doctrine of *mysticism.* Admittedly, as Shlomo Pines points out, an approach similar to Maimonides' emphasis on the importance of negative attributes in discourse about God "may be found in mystical writings." However, Pines says categorically, "Maimonides is no mystic," and his negative theology does not recommend any mystical or obscurantist detachment from the knowledge of things that are not God. Its intention and effect is rather the pursuit of the kind of knowledge of things that avoids "misplaced references to God's essence."[42]

The label "mystic" hardly befits Maimonides or Aquinas. Mysticism is a doctrine or a range of doctrines that espouse a variety of notions about the nature of God and assert that there are modes of apprehending God, such as direct intuition or other "mystical experiences." These mystical methods are putatively different from and more reliable than the "normal" empirical and rational methods of apprehending other entities. To assert that God is unknowable in no way entails the espousal of mysticism or the acceptance of its claims; in fact, the two are mutually exclusive. To say that God is unknowable to the human intellect is, indeed, to say, using the word in its narrow, lexical sense, that God is a "mystery." But this is only to say that we do not know or apprehend or understand the nature of God, and that we know only that he exists; and it is not to suggest or propound a doctrine of mysticism with all the claims that it would entail.

(3) *Negative theology leads to and entails agnosticism.* In the article referred to above, George Englebretsen concluded that "the way of negation is no new way to God," and that this negative theology is "indiscernible from agnosticism."[43] The charge of agnosticism is also made several times by F. C. Copleston, in his book on Thomas Aquinas: "Exclusive adherence to the negative way would lead to agnosticism about the divine nature."[44] "In Aquinas' account of our natural knowledge of the divine nature there is, then, a certain agnosticism."[45] "As Aquinas saw clearly, a certain measure of 'agnosticism' is inevitable."[46] However, Copleston appears to be equivocating here in two ways. On the one hand, he seems to be shuttling back and forth between the interpretation of Aquinas as saying that man can have *no* knowledge at all of God's nature, and the interpretation of Aquinas as saying that man can have *some* knowledge of the divine nature. Admittedly, there is evidence of such equivocation in both Aquinas and Maimonides — a subject to which we shall return. On the other hand, Copleston also appears to be equivocating in *his own* use of the term "agnosticism," using it at times as a disparaging name for an erroneous doctrine, but at other times as a label for a perhaps regrettable but unavoidable doctrine, the alternatives to which are beset by difficulties.

Clearly, Copleston acknowledges, affirming positive predicates of God inescapably leads either to anthropomorphism or to the reduction of statements about God to myths. But, "Aquinas was not prepared to accept either an anthropomorphic view of God or an interpretation of theological propositions as so many myths."[47] Copleston ends up with a question-begging declaration to the effect that

> Aquinas' agnosticism, then, is not agnosticism in the modern sense. He has no doubt about the existence of God, and he is far from saying that we can know nothing about the divine nature or that we can make only negative statements about it.[48]

This conclusion here is question-begging because, first, as was shown earlier, the logic of radical negative theology does not entail doubts about the *existence* of God. Secondly, it is question-begging because the full, authentic doctrine of Aquinas and of Maimonides (except for the equivocations to which we shall return) says clearly and precisely what Copleston cavalierly claims Aquinas did not say, namely, that "we know nothing about the divine nature," and "that we can make only negative statements about it." The two distinct issues, namely, *whether man can know that God exists* and *whether man can know God's nature or essence,* must be kept distinct from each other. To the former question the answer is clearly affirmative. To the latter, the answer is clearly negative: the nature of God is *unknowable,* and to call this doctrine "agnosticism" is not to refute it or to disparage it, but only to describe it. It is of some use, in this context, to rehabilitate the terms "agnostic" and "agnosticism" and restore them to respectable company in the philosophical lexicon. In their unadulterated, etymological sense these terms betoken an acknowledgment of *not knowing.* An agnostic position with reference to any issue is a position which says that the subject in question is unknown or unknowable. And this, *simpliciter,* is what the adherent of negative theology says about the nature of God.

(4) *Negative theology is subversive of religious doctrine, of "The Law."* The charge that negative theology is subversive of religion has been lodged principally against Maimonides and was repeated most recently by the late Leo Strauss, who stated that "the teaching that positive attributes of God are impossible . . . clearly contradicts the teaching of the law."[49] In this charge we hear reverberations of nearly eight centuries of anti-Maimonidean argument and polemic by some of the teachers and thinkers in the mainstream of Jewish religious and philosophical literature. In elaborating his charge, Strauss averred that:

> Maimonides' doctrine of attributes would be entirely negative and even subversive. For the doctrine culminates in the assertion that we grasp of God only that he is and not what he is.[50]

But this is very puzzling, coming as it does from Strauss, since the latter view, namely, "that we grasp of God only *that He is* and *not what He is,"* is precisely what was held by both Maimonides and Aquinas, as we tried to show above. Moreover, as Strauss surely knew, Maimonides anticipated these attacks, and took the offensive himself, as it were. For he in fact warned that, on the contrary, it is the ascription of affirmative attributes to God that is subversive of religion. In the *Guide* he stated categorically that "he who affirms that God has affirmative attributes . . . has abolished his belief in the existence of the Deity without being aware of it."[51] Baldly stated then, the paradox is that on the one hand Maimonides clearly rejected the ascription of positive attributes to God and characterized such predication as equivalent to the denial of God's existence, whereas Strauss, on the other hand, alleged that the teaching which denies affirmative attributes to God contradicts the teaching of the Law and is subversive.

It appears to me that what is involved here is a puzzling neglect or circumvention by Strauss, in this relatively recent work of his on Maimonides, of a fundamental, all-important aspect of Maimonides' thought that has eluded very many of his readers throughout the centuries since the publication of his *Guide*; but in systematically explicating this aspect Leo Strauss himself has generally been among the very few and among the most diligent and incisive readers in recent years.[52] In the passages quoted above from his "Introduction to the *Guide*," Strauss explains that Maimonides' doctrine of the attributes "is a secret doctrine."[53] Though a number of other scholars and commentators have made the same observation, including some contemporaries of Maimonides, this aspect of his philosophical theology is neither widely known nor well-understood. Regrettably, the limitations of this paper do not make possible an adequate exposition of it, and a brief and much simplified sketch will have to suffice here.

An understanding of this matter can be helped by noting, first, that throughout the text of the *Guide* there are scattered numerous admonitions by its author not to disclose certain truths to the masses, and second, that these admonitions are not limited only to his doctrine of attributes. Among the locutions conveying Rabbi Moses' wish for secrecy we find the following: "my purpose is that the truths be glimpsed and then again concealed"; "If we explained what ought to be explained, it would be unsuitable for the masses among the people"; "I adjure every reader of this Treatise of mine . . . not to explain to another anything in it"; "in speaking about very obscure matters it is necessary to conceal some parts and disclose others"; "these matters are only for a few solitary individuals of a very special sort, and not for the multitude"; "it is not permitted to divulge these matters to all people"; "these are obscure matters . . . they are truly the mystery of the Torah . . . matters that ought not to be spoken of except in chapter headings."[54] Specifically with reference to his doctrine of the attributes, Maimonides cautions that "this notion concerning them also should not be divulged to the masses."[55]

The important fact about Maimonides to which these caveats draw the attention of the careful student is that, under a variety of disguises and deliberate obfuscations, he propounded in the *Guide* two distinguishable though related and overlapping doctrines about God, a *manifest doctrine* and a *secret doctrine*; or a "double faith" theory consisting respectively, to use Maimonides own terminology, of (*a*) "*necessary beliefs*" and (*b*) "*true beliefs*."[56] "Necessary beliefs" embrace a wide range of religious observances and rituals, as well as ethical prescriptions and imperatives that in the aggregate make possible an orderly, civilized, tranquil, and just society and that presuppose belief in the traditional doctrine of a personal God who commands, gets angry, punishes and rewards, and responds to our actions and prayers. "True beliefs," on the other hand, include the de-anthropomorphization and even the de-personalization of God, recognition that the nature and essence of God are unknowable, that God is "wholly other," wholly unlike the things of the world, and is imperturbable and unaffected by human expressions. God, therefore, is an object of pure, disinterested love and contemplation, and man's most exalted worship and piety is this kind of disinterested, contemplative love. Few humans are capable of achieving this purely intellectual love and contemplation. Certainly the masses are not. For the masses it is the system of "necessary beliefs" that is important, and only if these beliefs are followed will there be a civilized society that will make possible the rise of the small number of rare individuals who will be capable of understanding and living by the "true beliefs."

"Necessary beliefs" therefore concern actions, behavior, societal interrelations and imperatives, and the system of "practical commandments" in the written *Torah* and in the transmitted Oral Tradition of Rabbinic teaching and codes. "True beliefs," on the other hand, concern what Maimonides calls "opinions" or "correct opinions," i.e., philosophical beliefs concerning the nature of the universe, created *ex nihilo,* the meaning of words that purport to refer to God, etc. Maimonides explains this succinctly:

> Sum up what we have said concerning beliefs as follows: In some cases a *commandment* communicates a *correct* belief, which is the one and only thing aimed at—at for instance the belief in the unity and eternity of the deity and in His not being a body. In other cases the belief is *necessary* for the abolition of reciprocal wrongdoing or for the acquisition of a noble moral quality—as, for instance, the belief that He, may He be exalted, has a violent anger against those who do injustice . . . and as the belief that He, may He be exalted, responds instantaneously to the prayer of someone wronged or deceived.[57]

In numerous instances the "true beliefs" or "correct opinions" clearly coincide with the the "necessary beliefs" which have as their goal the establishment of morality and social justice. One of the examples given by Maimonides is the statute of the Sabbath, the "first intention" of which is "the belief in correct opinions, namely, in the creation of the world in time," and "its contribution in fortifying this principle." However, "the intention also included the abolition of mutual wrongdoing among men."[58]

Now, it is belief in the unknowability of God, God's being "wholly other," imperturbable, depersonalized, not characterized by anthropomorphic attributes, etc., that is among the "true beliefs" to which philosophical thought and analysis will lead the religiously committed Jew who is able to engage in such inquiries. But the masses are unable to comprehend many of these beliefs. Indeed, the exposure of the masses to such beliefs may weaken their faith in and jeopardize their adherence to the imperatives that are part of the system of "necessary beliefs." *True beliefs* may be taught only to very special, singular individuals, and must not be disclosed to the masses. Such beliefs form a secret doctrine, limited to the intellectual elite who form the hypothetical audience to whom much of the *Guide* is addressed. For this elite group, the secret doctrine, including the denial of affirmative attributes in relation to God and the doctrine that we can know only *that* God is and not *what* God is, far from being subversive of their faith, is its very strength and its firm foundation, and the ground for their true contemplative love and worship of God. The secret doctrine does indeed contradict some of the traditional, popular "teaching of the Law" that is part of the system of "necessary beliefs" and is ordained by Divine decree in order to reduce mutual wrongdoing among humans and assure a moral society. It is precisely for this reason that the doctrine should not be disclosed to the multitudes who are unable to understand it and are likely to draw erroneous conclusions from it. Leo Strauss was among those who understood and explicated most acutely this obscure aspect of Maimonidean thought,[59] hence the perplexity evoked by his comments quoted above.

Now, two questions arise here in connection with Thomas Aquinas. First, was his negative theology among the elements in his thought that triggered controversy and opposition to him in his own day? Second, did Thomas feel or ever say that some philosophico-theological teachings should be considered secret doctrine and not be divulged to the masses? These are interesting historical questions, but I am not familiar with any of the published systematic research on them. However, one Aquinas text seems to indicate that the subject of secret truths to be concealed from the masses did receive some attention in Christian theological literature, and that St. Thomas leaned toward the view that some divine truths ought to be concealed from the masses to whom they might do harm. The discussion occurs in Thomas's *Commentary on the De Trinitate of Boethius,* in the article entitled "Whether Divine Truths Ought To Be Concealed By New and Obscure Words." After raising the question, and quoting biblical and other texts on both sides, Aquinas concluded

> But . . . there are other [truths] . . . which, if openly presented, cause harm to those hearing them. . . . If any subtleties are proposed to uncultivated people, these folk may find in the imperfect comprehension of them matter for error.[60]

Then, after quoting concurring views from Gregory and Augustine, Aquinas reiterates his view that "there is no denial of the fact that there are mysteries which ought to be concealed by obscuring words."[61] I leave this matter without further comment.

(5) *Negative theology leads directly to the Theology of Silence.* This charge, in these very words, was made by George Englebretsen whom we quoted earlier,[62] and the same charge was also made, but more dramatically and forcefully, by the logician Fred Sommers, in his essay entitled "What We Can Say About God."[63] In that essay Sommers claimed that, to the question "'what can we say about God?' the negative theologian answers, 'nothing!'"[64] There is a deceptive appearance of plausibility in this claim by Sommers, deceptive, I venture to suggest, for the author himself as well as the reader, because of the tacit, uncritical, and question-begging assumption that underlies it, namely, that rational discourse about God is possible *only* in terms of *affirmative divine attributes.* Naturally, therefore, on this assumption, since negative theology insists that affirmative attributes can not be predicated of God, the negative theologian appears self-condemned, strictly speaking, to saying nothing about God. The seeming plausibility of Sommers's charge can be further unmasked if we exhibit the unarticulated tautological syllogism into which he seems to have trapped himself, while trapping the negative theologian as well as the reader:

> Whatever we can say nothing affirmative about,
> we can say nothing about.
> We can say nothing affirmative about God.
> _____
> Therefore, we can say nothing about God.

But manifestly, the question-begging, tautological reasoning here is Sommers's, and is not to be charged to the negative theologian. For the latter, discourse about God is not only possible (though, of course, not via the ascription to Him of affirmative attributes), but is indeed mandatory (see below), and it is *negative discourse* about God that is mandatory. To the question "What can we say about God?" the negative theologian responds as follows:

> We have an inexhaustibly large number of things to say about God, namely, to say *what God is not!* Because erring mankind has for so long in the past been saying and repeating an infinitely large number of things about God in ascribing affirmative attributes to Him, and because mankind will continue in its erring future to make an infinitely great number of attributions of affirmative characteristics to Him, it is the task of negative theologians, and of those who have been persuaded by them, to "unknow" and "unsay" what has been claimed to be known about God, and what has been said about God, and to continue saying and repeating in an infinitely great number of ways *what God is not!*

Now, this can hardly be called a theology of silence!

And thus, by this path, we arrive finally at "rational theology" and its place within negative theology.

(6) *Negative theology is a* reductio ad absurdum *of rational theology.* This imputation also comes from the pen of Fred Sommers, in the same essay in which charge number 5 appeared.[65] The rejoinder here is essentially the same as the rejoinder above. For a long time, "rational theology" was taken to mean largely the systematic setting forth, analysis, and explication of *affirmative attributes* of God. This seems to be also Sommers's assumed definition, and, as explained earlier, understood in this way the enterprise is misguided and also idolatrous. If, however, the discipline of theology were understood to be the systematic pursuit of the countless ways of saying *what God is not,* then, what can possibly be more *rational* in that pursuit than to continue with relentless perseverance to deny and unsay the affirmative statements about God, and thus to spread understanding of God's utter differentness and ultimate incomprehensibility? To teach that every positive attribution that is predicated of God is distortion, is a reduction of God to human terms, and thus is idolatrous, this is the task of "rational theology." Let no one be under any illusion that this task is an easy one.

NOTES

1. Martin Buber, *Eclipse of God* (New York: Harper, 1952), pp. 16–17.

2. Thomas Aquinas, *On the Truth of the Catholic Faith — Summa contra gentiles,* trans. Anton C. Pegis (New York: Image Books, Doubleday Doran, 1955), book 3, chapter 49, par. 9, p. 170. Cf. Anton C. Pegis, *"Penitus Manet Ignotum,"* in *Medieval Studies* 27 (1965): 212–226.

3. Fred Sommers, "What We Can Say About God," *Judaism* 15 (1966): 61–73.

4. Moses Maimonides, *The Guide of the Perplexed.* The standard Arabic edition is *Dalalat al-ha'irin,* ed. Issachar Joel (Jerusalem: J. Junovitch, 1930–31). The most authoritative English translation is by Shlomo Pines, with an introductory essay by Leo Strauss (Chicago: University of Chicago Press, 1963), pp. 112–147.

(Moses Maimonides was born in 1135 and died in 1204. His philosophic *magnum opus* was the *Guide of the Perplexed,* written in Arabic but in Hebrew characters and completed about the year 1190. The first translation into Hebrew was completed in the year of the author's death. One or more translations into Latin were made from the Hebrew and were in circulation among Christian philosophers and theologians well before the middle of the thirteenth century.)

5. Ibid., Chapter 52, pp. 117–118.

6. Fred Sommers, "What We Can Say About God," pp. 63–65.

7. Maimonides, *Guide* I, 58, p. 136.

8. Ibid., I, 57, p. 132.

9. Ibid., I, 56, p. 130.

10. Ibid., I, 57, p. 133.

11. Rudolf Otto, *The Idea of the Holy,* trans. John W. Harvey (Oxford: Oxford University Press, 1926), p. 25ff.

12. Moses Maimonides, *Guide* I, 58, p. 135.

13. Ibid., III, 21, p. 485.

14. See Simon Rawidowicz, "*Adam Ve'eloha: Prakim b'toldot ha'elohut shel Harambam*" ("God and Man: Chapters in Maimonides' Theology"), in *I'yunim Bmahshevet Yisrael* (*Studies in Jewish Thought*) (Jerusalem: Rubin Mass) 1 (1969): 297–331, esp. pp. 297–303. There appears to be some confusion about the authorship of the apothegm, "If I knew Him, I would be He." Rawidowicz does not directly ascribe it to Maimonides, but says only that his formulated doctrine is Maimonides' version of the apothegm. However, Julius Guttmann does ascribe it to Maimonides, in his lecture "*Typussim Shel Havayah Datit*" ("Types of Religious Experience"), in *D'Varim Al Haphilosophia Shel Hadat* (*Lectures on the Philosophy of Religion*) by Julius Guttmann (Jerusalem: The Hebrew University, 1958), p. 93. I have not been able to find this apothegm, *in his verbis,* in any Maimonidean text.

15. Maimonides, *Guide* I, 59, p. 139.

16. Ibid.

17. Maimonides, *Guide,* trans. M. Friedlander (New York: Hebrew Publishing Company, 1881), p. 215.

18. Jacob B. Agus, *The Evolution of Jewish Thought* (New York: Abelard-Schuman, 1959), p. 189.

19. Richard McKeon, "Maimonides the Philosopher," in *Essays on Maimonides,* ed. Salo W. Baron (New York: Columbia University Press, 1941), pp. 2–8. See especially p. 7.

20. Etienne Gilson, *The Philosophy of St. Thomas Aquinas: Authorized Translation . . . of Le Thomisme* (St. Louis: B. Herder Book Company, 1925). This book contains numerous references to Maimonides. However, one lengthy footnote on page 34 is worth quoting in full:

> Apart from Christian thought, a special place must be reserved, among the sources of St. Thomas, to the influence of Moses Maimonides. On a good many points the position of the "Rabbi Moses" prepares that adopted by Thomism and their respective interpretation of Aristotle is often analogous. Maimonides is opposed to the Arabic "motecalemin" (theologians) just as St. Thomas opposes the Augustinian traditionalists; their mental attitude, positive and full of common-sense is singularly akin and the study of their relationship would be worthy of an exhaustive treatment.

Gilson's later book, *The Christian Philosophy of St. Thomas Aquinas* (New York: Random House, 1956) (which is a much expanded version of the earlier *Le Thomisme*), contains repeated references to Maimonides, with occasional identification of a Maimonidean idea as the source of a Thomistic passage.

21. M. Joel, *Verhältniss Albert Des Grossen Zu Moses Maimonides: Ein*

Beitrag Zur Geschichte Der Mittelalterischen Philosophie (Breslau: Verlag der Schletter'sschen Buchhandlung, 1863), p. 2. "What is actually involved is not isolated passages, but rather entire discourses in Maimonides' writings . . . that are reproduced in Albert's writings."

22. "Maimonides is the precursor of St. Thomas Aquinas, and *The Guide of the Perplexed* announces and paves the way for the *Summa Theologiae.*" Émile Saisset, "La Philosophie des Juifs: Maimonide et Spinoza," *Revue des Deux Mondes* 37 (1862): 296–325.

23. Anton C. Pegis, *"Penitus Manet Ignotum."*

24. Thomas Aquinas, *The Summa Theologica,* trans. Fathers of the English Dominican Province (New York: Benzinger Brothers, 1947), Q. 13, a. 2, vol. 1, p. 61.

25. Ibid., p. 62.

26. Ibid., Q. 3 (preamble), p. 14.

27. *Summa Contra Gentiles,* Book III, Chapter 49, par. 3, p. 168.

28. Ibid., Book III, Chapter 39, par. 1, p. 127.

29. Ibid., Chapter 49, par. 9, p. 170.

30. Ibid., Book I, Chapter 5, no. 3, p. 70.

31. Thomas Aquinas, *De potentia Dei,* Q. 7, a. 5, *ad* 14, concluding paragraph.

32. Thomas Aquinas, *In Librum B. Dionysii Nominibus Expositio,* ed. C. Pera (Rome-Turin, 1950), VII, Lectio 4, no. 731. (Quoted by Anton C. Pegis, *Basic Writings of Thomas Aquinas,* p. 225.)

33. Anton C. Pegis, "Penitus Manet Ignotum," p. 225.

34. Ibid., p. 219.

35. Ibid., p. 226.

36. *The New Scholasticism* 47 (1973): 231.

37. *The New Scholasticism* 49 (1975): 93.

38. Leon Roth, *Spinoza, Descartes, and Maimonides* (Oxford: Clarendon, 1924), p. 77.

39. Ibid.

40. Ibid.

41. Maimonides, *Guide* I, 35, p. 80.

42. Shlomo Pines, Introduction to *The Guide of the Perplexed,* p. xcvi.

43. George Englebretsen, p. 232.

44. F. C. Copleston, *Aquinas* (New York: Penguin Books, 1955), p. 128.

45. Ibid., p. 131.

46. Ibid., p. 134.

47. Ibid.

48. Ibid.

49. Leo Strauss, "How to Begin to Study The *Guide of the Perplexed,*" in Moses Maimonides, *The Guide of the Perplexed,* pp. xlviii–xlix.

50. Ibid., p. xlviii.

51. Ibid., I, 60, p. 143.

52. Leo Strauss, *Persecution and the Art of Writing* (Glencoe, Ill.: The Free Press, 1952). (See esp. "The Literary Character of *The Guide of the Perplexed,*" pp. 38–94;) reprinted in this volume. Cf. also Yaacov Becker, *Mishnato Haphiloso-*

phit Shel Rabbenu Moshe Ben Maimon (*The Philosophical Doctrine of Moses ben Maimon*) (Tel Aviv: J. Simoni Publishing House, 1955).

53. Maimonides, *Guide*, p. xlviii.

54. Ibid., pp. 7, 9, 15, 18; I, 34, p. 79; I, 35, pp. 80–81; I, 71, p. 175.

55. Ibid., I, 59, p. 142.

56. Ibid., III, 28, pp. 512–514.

57. Ibid., pp. 513–514.

58. Ibid., III, 32, p. 531.

59. See n. 52 above.

60. Thomas Aquinas, "Commentary on the De Trinitate of Boethius," Q. 2, a. 4. According to the standard edition, *Sancti Thomae De Aquino Expositio Super Librum Boethii De Trinitate,* 2nd., ed. B. Decker (Leiden: E. J. Brill, 1959), p. 99. I am grateful to John Wippel of Catholic University for bringing this Aquinas text to my attention.

61. Ibid.

62. George Englebretsen, p. 232 (see n. 36).

63. Fred Sommers, "What We Can Say About God," (see n. 3 above).

64. Ibid., p. 66.

65. Ibid.

Select Bibliography

COMPILED BY JOSEPH A. BUIJS

This bibliography is restricted to topics covered in this collection and primarily to recent discussions in English. With some exceptions its entries deal with philosophical issues in the thought of Maimonides, published over the past twenty years. Much of the earlier scholarship is in German or French. Extensive work continues to be done in Hebrew, and on other religious aspects of Maimonides' thought.

For more comprehensive bibliographical information on Maimonides and other medieval Jewish thinkers, see, for instance, the very detailed study of Georges Vajda, "Les études de philosophie juives du moyen âge depuis la synthèse de Julius Guttman" (*Hebrew Union College Annual* 43 [1972]: 125–147, and 45 [1974]: 205–241).

A more recent, introductory survey is that of Lawrence V. Berman, "Medieval Jewish Religious Philosophy" (*Bibliographical Essays in Medieval Jewish Studies* [1976], pp. 233–265). A helpful overview for a beginning student in the field is that of Norbert Samuelson, "Medieval Jewish Philosophy" (*Back to the Sources,* ed. Barry W. Holtz [1984], pp. 262–304). Norman Roth lists major Judaeo-Arabic editions, critical editions, and easily accessible English translations of the works of Maimonides in "Maimonides: Basic Bibliography and a Proposal" (*Maimonides, Essays and Texts, 850th Anniversary* [1985], pp. 155–162).

The following abbreviations are used:

AAJR – American Academy for Jewish Research
AJS – Association for Jewish Studies
CCAR – Central Conference of American Rabbis
HUCA – Hebrew Union College Annual
JMR Studies – *Jewish Medieval and Renaissance Studies.* Ed. Alexander Altmann. Cambridge, Mass.: Harvard University Press, 1967.
M & Phil. – *Maimonides and Philosophy. Papers Presented at the Sixth Jerusalem Philosophical Encounter, May 1985.* Ed. Shlomo Pines and Yirmiyahu Yovel. Dordrecht: Martinus Nijhoff Publishers, 1986.
Essays in J. Phil. – *Essays in Medieval Jewish and Islamic Philosophy. Studies from the Publications of the AAJR.* Selected with an introduction by Arthur Hyman. New York: KTAV, 1977.

Straight Path — *A Straight Path, Studies in Medieval Philosophy and Culture. Essays in Honor of Arthur Hyman.* Editor-in-Chief: Ruth Link-Salinger. Washington, D.C.: Catholic University of America Press, 1987.

I. WORKS

1. Arabic and Hebrew Editions

Dalālat al-Ḥā'irīn (Guide of the Perplexed). Arabic text based on S. Munk, ed. Issagar Joel. Jerusalem: Junovitch, 1929.

Iggeret Teman (Epistle to Yemen). Arabic text with three Hebrew versions, ed. with introduction (in Hebrew) by Abraham S. Halkin. New York: AAJR, 1952.

Iggerot ha-Rambam (Letters of Maimonides). Ed. David H. Baneth. Jerusalem: Mezike Nirdamim, 1946.

Iggerot ha-Rambam (Letters). Hebrew texts, ed. Mordecai D. Rabinowitz. Jerusalem: Mossad Harav Kook, 1968.

Iggerot, Rabbi Moshe Ben Maimon (Letters). Arabic original with new (Hebrew) translations and commentary by Joseph Kafiḥ. Jerusalem: Mossad Harav Kook, 1972.

"Letter on Astrology." Hebrew text, ed. Alexander Marx, *HUCA* 3(1926): 311–358 and 4(1927): 493–494.

Ma'amar Teḥiyyat ha-Metim (Treatise on Resurrection). Ed. with notes by Joshua Finkel, *AAJR Proceedings* 9 (1939): 57–105, 1–42 (Hebrew section).

Millot ha-Higgayon (Treatise on Logic). Original Arabic and three Hebrew translations, ed. Israel Efros. New York: AAJR, 1938. Revised edition. Israel Efros, "Maimonides' Arabic Treatise on Logic," *AAJR Proceedings* 34 (1966): 155–160, 9–42 (Hebrew section).

Mishneh Torah (Code). Hebrew text, ed. S. T. Rubenstein, M. D. Rabinowitz, et al. Jerusalem: Mossad Harav Kook, 1967–1973.

Moreh ha-Nebukhim — Dalālat al-Ḥā'irīn (Guide of the Perplexed). Arabic original and Hebrew translation by Joseph Kafiḥ. 3 volumes. Jerusalem: Mossad Harav Kook, 1972.

Moreh Nevukhim (Guide). Hebrew translation of Judah al-Ḥarizi. New edition based on S. Munk by S. Scheyer. Reprint. Tel Aviv: 1964.

Moreh Nevukhim (Guide). Hebrew translation of Samuel ibn Tibbon with commentaries by Efodi, Shem Tov, Crescas, Abravanel, and Hanarboni. New York: Om Publishing, 1946.

Perush ha-Mishnah (Commentary to Mishnah). Hebrew translation by Joseph Kafiḥ. 7 volumes. Jerusalem: Mossad Harav Kook, 1963–1969.

Sefer ha-Mitzvot (Book of Commandments). Arabic original and Hebrew translation, ed. Joseph Kafiḥ. Jerusalem: Mossad Harav Kook, 1971.

Sefer ha-Mitzvot (Commandments). Hebrew translation of Moses ibn Tibbon, ed. with notes by Hayyim Heller. Jerusalem: Mossad Harav Kook, 1946.

Shemonah Perakim (Eight Chapters). Ed. Joseph I. Gorfinkle. Reprint. New York: AMS Press, 1966.

Teshubot ha-Rambam (Responsa). Hebrew and Arabic texts, ed. Joshua Blau. 3 volumes. Jerusalem: Mezike Nirdamim, 1957–1961.

2. English Translations

The Book of Knowledge and *The Book of Adoration*. Tr. Moses Hyamson. Reprint. Jerusalem: Boys Town Publishers, 1962.

The Book of Knowledge from the Mishneh Torah of Maimonides. Tr. H. M. Russell and J. Weinberg. New York: KTAV Publishing, 1983.

The Code of Maimonides. Translated by various authors. Yale Judaica Series, general editor Leon Nemoy. New Haven, Conn.: Yale University Press. Books III, V, VI, VII, VIII, IX, X, XI, XII, XIII, XIV. 1949–1972.

The Commandments: Sefer ha-Mitzvoth. Tr. with notes by Rabbi Charles B. Chavel. 2 volumes. London and New York: Soncino, 1967.

The Commentary to Mishnah Aboth. Tr. with introduction and notes by Arthur David. New York: Bloch, 1968.

Crisis and Leadership: Epistles of Maimonides. (Epistle on Martyrdom, Epistle to Yemen, Essay on Resurrection). Tr. Abraham Halkin; discussions by David Hartman. Philadelphia: Jewish Publication Society of America, 1985.

Eight Chapters of Maimonides on Ethics. English translation and notes by Joseph I. Gorfinkle. Repint. New York: AMS Press, 1966.

The Guide of the Perplexed. Tr. with introduction and notes by Shlomo Pines. Chicago: University of Chicago Press, 1963, 1969.

"Letter on Astrology." Tr. Ralph Lerner. In *Medieval Political Philosophy: A Sourcebook*, ed. Ralph Lerner and Muhsin Mahdi, pp. 227–236. Glencoe, Ill.: Free Press, 1963.

Letters of Maimonides. Tr. and ed. with introduction and notes by Leon D. Stitskin. New York: Yeshiva University Press, 1977.

"Maimonides on Immortality and the Principles of Judaism" (*Perek Ḥelek*). Tr. Arnold J. Wolff, *Judaism* 15 (1966): 95–101, 211–216, 337–342.

Maimonides' Commentary on the Mishnah Tractate Sanhedrin. Tr. with introduction and notes by Fred Rosner. New York; Sepher-Herman, 1981.

Moses Maimonides' Commentary on the Mishnah: Introduction to Seder Zeraim and Commentary on Tractate Berachoth. Tr. and annotated by Fred Rosner. New York: Feldheim, 1975.

Moses Maimonides' Treatise on Resurrection. Tr. and annotated by Fred Rosner. New York: KTAV, 1982.

Selected Letters. In *Memoirs of My People*, ed. Leo W. Schwarz, pp. 15–20. New York: Ferrar and Rinehart, 1943.

Selected Letters. In *A Treasury of Jewish Letters*, vol. 1, ed. Frank Kobler, pp. 178–222. Philadelphia: Jewish Publication Society, 1954.

Treatise on Logic. English translation by Israel Efros. New York: AAJR, 1938.

3. Selections

Ethical Writings of Maimonides. Ed. Raymond L. Weiss with Charles E. Butterworth. New York: New York University Press, 1975; Dover Publication, 1983.

Maimonides' Mishneh Torah. Selections from all fourteen books. Ed. Philip Birnbaum. New York: Hebrew Publishing Co., 1967.

A Maimonides Reader. Ed. with introductions and notes by Isadore Twersky. New York: Behrman House, 1972.

Rambam: Readings in the Philosophy of Moses Maimonides. Selected and translated with introduction and commentary by Lenn Evan Goodman. New York: Viking Press, 1976; Schocken Books, 1977.

II. STUDIES

1. Issues of Interpretation

Berman, Lawrence V. "The Structure of Maimonides' *Guide of the Perplexed.*" *Proceedings of the Sixth World Congress of Jewish Studies* 3 (Jerusalem, 1977), pp. 7–13.

Brague, Rémi. "Leo Strauss et Maïmonide." In *M & Phil.,* pp. 246–268.

Davidson, Herbert. "Maimonides' Secret Position on Creation." In *Studies in Medieval Jewish History and Literature,* ed. Isadore Twersky. Vol. 1, pp. 16–40. Cambridge, Mass.: Harvard University Press, 1979.

Fox, Marvin. "Prolegomena" to A. Cohen, *The Teachings of Maimonides,* pp. xv–xliv. New York: KTAV Publishing House, 1968.

Guttman, Julius. "Philosophie der Religion oder Philosophie des Gesetzes?" *Proceedings, The Israel Academy of Sciences and Humanities* 6 (Jerusalem, 1974).

Hyman, Arthur. "Maimonides' Thirteen Principles." In *JRM Studies,* pp. 119–144.

Ivry, Alfred L. "Islamic and Greek Influences on Maimonides' Philosophy." In *M & Phil.,* pp. 139–156.

Kaplan, Lawrence. "Maimonides on the miraculous element in prophecy." *Harvard Theological Review* 70 (1977): 233–256.

Kellner, Menachem. "Maimonides's Thirteen Principles and the Structure of the 'Guide of the Perplexed.'" *Journal of the History of Philosophy* 20 (1982): 76–84.

Kluxen, Wolfgang. "Maimonides and Latin Scholasticism." In *M & Phil.,* pp. 224–232.

Kravitz, Leonard S., *The Hidden Doctrine of Maimonides' Guide for the Perplexed, Philosophical and Religious God-Language in Tension.* Queenston, Ont.: Edwin Mellen Press, 1987.

Mesch, Barry. "Principles of Judaism in Maimonides and Joseph ibn Caspi." In *Mystics, Philosophers, and Politicians, Essays in Jewish Intellectual History in Honor of Alexander Altmann,* ed. Jehuda Reinharz and Daniel Swetschinski, pp. 85–98. Durham, N. C.: Duke University Press, 1982.

Motzkin, Aryeh Leo. "On the Interpretation of Maimonides." *The Independent Journal of Philosophy* 2 (1978): 39–46.

Pines, Shlomo. "The Philosophical Purport of Maimonides' Halakic Works and the Purport of *The Guide of the Perplexed.*" In *M & Phil.,* pp. 1–14.

Ravitsky, Aviezer. "Samuel Ibn Tibbon and the Esoteric Character of the *Guide of the Perplexed.*" *AJS Review* 6 (1981): 87–123.

Samuelson, Norbert. "Philosophic and Religious Authority in the Thought of Maimonides and Gersonides." *CCAR Journal* 16 (1969): 31–43.

Shapiro, David Solomon. "A Note on the *Guide of the Perplexed.*" In *Meyer Waxman Jubilee Volume, on the occasion of his seventy-fifth birthday,* ed. Judah Rosenthal, pp. 113–121. Chicago: 1966.

Strauss, Leo. "How to Begin to Study *The Guide of the Perplexed.*" Introductory Essay to Moses Maimonides, *The Guide of the Perplexed,* tr. Shlomo Pines, pp. xv–lvi. Chicago: University of Chicago Press, 1963. The first part has been reprinted as "On the Plan of the *Guide of the Perplexed,*" in *Harry Austryn Wolfson, Jubilee Volume on the occasion of his seventy-fifth birthday,* ed. Saul Lieberman, vol. 1, pp. 775–791, English section. Jerusalem: AAJR, 1965.

———. *Philosophy and Law: Essays towards the understanding of Maimonides and his predecessors.* Tr. Fred Baumann. Philadelphia: The Jewish Publication Society of America, 1987.

Twersky, Isadore. "Some Non-Halakic Aspects of the *Mishneh Torah.*" In *JMR Studies,* pp. 95–118.

Vajda, Georges. "La pensée religieuse de Moïse Maïmonide: unité ou dualité?" *Cahiers de Civilization Médiévale* 9 (1966): 29–49.

2. Issues in Epistemology and Metaphysics

Broadie, Alexander. "Maimonides on Negative Attribution." *Transactions of the Glasgow University Oriental Society* 25 (1973–74): 1–11.

Buijs, Joseph A. "Comments on Maimonides' Negative Theology." *The New Scholasticism* 49 (1975): 87–93.

Englebretsen, George. "The Logic of Negative Theology." *The New Scholasticism* 47 (1973): 228–232.

Fackenheim, Emil L. "The Possibility of the Universe in Al-Farabi, Ibn Sina, and Maimonides." *AAJR Proceedings* 16 (1947): 39–70. Also in *Essays in J. Phil.,* pp. 303–334.

Fakhry, Majid. "The 'Antinomy' of the Eternity of the World in Averroes, Maimonides and Aquinas." *Le Muséon* 66 (1953): 139–155. Also in *Studies in Maimonides and St. Thomas Aquinas,* selected with introduction and bibliography by J. I. Dienstag, pp. 107–123. New York: KTAV, 1975.

Faur, José. "Intuitive Knowledge in Medieval Jewish Theology." *The Jewish Quarterly Review* 67 (1976–77): 90–110.

Goldman, Eliezer. "Rationality and Revelation in Maimonides' Thought." In *M and Phil.,* pp. 15–23.

Goodman, Lenn E. "Matter and Form as Attributes of God in Maimonides' Philosophy." In *Straight Path,* pp. 86–97.

Gottschalk, Alfred. "The use of reason in Maimonides — an evaluation by Ahad Ha-am." *Fifth World Congress of Jewish Studies,* ed. A. Shinan, vol. 3, pp. 7–16. Jerusalem, 1972.

Heller, Joseph Elias. "Maimonides' Theory of Miracles." In *Between East and West: essays dedicated to the memory of Bela Horovitz,* ed. Alexander Altmann, pp. 112–127. London: East & West Library, 1958.

Herrera, Robert A. "An Episode in Medieval Aristotelianism: Maimonides and St. Thomas on the Active Intellect." *The Thomist* 47 (1983): 317–338.

———. "Saint Thomas and Maimonides on the tetragrammaton. The 'Exodus' of Philosophy." *Modern Schoolman* 59 (1982): 179–193.

Hyman, Arthur. "Maimonides on Causality." In *M and Phil.,* pp. 157–172.

———. "Some Aspects of Maimonides' Philosophy of Nature." *La filosofia della natura nel Medioeva.* Atti del Terzo Congresso Internazionale di Filosofia Medioevale, pp. 209–218. Milan: Vita e Pensiero, 1966.

Ivry, Alfred L. "Maimonides on Possibility." In *Mystics, Philosophers, and Politicians, Essays in Jewish Intellectual History in Honor of Alexander Altmann,* ed. Jehuda Reinharz and Daniel Swetschinski, pp. 67–84. Durham, N. C.: Duke University Press, 1982.

Jevollela, Massimo. "Songe et prophétie chez Maïmonide et dans la tradition philosophique qui l'inspira." In *M & Phil.,* pp. 173–184.

Johnson, Harold J. "*Via negationis* and *Via analogiae*; Theological Agnosticism in Maimonides and Aquinas." In *Actos del V Congresso Internacional de Filosofia Medieval,* vol. 2, pp. 843–855. Madrid: Nacional, 1979.

Klein-Braslavy, Sarah. "The Creation of the World and Maimonides' Interpretation of Gen. i–v." In *M & Phil.,* pp. 65–78.

Macy, Jeffrey. "Prophecy in al-Farabi and Maimonides: The Imaginative and Rational Faculties." In *M & Phil.,* pp. 185–201.

Malino, Jonathan W. "Aristotle on Eternity: Does Maimonides Have a Reply?" in *M and Phil.,* pp. 52–64.

Miller, Clyde Lee. "Maimonides and Aquinas on Naming God." *Journal of Jewish Studies* 28 (1977): 65–71.

Nuriel, Abraham. "Remarks on Maimonides' Epistemology." In *M & Phil.,* pp. 36–51.

Pines, Shlomo. "Les limites de la metaphysique selon al-Farabi, Ibn Bajja et Maïmonide. Sources et antithèses de ces doctrines chez Alexandre d'Aphrodisè et chez Thémistius." In *Sprache und Erkenntnis in Mittelalter,* vol. 1, pp. 211–225. Berlin/New York: Walter de Gruyter, 1981.

Puig, Joseph. "Maimonides and Averroes on the First Mover." In *M & Phil.,* pp. 213–223.

Ravitsky, Aviezer. "The Anthropological Theory of Miracles in Medieval Jewish Philosophy." In *Studies in Medieval Jewish History and Literature,* ed. Isadore Twersky, vol. 2, pp. 231–272. Cambridge, Mass.: Harvard University Press, 1979.

Reines, Alvin J. "Maimonides' Concept of Providence and Theodicy." *HUCA* 43 (1972): 169–206.

———. "Maimonides' Concept of Miracles." *HUCA* 45 (1974): 243–285.

———. "Maimonides' True Belief Concerning God." In *M & Phil.,* pp. 24–35.

Roth, Norman. "Knowledge of God and God's Knowledge: Two Epistemological Problems in Maimonides." In his *Maimonides: Essays and Texts, 850th An-*

niversary, pp. 69–87. Madison, Wisc.: The Hispanic Seminary of Medieval Studies, 1985.

Saint-Laurent, George. "Avicenna, Maimonides, Aquinas and the existence of God." In *Festschrift in honor of Morton C. Fierman,* ed. Joseph Kalir, pp. 165–191. Fullerton, Calif.: California State University, 1982.

Samuelson, Norbert. "On Knowing God: Maimonides, Gersonides, and the Philosophy of Religion." *Judaism* 18 (1969): 64–77.

———. "The Problem of Future Contingents in Medieval Jewish Philosophy." *Studies in Medieval Culture* 6–7 (1976): 71–82.

Spero, Schubert. "Is the God of Maimonides truly unknowable?" *Judaism* 22 (1973): 66–78.

Touati, Charles. "Les Deux Théorie de Maïmonide sur la Providence." In *Studies in Jewish Religious and Intellectual History, presented to Alexander Altmann on the occasion of his seventieth birthday,* ed. Siegfried Stein and Raphael Loewe, pp. 331–344. University, Ala.: University of Alabama Press, London: Institute of Jewish Studies, 1979.

Weiler, Gershon. "Beliefs and Attributes." *Philosophy* 36 (1961): 196–210.

Weiss, Raymond L. "On the Scope of Maimonides' *Logic,* Or, What Joseph Knew." In *Straight Path,* pp. 255–265.

Wolfson, Harry A. "The Amphibolous Terms in Aristotle, Arabic Philosophy and Maimonides." *Harvard Theological Review* 31 (1938): 151–173. Also in Harry A. Wolfson, *Studies in the History of Philosophy and Religion,* ed. Isadore Twersky and George H. Williams, vol. 1, pp. 455–477. Cambridge, Mass.: Harvard University Press, 1973.

———. "The Aristotelian Predicables and Maimonides' Division of Attributes." In *Essays and Studies in Memory of Linda R. Miller,* ed. Israel Davidson, pp. 201–234. New York: Jewish Theological Seminary of America, 1938.

———. "Hallevi and Maimonides on Design, Chance and Necessity." *AAJR Proceedings* 11 (1941): 105–163. Also in *Essays in J. Phil.,* pp. 34–92.

———. "The Kalam Arguments for Creation in Saadia, Averroes, Maimonides, and St. Thomas." *Saadya Anniversary Volume,* vol. 2, pp. 197–245. New York: 1943.

———. "Maimonides and Gersonides on Divine Attributes as Ambiguous Terms." *Mordecai M. Kaplan Jubilee Volume on the occasion of his seventieth birthday,* pp. 515–530, English Section. New York: The Jewish Theological Seminary of America, 1953.

———. "Maimonides on Negative Attributes." *Louis Ginsberg Jubilee Volume on the occasion of his seventieth birthday,* pp. 411–446. New York: AAJR, 1945. Also in *Essays in J. Phil.,* pp. 180–218.

———. "Maimonides on the internal Senses." *The Jewish Quarterly Review* n.s. 25 (1935): 441–467. Also in Harry A. Wolfson, *Studies in the History of Philosophy and Religion,* ed. Isadore Twersky and George H. Williams, vol. 1, pp. 344–370. Cambridge, Mass.: Harvard University Press, 1973.

———. "Maimonides on the Unity and Incorporeality of God." *Jewish Quarterly Review* 55 (1965): 112–136.

———. "Notes on Proofs of the Existence of God in Jewish Philosophy." *HUCA* 1 (1924): 575–596. Also in Harry A. Wolfson, *Studies in the History of Philosophy and Religion,* ed. Isadore Twersky and George H. Williams, vol. 1, pp. 561–582. Cambridge, Mass.: Harvard University Press, 1973.

———. *The Philosophy of the Kalam.* Cambridge, Mass.: Harvard University Press, 1976.

———. "The Platonic, Aristotelian and Stoic Theories of Creation in Halevi and Maimonides." *Essays in Honour of . . . J. H. Hertz,* pp. 427–442. London, 1942.

———. *Repercussions of the Kalam in Jewish Philosophy.* Cambridge, Mass.: Harvard University Press, 1979.

Zac, Sylvain. "Le rationalisme de Maïmonide et ses limites." *Les Études Philosophiques* (1984): 205–216.

3. Issues in Ethics, Law, and Politics

Altmann, Alexander. "Free Will and Predestination in Saadia, Bahya, and Maimonides." In *Religion in a Religious Age,* ed. S. D. Goitein, pp. 25–51. Cambridge, Mass.: AJS, 1974. Also in Alexander Altmann, *Essays in Jewish Intellectual History,* pp. 35–64. Hanover, N. H.: Brandeis University Press, 1981.

———. "Maimonides' 'four perfections.'" *Israel Oriental Studies* 2 (1973): 15–24. Also in A. Altmann, *Essays in Jewish Intellectual History,* pp. 65–76. Hanover, N. H.: Brandeis University Press, 1981.

Berman, Lawrence V. "The Political Interpretation of the Maxim: The Purpose of Philosophy is the Imitation of God." *Studia Islamica* 15 (1961): 53–61.

———. "Re-examination of Maimonides' Statement on Political Science." *Journal of American Oriental Society* 89 (1969): 106–111.

———. "The Structure of the Commandments of the Torah in the Thought of Maimonides." In *Studies in Jewish Religious and Intellectual History, presented to Alexander Altmann on the occasion of his seventieth birthday,* ed. Siegfried Stein and Raphael Loewe, pp. 51–66. University, Ala.: University of Alabama Press, London: Institute of Jewish Studies, 1979.

Bland, Kalman P. "Moses and the Law according to Maimonides." In *Mystics, Philosophers, and Politicians, Essays in Jewish Intellectual History in Honor of Alexander Altmann,* ed. Jehuda Reinharz and Daniel Swetschinski, pp. 49–66. Durham, N. C.: Duke University Press, 1982.

Blumberg, Harry. "Theories of Evil in Medieval Jewish Philosophy." *HUCA* 43 (1972): 149–168.

Breslauer, S. Daniel. "Philosophy and Imagination: the politics of prophecy in the view of Moses Maimonides." *Jewish Quarterly Review* 70 (1980): 153–171.

Davidson, Herbert. "Maimonides' *Shemonah Peraqim* and Alfarabi's *Fuṣūl al-Madanī.*" *Proceedings of the AAJR* 31 (1963): 33–50. Also in *Essays in J. Phil.,* pp. 116–133.

Faur, José. "The Origin of the Classification of Rational and Divine Commandments in Medieval Jewish Philosophy," *Augustinianum* 9 (1969): 299–304.

Fox, Marvin. "Maimonides and Aquinas on Natural Law." *Diney Israel* 3 (1972): v-xxxvi. Also in *Studies in Maimonides and St. Thomas Aquinas,* selected with introduction and bibliography by J. I. Dienstag, pp. 75-106. New York: KTAV, 1975.

Frank, Daniel H. "The End of the Guide: Maimonides on the Best Life for Man." *Judaism* 34 (1985): 485-495.

Gellman, Jerome. "The Philosophical *Hassaqot* of Rabad on Maimonides' *Mishneh Torah.*" *The New Scholasticism* 58 (1984): 145-169.

Goldman, Solomon. "The Halachic foundation of Maimonides' Thirteen Principles." In *Essays presented to Chief Rabbi Israel Brodie on the occasion of his seventieth birthday,* vol. 1, pp. 111-118. London: Soncino Press, 1966-1967.

Goodman, Lenn Evan. "Maimonides' Philosophy of Law." *The Jewish Law Annual* 1 (1978): 72-107.

Hartman, David. *Maimonides: Torah and Philosophic Quest.* Philadelphia: Jewish Publication Society, 1976.

Harvey, Warren Zev. "Ethics and Meta-Ethics, Aesthetics and Meta-Aesthetics in Maimonides." In *M & Phil.,* pp. 131-138.

Hyman, Arthur. "A Note on Maimonides' Classification of Law." *Jubilee Volume of the AAJR, Proceedings* 46-47 (1979-1980): 323-343.

Kellner, Menachem Marc. "Maimonides and Gersonides on Mosaic Prophecy." *Speculum* 52 (1977): 62-79.

Lerner, Ralph. "Moses Maimonides." In *History of Political Philosophy,* ed. Leo Strauss and Joseph Cropsey, pp. 203-222. 2nd ed. Chicago: University of Chicago Press, 1981.

Levine, Michael P. "The Role of Reason in the Ethics of Maimonides; or why Maimonides could have had a doctrine of Natural Law even if he did not." *Journal of Religious Ethics* 14 (1986): 279-295.

Macy, Jeffrey. "The Rule of Law and the Rule of Wisdom in Plato, al-Farabi and Maimonides." In *Studies in Islamic and Judaic Traditions,* ed. W. M. Brinner and S. D. Ricks, pp. 205-232. Atlanta, Ga.: Scholars Press, 1986.

Reines, Alvin J. *Maimonides and Abrabanel on Prophecy.* Cincinnati, Ohio: Hebrew Union College Press, 1970.

Rosenthal, Erwin I. J. "Torah and 'Nomos' in Medieval Jewish Philosophy." In *Studies in Rationalism, Judaism and Universalism,* ed. Raphael Loewe, pp. 215-230. London: Routledge & Kegan Paul, 1966.

————. "Maimonides' Conception of State and Society." In *Moses Maimonides 1135-1204,* ed. I. Epstein, pp. 191-206. London: Soncino Press, 1935.

Samuelson, Norbert. "The Problem of Free Will in Maimonides, Gersonides, and Aquinas." *CCAR Journal* 17 (1970): 2-20.

Schwarzschild, Steven S. "Moral Radicalism and 'middlingness' in the ethics of Maimonides." *Studies in Medieval Culture* 2 (1977): 65-94.

Sherwin, Byron L. "Moses Maimonides on the Perfection of the Body." *Listening* 9 (1974): 28-37.

Spero, Schubert. "Maimonides and our love for God." *Judaism* 32 (1983): 321-330.

Stern, Joseph. "The Idea of a *Hog* in Maimonides' Explanation of the Law." In *M & Phil.,* pp. 92–130.

Strauss, Leo. "Maimonides' Statement on Political Science." *AAJR Proceedings* 22 (1953): 115–130. Also in *Essays in J. Phil.,* pp. 164–179.

Twersky, Isadore. *Introduction to the Code of Maimonides (Mishneh Torah).* New Haven, Conn.: Yale University Press, 1980.

Weiler, Gershon. "Politics, authority and prophecy in Maimonides." *Religious Traditions* 3 (1980): 53–73.

Weiss, Raymond L. "Language and Ethics: Reflections on Maimonides' Ethics.'" *Journal of the History of Philosophy* 9 (1971): 425–433.

4. The Influence of Maimonides

Altmann, Alexander. "Maimonides and Thomas Aquinas: Natural or Divine Prophecy." *AJS Review* 3 (1978): 1–19. Also in A. Altmann, *Essays in Jewish Intellectual History,* pp. 77–96. Hanover, N. H.: Brandeis University Press, 1981.

Blumberg, Harry. "The Problem of Immorality in Avicenna, Maimonides, and St. Thomas Aquinas." In *Harry Austryn Wolfson, Jubilee Volume on the occasion of his seventy-fifth birthday,* ed. Saul Lieberman, vol. 1, pp. 165–185, English Section. Jerusalem: AAJR, 1965. Also in *Essays in J. Phil.,* pp. 95–115.

Blumenthal, David R. "Was there an Eastern tradition of Maimonidean Scholarship?" *Revue des études juives* 138 (1969): 57–67.

Broadie, Alexander. "Maimonides and Aquinas on the Names of God." *Religious Studies* 23 (1987): 157–170.

Brüngel, Ferdinand. "Maimonides' Agnosticism and Scholasticism." *CCAR Journal* 19 (1972): 65–68. Also in *Studies in Maimonides and St. Thomas Aquinas,* selected with introduction and bibliography by J. I. Dienstag, pp. 165–168. New York: KTAV, 1975.

Burrell, David B. "Aquinas and Maimonides: A Conversation about Proper Speech." *Immanuel* 16 (1983): 70–85.

———. "Aquinas's Debt to Maimonides." In *Straight Path,* pp. 37–48.

———. *Knowing the Unknowable God: Ibn Sina, Maimonides, and Aquinas.* Notre Dame, Ind.: University of Notre Dame Press, 1986.

———. "Maimonides, Aquinas and Gersonides on Providence and Evil." *Religious Studies* 20 (1984): 335–352.

Dunphy, William. "Maimonides and Aquinas on Creation, A Critique of their Historians." In *Graceful Reason, Essays in Ancient and Medieval Philosophy, Presented to Joseph Owens CSSR,* ed. Lloyd P. Gerson, pp. 361–379. Toronto: Pontifical Institute of Medieval Studies, 1983.

Feldman, Seymour. "Did the Scholastics Have an Accurate Knowledge of Maimonides?" In *Studies in Medieval Culture* 3, ed. John R. Sommerfeldt, pp. 145–150. Kalamazoo, Mich.: The Medieval Institute, Western Michigan University, 1970.

Goodman, Lenn E. "Maimonides and Leibniz." *Journal of Jewish Studies* 31 (1980): 214–236.

Gottschalk, Alfred. "Maimonides, Spinoza, and Ahab Ha-am." *Judaism* 21 (1972): 303–310.

Harvey, Warren Zev. "Crescas versus Maimonides on Knowledge and Pleasure." In *Straight Path,* pp. 113–123.

———. "A Portrait of Spinoza as a Maimonidean." *Journal of the History of Philosophy* 19 (1981): 151–172.

———. "The Return of Maimonideanism." *Jewish Social Studies* 42 (1980): 249–268.

Laks, H. J. "Re-appraising Maimonides." *Judaism* 23 (1974): 183–192.

Levinger, Lee J. "The Influence of Maimonides on scholastic thought." In *Jews in the Arts and Sciences, Jubilee Volume, Jewish Academy of Arts and Sciences,* ed. Mordecai Soltes, et al., pp. 99–103. New York: Herald Square Press, 1954.

Luby, Barry Jay. *Maimonides and Spinoza: Their Sources, Cosmological Metaphysics, and Impact on Modern Thought and Literature.* New York: Anaya, Las America, 1973.

Manekin, Charles H. "Problems of 'Plenitude' in Maimonides and Gersonides." In *Straight Path,* pp. 183–194.

Maurer, Armand A. "Maimonides and Aquinas on the Study of Metaphysics." In *Straight Path,* pp. 206–215.

Pines, Shlomo. "Maïmonide et la philosophie latine," in *Actos del V Congresso Internacional de Filosofia Medieval,* vol. 1, pp. 219–229. Madrid: Nacional, 1979.

———. "Spinoza's Tractatus Theologica-Politicus, Maimonides, and Kant." *Scripta Hierosolymitana XX, Further Studies in Philosophy,* ed. Ora Segal, pp. 3–54. Jerusalem: Magnes Press, 1968.

———. "Saint Thomas et la pensée juive médiévale: Quelques Notations." In *Aquinas and Problems of His Time,* ed. G. Verbeke and D. Verhelst, pp. 118–129. Leuven: University Press/The Hague: Martinus Nijhoff, 1976.

Popkin, Richard H. "Newton and Maimonides." In *Straight Path,* pp. 216–229.

Roth, Norman. "Maimonides' Impact on World Culture." In his *Maimonides, Essays and Texts, 850th Anniversary,* pp. 17–41. Madison, Wisc.: The Hispanic Seminary of Medieval Studies, 1985.

Wilensky, Sarah Heller. "The *Guide* and the *Gate:* The Dialectical Influence of Maimonides on Isaac ibn Latif and Early Spanish Kabbalah." In *Straight Path,* pp. 265–278.

Yovel, Yirmiyahu. "God's Transcendence and its Schematization." In *M & Phil.,* pp. 269–282.

Zac, Sylvan. "Spinoza, critique de Maïmonide." *Les études philosophiques* 3 (1972): 411–428.

———. "Spinoza et la théorie des attributs de Dieu de Maïmonide." *Archivio di Filosofia* 1 (1978): 11–27.